£ 7.50

I0918747

# Housing, States and Localities

# Housing, States and Localities

*Peter Dickens, Simon Duncan,*
*Mark Goodwin and Fred Gray*

*METHUEN*
London and New York

First published in 1985 by
Methuen & Co. Ltd
11 New Fetter Lane, London EC4P 4EE

Published in the USA by
Methuen & Co.
in association with Methuen, Inc.
733 Third Avenue, New York, NY 10017

Typeset by Scarborough Typesetting Services
and printed in Great Britain
at the University Press, Cambridge

*British Library Cataloguing in Publication Data*

Housing, states and localities.
1. Housing policy – Great Britain 2. Housing
policy – Sweden
I. Title II. Dickens, Peter, *1940–*
363.5'8'0941 HD7333.A3

ISBN 0–416–73780–3

*Library of Congress Cataloging in Publication Data*
Main entry under title:

Housing, states, and localities.
Bibliography: p.
Includes index.
1. Housing – Great Britain. 2. Housing – Sweden.
3. Housing policy – Great Britain. 4. Housing policy –
Sweden. I. Dickens, Peter, 1940–
HD7333.A3H6965 1985 363.5'0941 85–5020
ISBN 0–416–73780–3

# Contents

# List of tables

# List of figures

The authors and publishers are grateful to the following for permission to reproduce copyright material in this book:

Macmillan, London and Basingstoke, for figure 1.2, from J. Urry *The Anatomy of Capitalist Societies*, p. 116; and Andrew Sayer, for figure 7.1, from *Radical Philosophy*, 28.

# Preface

This book is about a series of interrelated social processes and issues that surround the production, provision and use of housing in Britain and Sweden. Not only is the volume concerned with the more orthodox areas of housing distribution to social groups and the tenure policies of governments – the conventional concern of many 'housing books' – but also with how houses are built and the manner in which people, as housing consumers, respond to their housing experiences. In all this, variations over time and space are argued to be particularly important. As such, 'states' and 'localities' (not 'state' and 'locality') are key themes. However, in themselves such terms explain little. Consequently, throughout the book a central objective is the search for an explanation of the causal processes at work determining housing provision, accounting for state activity (or the lack of it) and producing different outcomes in different localities.

The research began in the late 1970s with the then seemingly relatively straightforward aim of comparing the forms and processes of housing provision in Britain and Sweden. The objective was not just to compare housing in the two countries, but to use the comparison to answer a specific question about how housing was provided in social democratic style capitalism. How and why did state intervention into housing provision develop, and what did this tell us about the nature and role of the state? Why, for example, are certain policies followed and not others; why are particular strategies and not others taken up in pursuing these policies? This question was seen as crucial, for previous work – including our own – had suggested state activity as the key factor in explaining variations in housing allocation and consumption over space and time. At the start of the research it seemed that one fruitful way to answer this question would be to examine the way different national states actually did act in response to similar situations.

As the research progressed it became apparent that there are severe limitations to this original view. It is our reactions to these limitations that form the basis of this book. For example, comparative analysis must be as much conceptual analysis as empirical juxtaposition; 'the state' is not unitary and we need to look at localities and local states as much as central government to understand the processes of housing provision; it is necessary to examine production and protest just as much as state policy about consumption; to integrate and control these redefinitions we would have to use a realist view of explanation; and so on. Such themes combine to provide an answer to our initial question, but not in the way we originally expected.

Chapter one introduces these research issues in greater detail. It describes how we developed a conceptual starting point to housing provision, states and localities. One particularly important section discusses what comparative analysis can, and cannot, do in helping to understand complex social changes. Chapter two relates these themes to our choice of comparative case studies and also provides a brief analysis of Swedish society and its development.

Chapters three and four ask how the supply and demand for housing are socially organized. Chapter three shows how the production of housing as a commodity has taken different forms in Sweden and Britain, with considerable effects on housing costs, conditions and access. The chapter also attempts to show why this has been the case. The 'economic level' of commodity production is seen as a social process and as such how housing is built is just as deeply affected by the 'external' social relations of the construction industry (e.g. with land ownership or state power) as by 'internal' capital-labour relations. Chapter four follows a similar path with reference to the evolution of national housing policy in the two countries. Again, this cannot be seen as a purely 'political' level in isolation.

One of our conceptual starting points addressed in chapter one concerns the importance of localities. Chapters five and six follow up this theme more closely in relation to housing provision. Chapter five examines to what extent and why housing provision can vary within one nation state, using Sheffield and inter-war rural Norfolk as case studies. In both these cases there were much higher rates of council house building than the national average, yet these two areas were quite different in social and economic terms. Again, the determinants of how housing is provided reach far outside housing itself, and these determinants can have significant local specificity. Chapter six continues this theme in concentrating on the range of actions by housing consumers themselves, and in particular housing protest. This chapter uses the examples of squatting in Brighton, opposition to the establishment of Crawley New Town and conflict over rent levels when the new town had been established. Not only is housing protest a widespread social phenomenon, but it cannot be properly understood without analysis of local states and localities.

Finally, chapter seven returns the discussion to the themes we began with. What sort of explanation was most useful in the research and where can we go from here?

The writing of the book has very much been a joint product by all four authors. However, **Peter Dickens** has taken major responsibility for the research on housing provision in Britain on a national level, written up in chapters three and four, and also the research on housing protest in Brighton, written up in chapter six. **Simon Duncan** was responsible for the research on Sweden, written up in chapters two, three and four, and also for the work on housing research, housing provision, localities, comparative analysis and realism written up in chapters one, two, three and seven. **Mark Goodwin** was largely responsible for the research on local variations in housing provision in Britain, including the studies of Sheffield and Norfolk written up in chapter five, while **Fred Gray** undertook the bulk of the work on housing protest, including the Crawley case studies, in chapter six. The book is one result of a five-year research project (1978–83) on 'Housing and the state in Britain and Sweden' and some of its more detailed results on issues secondary to the main themes of this book are published in journal articles or working papers. These are listed in the Appendix.

Throughout the volume all translations from Swedish to English are our own. In the text 'Britain' is taken to mean England, Wales and Scotland. However, the statistical information for Britain often refers to the United Kingdom (including Northern Ireland) or England and Wales alone.

We would like to thank the many people who helped us write the book. Mike Ball, Berth Danermark, Jane Darke, Ingemar Elander, Graham Ive, Steve Merrett, Andrew Sayer, Thord Strömberg and John Urry have been generous with their time and have commented on earlier chapter or section drafts. Peter Williams, as reader for Methuen, read the whole book in a rough draft form and made some valuable strategic suggestions. Tom Ritchey assisted us with local studies of housing provision in Sweden, while the Urban and Regional Studies Division at Sussex University has always been a stimulating base for the research. Thanks also to the drawing office at the London School of Economics, in particular to Jane Pugh, for the artwork, and not least to everyone at Methuen who helped make the research results into a book. Finally we gratefully acknowledge the financial help of the Social Science Research Council (now the Economic and Social Research Council), the Swedish Council for Building Research, the British Council and the Northern Studies Fund at the LSE.

Sussex University, April 1984

## CHAPTER ONE

# The variability of structure, housing provision and comparative analysis

## 1.1 Housing provision and the variability of capitalism

Capitalism is both an overarching social structure and an international economic system. This is fundamental to the way people conduct their everyday lives and build their societies. The provision of housing, and by provision we mean its production as well as its distribution and consumption, is one part of everyday life and its social organization. It is, therefore, quite possible to elaborate theories which explain how housing is provided by reference to the basic dynamics of capitalist society. Even with the qualification that these basic dynamics are not yet fully understood, and that capitalism is not the only structural determinant of social life, these theories can be very illuminating. They allow us to delineate some general explanations of how and why housing is provided in capitalist societies. The works of Engels, Lefebvre, Castells and Harvey are perhaps the most well known.

Despite their value, theories like these fail when they are used to explain what actually happens in the reality of particular societies, in particular places at particular times. For instance, we can understand that the social conditions of capitalism must be reproduced if it is to continue; it seems very likely that state intervention to provide subsidized housing will be one part of this reproduction. But this says nothing about how this happens, about the forms it produces, nor even – except at a very general level – why this happens. Social reproduction need not necessarily involve the provision of state subsidized housing; indeed, the reproduction may itself cease. To identify structural mechanisms of capitalism is not the same as explaining what happens in particular capitalist societies. It is the characteristics of these societies, the multifarious ways of institutionalizing practice, that determine how, in what ways, or if at all, such structural mechanisms work. Furthermore, many of these features do not have their origin in capitalist social structures. In turn, these characteristics have been created by people. People may not be able to act independently of others, nor in circumstances of their own choosing, and the nightmare of the past certainly bears down upon them. But they do act, in accordance with their evaluation of the circumstances and often with considerable skill and force. It is not so surprising, therefore, that what are identified as basic structural mechanisms actually produce widely variable outcomes in different times and at different places.

We cannot hope, consequently, to read empirical events directly out of abstract theory. Those theorizations of housing provided by Engels, Castells, Harvey and others (even assuming they are adequate at their abstract level) can only provide starting points for the explanation of why and how events occur. Nor can we leave explanation of social change in some timeless or non-spatial void, as some theorists are now belatedly discovering (notably the recent work of Giddens, e.g. 1981). Societies can only exist spatially and temporally. On the other hand, this recognition that social forms (like housing provision) and their causes can only be completely understood in the particular does not mean that we should reject any identification of structural mechanisms. This would leave us in the fake world of voluntarism, where people do whatever they independently happen to think of next, as though no other people or society had ever existed. At the very least, we would be in the unsatisfactory position of eschewing explanation and trying to describe a world of myriad assorted and apparently random events; inevitably, we would end up using unconscious or implicit theoretical presuppositions just to decide what was important enough to describe. Rather, we must accept that social structures are both the medium and the outcome of social practices; both structural and 'practical' must be combined in explaining social forms and understanding how they change. Capitalism has both a geography and a history. But, similarly, geography and history are created through capitalism. And the same holds for housing provision.[1]

The purpose of this book is to advance such a 'historical geography' of housing provision in capitalist society. How is it that the political economy of capitalism produces important variations in housing provision? Previous work has stressed the scale of historical transformations in housing provision in these societies, and shown the importance of national and sub-national variations at any one time (e.g. Merrett 1979, Merrett with Gray 1982, Heady 1978). Other, more theoretical work had provided good accounts of the position of housing within capitalism in general (e.g. Castells 1977, Ball 1978). The need remains of linking the two and this book makes one contribution.

One strategy in establishing such connections between 'the theoretical' and 'the empirical' is to use comparative research.[2] This posits the question 'how have specific variations emerged in relation to general structures?' in terms of particular, real cases where the attempt is made to distinguish how elements common to those cases have become unique to one case. This is the approach taken in this book with reference to housing provision. Why do nation states, apparently with similar structural positions in international capitalism, end up with substantial variations in housing provision? Why do local states within the same nation states exhibit local variations of housing provision? If we accept that events are socially caused, and hence that explanation must refer to socially logical causality ('social processes' and 'mechanisms') then such differences cannot be reduced to random or voluntaristic variations on a structurally determined constant. They must reflect the interaction of structures with practices.

How is this conclusion developed in this book? First of all, we compare aspects of housing provision in Britain and Sweden, both social democratic nation states in advanced capitalism,[3] but exhibiting dramatic contrasts in both the production

and consumption of housing. In Sweden, the building industry is much more productive and more closely follows the normal model of capitalist rationality. More
housing can be built for less cost. Similarly, the supply of housing land is separated from the private ownership of land; the appropriation of development gain
by builders or landowners is minimized. These factors are related to a huge
improvement in housing quality, quantity and access since 1945 which, unlike in
Britain, has been achieved with relatively controlled housing costs and – where
housing consumption has also been traditionally more socialized than in Britain –
without anything like the same degree of social polarization. We will attempt to
show how the same mechanisms of commodity production and class relations in
capitalism have produced these different outcomes. Sweden, it should be noted,
can be taken as the exemplar of social democratic capitalism.

Next, we compare Sheffield and a part of rural Norfolk as major examples of
variation within one nation state. Here the basis for comparison is reversed, for at
the periods chosen for comparison (Sheffield in the post-war period, Smallburgh
RDC in the inter-war period) both these local states exhibited the same housing
provision strategy – heavy reliance on subsidized public renting. The problem
here is to explain how two very different places within Britain ended up with the
same housing outcome. There are three possibilities. It could be the case that the
structural mechanisms of commodity production and class relations in capitalism
predetermine tenurial variations in housing provision. Given the large differences already found for Sweden and Britain, it would be hard to accept the determinism necessary to support such a conclusion; at the very least the proposition
needs empirical demonstration. Second, it could be that the existence of the same
central agencies of the British state, and the same overall structures of British
society, would completely dominate local social variations and so impose the same
outcome on two quite different places. Again, this begs the question – such
dominance would have to be shown working in practice, and we know that the
state is not unitary and that 'overall' social structures disguise dramatic local and
regional variations. Indeed, there are good grounds for suspecting that national
structures were not completely dominant, for during the periods chosen both
Sheffield and rural Norfolk were *exceptional* in the British context. In both much
more council housing was built than normal. The third possibility, that locally
specific social processes were significant in explaining this exceptional variation,
becomes more likely. Our examination of both localities lends support to this
conclusion.

Finally, we go on to compare three cases of protests by groups of consumers
over housing access, conditions and costs, looking in turn at squatting in
Brighton, legal protest in Crawley and a rent strike, again in Crawley. These cases
are illuminating because of the way in which central directives were brought face
to face with local practices. Because of the fundamental issues of property ownership at stake in the case of squatting, and because (in the case of Crawley) of the
special status of British new towns, the intermediary level of electoral local
government was much less important than normal. The interaction of local and
national, although abnormal, is clearer. In chapter two we describe these six case
study areas a little more closely. Figure 1.1 maps their locations.

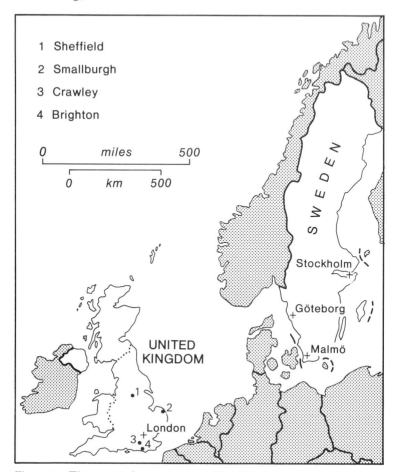

*Figure 1.1*   The case study areas: state and localities

What is the point of these particular case studies? First of all, the events and circumstances we go on to examine contain an intrinsic interest. It is useful to try and find out why housing production in Sweden is more socially and economically efficient than in Britain, why different social groups in industrial Sheffield and rural Norfolk saw council housing as an answer to social conflict, or how the vaunted British new town model in Crawley actually produced protest over housing. The 'housing question' as a whole, for both political and intellectual reasons, is a fascinating and important topic (see section 1.3). Second, the case studies demonstrate the importance of variation within common structures. It is not possible to reduce empirical questions to structural assertion and the comparative material makes this point quite strongly. But the overall aim of the cases is to erect some signposts to how the 'interaction of structures with practices' can be researched and understood; how is it possible to move out of sterile structure versus agency debates towards some resolution of the two?

To take some examples from research on housing – is it the 'balance of class forces' that determines changes in housing policy, or is this just timetabling an essentially pre-determined response to the difficulties of producing housing as a commodity which produces a structural crisis for capitalism? Was the introduction of council housing in Britain a working-class victory or a sop by capital? The attempt to answer these questions has led to some acrimonious debate (for a discussion, see chapter six). But these questions are essentially ill-founded. This is not just because the answer is usually 'a mixture of both', but more because we cannot expect very particular empirical circumstances to give general answers to abstract questions, or vice versa. Partly then, the answer is to unscramble these levels, and, having done so, to relate them to one another logically rather than chaotically. But how is this to be done? How is the precise 'mix' of structure and practice to be established? This problem is approached in more philosophical and theoretical terms in chapter seven. The case studies give this philosophical question more point and empirical relevance. They do so by problematizing, through comparative research, the question of structure and agency for some key processes of housing provision – construction, distribution and consumption.

## 1.2 Housing provision and social causation – developing an approach

In order to carry out the tasks identified in the last section it was clearly necessary to develop some means of theorizing the case study material. That is, it was necessary to develop overall concepts about the role of housing provision and how it occurred so that explanatory questions could be asked and to provide an initial guide about how to answer them. This section discusses how we reached this take-off point. It provides, by this means, a discussion of theoretical alternatives. Although inevitably more limited than a formal discussion of theory, this strategy also holds the not inconsiderable advantages of being shorter and less dense. Some more formal theoretical discussion of alternatives takes place in chapter seven, with the advantage of the empirical hindsight provided by the case studies. Readers who are not interested in why we reached one particular conceptual starting point, but just want to know what it is, are advised to skip this section and move on to 1.3. Those who are impatient of conceptual discussion as a whole should turn straight away to chapter two.

There is no single right way to understand the development of social systems and social practices; different theories can complement one another and work better in relation to different questions. There are, however, some wrong ways and theories can contradict as well as complement (see Duncan 1977, 1981; Sayer 1979 for our views). We have worked from a Marxist conceptualization of social enquiry. Appropriately modified and extended, this seemed to us to offer the best chance of relating structure to particular practice, and therefore of understanding change and variability in both. This is perhaps one of Marxism's central projects as a strategy for social science and this links in well with recent developments in the realist philosophy of science (see chapter seven). The departure point of

Marxism also meant that we would not be restricted to the narrow confines of particular disciplines, nor would we be confined to broader, but still limiting divisions such as 'the social' (as with much Weberian informed research) or 'the economic'. If anything, our research has shown us how the political and the economic, the social and the spatial, are interlinked. Indeed, it is the links which are probably most important in explanatory terms. Notably, of course, Marxism also provides conceptual insights on capitalist economies and much empirical analysis on how capitalist societies have developed and worked.

Much weaker is Marxism's conceptualization of capitalist states and of 'civil society'. With regard to the latter the neglect of gender roles and the domestic economy is remarkable (and our book suffers in the same way here). However, other possible conceptual departure points are at least just as bad in this respect and most are actually worse in not allowing the integration of these subjects into an overall view of society, or not even allowing their conceptualization at all. Furthermore, these limitations are slowly being resolved, not without considerable debate and diversion. The nature of capitalist states, and the interaction of patriarchal and economic structures, have been two of the foremost research problems in social science over the last decade.

Despite this, much of Marxism since Marx – at least up to the last ten or twenty years – has tended to underrate the importance of social variability within social (capitalist) structures, and this means that Marxism was limited in appreciating the varying ways in which real capitalist societies have accommodated the self-destructive forces and contradictions of capitalism. There are several reasons for this limitation, both internal and external to Marxism. In part, the evolutionist tendencies in Marx's own work have given a false lead, and the need to build up basic structural accounts has sometimes overshadowed the question of how these structures work in practice. The political vicissitudes of Marxism and Marxists have not helped, producing gaps, isolation and distortions in ideas as well as between the people involved. However, Marxists have also over-reacted to the inadequacies of conventional social science, which for so long operated in practice without any conception of society and causally linked social structures. Even those formal attempts to acknowledge social totality were usually functionalist and so were usually ignored in empirical research.

Marxism offered one powerful way out of this blinkered position but, as happens so often in social science, this led to one extreme being followed by another with the onslaught of Marxist informed structuralism in the 1960s and 1970s. Ironically enough, in leaving explanation at the identification of basic social structure, the problems of functionalism were re-introduced. Ultimately depending on circular and effectively deterministic, non-social explanations, the inability to account for the variability of social practices remained. It was possible to agree, for example, that local states were involved in social reproduction, but it remained difficult to understand why this happened in particular ways or even why it came to happen at all without recourse to circular arguments ultimately predicated on some mystical idea of capitalism as an all-powerful being. Although our own work is written in reaction to this phase, it was perhaps necessary enough just to reintroduce particular notions of structure into social science. In some ways our problem was that of not throwing out the structural baby in the functionalist bathwater, and comparative research was one strategy for achieving this.

For this reason it is a pleasure to be able to quote Marx on variability in capitalism and comparative research. Contributing to the late nineteenth-century debate on whether traditional Russian village organization contained the seeds of communist society, and hence contributed something missing in his own work, Marx wrote that 'events strikingly analogous but taking place in different historical surroundings lead to totally different results'. He went on:

> By studying each of these forms of development separately and then comparing them one can easily [sic] find the clue to this phenomenon, but one will never arrive there by using as one's master key a general historical-philosophical theory, the supreme virtue of which consists in being supra-historical.
>
> (Quoted in Sutching 1972, 242)

This is a convenient way to mark the significance of our theme; the comparative analysis of historical and geographical variability within capitalism, in our case for housing provision. But we must stress at the outset that comparative analysis is not a panacea for a lack of theory; it is not an explanation in itself even if Marx almost implies as much. In order to carry through the work we had to re-evaluate an initially overhopeful view of the potentialities of comparative study, and also to provide theorization of particular social relations in its place. Our work on the local state is a major example, although we are very conscious of the gaps that remain. But before discussing the use and potential of comparative analysis in more detail we will first sketch out how our ideas about research design changed over the life of the project, for our view of comparative analysis was part and parcel of these changes.

The study began by taking housing provision as its given problem. This reflects the social significance of housing, and this significance was mirrored in both academic and policy debate at the time. Our own previous work was concerned with housing where this was an 'authorized' subject for geographical research, for our own backgrounds (at least for three of us) and our funders were in geography. The obvious spatial variations in housing provision as well as the no less obvious social causes of this variation gave some leeway to a subject which was recoiling against its own 'spatial fetishism' (spatial differences produce social differences) at the same time as it attempted to keep in contact with its own spatial rationale. The research actually became a route away from the artificial disciplinary boundaries of social science. (After all, these were invented in the heyday of Imperial Britain for very specific reasons.) Cohesion would instead be provided more by the object of research, housing as a social and political problem – and by the way of explaining it – a commitment to Marxist-informed analysis of social causes and processes. Geography would remain as something to be explained, but would disappear as a way of explaining.

Within this overall focus, the original research plan drafted in 1977 aimed to compare directly forms of housing consumption in Britain and Sweden, concentrating on the differences in state intervention assumed to lie behind these differences. This was because previous research, including our own, had shown up the importance of state policy in accounting for the fact that different sorts of people, in different areas, ended up with different sorts of housing. (See Bassett and Short 1980 for a review.) Analysis of state policy would be crucial to an understanding of the social geography of housing consumption. Furthermore, state intervention was one crucial means by which capitalist societies had survived.

We would take the provision of 'social housing' (that is 'non-profit' rented housing like council housing) as a lodestone and comparatively chart its changing importance, and also the variations in how it was provided, for both Britain and Sweden. This would allow us to isolate those variations in state intervention that were assumed to cause differences in the availability, forms and conditions of social housing between the two countries. But we were well aware that national differences could conceal huge sub-national variations. A second stage of the research would deal with this problem by comparing a number of local authorities within each country. It was in the local authority, we assumed, that local decisions about housing provision were taken. Subsequently, the analysis would attempt to discern why state policy was different in these different places. We knew that the labour movement in Sweden was the strongest in any capitalist country, with a history of substantial influence on state policy formulation. This was taken as the dynamic behind Sweden's emergence as social democracy's exemplar. The varying strength of labour might provide a key in explaining variations in housing provision both nationally and locally.

Elements of this research design persist in the research actually carried out. But in several key ways this initial plan was empirically and methodologically limited. It could provide a description of national and sub-national variations in social housing. This would be useful enough given the stark contrasts in housing conditions and state policies between Britain and Sweden, and between local areas in both countries. However, the design would not be adequate in explaining how these contrasts were produced. We will spend a little time here looking at these research limitations, and the resulting changes to our view of housing provision.

The initial research plan was limited for two main, linked, reasons, which we can label 'empirical' and 'conceptual'. In empirical terms, the focus on housing as tenure and as a distribution/consumption process choked off the analysis of housing *production* and all those other social processes outside 'housing' (defined in narrow consumption terms) which are so important in accounting for variations in housing provision. Particular social relations in state institutions or over land ownership, are just two examples. The pre-conceived cut-off points in the research plan did not coincide with those existing in the social world. We thought it better to change the former rather than ignore the latter. The analysis would be as much about capitalist states and construction industries as about housing consumption and state housing policy. Having widened the empirical net of the study and thus broken with conventional disciplinary boundaries of the time, it gradually became clear that analysis of housing provision should be related to an overall conceptualization of social relations in capitalist societies. In turn, this meant re-evaluating the epistemological basis of the research; how explanation could proceed. Finally, these linked empirical and conceptual modifications would alter our views of comparative study. We will deal with these modifications in turn.

Starting with immediate empirical issues, it became clear that to understand housing provision one would have to consider construction and land ownership as well as distribution and allocation. Put simply, any amount of policy is meaningless if you cannot build the houses or acquire land to put them on – and various governments have found this out the hard way. This point was being made quite forcefully in the academic debate around the time when the research began (e.g. Ball 1978, Bartlett School 1980), and our own pilot research on housing in Sweden showed some very significant differences to Britain in these respects. It was these differences in housing production, as well as in state housing policies, which seemed connected with the differences in housing provision in the two countries. Indeed, housing policies could themselves depend very much on differences in construction or land. Similarly, distribution pure and simple (usually a focus on allocation and condition by tenure) misses out how consumers respond to these situations. Their actions, including direct protest, could be very influential on both state policy and housing provision. Not only were these issues outside the remit of 'housing' seen as distribution and state housing policy, but analysing them meant in turn dealing with social relations and social histories at some remove from this initial focus.

For instance, in contrast to Britain, the Swedish building industry shows a high level of industrialization (on-site as well as off-site), technical innovation and product development, all leading to relatively dramatic productivity increases in the post-war period. This was predicated on changes in the labour process in construction work. In turn this depended on management–labour relations and capital ownership in construction, but also on the way these internal features were affected by social relations outside construction itself. In Sweden house builders could not easily make profits through land development gains, labour for building was relatively expensive and well organized, construction was part of an integrated finance and industrial capital leading to high rates of internal investment, and so on. All these factors could be related to the particular form of social democracy developed in Sweden; the precise balance struck between labour and capital. To understand housing provision it would be necessary to move outside housing itself.

Similarly, academic debate in the late 1970s stressed that 'the state' was not unitary. 'Local states' were also important although their precise role was as yet contentious (e.g. Cockburn 1977, Saunders 1979). This fitted in with our own empirical concerns on local variations, and furthermore using Sweden and Britain as two cases showed forcefully that there was not any one capitalist state except in the most general terms; there were different forms of capitalist state existing in specific, spatial and temporal contexts.

This directly contradicted the original notion of analysing state housing policy in relation to a general 'capitalist state'. Furthermore, variability in capitalist states also had social causes, as the literature on the development of social democracy in Sweden made clear. Finally, we realized that the effects of housing policy, just as much as its causes, reach outside 'housing' itself. For instance, research using feminist perspectives was already showing how housing form helps create and support gender roles (see Mackenzie and Rose 1983 for a general review). Again, housing consumption was just one component of wider social relations. In like manner, it became clear that it was over-simplistic to isolate labour as the key social variable accounting for variations between and within nation states. In the evolution of Swedish social democracy, for instance, it was the interaction of *specific* constellations of labour *and* capital which was crucial (see section 1.6).

Extension in empirical context highlighted the need for the research to be set within some conceptualization of social relations. On the one hand, housing could not be isolated as a self-sufficient element which could be easily extracted from society; on the other hand we needed to be able to place limits on what we would research, and these limits should have some conceptual correspondence with how housing worked in society. This threw into relief the concomitant conclusion on the need for detailed study of how the structural becomes the particular. Historical description should not be used as a sort of 'error term' to cover observed but otherwise unexplained differences. Rather than merely link events in time, any explanatory analysis needs to abstract what was crucial, what was contingent, what was irrelevant and so on. Historical description does not in itself provide the concepts necessary to carry out this sorting procedure – even if it can be suggestive as the reader and writer inevitably insert their own – perhaps unconscious – conceptual apparatus in reading and writing. Again, structuration and determination should not be thrown out because of the (commendable) recognition of the importance of the particular.

This was one conclusion of the debate over the work of 'culturalist' historians like Thompson and Hobsbawm in relation to their attacks on the theoreticism of structuralists (see, for example, Johnson 1978). And, as with our own work, the realist philosophy of social science seemed to offer a practical way to follow this 'happy medium', to carry out conceptually informed historical research (Sayer 1981, 1984, Johnson 1982, see also chapter seven). Unfortunately, we only became aware of the potentialities of a realist concept of explanation towards the end of the research project. Nor, it must be admitted, is realism sufficient, unproblematic or even ready-finished as a guideline for research conceptualization – although again it is a case of the most adequate way of working available for our purposes. But for most of the study we were left with our own primitive realism, formed in reaction to the earlier phases of empiricist and structuralist research on housing; a commitment to discovering underlying social processes which caused social forms, where discovery would proceed by conceptually informed historical research (see Duncan 1977, 1981). Comparative analysis was one strategy for carrying out such work in practice.

## 1.3 Housing provision, capitalist society and localities

The previous section relates how we developed an overall framework on what housing provision is and how this might best be analysed. One conclusion was that to understand housing we must move outside housing itself, and relate its provision to an overall theorization of social relations. This section provides a general statement on how we see housing provision in capitalist society, and on how this relates to the idea of 'the locality'. These generalizations may strike the reader as rather assertive; we should stress that these are introduced as no more than initial working positions. It is the book as a whole which develops and justifies them. We will deal in turn with housing provision in capitalism, the anatomy of capitalist society (including the role of capitalist states), and the importance of localities.

*Housing provision*

Readers may remember that our research began by taking variations in housing provision as a given problem to be explained. This initial impetus was provided by the social significance of housing and the way in which this was reflected in academic debate.

Why is housing provision so important? First of all, it is crucial to individuals. This is not just a matter of shelter and space, but also access to other material resources and to social rewards. The dwelling becomes a meaningful cultural object expressing feelings and social relations as well as depending upon them. It is crucial for the social individual's life trajectory. Even at the individual level, then, housing provision is one aspect of social relations. This becomes all the clearer in turning to direct economic relations. In capitalism housing is a source of income for builders, landowners, financiers, rentiers, middlemen of various sorts, among others; less directly housing construction, maintenance, equipping and servicing have far-reaching effects on industrial production, on consumption patterns and on household incomes. Housing provision is very important for both capital accumulation and employment generation in capitalist economies.

But the economic role of housing provision stretches even further than this. The costs of labour for employers are partly determined by the costs of housing for employees; even the latter's continued existence and quality as a commodity are strongly influenced by the costs, quantities and sorts of housing available. Workers have to be produced, and they are produced outside capitalist social relations themselves – in the home and in the 'community'. However, housing does not only represent dwellings for workers, but also homes for people; housing provision has a central social role as much as an economic function. The home has a crucial part to play in reproducing social structures in terms of its significance for socialization, social control and social interpretation. This role extends far beyond the economic function of managing the social nature of labour as a commodity. Moreover, that surplus labour, domestic workers and all those who are not directly involved in capitalist production are also vitally linked to the process of social reproduction as well as economic management. It is not surprising that housing often plays a key role in social conflict, economic organization and political mobilization. Crucially, the processes of housing provision cut through and bring together the major conceptual and everyday divides of production and consumption, politics and economics, material and ideological. Housing is work, home and politics.

*The anatomy of capitalist societies*

If housing embodies work, home and politics, housing provision straddles the major spheres of social structuration in capitalist societies – social relations of production, of state institutions and 'civil society' (the home, the community). This is, of course, equally true of many other social activities, although most (e.g. sport, work, family life) are centred in one sphere and few have such an important role in each. It will be useful here to outline how our research fits into this picture. First it will be necessary to expand a little on this conceptualization of capitalist society. Our account is largely taken from Urry (1981a, 1982).

In identifying three spheres of social relations, we should not imagine these as separate levels or instances, nor as economic base and social superstructure. Rather we are conceptualizing sets of bases for social actions, abstractions of 'areas of social life', and it is most appropriate to visualize interrelating circuits of social relations. Furthermore because capitalist societies are premised upon continual change, the form of these circuits and the links between them are constantly being restructured. Although no one sphere can be seen as a societal base, capitalism as a particular social structure is premised upon exchange relations and the production of commodities. It is because production is separated from circulation (including consumption here) that surplus labour can be realized in value form. The products of labour are separated – by ownership and by the market – from consumption on the part of the labourers. Housing construction is just one production/valorization process by which this can occur; likewise land development gains or house rents are one means by which particular social groups can intervene in this process of valorization (landowners may be able to appropriate part of builders' profits, rentiers part of workers' wages). Labour power itself is bought and sold as a commodity, and money – as one, fetishized representation of value – helps knit production relations into civil society through that crucial factor of everyday capitalism, the wage.

The analysis of production relations was of course the major aim of Marx's *Capital*. But what of civil society and the state? *Capital* neglects three crucial points. First, only a minority of the population is directly involved in capitalist production; surplus workers, domestic workers, children, the old, do not appear as 'bearers' of the functions of capital and labour. This was less true, perhaps, in the Britain of 1848 but is certainly the case now. The position of some state service workers is also an ambiguous one. (In speaking abstractly here, we also ignore the complicating factor of commodity and subsistence production outside capitalist relations, such as in a peasant sector. The case of Sweden (see section 2.2) shows how this can be a telling contingent factor in real societies.) Second, even when individuals do bear the social relations of capitalist production, part of their lives is lived outside paid work and even within it they are endowed with consciousness and will. Finally, wage labour itself is obviously a presupposition of capitalist production, but it is not produced by capitalism. Hence the telling criticism of Marx's neglect of domestic labour and the production of people. It is a precondition of capitalist relations of production that there is a realm of social practices outside it where people, and individual subjectivities, are made and reproduced. It is here they develop consciousness and will just as much as (if not more than) in capitalist workplaces. These diverse social practices can be categorized as 'civil society'.

Urry distinguishes three sorts of practices which comprise civil society; these are the social relations of circulation, of reproduction and of social inter-vention (called social struggles by Urry). Examples with relevance to our research are housing tenure itself (a means of circulation), housing as a vital element for the domestic economy, and finally voluntary organizations such as tenants' associ-ations, community groups and political parties which seek to intervene in housing production, its circulation and its consumption (largely, in social-democratic societies, through action aimed at state institutions). This plethora of social practices is partly, and to a varying degree, independent of capitalist production – it may even threaten the latter. None the less, we repeat, it is essential to capital-ism's existence (see figures 1.2 and 1.3).

Civil society is also highly differentiated; by gender, religion, ethnicity, gener-ation, and spatially. As recent research has stressed, these differences are also important to the capitalist economy and again are partly used by and partly formed by production relations (e.g. Friedman 1977, Massey 1983). Urry goes on to categorize civil society as being predominantly 'vertically' organized when these diverse social groupings and relations are predominantly class specific, that is formed around production relations, with relatively little independent organiz-ation. On the other hand, civil society is 'horizontally' organized when groupings and practices are relatively non-class specific.

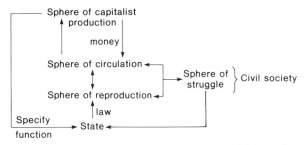

*Figure 1.2* The basic structure of capitalist social formations

*Source:* Urry 1981, 116.

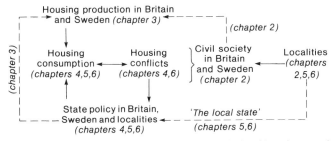

*Figure 1.3* Structure and variation in our analysis of housing provision

It is useful to categorize our own case studies in this way. As we shall see, Sweden, Sheffield and inter-war Norfolk are good examples of the vertical organization of civil society (and the very existence of these examples demonstrates the importance of spatial differentiation). In Sweden, capital and labour, themselves two organized blocs, together dominate civil society and state behaviour. In Sheffield organized labour, mainly through trade unions and the Labour Party, has long dominated local politics and hence influenced circulation and reproduction relations in that locality. Inter-war rural Norfolk was similar, except that here farmers and landowners dominated organized agricultural labour. On the other hand, civil society in Brighton, at least during parts of the post-war period, is probably one example of horizontal organization – our squatting case study suggests this at least, while it is certainly arguable that civil society in Britain as a whole is becoming increasingly 'horizontal'. This change does not necessarily mean a shift to the political right, incidentally. Brighton has shown a long-term shift to the left, and arguably this is partly one result of the 'alternative politics' of a wide range of densely organized, if 'horizontal', groups. Crawley has been in something of a see-saw position, complicated by the anomalous position of the local state in a new town.

But, whatever the form of civil society, the capitalist economy is still organized around the relations of capital and labour; even if both capitalists and labourers experience 'horizontal' groupings in civil society as a prime basis for their subjectivity. (None the less, even though they must enter capitalist social relations 'against their will' their behaviour in exercising these relations may then well differ.) However, the nature of civil society cannot be read directly from the form of the economy, the links between both spheres are contingent upon social struggles originating in both. For instance, whether and how far the capital–labour division is reflected in the dominant politics of civil society (Sweden versus USA, Sheffield versus Brighton) depends upon struggles which establish and sustain the salience of class as opposed to other bases of popular mobilization.

Capitalist states have emerged as that sphere of social relations which mediates between civil society and the capitalist economy. Usually developing from existing pre-capitalist states in the advanced capitalist countries, the minimal function exercised through capitalist states was, and still is, the attempt to ensure continued capital accumulation within its territory. (This attempt may well fail.) The organization and orchestration of civil society, and the response to struggles taking place there, is one chief means of attempting to sustain capital accumulation. This is promoted through the development of a set of institutions ultimately based on the regular and centralized monopoly of physical coercion, although generally transmuted into law and state organized social rules. This intervention and response role places state institutions in a contradictory position and this is one important reason why state action is confused, fragmented and internally contradictory. This situation is more complicated in franchise societies and particularly in social democracy where the representatives of labour have increased influence on state institutions. In some cases, as in Sweden, labour exerts influence from within the state. Indeed, as we shall see in section 2.2, many important state institutions in Sweden were developed through labour's political hegemony and represent its interests closely. This contradictory position does not necessarily mean that the capitalist economy suffers; Swedish social democracy clearly represents a thoroughly institutionalized class compromise, where struggles have produced complex, elaborate and fairly secure means of stabilizing and regularizing social conflict. None the less, the potential for reforming or even for removing capitalism is established to some extent.

How do state institutions carry out this role? Partly this is a matter of what they do, developing activities to manage labour directly (the Poor Law), reproduce it (housing, health), or support capital accumulation direct (state infrastructure, property rules and rights). These functions are not necessarily functional in origin; nor are they always dreamt up by an all-powerful state or capitalist class. Most are in fact produced by social struggles and have complex transforming effects as well as sustaining effects; they work both ways as it were – for capital and labour, for stability and change. The vote, or state subsidized housing, are two notable examples.

Crucially, however, the importance of state institutions lies not only in what they do, but how they do it. State activity is as much a matter of interpreting society as physical management. In franchise and social democratic states in particular, state institutions act to transcend class relations and the other relations of civil society into supposedly equal and non-social legal relations of individual citizenship (see Duncan and Goodwin 1982b). This is sometimes called the 'state form' of the capital–labour relation. It is analogous to the wage relation developed in that other central capitalist institution, the firm, where class relations are transcended into the supposedly equal legal relations of employer and employee. Citizenship is analogous to the wage. Neither transcendence is, of course, at all secure or given. People have to work hard to maintain them and equally people work against them; not just that, but these fetishized relations have to be maintained against a more real world where class relations are a basic experience and where class can be a threatening and attractive way for people to conceptualize society. Social democracy is one compromise position – a position which some commentators argue to be in danger of collapsing in Britain. In Sweden, both social democratic institutions and the social compromises and structures supporting them are stronger, but even so the period since 1973 has seen increased tension and inadequacy in 'the Swedish model'.

Where does the 'local state' fit in? As well as providing local administration, one key role of local state institutions is to manage, respond to and, if possible, transcend (into legal relations) local class relations and other local social relations. For, as we have pointed out, civil society is unevenly developed and hence spatially differentiated.

How are we going to use the terms state, local state, government, etc. in this book? These terms are often used in a confusing way; we shall at least attempt to use them consistently. To start with the easiest case, we define *local government* as those sub-national institutions ostensibly run on the principles of representative democracy and electorally accountable to all citizens within their territorial limits. Examples in Britain are the district councils, the county councils, London boroughs, metropolitan counties and the Greater London Council. (Typically, legislation in 1984 seeks to abolish the last two.) In Sweden the communes and the county assemblies (*kommun* and *landsting*) are the major local government institutions. It is the district and county councils (including London boroughs) in Britain and the communes in Sweden which supposedly have responsibility for local housing policy. There are also, however, a wide range of *non-electoral* local government institutions. These vary from local offices of central departments to a bewildering array of autonomously constituted local and regional corporatist bodies. Health and Water Authorities are good examples in Britain. The County Boards (*länstyrelse*) in Sweden are important in devolving central policy and resources to local communes, including housing. In Sweden, incidentally, health services are administered by the electoral *landsting* on a regional (sometimes metropolitan) level. All of these sub-national institutions of government and administration can be lumped together as 'local state institutions'.

It is more difficult to provide precise definitions at the national level. We use *central government* to refer to the cabinet–ministry–civil service department nexus of executive and administrative state power, where a parliamentary majority is just one condition for the exercise of such power (see Jessop 1980). This includes ministries and ministers responsible for overt housing policy. Again, *central state institutions* are seen as wider than this, encompassing the vast range of autonomous bodies sometimes loosely referred to as quangos, some with considerable power. The Manpower Services Commission in Britain, or the National Housing Board in Sweden (which eventually became a ministry) are good examples. We take the term *the British* (*or Swedish*) *state* as a collective description for all these institutions, local and national. Note also the emergence of international executive 'state' bodies, often powerful economic and military institutions (EEC, NATO), but also encompassing a wide range of agencies (UNESCO, Council of Europe). Direct electoral influence is almost shadowy at this level.

Finally, what of the terms *capitalist state*, *local state*, and *the state*. These we take as more abstract terms, real enough but not referring directly to empirical institutions and procedures. They refer also to the social relations between people and groups which fuel these institutions. The 'capitalist state', then, refers to those relations distinguishing this form of the state from those connected with other modes of production (the feudal state, etc.). 'The state' is of course an extremely general and transhistorical term (like 'production', 'the family' or 'society'). 'The local state' is most difficult to define, partly because of its origin as a polemical term. We take it to refer, abstractly, to the specificity of the state form at sub-national level – if any.

We are now in a position to link this discussion back into our project for comparative analysis of particular forms of housing provision in capitalist society. Going back to our initial discussions of why housing provision is important in capitalist societies (pages 10–11), we can see how housing provision threads through capitalist economies, civil societies and state institutions.

It is quite possible to pursue these interconnections at this abstract level. Ball (1978) undertook this task with reference to the 'economic level' in isolation.

Similarly Harvey, in a number of essays (e.g. 1978) has linked transformation in the built environment to the circuiting of capital. Castells (1977) made a major attempt in *The Urban Question*, although this time analysis was artificially restricted to an urban political level (see Duncan 1978a, 1981 for a critique of the 'levels' approach). Neo-Weberian theorists restrict themselves to the analysis of consumption sectors in relation to state institutions (e.g. Saunders, 1980); feminist based analyses concentrate on gender roles, the domestic economy and the production of people (e.g. Mackenzie, 1980). The stage is still set for a unifying, abstract theorization of housing in capitalism. A less economistic version of Cleaver's (1979) notion of society as a 'social factory' complemented by analyses of the production of people might do the trick. However, although capitalist societies are distinguished by distinctive functional relations between capital, labour and the state, these formulations tell us relatively little about the detailed contingent characteristics of such societies. The human world of action is temporal and spatial, located in unique circumstances which give a specific action its character. One reason, then, for the failure of Castells's project was just that he attempted to read off specific characteristics from this structural analysis, even though many of the objects and relations he studied do not have any general form. This approach is also quite inadequate in apprehending how necessarily contingent social struggles impinge on structures.

So, rather than provide this possible abstraction of housing in capitalism, we have attempted to follow through some of the contingent links made by housing provision, in such societies, between the economy, civil society and the state. In abstract terms, we concentrate on housing production as one element of the capitalist economy, on social struggles over housing in civil society, and on the resolution of these struggles in state institutions. We take one major cause of differentiation of civil society and examine its effect on social conflict – including its uneven development spatially and over time. This leads to the creation of socially specific localities within overall structures of change and continuity. Figures 1.2 and 1.3 summarize the relation of our study to this discussion of the anatomy of capitalist societies.

*Localities*

In figure 1.3 some particular stress is placed upon 'localities' as a major dimension of civil society. We will end this section by discussing what this designation means. Readers may remember that we began our initial project formulation with an awareness of the importance of local variations. Indeed, national figures on housing consumption say, only aggregate and average out local variations. It is unrealistic to suppose that local variations have no local effects, and they might be important in understanding local housing conflict for instance. But more serious than this, national level analysis in isolation could miss specifically local mechanisms, local social processes, which help produce social changes in particular places. Indeed, there is evidence to suggest that even national policy changes have been fundamentally affected by sub-national social relations. Housing policy

(Melling 1980), regional policy (Massey and Meegan 1982) and the evolution of state institutions themselves (Duncan and Goodwin 1982b) are cases in point.

Before discussing possible social bases for locally specific processes, it is important to distinguish between local variation and local process. (We use 'local' as a synonym for the rather ungainly 'sub-national'.) It is only the latter which would have causal status in *producing* social change, rather than reflecting it. The natural and social worlds are unevenly developed, and the economic and social processes of capitalism accentuate this. Thus it is not surprising that we find concentrations of economic activity, classes, consumption patterns etc., over space. The contrasts on a world level are most dramatic, but those existing on sub-national scales are not unimportant. Variation in itself, however, does not amount to locally specific causal social process – although it will be a contingent factor to how causal processes work. For example, policies for building more council housing would mean something different when applied in areas with many low income families compared to those without and local deviations to a nationally produced policy would result. Alternatively, local factors may cause local variation. The key difference is the local specificity of causal action. The particular state of local class relations in a 'red island' of strong labour organization, for instance, might result in specific local action to build more council housing. (In the same way, national level processes are nothing more than specific 'local' processes in the context of international capitalism.) A local social process worthy of the name must refer to something active and specific to localities, although not necessarily unique to one locality, rather than local deviations to national level processes. Similarly, a national process worthy of the name must not merely be the average of a mass of local ones; rather it should apply to all areas in practice. A 'locality', then, is not just any sub-national territorial unit exhibiting a degree of variation. Rather, 'locality' refers to a socially defined unit, distinguished by active and specific local differences in causal process.

So much for a formal, abstract distinction between local variations pure and simple and local causal processes. But the question still remains, are there significant and widespread social bases for the existence of locally specific causal processes in reality? This can be answered on two levels. First, are there structural conditions which *could* generate such processes? Second, *if* there are, are conditions such that these processes actually are generated? Or do national and international forces reign supreme in practice even though the potential for locally specific social processes exists structurally?

To answer the structural question first, and very briefly. There seem two broad structural conditions which link together to create a potential for locally specific causal process. First of all, capitalism is both a transforming and unevenly developed social system. These characteristics are structurally based features of the social and economic functioning of capitalism. This is not, then, a matter of some passive mapping of inevitable variation over time and space. Rather uneven development in time and space is central to the processes of capitalist production and social reproduction. Development at one place and time is linked causally to underdevelopment elsewhere, development in one area of life is linked causally with underdevelopment in another, the conditions both produce lead causally to further uneven development. Second, social relations are just what the name suggests (although this is often forgotten) – relational between people and actively developed in practice. They have to be developed and may undevelop, and this will happen contingently in the context of an already unevenly developed social system. How, and indeed if, particular social relations develop will partly depend on time–space links established between social actors.

On logical grounds, therefore, we would expect uneven development to be a prominent part of the capitalist world, both as a socio-spatial result and as a causal socio-spatial process. Two questions follow. What are the actual mechanisms by which uneven development occurs and do these have significant sub-national ('local') dimensions?

At the global level, the dramatic differences and opposing trajectories of First and Third World are so obvious as hardly to need comment. Uneven development has, in response, become the focus of a whole corpus of thought – 'development studies'. The fact that capitalism as a world system is so clearly uneven is useful for our argument; it is a corrective to that sociological and economic reductionism which so easily misidentifies 'society' with 'nation state' and, having done so, proceeds to analyse as though action took place in a timeless void. In fact, as sociology at least is belatedly rediscovering (cf. Giddens 1981) action is specified through time-space linkages, and the nation-state is only one – if possibly very significant – institutionalization of this. And, where the clear fact of uneven development at the world scale has resulted in development studies, uneven development at a sub-national scale underlies urban and regional studies.

But if there is little disagreement about the importance of uneven development at a world scale, exactly how it occurs and, even more, how it is caused, is more contentious. Concepts of dependency, unequal exchange, the articulation of modes of production and the international division of labour have all been employed in the attempt to explain how capitalism becomes so hugely differentiated. Each stresses various combinations of political domination, economic dependency and social subordination to explain how uneven development occurs. (See Roxborough 1979 for a review.) Interestingly, from our point of view, one major conclusion of this work is that, in order to explain how real societies become unevenly developed in practice, it is necessary to relate these more abstract theorizations of causal structure to the particulars of specific societies and conjunctures (e.g. Leys 1975, on Kenya). Similarly, it is clear that the variations between so-called Third World countries are as huge as between First and Third World, while variations in particular countries can also be causally significant in explaining how uneven development actually takes place. 'Articulation of modes of production' theory is indeed an attempt to situate these conclusions on a structural level. (See Taylor 1979 for one review.)

Given conclusions like these, it is not surprising that these theories of global uneven development have been adapted for use on the sub-national level of urban and regional studies – just as development studies itself began to stress the importance of particular localities within the capitalist world order. To take some representative examples, Carter (1974) used Frank's dependency theory to explain the emergence of the Scottish Highlands as an underdeveloped region,

Carney and Hudson (1978) tried to understand the decline of north-east England through concepts of unequal exchange, and Geddes (1979) criticized and complemented Carter's study on the Scottish Highlands through the medium of articulation of modes of production theory. Echoing Hymer (1972), Murray (1972) and Mandel (1963), Massey and Meegan (1982) and others adopted ideas of the international division of labour as a cause of uneven development. The normal processes of economic restructuring in capitalism would create new *spatial* divisions of labour at the same time as they created new social divisions of labour, and this was just as evident at the sub-national scale as it was at an international scale. Similarly, just as control over labour-power was crucial for economic and social restructuring in capitalism (e.g. Braverman 1974, Cleaver 1979), this control had spatial effects and components (e.g. Friedman 1977, Byrne and Parson 1983). The same can be said for gender relations in capitalist societies; as the relation between genders changes so does urban and regional development, *and* vice versa (e.g. Mackenzie and Rose 1983).

As the discussion so far implies, this spatial component is not only a simple and passive 'mapping' of social and economic changes. Local differentiation becomes one element of a linked and circular process of uneven development. It is perhaps easiest to demonstrate this point by reference to recent examples of this process in Britain, using Massey (1983) as a source. In this paper, Massey examines the links between economic restructuring, class restructuring and spatial change, employing Cornwall and the coal mining areas of South Wales as examples. In South Wales, relatively rapid, dramatic and one-sided development in the 1870–1910 period ensured a pattern of economic militancy and labourist local politics in an industrial 'radical region'. This was supported by a number of conditions: a relatively undifferentiated working class often labouring in egalitarian and co-operative ways and working for a distinct bourgeois class and then the state, political and economic domination by outsiders, a single union, pride in the masculine character of skilled heavy work, the lack of a middle class or small entrepreneurs, the lack of alternative forms of labour. (See also Cooke 1983.) However, recent changes in the international division of labour have led to the decline of coal mining in South Wales and the creation of a pool of surplus labour there. This is not only composed of male ex-coal miners but also women where the latter are now less fixed in subordinate domestic labour (even if they still carry out most of it). This concentration of deskilled, partly unskilled and partly inexperienced industrial labour is an inducement for multi-national companies to locate branch factories in the region, concentrating on semi-skilled and unskilled assembly work and often favouring the employment of women. Together with the expansion of state service of jobs, also favouring female employment, the social and political character of the region has been modified. Increases in the size of the new middle class and a decrease in work socialization (e.g. in the coal miners' union) has blurred labour–capital lines of conflict, while changes in the labour force have undermined the homogeneity, uniqueness, maleness, income and status of the previously dominant labour force. These changes have a knock-on effect on local industrial and political relations, placing the region in yet another category for developing divisions of labour.

Massey then looks at the impact of superficially similar branch plant location in Cornwall. Location in this area was also a process of searching for relatively cheap and unorganized labour without jettisoning the infrastructural, social and political advantage of a First World location. But space is not a clean slate; Cornwall already had a specific social character and consequently opposite effects to those in South Wales have occurred. Wage labour and wage levels have increased, the working class has become more homogeneous, traditional small capital is threatened in both commodity and labour markets and lines of conflict between labour and capital become less blurred. The character of Cornwall is becoming quite different as a basis for future action. The same process of economic restructuring has had quite different results because of specific spatial and temporal linkages; furthermore, spatial differences are not only socially caused but become a component of future uneven development.

There is no logical reason why processes of uneven development should be restricted to the supra-national level; examples such as Massey's show how processes of uneven development have sub-national components and effects in practice. Urry (1982) suggests why. Simply put, capitalism may be an international system and its chief economic institution – the firm – is increasingly multinational and increasingly freed from time/space constraints. Labour, however, is not, nor are people's daily individual and communal lives. People live in households grouped together in various localities (with various degrees of density which we can label urban, rural, small town, etc.). These localities are defined in terms of the overlapping co-presence of residents, in familiarity and attachment including important ontological dimensions in people's lives, in a particular relationship to nature and with regard to shared social practices, including (but of course not only) those practices set round local state institutions. As Urry puts it drawing on the work of Giddens (1981) 'Localities are thus the prime site in which social practices are made and sustained, social practices which constitute social systems' (1982, 39). These localities are essentially based on a relatively self-sustaining organization of labour.

Urry categorizes the socio-spatial relations of localities as composing three major components. First of all the regularities and routines of everyday life, second, the spatial relations of a given social structure (e.g. household organization) and, third, the spatial effects of relations between distinct social structures (and hence also distinct social and spatial structures). Massey's work discussed above shows examples of this, the relation between world-wide forms of capital accumulation and relatively bounded, immobile and individualized households of civil society. Relations between national state structures and localities are another example. For Urry, therefore, it is local labour markets which best define localities (albeit approximately). However, this conclusion is based on a primarily economic analysis which does seem reductionist *vis-à-vis* the suggested components of localities. If we were to introduce political and cultural relations more strongly (e.g. national state – locality, national culture – locality) local government areas and regional areas could also be recognized as overlapping operational definitions of locality. None the less, Urry's major conclusion remains:

The consequences of a particular social practice depend upon the manner in which distinct social structures are spatially interdependent over time. Assessment of such spatial effects thus depends upon analysing the particular temporal relations between the causally pertinent social structures.

(1982, 40)

Urry goes on to flesh out this argument through summarizing some particular, current transformations in social structure which, in their consequent spatial and temporal interdependencies (i.e. as they become locally specific social processes) produce particular spatial consequences. Especially important, he claims, are the increased concentration and centralization of capital and the increased role of state expenditure and employment. Paradoxically, because of these spatial and temporal interdependencies, these processes are probably *increasing* the variety and variability of local social structures and practices; localities are becoming more important, not less (cf. Massey's examples of South Wales and Cornwall). This is an interesting conclusion to come up with, particularly because it flies in the face of much conventional political science analysis (both pluralist and structuralist). Not only did conventional political science (like much of social science as a whole) ignore the importance of spatial interdependencies in social relations, but they were probably safest in doing so during the 1950s and 1960s. The important economic and social transformations of the last decade or so were then only nascent, hence the spatial effects and components of transformation were less apparent. The inaccuracy of taking everywhere as being more or less the same, as a sort of subset of the national average, might not have mattered quite so much. In a paradoxical way the current 'crisis of local government' in Britain bears this out. (See Duncan and Goodwin 1985 for a description.) The changing spatial division of labour together with a heightened (and often locally threatening) variety of localities has given a political basis for local governments to act in widely different and sometimes challenging ways. This is one reason why the centre now spends so much effort in trying to control them. In this way the crisis of local government is one component of the process of uneven development.

This recognition of the significance of localities and local social processes has implications for the debates concerning the significance of space *vis-à-vis* society. It does not follow from the argument that local processes have their own specificity that spatial processes operate in some way independently of social process, nor that spatial areas or localities can be analysed in isolation. It is not space *per se* which has a social effect, rather it is the uneven development of social relations. Yet again, Urry puts this rather well:

space *per se* has no general effects . . . it only has effect because the social objects in question possess particular characteristics, namely, different causal powers. Such powers may or may not manifest themselves in empirical events – whether they do or not depends upon the relationship in time–space established with other objects.                                    (1981b, 458)

Spatial patterns are not autonomous from social organization, nor does space determine social organization and activity. This point is now generally accepted within urban and regional studies (e.g. Castells 1976, Saunders 1980). But having said this, it is important to recognize that spatial interdependencies – i.e. uneven development not space *per se* – remain crucial for social processes. Uneven development cannot be ignored in explanations of social change and localities will usually be an important component of this.

Much research has been carried out in recent years on the economic and political processes operating at the global and national levels (e.g. Jessop 1980, Gamble 1981 for analyses of the British state and British economy respectively). At the opposite end of the spectrum, geography, urban sociology and urban history have directed much research activity at the question of local processes. (See Bassett and Short 1980; Saunders 1979, 1981, for reviews.) What is less established, however, is research which focuses on the interaction of these levels. There have been some outstanding pioneer studies of this type in social history (e.g. Stedman-Jones 1971 on economy and housing in Victorian London; Foster 1974 on economy and local state in Oldham; Neale 1981 on social consciousness in Bath). This work has more recently been echoed in urban and regional studies (e.g. Friedman 1977, Massey 1983, Cooke 1983a and b). It is this focus which, we claim, is necessary for understanding how change occurs and its neglect will be particularly serious if we seek to produce explanations of urban and regional problems.

In making this claim, it follows that the approach followed in this book reacts against both simple 'top-down' and 'bottom-up' approaches. Sometimes the primacy of top-down or bottom-up is merely a matter of scale (especially for the former). The primacy of a particular level is asserted on a priori grounds, or simply taken for granted. Very often in sociology the national level is given this role where this particular spatial configuration is misidentified with 'society'. The sub-national level is reduced to impotence (e.g. Dunleavy 1980, 1981). Alternatively, especially in economics, it is capitalism (or 'the market') as an inter-national system which reduces the national level to impotence (e.g. Mandel 1975). This primacy may be the case but we can now see that this must be an empirical question rather than an a priori given, or the disciplinary Mosaic law it often becomes.

Sometimes this simple 'scale primacy' top-down approach has been com-pounded by a commitment to structuralist theory and methodology. This inevi-tably leads to a focus on the general rather than the specific, the 'system' rather than the particular, the abstract rather than the concrete, and structural determi-nation rather than human agency. At the other side of the coin is empiricism's bottom-up approach. Both approaches are clearly contradictory with a concern to investigate the ways in which the uneven development of social process – local action, local consciousness, local culture, local history – mediate processes gener-ated in wider structural systems. The next chapter will follow up this theme in describing our own case studies of housing provision, states and localities.

### 1.4 Comparative analysis: tool or panacea?

One major conceptual task remains before we can move on to the empirical research – what role can, or should, comparative analysis play in explanation? As discussed in section 1.2, the changes in empirical focus and conceptual approach produced by our researches also led us to re-evaluate the roles, methods and potentialities of comparative analysis. Yet the whole research project had been founded, at least partly, on the notion of comparison between Britain and Sweden, and between various sub-national units. It was not just that variations were important, but the idea was that comparison would in some way make explanation easier. This internal re-evaluation was paralleled and heightened by an emerging 'paradox of comparative analysis' in urban and regional studies as a whole. The 'paradox' was as follows. Researchers in a number of areas – not least in housing work – came to the conclusion that 'comparative research' was necessary to solve their problems, and by and large the research community supported them in this. Funds were granted, the research got under way, and the results were awaited with anticipation. But when the results appeared they were greeted with considerable disappointment. Not only had the comparisons failed to clear up the initial problems, but they had introduced further difficulties (see Harloe and Martens 1984, for one recent indictment).

Why has this been the case, and can comparative analysis make some sort of explanatory contribution despite this unimpressive track record? We attempt to answer this question in three stages. We start off by asking what it is that researchers have expected comparative analysis to do. We go on to demonstrate how these expectations are unrealistic; hence the disappointments. And we end by discussing what, in the light of these arguments, comparative analysis may actually be able to achieve.[4] Underlying this whole discussion is a debate about explanation in social science, about what explanation aims for and how this can best be carried out. The perceived role of comparative analysis is deeply affected by one's position in this debate and our own perceptions are no exception. However, this underlying debate is not strictly necessary to our task here, that of evaluating the role of comparative analysis in relation to our empirical work. We return to this wider discussion in chapter seven.

What are researchers trying to do in using comparative analysis? It seems to us that, usually, although more often unconsciously rather than consciously, they have attempted to replicate the experimental method in natural science. Here the aim (practice is often deficient) is that the experimental conditions and their changes are subject to the will of the researcher. She is *physically* able to control the experiment in conditions that should leave only one unknown – the phenomenon under investigation. As everything else is controlled the nature and effect of this phenomenon can be observed and measured.

The conventional fruit fly experiment is a good example. We know almost everything there is to know about fruit flies and anyway, the researcher knows exactly under what conditions a particular batch of flies has developed. Furthermore, every fly in this batch has developed in the same way. This identical population can be broken into two or more groups, one control group and one or more groups where a single condition is physically altered at the will of the researcher. The effect of changing this single condition, in terms of variations to the different fruit fly populations, can then be measured as precisely as the apparatus allows.

It is important to note that this is not necessarily an empiricist model of scientific behaviour. Interpretation and theory are vital ingredients. How should variable and constant factors be picked? What do the experimental measurements mean? Why do a particular experiment at all? The measurements produced by the experimental comparison are only an aid to the interpretive process of analysis – reasonably precise observations are available for a range of situations when the researcher knows exactly which experimental condition has been changed, when this happened and by how much. This does not in itself produce explanation. The scientist still has to interpret why these recorded changes occur.

Misapprehension on this point is one source of error in social science comparison. The empiricist model idealizes what it takes as the scientific method – the experiment – forgetting that the experiment can only take place and be given some meaning through the researcher's value-laden interpretation. However, our criticisms are not solely directed at the empiricist fallacy (although this certainly doesn't help). The problems of social science comparative analysis run deeper than that.

This is because it is not just the empiricist version of the test-tube experiment which provides the model (conscious or not) for comparative social science. The non-empiricist version – fully acknowledging the crucial role of theory and interpretation – is still based on the experimental method. And, equally, it is just as important to establish complete control over experimental populations. A large part of natural science research in fact consists in checking that this is indeed the case, that it is only the factors which are meant to vary that have actually varied, that populations are truly independent. Perhaps defective apparatus has not allowed proper control, or interactions are occurring about which the scientist has no prior knowledge. Ironically, at the time of writing, a whole generation of biological research has been plunged into chaos by the discovery that populations of laboratory mice have not been truly independent; rogue mice have escaped captivity and transfered genetic characteristics willy-nilly.

Clearly, this degree of physical control is not possible for social science research; the social world cannot be put into test tubes or laboratory cages. Even supposedly real world equivalents, like those so often used (e.g. populations of students, military personnel or prisoners), are not nearly good enough, even if ethical problems could be overcome. For human populations very easily create their own social mechanisms which will disrupt experimental control and even mediate the researcher's manipulations (prison hierarchies are a good example). The subject population can actively alter the conditions of the experiment in a way that the researcher cannot control; they can alter their own social world.

This is where comparative analysis comes in. It seems to offer a way out – the possibility of finding real world test tubes where history and geography have set up the experiment. Situations can be found where certain conditions have been constant, and where others have varied. At the very least, particular conditions may have developed to extremes and so their effect can be effectively isolated and measured. Our own research comparing Britain and Sweden can be seen in this way; thus the labour movement in Sweden has had effective access to state power over a sustained period, while landed capital is politically and economically weak.

More or less the converse is true of the situation in Britain. These variables are 'controlled' in a real world test tube.

There are, however, considerable inadequacies with this 'imitation test tube' view of comparative research. This is not just because of its inherent limitations, where comparative analysis in social science can in no way emulate the level of success reached by the experimental method in natural science. These inadequacies have been exacerbated by the method of imitation itself; accepting the test tube model has been facilitated by an empiricist view of explanation which has fed into misapprehensions about the relation between comparison and explanation.

We have, therefore, two grounds of criticism of the 'imitation test tube' approach to comparative analysis – the way it has usually been carried out has been inadequate, and over and above this it anyway founders on its own epistemological grounds. The one reinforces the other. Critical comment has mostly been levelled at the former, the most obvious failing, but it should be clear that, even if the research method was itself exemplary the epistemological limitations of the whole approach would prejudice the comparison. We will consider these epistemological failings first.

There are three fatal and inherent weaknesses of the 'imitation test tube' model of comparative analysis. First of all, abstraction can rarely be developed empirically in social science. Unfortunately, this is the goal of the experimental method – the experiment allows physical control over variability and it is then possible to objectify abstraction. (Indeed, particle physics seems to have reached the stage of physically creating its own abstractions in the experiments themselves.) But it is not possible to objectify physically, for example, a pure capitalist mode of production, a pure ground rent or gender relation.

Second, there is a world of difference between the comparisons undertaken in controlled experiments and in social science comparative research. In the former, the experimenter takes a homogeneous sample of population, applies different treatments to different parts of this one group, and then sees what happens. Only the treatment should vary according to the researcher's physical control. However, social science comparison is quite different. Here the investigator picks two or more highly heterogeneous and *already* constituted separate populations, and is unable to treat them in different ways. Furthermore, in aping the experimental method, conventional comparative analysis assumes that the differences observed in the cases are simply going to be caused by the differences referred to in the criteria used in picking these cases (e.g. industrial/non-industrial, communist/non-communist, labour/conservative). This is quite likely to be a false assumption. The ex-post division of a non-experimental situation is in no way the same as experimental control. (Similarly, statistical control is not the same as physical manipulation, although the opposite is often assumed.) These divisions *might* be the 'crucial variable', but this conclusion depends on showing, empirically, how this is so – how the social processes involved are fundamental in explaining the observed differences between the cases.

Finally, there are the added problems in social science of separating the researcher from the object of research – the social world. The problems of interpretation are difficult enough in natural science, where the researcher has to understand scientific interpretations (concepts and theories) and use them to set up experiments, define measurements and make sense of results. But at least the natural world is usually impervious to these interpretations and separate from them. This is not the case for the social world where the researcher does not only have to understand scientific interpretations but also social interpretations made by the object of study (understandings of class, the role of planning or the housing problem, for instance). Add in the facts that scientific and everyday interpretations very often overlap in an unclear way, that scientific interpretations can change everyday conceptualizations, that the researcher is not outside the object of study and indeed is deeply influenced by it, and the problems for the test tube model become immense. This relates to the well known difficulty of actually comparing different social situations. 'Owner-occupation' as a social concept does not mean the same, or have the same effects, in Sweden and Britain or in Accrington and Epsom. Not only is it impossible to put society into test tubes (our first two objections) but the researchers contaminate the test tube and even live in it.

All this is serious enough, but the way research has been carried out has often exacerbated these inherent limitations. For comparative analysis is frequently used as little more than a device to sidestep the overall failure of empiricism – the attempt to establish abstraction and causal inference without overt theory. We say 'overt' for it is not possible to avoid theory when all observation is theory-laden. But unconscious or post-experimental theory will normally be weak and under-developed. In fact most empiricists do feel the need for theory, and grope towards it as far as possible – it is just that they remain hamstrung by an epistemology that denies the role of theory in empirical research.

So what does the empiricist do in this self-defeating situation? We will take one recent research project on the inner-city problem as an example (Hall (ed.) 1981; see Duncan 1982c for a critical review). One response is to smooth over the dilemma by appealing to unexamined, and often analytically superficial, common-sense theories. These are merely tacked on to the end of the research as a sort of desperate afterthought when the need for abstraction cannot be palmed away any longer. So Hall and his contributors use the notion of a life cycle of cities to explain the inner-city problem; they present masses of useful information, but the explanation proffered does not interact with this information except in the most superficial way and so remains simplistic. There is, furthermore, no coherent rationale for presenting just that information and what it means remains uncertain. Another and very similar response is to lift theories from other disciplines, a sort of 'social science common sense' and again uncritically and superficially tack them on to the end of the 'data' (which has already been collected according to some other unexamined and implicit theory). Neo-classical economies is one favoured source, probably because of its socio-academic standing. So the utility function of inner-city locations is held to have declined and this, deterministically, is taken as explaining the data. (Occasionally, no doubt as unconscious complement to the rising social status of Marxism, Hall uses the 'dominant ideology' in a similar role.)

Finally, and this is the point of our critique of Hall so far, comparative work can perform the role of explanatory panacea. The hope is that comparative empiricism can somehow produce explanatory theory when simple empiricism cannot. To go on using the same example, Hall assumes that in comparing cities with different social and economic trends (e.g. Glasgow and Bristol) the crucial variable causing these differences will, somehow, emerge. The idea is that comparison will itself produce theory and hence explanation. Setting up the test tubes is enough; we do not have to bother with interpretation, with carrying out the experiment. This is a chimera.

Our conclusion is that the 'imitation test tube' approach to comparative analysis is quite misleading. The epistemological inadequacies of this approach are severe, and are all the worse for usually remaining unrecognized. Such comparisons will promise much, but will not be able to deliver. And to cap it all, the imitation test tube approach most easily leads to an empiricist research strategy which can only exacerbate these inherent inadequacies. Section 2.3 follows up this line of reasoning in relation to some actual examples of comparative research on housing provision in Britain and Sweden.

However, this sort of conclusion leaves social science (not to mention our own project) with a difficult problem. For comparative analysis is actually a central research strategy – even if this centrality very often remains unacknowledged and its implications neglected. This role is indicated quite well by the frequency of the question among researchers – 'What are your case studies?' Case studies are essentially an investigative method of controlling real world complexity and variation, and involve a strong comparative element. In this sense, comparative analysis is not restricted only to international comparison (although this is often taken for granted) – it is merely then that the problem of the approach becomes most obvious. Research can be just as comparative in examining different places in one country, or the same place at different times. Taking just one case study is also comparative, although here the comparison often remains implicit – with an assumed national or social norm perhaps.

The central role of comparative research, implicit or explicit, is likely to be especially important in urban and regional research. An important task is to understand how particular cities and regions have developed in particular ways, in relation to wider generative processes of social change. The so-called 'inner-city problem' for instance, is as much a problem of the new international division of labour, or of Britain's political and economic impasse, as it is of inner cities *per se*. The overall social science problem of explaining variation within broad trends, of relating spatially and temporarily specific changes to wider processes, is writ especially large for urban and regional studies. Hence the attraction of comparative analysis. It offers the hope of controlling some of these variations. If particular circumstances can be standardized through comparative studies, the effect of wider processes of change can be assessed, or the experiment can be reversed to standardize the wider processes and assess the role of particular conditions.

How can we move forward out of this impasse, where the promise of comparative analysis is faced by the failures of the 'imitation test tube' approach? The answer is that this approach is not the only possible role for comparative analysis, there is something left and comparison can still play an important role. It is only that comparative work can no longer be seen as a talisman to make up for the deficiencies of empiricism, nor the social science equivalent of the experimental method. We see two major roles. First, an 'undercutting the taken for granted' and 'abstraction checking' role. Second, and more problematically, a 'variability reduction' role. Fundamentally, comparative analysis should only be seen as a methodological aid, not as explanation. To carry on the natural science metaphor, it is more like the experimental situation than the experiment itself. Comparison cannot in itself produce conceptual knowledge.

We have termed the simplest use of comparison 'the undercutting the taken for granted role'. Quite often situations which are socially and historically created are taken for granted – that is assumed to be unproblematical and sometimes natural, inevitable or universal – by particular social groups including research communities. The classic case in housing work is the acceptance, in Britain, of owner-occupation as a natural, inevitable and superior tenure which is in some way a function of increased living standards. But in Sweden, owner-occupation declined as a proportion of stock between 1945 and 1975 (it is now increasing again), although at the same time real household incomes increased substantially above the British level while housing standards also improved considerably. This is not to say that owner-occupation does not have some 'organic' connection with advanced capitalist society – but if it does this now has to be demonstrated or (for policy makers) justified.

The comparative shock regarding owner-occupation has of course had some effect by now, although more among researchers than policy makers. More pervasive is the notion that private-sector housing construction in capitalist societies must necessarily be speculative. In fact Britain is very much the odd person out on this score, at least as far as western Europe is concerned where speculative housing production is usually of negligible importance (see Barlow and Dickens 1984). In Sweden only 13 per cent of housing built since 1940 has been built in this way; most private-sector housing is built to local authority tender where state authorities regulate where, when, how and to what price the dwellings are to be built – and even allocate them through waiting lists. If this arrangement works well socially and economically in Sweden – which it does (see chapter three) – why not in Britain?

A stage further on is what we call 'generalization and abstraction checking'. This involves the generalization of particular cases as universal, or their elevation to the status of abstract, context-free statements. Incorrectness in this process is especially a danger when the cases involved are socially immediate to both researchers and research-users. As far as these groups are concerned, the society, nation or locality in which they live or have been brought up in is normal, and that conclusions drawn from research on any of these entities therefore have general application.

This may be the case, but should not be taken for granted. Problems of un-warranted generalization or abstraction can arise when the assumed normality of a given case outstrips empirical and conceptual examination of generality. Indeed the case study (for that is what it is) may be a deviant one – this is actually quite likely for research based in Britain. A good example is the 'British model' of housing production. This is based on detailed research which has established that the British house building industry is relatively undercapitalized, with low productivity levels and, in one sense, 'abnormally' capitalist in that restructuring of the labour process or technical innovation is not seen as the key to profitability (Ball 1978, 1983; Merrett 1979). To some extent these authors have assumed that this is inevitably the case for house building in capitalist societies, either for technical reasons (the complexity and difficulty of the building process, etc.) or for social reasons (the role of land ownership and hence development gain is one example). Yet the alternative 'Swedish model' (which may perhaps be equally abnormal but in a different way) shows that the British case is certainly not an inevitable one. The house building industry in Sweden is relatively well capitalized, with relatively high productivity and considerable labour process restructuring and technical innovation (see chapter three). The relations of house building are clearly socially created even within the bounds of capitalist societies (see Duncan 1978a for an earlier critique along these lines). Research on local states is perhaps the classic example of this process. Investigators have spent a lot of time describing and categorizing the British situation, and then go on to attach general descriptive labels to these categories. It is then assumed that this provides an explanatory theory of *the* local state. But this is not necessarily – and in fact is probably not – the case (see Duncan and Goodwin 1982a).

In these ways comparison can provide a conceptual challenge to accepted positions. Undercutting the taken for granted poses new questions about 'how' and 'why'. Generalization has to be checked and abstractions refined. But comparison has not provided any of the answers. Researchers still have to go on to investigate how and why. Chapter three begins this task when considering the problem of variations in housing production in capitalist societies.

This role for comparative analysis is useful enough. But how far can it undertake a more positive role? We believe that there is such a role and that this consists of a methodological aid for the abstraction of explanatory concepts in empirical research. Explanation is all about holding off supposed peripheral factors so as to isolate the supposed crucial factors, and so allocate causal significance. Comparative analysis can find appropriate combinations of real world similarities and differences to allow a measure of control over complexity and variability. For instance a particular factor may be taken to an extreme in one case, or conversely particular circumstances are the same in two or more cases. It is then more possible, using such comparison, to isolate the effect of particular and general and to aid the process of attributing causal significance. Put another way, comparative analysis can achieve some control over real world variability and so contribute in establishing the process links between structural mechanisms and historical events. And this is a central concern of this book.

At first sight, this might appear like 'The test tube is dead, long live the test tube'. But there are essential differences between this view and the 'imitation test tube' approach. This is not just a matter of freeing ourselves from unwarranted explanatory ambitions where there can be no pretence that a simple juxtaposition of empirical outcomes will produce explanation in itself, out of the blue. For although comparison does not give the ability to *control* real world variability in what are open social systems, it does allow some *reduction* in object variability – even though this reduction is not open to control by the researcher.

This brings us to two further reservations about comparative analysis. First, although comparison can be useful in showing cases where actual contingent conditions present differ, these conditions will vary simultaneously and not in a controlled fashion. It will not be easily possible, and may be impossible, to identify particular differences with particular conditions. Second, much of human action is highly context dependent. Social and political consciousness is one example with relevance to our research. Sheffield could hardly be a 'red island' of social consciousness without Sheffield as a place, history and cultural association. Political consciousness cannot be easily treated as an isolatable factor which can be added or subtracted at will. Experimental method assumes that this is the case, that the specific components of behaviour are found independent of context.

It is for reasons like this that it is the unusual case that is often the most valuable for social science comparative work. It is here that the conceptual challenge, 'undercutting the taken for granted', or, checking generalization is more likely and more effective. The 'variability reduction' role of comparison is also more possible when using unusual or extreme cases. These cases will, by definition, 'spontaneously' hold off contingent factors common elsewhere. (As Sweden 'holds off' concentrated and powerful land ownership, for example.) If these apparently unusual cases can then be shown to be produced by wider common structures and to be linked with other unique cases we shall have achieved some resolution of the structure-variation problem. Structures and contingencies can be isolated. This was one reason for choosing our case studies.

Our overall conclusion is that comparative analysis can only be used as a low order methodological aid. Hence our use of the term 'comparative analysis', rather than 'comprehensive research'.[5] It can provide a conceptual challenge to accepted positions and possibly enable some relative and largely uncontrolled reduction of real world variability. In this way comparison can contribute to conceptually informed causal analysis. We will now go on to try and do some of this for our own research on housing provision in capitalist society.

## CHAPTER TWO

# State and localities – the case studies

## 2.1 Choosing the case studies

We have so far established the importance of variability in four major ways. First of all, social process and structure take effect as they interact contingently in space and time. Indeed, these interdependencies are fundamental to *how* they act. Second, capitalism is unevenly developed in its very structure. Third, although national variations are a major historical configuration of spatial interdependence, sub-national configurations (localities) may also be significant. It is even possible that localities are becoming more important as the pace of social transformations heightens. The local dimensions of housing as a material construct and the home as ontological device, as a means of shaping and defining personality, will emphasize these factors. Finally, a comparative methodology can be a useful research strategy in examining this variation. While not the quasi-experimental panacea it is sometimes assumed to be, comparative research can allow some degree of control over variability. More pragmatically, only very long-term or well financed research projects can attempt to be simultaneously general and detailed. Understanding social processes in practice means detailed work which thus usually dictates case study.

What of the particular cases – Britain, Sweden, Sheffield, rural Norfolk, Crawley and Brighton? Britain had effectively chosen itself; it was the political and academic context for the research. Given this, the aim was to find exemplary comparisons where the effect of contingencies on structural mechanisms would be more obvious. These cases were most likely to be unusual, rather than typical. In this way Sweden was chosen as a comparative exemplar of social democracy. At first, using our British lenses, we saw Sweden as an extreme. However, the research soon suggested that if either country can be seen as deviant from some assumed normal, that country would surely be Britain. It was in Sweden that social relations appeared more normally capitalist – in the economy, in civil society, in the building industry, in land ownership. (Normal, that is, according to a Marxist understanding of social relations – see section 2.2.) We ended up, therefore, using the normality of Sweden to show up the effect of 'deviant' contingent factors in Britain. This comparison was used for those situations where the national configuration of variability was assumed to be strongest, in examining the processes of housing production (chapter three) and national housing policy (chapter four). Of course, as these chapters show, this configuration is by no means exclusive of international or local effects. The sub-national case studies were used for comparative examination of those social processes of housing provision where locally specific causes would be likely to have greater importance – especially for local policy implementation. (Note again, 'greater importance' does not mean 'exclusive', or even 'predominant'.) In other words, we thought it likely that these cases, particular instances of the variation in housing provision, would also be localities – places where locally specific social relations had causal significance.

Discussing current changes in social and economic structures currently affecting Britain, Urry (1983) develops an illustrative typology of resultant local stratification and its likely political effects. His chain of reasoning is as follows: a) changes in capital and states leading to b) spatial consequences including the development of new local variations in stratification structures leading to c) a heightened variety of localities leading to d) local political effects including changes to structural mechanisms. These localities are distinguished on economic role/economic class structure criteria, implicitly focused around the local labour market as spatial mediator. This typology is reproduced below (and see also Urry and his co-workers at the Lancaster Regionalism group for the details of one particular case):[1]

1　Large national or multinationals as dominant capital – small service class and deskilled white-collar workers – large working class, either mainly male or female, depending on supposed skill levels.
2　State as dominant employer – largish service class – many deskilled white-collar workers – declining working class – high employment of women.
3　Traditional small capitals as dominant employers – large petit bourgeois sector – small service class – few deskilled white-collar places – largish male working class – lowish female employment.
4　Private service sector capitals as dominant employers – large service class – many deskilled white-collar workers – many female workers – smallish working class.　　　　　　　　　　　　　　　(Taken from Urry 1983, 41)

Although only illustrative, it is clear that such a process-derived place typology would be superior to the purely epiphenomenal, statistical typologies usually constructed (e.g. Moser and Scott 1961; Donnison and Soto 1980). The latter certainly have their uses, but suffer from the overall limitation to statistical deduction – it is difficult to argue from form to process and this often comes to depend on common sense, intuitive ideas which remain unexamined. In this case, they may also be quite out of date. How much validity does the implicit process explanation 'Yorkshire and Lancashire textile towns' still possess for instance? If such a process-based typology of the type Urry proposes did exist (and at least one current research project is attempting this task), this would provide one basis for choosing case studies. As it is, Sheffield and Crawley New Town seem nearest to Urry's category 1, Crawley before 1950 to category 4, Brighton to category 2 and rural, inter-war Norfolk to category 3 – although none fits exactly.

But in choosing our case studies, we were searching for instances which could fulfil the comparative 'contingency control' role with respect to political relations and, at the same time, the level and type of housing provision. Urry's illustrative typology remains firmly based in the realm of economic change as structural cause (including the role of the national state in this – although Urry tantalizingly notes that he ignores ethnic differences). For our purpose the criteria for case study comparison would have to place greater stress on the role of pre-existing political and cultural processes, derived from already created variations in local civil societies. The differences between Britain and Sweden are not only economic in origin, and the same for localities. Again, this is not to underestimate the importance of national political and cultural structures. These will be very powerful, both in terms of institutional power (state agencies, the media, etc.), and in terms of a shared consciousness of the nation (cf. Anderson 1983). But where Anderson stresses the importance of the 'imagined community' of the nation in cementing everyday lives in a capitalism which is potentially anarchic, both materially and spiritually, it is likely that 'imagined communities' of the locality or region may have some effect. Certainly many social histories and sociologies support this possibility although only now are the connections being made overtly. (See, for instance Foster 1974; Neale 1981 on the locality and social consciousness, Cooke 1983 on the region.) Similarly, local institutions also exist, and it would be unwise to assume in advance of empirical evidence that these have no autonomous social power (e.g. Duncan and Goodwin 1982a,b, on the local state). These considerations also suggest that for some purposes regions or local government areas would be just as suitable for operational definitions as local labour markets. For our research, where local government retained some official and practical autonomy over housing provision, local government units were most suitable – although, as we shall see, local labour market and regional concerns were not without importance.

The first criterion for choosing sub-national case study areas in Britain was variability in housing provision. An initial survey of new house building in England and Wales since 1919 (chapter five) revealed areas with a sustained level of council house building over certain periods. Trends in the locality were often quite different from national trends; the latter could not be assumed to be inevitably dominant. Furthermore, analysis of the survey suggested that in some cases this was more than a function of local deviations caused by a passive mapping onto an already unevenly developed surface. (For instance, in a social democracy with a capitalist building industry we would expect that the national level processes of house provision would cause more council house provision in areas of higher unemployment.) Rather, in some cases local social processes seemed to be important, affecting the quantity, tenure, and quality of housing provided. Moreover, this was not explicable by simple party political differences in local government. Two such cases were taken as exemplars, both showing high rates of council house building at particular periods but having markedly different local social structures – post-war Sheffield and inter-war Norfolk. In Sheffield organized labour had long dominated local politics and had achieved a *local* hegemony over local government. In this sense, Sheffield could figuratively be described as a 'red island'. Local civil society in inter-war Norfolk was also vertically organized around class dimensions, but in the opposite way. Local government there resembled a local executive of the local bourgeoisie; it was run by farmers and landowners and this dominance was part of their strategy in dealing with a numerous, organized and class-conscious rural proletariat. The contingent factor of local political control and struggle would be exposed through this comparison.

Crawley was chosen as a case study where the role of electoral local government itself would be exposed (following earlier research, e.g. Gray 1983). For, over a long period, electoral local government was effectively bypassed in favour of a local organ of the central state – the New Town Corporation, and subsequently the Commission for the New Towns. Interestingly, this alternative structure for local administration seemed to encourage the vertical organization of civil society, especially in respect to housing issues. This was despite the role of the New Town concept which aimed to replace class by 'community'. For Crawley, therefore, we are able to examine two consequent localities in the one place. The pre-new town locality was forcibly replaced and indeed the conflicts over this transition provide us with one example of social struggle over housing provision.

Brighton, our final sub-national case study, was originally chosen as a less atypical comparative foil; we would be aware of how things worked out in a Conservative dominated local government where local civil society seemed horizontally organized. Brighton was convenient for our Sussex base and we could draw on previous research on the town (e.g. Ambrose and Colenutt 1975). However, in some respects Brighton turned out to be a bad choice to fulfil this 'normal control' function. Not only do all localities have their peculiarities (by definition) but Brighton provides a good example of one particular form of local political process; local government was still dominated by a local petite bourgeoisie. This group is potentially vulnerable – and hence often hostile – to reformist restrictions on property rights imposed by the national state in the wider consensual interest, such as land use planning. This was especially the case if these restrictions also impinged on labour costs, as is the case with council house provision. For Brighton's politically dominant petite bourgeoisie is heavily involved in small scale property investment and the use of cheap labour.

What makes Brighton unusual, therefore, is the survival there of an 'urban bourgeoisie' in control of local government. This was the class that dominated 'urban' local government in the late nineteenth century, but since then has been replaced almost everywhere. It was 'urban' in being territorially based in urban areas as well as being socially and materially reliant on the 'urban' economic processes of labour reproduction, especially housing provision, in a way that industrialists, farmers and aristocratic landowners were not. The urban bourgeoisie was made up of property developers, small builders, rentiers, estate agents, conveyancing solicitors, and the like. In industrial areas like north-east England or central Scotland the local power of this group was ousted by a reformist section of local working classes during the 1890–1920 period; petty reaction was replaced by labourism (see N. Tyneside CDP 1978, Byrne 1980a for examples). In some other industrial areas a more progressive and industrially based bourgeois interest became more important; the classic case is Chamberlain's Birmingham. In some other industrial towns local magnates dominated local politics as well as the work place long into the present century (e.g. Murgatroyd and Urry 1983, on Lancaster) while in middle-class suburban local governments a defensive and conservative residential interest has become powerful (cf. Saunders 1979, on Croydon, Young and Kramer 1978 on the politics of suburban exclusion in London). Although the political importance of local property interests remains, especially in small towns and suburbs with weak labour organization, only Belfast among the large industrial towns still shows a well developed urban bourgeoisie in local government (cf. Byrne 1980b).

The local political survival of Belfast's urban bourgeoisie has been predicated upon Orange–Green divisions overwhelming the politics of labour reproduction. We can speculate that survival in Brighton owes something to the availability of alternative economic opportunities outside this mainstream – the holiday trade and more recently office speculation and the antique trade. In Crawley, the incipient power of this group and of the suburban interest (which had themselves only recently squeezed landed interests out of local government in what was a newly urbanized area) was broken by the short but nasty battle over the imposition of the New Town Development Corporation in 1947. In Sheffield an urban bourgeoisie has only provided a brief interlude on the stage of local government politics – this has usually been a matter for local industrialists or local unions (cf. Pollard 1959, Smith 1982). And of course in rural Norfolk, like almost all of rural England (Scotland and Wales are another matter), the landed bourgeoisie of farmers and landowners remains well entrenched in local government (cf. Newby *et al.* 1978).

We will leave a more detailed description of these local case studies until chapters five and six, which is where we take up the issue of locally based causal processes with reference to housing provision. The next two chapters, however, concentrate on the international comparison between Britain and Sweden. The bulk of this chapter, therefore, consists of a comparative account of Swedish society which can form a preparation and context for what is to follow. We will save space and effort in assuming that most readers will be familiar with the British case, at least in general terms – although viewing Sweden comparatively will in itself produce some pointers. (See also Jessop 1980 and Leys 1983 for useful accounts of British society and politics.) Here again, we are looking at locally specific processes within unevenly developed international capitalism, but now at a national level rather than a sub-national one. In this sense national differences are just as much local variations as sub-national differences; the nation state should not be confused with 'society'.

## 2.2 A purer form of capitalism: the development of Swedish social democracy

In August 1852 Marx wrote:

> Universal suffrage is the equivalent of political power for the working classes
> . . . where the proletariat forms the large majority of the population . . . and

where it has gained a clear consciousness of its position as a class . . . its inevitable result . . . is the political supremacy of the working class.[2]

Given political history since universal suffrage was attained in the core capitalist countries, some considerable scorn has been levelled at this statement (although we should remember that universal suffrage was only consolidated as late as 1945 even in most of these countries although both Sweden and Britain were among the pioneers). However, a great deal of this scorn has been misplaced. First, Marx draws attention to two vital conditions if working-class supremacy is to emerge: the proletariat must form the large majority, and it must gain a clear consciousness of its position. Many countries would fail either or both of these 'contingent conditions', for example France certainly fails the first up to the 1960s, Britain the second – not least at the present. Second, commentators have often misunderstood what Marx says. He talks about *political* power and the *political* supremacy of the working class. Economic and social power is something else again; even political power is not solely a matter of the ballot box and Parliamentary legislation (even if much of political science has assumed that this *is* the case).

Ironically enough the Swedish Social Democratic Workers' Party, constantly 'in power' (as we usually put it) from 1932–76 and again from 1982, began to conceptualize these differences in its short period of opposition. Although the Party was still based around legislating capitalism into subordination, three distinct tasks were distinguished before this could be achieved. Two had been essentially completed. Political democracy and citizenship rights had been gained in the Party's heroic agitational period, from 1890 to 1917. Social democracy, giving these rights physical meaning in consumption, had been established with the creation of a comprehensive welfare state between the 1940s and 1970s – the classic period of Party dominance over government. This included the socialization of housing distribution in non-profit tenures, supported by a widespread system of housing allowances and state intervention in housing finance, land supply and development. But economic democracy – establishing popular control over working life and the use of labour power – was still to be achieved.

The identification of these phases is not as sloganistic as it might first appear. For Sweden is probably that society where historical outcome deviates least from Marx's abstract analysis of capitalist society, not just in political terms but also with regard to the pace of concentration, centralization and restructuring by capital. In most other capitalist countries – including Britain – the generative motors of capitalist society have combined with contingent relations in such a way as to produce more complex and impure social outcomes. In Sweden the combinations with contingent relations have, if anything, kept historical development on the lines predicted by the abstract analysis in isolation.

Why, then, does Sweden show what is probably the most developed form of reformism among the advanced capitalist countries, seen by both opponents and proponents alike as the 'ideal-type' social democracy?[3] This is not the result of an especially benevolent and correct spirit of reform lurking in the Swedish woods, nor even the racial characteristics of Swedes. Rather, as soon as we study the actual development of this 'ideal-type', we find a particular history of social relations which creates this reformism. And these are the social relations of this purer form of capitalism.

Marx elaborated at length how the vicious circle of self-destructing tendencies set up by capitalism's social and economic structure would ultimately threaten its existence. Any broad evaluation of world history since 1800 would surely support this statement. But what Marx – and less excusably subsequent Marxists – failed to elaborate was the relative success of the core capitalist societies in accommodating these self-destructive tendencies. One of the most important components of this success has been increasing social and economic management by the means of state intervention, management which has meant the production of new social forms and balances – social democracy – as well as shoring up old ones. As Keynes is supposed to have said, the question has been successfully changed from whether people should exploit one another to how this exploitation might best be regulated. (Other answers have included reliance on the family to absorb class exploitation in patriarchal exploitation, and the export of exploitation's more brutal edges to peripheral societies.)

One recurrent theme in explaining the decline of Britain and its economy has been the inability to achieve this modernization. Usually this is seen as the result of an entrenched, but conservative and ultimately feeble ruling class facing a defensively strong but politically emasculated labour movement. Neither is strong enough, organized enough or capitalist enough to create a durable and workable social democratic compromise as a means of effectively running an advanced capitalist country. (See, for example, Nairn 1978; Jessop 1980.) The opposite has been the case in Sweden. And it is indeed post-war modernization, in civil society and the economy just as much as in state policy, that provides the most immediate contrast with Britain. (To take just one example of particular relevance to this research, 70 per cent of Sweden's dwellings have been built since 1940, compared with 50 per cent in Britain.)

The thesis taken here is that the determining influence on the development of Swedish society is a relatively early, rapid, thorough and uncomplicated establishment of the capitalist mode of production. It is this which created a particular class structure which – interacting with capitalism's international development – allowed the emergence of a particular social form of advanced capitalism. Labour and capital, as labour and capital (not as, say, Tory landowners, the City and liberal-voting labour aristocrats) had the field fairly much to themselves. Both maintained a strong international competitive position (at least until recently) and, where other social classes were peripheral to this confrontation, the stage was set for capital and labour to compromise. This created the conditions in which the 'progressive modernization' of Swedish social democracy could occur. And, as we shall see, this has had some considerable implications for the way in which housing has been provided. We are, in terms of our need for comparative research, taking the case of a purer (if exceptional) form of capitalism. The rest of this section will briefly sketch out this historical development and some of its results.[4]

Rostow dates Swedish 'take off' to 1879, the sixth country in the world to reach 'industrial society'. By 1857 the Swedish economy began to follow the slump and boom of the international capitalist trade cycle, and by 1861 agriculture accounted for only 37 per cent of national product. But labour and capital did not only develop rapidly after the 1860s, they also developed without any important limitations or deviations imposed by the strength or pervasiveness of earlier social forms. First of all, Swedish capitalism was socially established 'from below', through the rise of a native industrial bourgeoisie even if Britain's industrial experience was the ultimate economic cause (as well as a source of both investment capital and free trade ideology). At the same time both the feudal nobility and the freeholding peasantry had already dissolved as cohesive social units, because of the internal relations of pre-capitalist Swedish society. In particular, unlike Britain, there was no strong landed aristocracy which could incorporate and define the political and cultural consciousness of the industrial bourgeoisie. Indeed, the first capitalists were by origin industrial merchants, state servants or 'gentlemen peasants', and by 1870 over 70 per cent of the agricultural population were landless or semi-landless. Capitalist social forms could escape absorption into earlier social forms and national antagonism would not dilute class antagonism. Similarly, unlike Britain, Sweden was an early follower rather than pioneer. In Britain the long development of capitalist social relations encouraged the development and fossilization of a multitude of archaic industrial forms and practices – the divisions between craft workers, the persistence of pre-capitalist working practices, and so on. This led to a strong diversification of both working-class and industrial interests missing in Sweden's rapid transformation.

Not only this, but Sweden's 'cleaner' class structure was consolidated in its almost immediate progress into monopolistic capitalism after the 1880s, a development which coincided with the transition from absolute to relative labour exploitation. By 1905 free competition 'had, in large part, disappeared from important sectors of industry and commerce',[5] banking capital was increasingly integrated with industrial capital, machine minding replaced craft work. If in 1860 Swedish labour was equated with Russian labour, by 1908 the working day had decreased by 40 per cent, wages were second only to English rates in Europe, and manufacturing productivity had increased by about $3\frac{1}{2}$ per cent per annum from 1880 to 1913. Only in the USA and Japan were growth rates as rapid, although Germany was not far behind. Figure 2.1, showing relative changes in profitability, exploitation and capitalization between 1870 and 1970, indicates this transition quite well. Factories were larger, paternalistic labour relations less possible and unionization grew apace. Over 60 per cent of workers were unionized by 1909, compared with about 25 per cent in Britain and one source estimates that the percentage of industrial workers experiencing paternalistic management declined from 70 to 30 per cent between 1870 and 1930. The great mass of the semi-landless rural population migrated to the towns or disappeared to America. (Numbers equivalent to fully 38 per cent of the 1860 population had left Sweden by 1914. As the saying went 'Which is better, Swedish flesh and blood in America or Swedish skin and bone in Sweden?'.) This second stage of industrialization consolidated and furthered the emergence of purer forms of labour and capital.

Classes do not, of course, exist in economic relations alone, as our earlier discussion of the anatomy of capitalist societies pointed out. Crucially, in Sweden

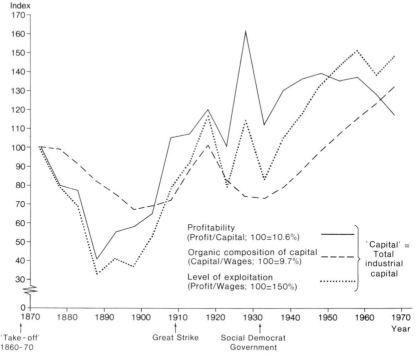

*Figure 2.1* Profitability, capitalization and exploitation in Swedish manufacturing, 1870–1970

*Source:* Adapted from Wibe *et al.* 1974.

political and ideological movement reinforced these strong economic divisions. Civil society was very much organized vertically, in Urry's terms. Second International style Marxist social democracy, based on the German model, rapidly became ascendant as a coherent, unifying political programme and social theory for the industrial working class, confronting the Manchester Liberalism of the industrial bourgeoisie. The Social Democrats became the largest electoral party shortly after universal male suffrage was attained in 1908, a position they have never lost. An overt political consciousness was only one strand in autonomous working-class experience of collective democratic action – by 1920 one in four adults were members in at least one of the 'people's movements' (the trade unions, the co-operatives, nonconformism, temperance). The cultural side of class is often neglected in the analysis of social structure, but in Sweden the pace was set by the people's movements on one hand and the capitalist dynast families who controlled monopoly capital on the other (Sweden's version of the Rockefellers or Vanderbilts). Culturally, politically and economically capital and labour were relatively pure and relatively conscious. In 1909, organized as the Confederation of Manual Trade Unions (LO) and the Confederation of Employers (SAF) they faced one another in the 'Great Strike' and lock-out.

This relatively pure formation of labour and capital was reinforced by the development of other classes and class interests. Not only were landed aristocratic interests weak, but the position of the freeholding peasantry and small farmers provided crucial political support for labour's attack on industrial and financial capital. Historically a strong class in political terms (one reason why the landed aristocracy was weak!), by 1870 the freeholding peasantry were economically threatened by the abyss of losing their subsistence holdings. They joined in the struggle to control big capital (for instance, their intervention secured limitation over financial investment in land) and were prepared to support social reform (if not socialism) in return for financial, tax and agricultural price guarantees. The political strength of the 'Red–Green' alliance, crucial to Social Democratic Government programmes in the 1930s and 1950s, was mirrored by the weakness of right political parties. The Conservative party last formed a government in 1930. Since 1908 it has never been the leading party in terms of votes cast at national elections, indeed it has passed 20 per cent only three times since 1934; government power for the right can only be found through coalition with the Liberals or Centre (previously Farmers') parties.

This weakness of the landed aristocracy was also to have a particular import-ance for housing provision. But, as this group had little concerted economic power, political influence, or even a major land holding role, the 'rural interest' became that of small and medium-sized freeholding farmers. This interest was centrist in political terms, opposed to big business and land speculation. Its economic interests were based on production; food prices and inheritance rights rather than rent and development gain were the major issues, and only rarely did any small group of owners dominate land ownership in local urban areas. In other words there was no political veto or ownership stranglehold over land supply for building (see Duncan 1982a, 1984). This provides another strong contrast with Britain, where much land is owned by landed property or large financial insti-tutions, where the Country Landowners' Association and property/developer interests act as influential lobbies, and where the Conservative party retains important links with these interests. Above all, in Sweden the dominant cultural and political ideologies of modernizing capital and reformist labour have not been absorbed into the remit of landed society.

In all these ways, labour and capital developed relatively freely as coherent and dominant economic, political and organizational blocs. This could be a recipe for class collision, and indeed this was what happened during the politically fraught 1890–1930 period. But this tendency was balanced by economic and political space within which both blocs could manoeuvre. Together with the blocs' own internal characteristics, this allowed resolution by compromise – the 'historical compromise' between capital and labour institutionalized as social democracy. This attempted resolution is not of course unusual; it is just that the particular nature of class relations in Sweden made this compromise particularly secure and thorough. It is the degree of success that makes Sweden unusual.

First of all, big capital had freedom of manoeuvre. The monopolistic fusion of finance and industrial capital achieved by the early 1900s was commercially successful in concentrating on supplying industrial materials and machinery to

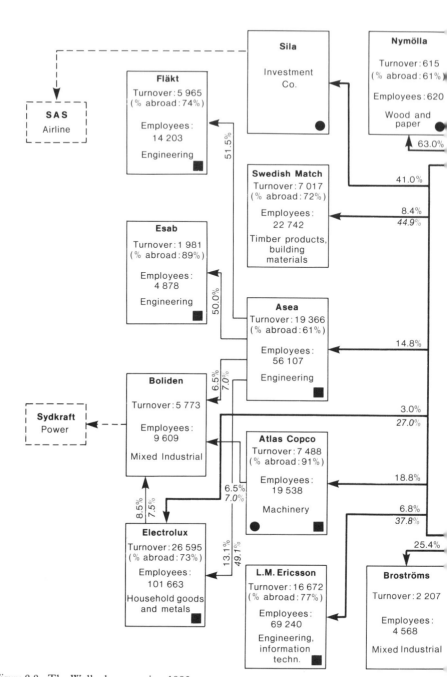

*Figure 2.2* The Wallenberg empire, 1982

*Notes:*

● Director and/or Chairman is a member of the Wallenberg family

☐ Director and/or Chairman is in the Wallenberg 'inner circle'

Turnover is in m Swedish kronor

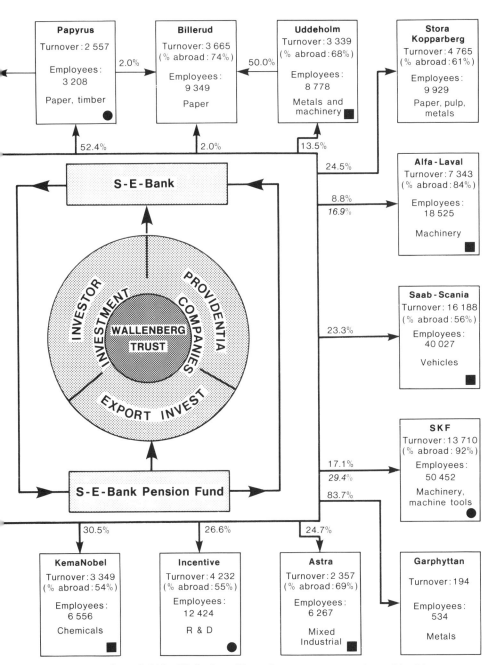

| Papyrus | | Billerud | | Uddeholm | | Stora Kopparberg |
|---|---|---|---|---|---|---|
| Turnover: 2 557 | | Turnover: 3 665 (% abroad: 74%) | | Turnover: 3 339 (% abroad: 68%) | | Turnover: 4 765 (% abroad: 61%) |
| Employees: 3 208 | 2.0% | Employees: 9 349 | 50.0% | Employees: 8 778 | | Employees: 9 929 |
| Paper, timber | | Paper | | Metals and machinery | | Paper, pulp, metals |

**S-E-Bank**

52.4%   2.0%   13.5%   24.5%

**WALLENBERG TRUST**
INVESTOR · INVESTMENT · PROVIDENTIA · COMPANIES · EXPORT INVEST

8.8%
16.9%

**Alfa-Laval**
Turnover: 7 343 (% abroad: 84%)
Employees: 18 525
Machinery

23.3%

**Saab-Scania**
Turnover: 16 188 (% abroad: 56%)
Employees: 40 027
Vehicles

**SKF**
Turnover: 13 710 (% abroad: 92%)
Employees: 50 452
Machinery, machine tools

17.1%
29.4%
83.7%

**S-E-Bank Pension Fund**

30.5%   26.6%   24.7%

| KemaNobel | Incentive | Astra | Garphyttan |
|---|---|---|---|
| Turnover: 3 349 (% abroad: 54%) | Turnover: 4 232 (% abroad: 55%) | Turnover: 2 357 (% abroad: 69%) | Turnover: 194 |
| Employees: 6 556 | Employees: 12 424 | Employees: 6 267 | Employees: 534 |
| Chemicals | R & D | Mixed Industrial | Metals |

6.5%   % shares held by Wallenberg Trust, investment companies and banking interests

7.0%   % votes held by Wallenberg Trust where different

*Source:* Adapted from Affärsvärlden, 38, 22 September 1982.

Western Europe, especially Britain and Germany. Monopoly capital could afford to compromise, especially as profit had become locked in to the relative labour exploitation of technical innovation and productivity increase by this time (see figure 2.1). Small firms were relatively weak both politically and economically. From the late nineteenth century industry and finance had been dominated by a small group of 'robber barons' who controlled major banks. Their successors are still dominant, where Swedish industry and finance is highly concentrated, as measured by market shares, employment, ownership and control (figure 2.2 is the classic example). In 1970 50 per cent of all product groups showed monopolistic or oligopolistic market situations, and 70 per cent were dominated by large firms. By 1975 the fifteen largest firms employed 25 per cent of all employees in the private sector (fifty employed nearly 50 per cent) although as befits 'the most multinational country in the world' over half of these top fifteen firms' work-forces was outside Sweden. In most companies, only two or three shareholders own a majority of shares, and in 1963 (the last effective survey) seventeen groups of owners effectively controlled over a third of manufacturing industry measured by output. One family, the Wallenberg bank, alone controlled 17 per cent and figure 2.2 shows how this financial interest straddles Swedish industrial capital. The construction and building materials industries are part of this integrated and concentrated structure. For instance, Swedish Match on figure 2.2 is partly concerned with building materials, and has subsidiaries directly involved in construction. Electrolux and Stora Kopparberg have important building materials and housing consumption interests, and several more Wallenberg firms would be closely affected by changes in construction rates, methods and costs. As we shall see, this integration into manufacturing–finance interests has important effects on the behaviour and structure of the construction industry.

Growing industrial concentration is not unusual, quite the contrary. But in Sweden this concentration is greater than in most other capitalist countries – including Britain – and was well established at a very early stage. Nor is this just concentration, as production innovation and labour use are just as advanced. And, just as important from the point of view of compromise with labour, there was no politically important but backward ruling-class group to dilute the 'progressive capitalist' interests of big capital, nor even any political institutions of any importance to represent such interests. There was no latifundiast class; landowners were of little importance; there was no House of Lords. (Although the parliamentary reforms of 1866 did bring in a two chamber system, one of which was elected through municipal government and other interest organizations expressly to represent conservative interests and, after 1908, to dilute the effects of universal suffrage. This was effectively reformed by a Social Democrat–Liberal coalition in 1917. It is something of a telling contrast with Britain that what seem the most practical current proposals to reform the British House of Lords mean the establishment of Sweden's 1866–1917 system!)

So although big capital had some freedom to manoeuvre, it was also forced onto the compromise path – not just because of the political and organizational strength of labour, but because of a lack of alternatives. There were no preferential colonial markets, no City of London. Return on investment could only be secured by innovation and productivity gains in manufacturing. This meant dealing with labour to secure investment in domestic manufacturing industry, and by 1930 experience had made it plain that this could only proceed by agreement, not by compulsion. We should also add that this involvement by finance capital in domestic production gives the former a wholly different attitude to housing provision, housing land and construction. The issue is much more production oriented than in Britain; much less an issue of finance or property values in isolation from production.

On the other side of the potential barricade, the labour movement was already predisposed to accept this. This was not just because the economic heights were held by a well-organized and powerful group of capitalists, but because of its own traditions and ideologies. The statism of Second International social democracy (socialism could only be legislated in place of capitalism gradually) fitted in well with existing traditions of a strong, interventionist state and the experience of paternalism of the earlier stage of industrialization.[6] The revolutionary strand of the labour movement, stressing the socialization of means of production, had anyway received a severe setback with the failure of the 1909 Great Strike which was aimed at the bourgeois state as much as employers (although it was actually provoked by SAF lock-outs). Like 1926 in Britain, this failure encouraged the primacy of 'moderate' piecemeal reform. In effect this became an ideology of paternalism socialized through the neutral state, as distributive socialism, leaving production and the control of labour power in the hands of capital, even if these were no longer unguarded or unchecked.

The contradictions of such a *modus vivendi* are potentially severe. The desire to remove social inequality and oppression can only be followed through by neglecting one of its major causes – exploitation at work, and thus losing leverage over major social problems such as uneven development over space as well as the nature of working life itself (see Elander 1978; Palm 1977). However, as long as Swedish capital was reasonably successful in generating profits and jobs this contradiction could be smoothed over. Since 1975 the situation has not been so easy – and the settlement has weakened. The miners' strike of 1969–70 has been seen as the 'alarm-clock' for social democracy in Sweden, an impression reinforced by the increasing frequency of both wild-cat and official strikes since then.

Finally, two other consequences of this particular social structure stimulated the emergence of a successful and long lasting 'historic compromise'. First, both big capital and labour were well organized and pervasive in their respective spheres. Labour through the high density and hierarchical structures of linked party, union and consumer organisations, big capital in the employers' federation (SAF, founded 1902) and the Industry Confederation (SI), not to mention the control structure of market, financial and ownership domination. Unlike Britain, both sides would be able to deliver as well as promise. And second, for both partners (as they would become) the economic and political weakness of small firms and the 'non-capitalist' bourgeois groups (like landowners, house landlords or small shopkeepers) provided an easy target to give reformist substance to the historical compromise. As we shall see, this situation became writ large in the area of housing provision.

*Table 2.1*  The old and new Sweden: industrial and political stability 1909–82

|  | Average person-days lost in strikes and lock-outs (000s p.a.) | No. of party government changes |
|---|---|---|
| 1903–09 | 2579 (1909 65%) | 2 |
| 1910–19 | 722 | 3 |
| 1920–9 | 3257 | 7 |
| 1930–9 | 1451 | 4 |
| 1940–9 | 1219 (1945 93%) | — |
| 1950–9 | 151 | — |
| 1960–9 | 55 | — |
| 1970–9 | 213 | 1 |
| (1980–2) | (2340) | (2) |

*Sources:* Calculated from SOS.

So, while the period between 1890 and 1930 was one of industrial and political conflict we can, with hindsight, see the establishment of compromise between labour and capital as a logical conclusion. Short-lived governments, strikes and lock-outs, demonstrations (symbolized by the 1909 Great Strike, the crowds besieging the Parliament building and the royal palace in 1917 demanding bread, freedom and a law against housing profiteers, the shooting of five demonstrating workers at Ådalen in 1932) were succeeded by Social Democrat government hegemony for forty-four years and the relative industrial peace of 'Harpsund democracy' – the country estate where LO, SAF and the Social Democrats met to discuss how to govern. Table 2.1 gives some quantitative indications of this sea change.

The actual 'timetabling' of this 'historically logical' conclusion was determined by two events, the Great Depression and the election of the Social Democrats in 1932. The former weakened labour's position in the labour market, but the latter strengthened labour politically – unions and especially LO were involved in economic and social policy-making, legislation could sometimes achieve what collective bargaining could not. Both events made the industrialists' need to do a deal with the labour movement all the more pressing, as well as strengthening the emergent divide between social intervention in distribution on the one hand and capitalist production on the other; between the 'political' and the 'economic' spheres. 'Political power', founded on labour organization would provide a counterweight to 'economic power', founded on control of capital (Korpi 1978). LO were put in the position of agreeing to the 1928 'industrial peace' Collective Agreements Act, which guaranteed the employer's right to control the labour process and to hire and fire, in return for a degree of union consultation. Strikes outside collective agreements became illegal, a situation remaining today, and a labour court was introduced. The 1932 election and the Saltsjöbaden Agreement of 1938 strengthened the union position but only on the basis of 1928. LO and SAF established a code of practice for regulating industrial relations at the sector, company and plant levels, with rules and regulations over employment contracts, working conditions, the direction of labour, union consultation, etc. One result of this agreement was to strengthen further the centralized power of LO over individual unions and plant organization, and the position of SAF *vis-à-vis* individual sectors and employers. The means of compromise were strengthened as well as the content. The 1939 'Co-operation Conference' between the Social Democrat state planners and SAF, establishing ground rules for economic policy-making, cemented the compromise in the political sphere.[7] During the same period the Social Democrats themselves expelled left-wing splinters and effectively marginalized communist and syndicalist movements – the apple cart was not to be disturbed.[8]

In this way class conflict between labour and capital became thoroughly institutionalized, and absorbed into the corporatist rationality of social democratic capitalism. This system was not without movement. For instance, the Harpsund agreements of the 1950s fine-tuned this system for the post-war era and another series of agreements in the 1970s enlarged employee influence at the margins (e.g. the 1976 'Codetermination at Work' Act). But movement was set firmly within the Saltsjöbaden framework right up to the 1980s when deeper cracks appeared. (In September 1983 LO even refused to talk to SAF who, they claimed, had become a right-wing institution, and for the first time since the 1930s there has been no *central* labour–capital agreement on wages.) Conversely, when this system did break down momentarily then the whole economic and social system was suspended. The very few cases where LO (as in 1981) did walk out meant complete stoppage of almost everything. Agreement was vitally necessary if Swedish social democracy was to continue.

The emergence of the Labour Market Board (AMS) 'probably the most influential of all Swedish economic institutions' (Scase 1977) well symbolizes this process. It intervenes in all aspects of economic planning: occupational training, manpower planning, employment services, unemployment benefits, industrial location, long-term planning, fiscal and economic policy, and so on. Not only has AMS greater scope than the Manpower Services Commission or NEDO in Britain, but it has been around much longer and is more important to policy formulation as well as implementation. It is also much more an institution of class compromise. For example, the AMS board consists of three SAF members, three from LO, two from the white-collar union confederation, one from the professional workers' union confederation, and two members representing women and agriculture.

In this way a social democratic form has been given to state institutions built up since 1933; their rules, practices, members and ideologies reflect the social consensus of the 'historic compromise'. This applies particularly to the institutions of the welfare state; older agencies (like the Foreign Department) remain more conservative, but, and this is very important, the Social Democrats have not hesitated to build alternative institutions in their own image, so as to bypass these inherited impediments where necessary. AMS and its equivalent in housing, the National Housing Board, are prime examples of allowing reform to circumnavigate the Finance Ministry.

None the less, one substantial caveat spoils this reformer's dream. The contradictions of this form of social democracy – increased social justice based on increased labour exploitation – remain. So in the 1960s AMS became known as the 'everyone must move south' organization among those living in small industrial villages in the north and centre of Sweden (*'alla måste söderut'*). These were 'rationalized out' in favour of the greater industrial and social efficiency to be gained by concentration around the three conurbations of Stockholm, Gothenburg and Malmö. This uneven regional development and massive suburban growth also had considerable effects on housing provision and on methods of constructing it, encouraging state intervention to procure large production series with economies of scale. The policy of 'wage solidarity' agreed by LO and SAF shows similar results. Under this policy, not only would wage differentials between workers be decreased, but high wage demands would deliberately be used to put small firms out of business. They could then be absorbed into technically innovative, high wage, big firms with a more secure future. Labour and big capital would both gain, at the expense of small firms – even if it meant families moving to high rise flats in the conurbations. An equivalent process occurred with housing policy itself, as we shall see. Labour gained in terms of costs, access and quality; big building firms could dominate the market and benefit most from state intervention to produce more efficient construction; landowners, landlords and smaller firms were frozen out (see Duncan 1978b).

Perhaps this whole era can best be symbolized by the reaction of leading social democrats to Marcus Wallenberg's death, in September 1982. Wallenberg was Sweden's dominant financial–industrial dynast and a key agent in running 'Harpsund democracy'. According to Sträng, who had been finance minister over most of the 1950s and 1960s (Wallenberg had been a member of his economic policy group and both men used to meet weekly over a private lunch): 'Despite disputes, we had the same goal – to build a strong Sweden'. Or, according to Tage Erlander, prime minister during the same period: 'Marcus Wallenberg himself had a bourgeois outlook, but he always maintained good contacts with both the union movement and with social democracy. Wallenberg built Sweden with us.' (*Dagens Nyheter* 15 September 1982).

If the politics of Swedish social democracy meant increased state spending, employment expansion and a profitable private industry, this agreed very well with the economic dogma of the post-war boom – Keynesianism. In fact not only was Keynesianism politically more possible in Sweden (arguably, it has never been applied wholeheartedly in Britain) but it had already been prefigured by Swedish economic and social theory. The 'Stockholm School' of Ohlin had produced a version of Keynes by the early 1930s, while the Myrdals in their *Crisis in the population question* (1934) anticipated most of the social reforms of the next thirty years. Not only would social welfare spending combine 'social merit and economic sense', but social reform could replace the missing 'natural demand' of population growth with increased 'social demand'. Housing was a favoured vehicle for these reforms, for linked economic, social and political reasons (for example, it was a labour intensive home-based industry, raising housing standards was an easy way to produce social demand, better and cheaper housing allowed family expansion, housing standards had been poor and this was an obvious way to give social democratic ideology some reality). So even though social reform measures were unexceptional before the war (for example introducing the first effective old age pensions and unemployment insurance) and Keynesianism was irresolutely applied (German rearmament was probably just as important) state expenditure on housing increased by 159 per cent between 1929 and 1939.[9] The same economic experts forecast a depression immediately after 1945, and saw housing expansion as the best means of counteracting it (as well as compensating for the wartime neglect of housing when capital had preferred the high profit rates of war-based export industries). In a depression, it would be the state which would have to organize counter-cyclical production investment, and this concern linked in well with the social democrat politics of lower costs and greater social justice in housing consumption. Housing investment and the development process itself would be state managed, and there would be state intervention through housing consumption subsidies and concentration on public and co-operative renting. Although this system in fact coincided with the post-war boom, not a depression, and indeed its financial support was weakened when this became clear, the 1946 reforms set the guidelines for Swedish housing provision up to the 1970s.

This suggests two things. First, housing was not *just* an instrument for capitalist management, and the 'Labour movement housing coalition' (the building unions, the tenants' association, the housing co-operatives, the larger urban authorities) were strong enough to see that this remained the case. Second, however, this system was not unfavourable to large building firms and the building materials industry. (One illustration is provided by the 'neutral market' – when the Social Democrats retook parliamentary power in 1982 share prices of construction and material firms rose considerably!) Interestingly, when this housing system finally faltered under the impact of a new economic epoch, after 1973, there was no return to the pre-war free enterprise system. Housing consumption has been increasingly privatized since 1973, but it rests on – and benefits from – a pervasive state capitalism in construction and land supply. But more of this in chapters three and four.

The consequences of all this on the level and form of housing provision have been fairly dramatic. Up to the 1930s Sweden had what was probably among the worst housing conditions in any industrial country. (For example, in 1933 40 per cent of families of five or more lived in one room, 62 per cent of all households were overcrowded on the generous definition of two persons per room, although this did show some improvement since the first housing census in 1912.) Indeed, a 1924 ILO survey found that Sweden had the highest rents for the lowest quality in industrial Europe. By the 1970s, housing conditions were among the best measured in terms of access, cost and quality. This was achieved, among other things, by what were consistently the highest per capita rates for housing investment and construction in Europe.

This same combination of economic sense and social merit is reflected in other social policy areas, of course. In the 1970s per capita social welfare expenditure was 30 per cent higher than in Britain, and in some areas contrasts between the two countries are startling. For instance, pensioner poverty is almost eliminated

*Table 2.2* State social transfer payments as a proportion of national income

|      | %    |
|------|------|
| 1929 | 3.0  |
| 1935 | 4.9  |
| 1940 | 5.1  |
| 1950 | 9.9  |
| 1956 | 13.0 |
| 1974 | 17.5 |

*Source:* Adapted from Samuelson 1968, Uhr 1977.

in Sweden; child-care facilities are much more widespread; and average un-employment benefit is around 80 per cent of average weekly income as opposed to around 35 per cent in Britain. Table 2.2 shows the increasing use of the state to achieve these sorts of social transfer. Note the quantitative leap shown in the table in the 1945–55 period, a time when the Social Democrats were fighting for welfare expansion against sometimes fierce opposition from the right and from some industrial interests (especially over taxation policy and pension funding). But here again, the split in the 'bourgeois' (centre-right) parties was crucial. Not only were the political waters muddied by a three way split, where 'red', 'green' (centre) and 'blue' alternatives were on offer, but the red–green alliance was dominant and even if it broke down the social democrat version was usually weightier than either green or blue in isolation.

These achievements are not to be sneered at. For instance one of the first things that strikes the visitor to Sweden, apart from the newness of its housing stock, is the relative vitality and comfort of old-age pensioners. Unlike Britain, there is no annual winter epidemic of hypothermia. But we should be plain that social welfare has not altered social structure, only – partially – the way it works. (And this includes how people think about it.) Income and wealth distributions are almost as unequal as in Britain, social mobility is almost as low, and as we have seen the concentration of economic power is greater (see Scase 1976a, 1977). In 1968 the members of Social Group I (8 per cent of the population) owned as much wealth as Social Group III (58 per cent); the wealth owned by company directors was equivalent to that owned by all employees, and the top 2.5 per cent earned as much as the bottom 50 per cent. Similar contrasts are evident in health and social indicators. Table 2.3 gives a flavour of these social differentials – an amalgam of the results of income distribution, social access and the experience of everyday life. (Only with regard to alcohol consumption are Social Group I worse off – but because of too much access!) According to one recent government inquiry, 'any equalization (of income) that did occur was extremely modest and took place in the years immediately before the 1950s; . . . in the 1960s there was a tendency for

*Table 2.3* Social and economic inequality: Sweden, 1968

| Social group* | % adult population | Average wealth (1967, kr) | Average income (1967, kr) | Average years of education | % overcrowded |
|---|---|---|---|---|---|
| I | 7.8 | 53,300 | 31,345 | 13.2 | 3 |
| II | 34.7 | 19,700 | 16,728 | 8.8 | 15 |
| III | 57.5 | 7,500 | 12,174 | 7.2 | 26 |
| All | 100.0 | 15,300 | 15,257 | 8.2 | 20 |

| Social group | % without car | % politically deprived** | % with movement difficulties | % with bad teeth | % with nervous troubles | % with too high consumption of alcohol |
|---|---|---|---|---|---|---|
| I | 28 | 3 | 7 | 3 | 16 | 8 |
| II | 37 | 11 | 11 | 6 | 19 | 3 |
| III | 54 | 24 | 18 | 13 | 23 | 1 |
| All | 47 | 18 | 15 | 10 | 21 | 2 |

*Notes:*
* Social Group I consists of senior civil servants, owners of large firms, large farmers, professionals and senior management; Social Group II of lower-grade non-manual workers, owners of small businesses and farms, independent artisans and foremen; Social Group III of manual workers.
** 'Politically deprived' was a composite definition, with criteria such as the condition of not belonging to any organization, of not knowing how to complain over an official act, etc.

*Sources:* Levnadsundersökningen (1968); unpublished report, SOS.

wealth to become more concentrated' (SOU 1968: 7 in Scase 1976a, 47). This is all reminiscent of Britain, and, like Britain, this situation is quite stable and had altered little by 1980 (SOS 1981).

Similarly, despite the well known progressive aspects of Swedish welfare legislation, the overall distributive effects are not unlike those of similar European countries (table 2.4). Rather, it is perhaps more the case that Britain will fall out of the group of 'high welfare states' during the 1980s.

Clearly, the situation in Sweden is a great improvement over the late nineteenth century, when $6\frac{1}{2}$ per cent of wealth holders owned 70 per cent of wealth; paupers were auctioned as servants to those who would accept the *lowest* poor relief to support them; and only 4 per cent of GNP was consumed publicly. Few mechanisms then existed for income transfer even within classes, and life cycle poverty was endemic for the working class. Absolute real incomes and service levels have increased dramatically since then. But social position and relative 'levels of living' still largely depend on relations in the labour market and the family, and thus on the movement of Swedish capitalism in the international economy and on gender

*Table 2.4*   National expenditure by sector in advanced capitalist countries, 1975 and 1980

| | Total GNP per capita (1975) US $ | % gross fixed investment | | % private consumption | | % public consumption | |
|---|---|---|---|---|---|---|---|
| | | 1975 | 1980 | 1975 | 1980 | 1975 | 1980 |
| 1  W. European 'high-welfare' states | | | | | | | |
| UK | 4031 | 19 | 18 | 58 | 60 | 21 | 22 |
| Sweden | 8415 | 20 | 20 | 49 | 52 | 24 | 29 |
| W. Germany | 6851 | 20 | 24 | 53 | 55 | 20 | 20 |
| 2  'low-welfare' states | | | | | | | |
| Switzerland | 8406 | 24 | 24 | 60 | 64 | 10 | 13 |
| Italy | 3027 | 21 | 20 | 67 | 62 | 14 | 16 |
| Japan | 4431 | 30 | 32 | 56 | 58 | 11 | 10 |
| 3  USA | 7044 | 13 | 19 | 65 | 64 | 23 | 17 |

*Sources:* Data from UN Statistical Yearbooks 1976 and 1981.

relations. In this sense there has been little fundamental change in the class structure of Swedish society since the 1930s – it is how this relationship is articulated that has changed with social democracy. As Therborn's mapping of class structure in economic terms shows (table 2.5) the major changes in composition have been the decline of the petite bourgeoisie and their replacement by the 'class contradictory' middle strata (especially of technicians, administrators and welfare workers). Other schemes using different theoretical and statistical definitions (e.g. Söderfelt 1980) come to similar conclusions. Certainly there has been little 'embourgeoisement' in terms of the jobs people do.

Indeed Therborn claims a substantial proletarianization based on the fact that the ratio of working class (strictly defined) to bourgeoisie (including part of the petite bourgeoisie) has changed from 4:1 to 10:1 between 1930 and 1975. Similarly, the proportion of working class broadly defined and the proletarianized middle strata, taken together, have increased from 58 per cent to 61 per cent of the economically active over this period (39–40 per cent of population), while the proletarianized 'pole' – these two groups plus the 'half-proletarian' petite bourgeoisie, amounted to 64 per cent of the economically active in 1975. This overall stability in economic class relations is not dissimilar to most other advanced capitalist countries. In Sweden, however, without significant religious or ethnic divisions, and where the economic poles of bourgeoisie and working class are more directly translated into the dominant organization poles of LO and SAF in

*Table 2.5* The class composition of Swedish society, 1930 and 1975

| | 1930 | | | 1975 | | |
|---|---|---|---|---|---|---|
| | *000s* | *% 'economi- cally active'* | *% population* | *000s* | *% 'economi- cally active'* | *% population* |
| Working class broadly defined | 1530 | 56 | 38 | 1840 | 53 | 35 |
| (Working class strictly defined) | (1035) | (38) | (25) | (1085) | (31) | (20.5) |
| Bourgeoisie | 52 | 2 | 1 | 30 | 1 | 0.5 |
| Special categories affiliated to the bourgeoisie | 25 | 1 | 0.5 | 40 | 1 | 1 |
| Petite bourgeoisie | 755 | 29 | 19 | 260 | 7.5 | 5 |
| Middle strata | 310 | 11 | 8 | 1300 | 37.5 | 25 |
| Pre-capitalist | 25 | 1 | 0.5 | — | — | — |
| TOTAL | 2697 | 100 | 67 | 3470 | 100 | 67 |

*Definitions:*
Working class strictly defined: manual workers in production and distribution.
Working class broadly defined: includes shop assistants, etc.
Bourgeoisie: owner-employers employing more than five workers, other executive directors.
Special categories affiliated to the bourgeoisie: managers, technical and economic experts, higher state and municipal officers, police and military officers, heads and officials in advertising, the media and education.
Petite bourgeoisie: self-employed and family workers, including farmers.
Middle strata: technicians and foremen, office personnel, commercial functionaries, teachers, welfare workers, white-collar service workers, security officers, intellectual functionaries.
Pre-capitalist: crofters and sharecroppers.

*Source:* Adapted from Therborn 1976, 1981 and national censuses.

the labour market, the socialist bloc and the bourgeois bloc in politics, this stability has particular significance.

Nevertheless, if class relations are essentially stable, important internal adjustments have occurred. Patriarchal working relations (for family helpers and servants) have declined from 20 per cent of the economically active in 1930 to less than 1 per cent in 1975, while women accounted for 45 per cent of the work-force (by 1980). Over 60 per cent of all women are now 'economically active' and although benefiting from less overt discrimination in the job market than in Britain (as well as far greater access to child-care facilities) are still concentrated in particular sectors, occupations and in part-time work. Average hourly rates for women are still around 10 per cent less than for men (cf. 30 per cent less in Britain). Similarly, a significant immigrant work-force is still concentrated in particular unpleasant manual occupations and low status housing areas in the big cities. They make up 8.5 per cent of the population, although 5.5 per cent come from other Scandinavian countries (especially Finland). Finally, as many as 30 per cent of the work-force was employed directly by central and local government by 1980. Although in functional terms many have replaced (and expanded) the role of the old petite bourgeoisie, direct employment by the state makes a significant change in economic and social relations.

So far, however, these changes have been absorbed within the structures of organized labour and the existing institutions of corporatist compromise – not without some dissatisfaction because of the group marginalization this can produce. The middle strata have followed the existing ground rules in forming their own trade union bloc, TCO (although significantly they have largely moved from rented/co-op housing to owner-occupation over the last ten years). Unionization is still increasing even over existing very high levels (currently 95 per cent for manual workers, 75 per cent for white-collar workers).

The same basic stability is apparent for capital as well. Although the co-operative movement, the unions and the state have important holdings in some sectors, nearly 90 per cent of production value is accounted for by privately owned firms. State holdings are concentrated in less profitable restructuring sectors like steel and textiles, and as we discussed earlier ownership and control concentration in private industry is extreme. If anything, increasing concentration and centralization increase the stability of capital as a social force in Sweden, although multinationalization may counteract this. Public services still account for little more than 20 per cent of GDP and it is the large, private firms that dominate the crucial export sector. The major social actors are still organized labour and big capital; it is the relative strength and cohesiveness of these actors that remains the major social fact of Swedish society.

It is for this reason that Social Democratic attempts to portray the new (post-1932) and old Swedens as fundamentally different have been dismissed as ideology (cf. Wibe *et al.* 1974, Sunesson 1974, Elander 1978). This is correct – but on the other hand this should not blind us to the social results of those reformist changes which have occurred, nor to the real effects of ideology itself, however 'false'. Indeed, rather than the new Sweden being particularly socialist it is perhaps more the case that Britain's rulers – unlike Sweden's – have been unable to construct an effective reformism. Even the limited reformism of social insurance (old-age pensions, sickness benefits, maternity benefits, unemployment benefit, child care, etc.) which is largely a matter of transferring income between different periods of a person's life and only marginally a transfer between classes, has been sporadically and relatively weakly developed in Britain. The enthusiastic application of this 'life-cycle reformism' in Sweden, as one part of the bargain struck between capital and labour, has led to a considerable reduction in life-cycle poverty. This material success is important politically, for the proof of an ideological pudding seems to lie primarily in its eating.

The same is true of housing policy, where the contrasts between the old and new Swedens are vividly remembered by many of the older generation as well as becoming the standard fare of textbooks and university courses. A Swedish commentator put this presciently in 1945:

To this generation of Swedes, housing is becoming the panacea for all social evils. What the cathedral was to their ancestors, the bible to their grand-fathers, and Kreuger debentures to their fathers, the modern spacious home (filled of course with stainless steel and labour saving gadgets) has become to them. (Sandström 1945, 73)

Nor is it the case that Swedish social democracy has been merely lucky enough to appropriate the political benefits of successful capitalism, high wages and full employment. It is compromise and its results (easier restructuring, the pressure for productivity increase, higher investment rates, state planning, etc.) which have partly underlain this success and its politically happy results. Thus social democracy has also meant the creation of *new* social forms and the mediation of social relations in *new* ways, not just in the institutions of compromise themselves like AMS, but also with regard to structural conditions. The state run National Pension Funds (ATP) give one example. Introduced after fierce resistance from the bourgeois parties in the 1950s, they counterbalance private capital in the finance market. Amounting to 40 per cent of gross savings in the Swedish economy, ATP can be used for long-term economic investment and to help secure the social conditions that support this. ATP provides long-term loans for industrial restructuring, technical innovation and housing construction, for instance. To an extent ATP must be used in this way for its future survival depends on high domestic employment with high wages (or how else could it pay out millions of pensions in decades to come). This is far from arguing that ATP is used in some socialist sense, far from it; however, it is being used for long-term domestic modernization and it is just this function that the City of London is apparently unable to provide. (Other more successful capitalist countries manage this in other ways; Japan's banks allow long-term fixed interest loans to domestic firms for instance, again in a way unknown in Britain. As we might expect however, ATP must stress some social merit in addition to this economic sense.)

The current plans for wage-earners' funds, to consolidate and extend the role of ATP, might even end up with the collectivization of capital accumulation. Originally to be based on a wage levy and the appropriation of some excess profits, they would soon completely dominate the Swedish investment market. One reason for these plans is just that of neutralizing the huge economic power exercised by a few individuals like Wallenberg (they would be replaced by state/union/citizen boards with some electoral input). Certainly the wage-earners' funds and ATP reforms represent more of a threat to capital than social insurance policy and distributive reform, as is shown by fierce resistance to the former and acceptance – even welcome – of the latter. The initial implementation of the wage-earners' funds in 1983 was much more cautious than the original proposal presented to the LO Congress in 1975. The only trouble for capitalists' oppo-sition to the funds is that they are desperate for long-term finance, to face the new international division of labour. How far and in what form the funds are eventu-ally put into practice is still a matter of considerable doubt – but it is intriguing whether this is the point where quantitative change *within* a system tips over to become qualitative change *to* that system. The opposition by Swedish capitalists may be very well founded.

An example from housing provision itself shows very well the economic importance of a successful reformism. In 1964 the Social Democrats received a severe electoral shock where one major issue had again become housing costs and access. The party were jolted from any idea that their electoral and ideological success was self-fulfilling and promised some material proof – to build one million new houses by 1974. (They succeeded, for Britain the equivalent of building over 600,000 houses every year for ten years!) What were the results of this 'million programme'? First of all, huge investment in housing construction combined with considerable attention to its efficiency. State organizations, partly through existing control of housing investment and development, stimulated productivity increase in building and this combined with the effects of large economies of scale and the efforts of building firms themselves – for they were faced with a well-organized and politically well connected work-force with above average wage-rates. Construction costs declined by about 25 per cent in real terms between 1964 and 1975 and labour productivity doubled. At the same time, however, elements of the labour movement became more radical (not unconnected with 1964 as well as 1968) while the success of the 'million programme' seemed prejudiced by a resurgence of the land question in building. Evidence suggested that the larger building firms were establishing large land banks which would – through their potential appropriation of development gain – threaten the whole strategy of providing masses of cheap housing. A counter-attack was mounted under the political hegemony of the Social Democrats (where the 'labour movement housing coalition' of unions, co-operatives, renters and urban authorities had kept tabs on housing issues). Several government inquiries provided a basis for legislation aimed at separating land ownership from land development, and so stop building firms getting their hands on development gain. Nearly all housing is now built on publicly owned land, acquired relatively cheaply with the aid of expropriation and other powers which give local authorities a dominant position in local development land markets. Apart from cheapening housing costs and directing development gains at consumers, this land policy has had one other important knock-on effect – it has intensified the need for building firms to find productivity gains and technical innovation in construction itself. Profits have to be made through the building process rather than development. (See Duncan 1984 and chapter three.) Political and ideological relations intervene in economic change, and vice versa. The result is not that social democracy dominates an isolated ideological level, but that relations in production and ownership are also changed. The one feeds off the other.

Up to the mid-1970s this dialectical feeding process between big capital and organized labour was, as we have suggested, relatively stable. But its continuation depends on the competitive success of Swedish capital as well as the strength and cohesiveness of the two blocs – indeed, the latter is also deeply influenced by the former. Since 1975 this success has no longer been so secure. Private business investment declined by 2 per cent per annum between 1975 and 1980 (compared to growing at 5 per cent per annum during 1970–5). Profit rates in manufacturing were halved and growth in industrial production declined to 2 per cent per annum between 1970 and 1980 (compared to 6 per cent in the 1960s). The Swedish share of the crucial OECD manufactured goods market declined by 15 per cent over the decade, GDP grew by only 1.6 per cent per annum while real wages stagnated after 1976. At the same time the average inflation rate during the 1970s was double the 1960s level and registered unemployment had doubled to 3.5 per cent by 1980. This was not without effect in housing provision, as both housing investment and construction declined considerably, accompanying a shift towards owner-occupation and upgrading at the expense of non-profit renting and new build.

Nevertheless it is clear that, as yet, the economic and political crisis is not of British proportions. Indeed, there has been a recovery since 1979, and the 1975–8 period seems to have been the deepest trough so far. In manufacturing, while steel, shipyards and textiles received severe shocks, and forestry products faltered, the no less basic engineering sector increased production considerably and now accounts for nearly half Swedish exports. The Social Democratic government elected in 1982 ended up gambling on a modified Keynesian reflation combined with increased investment and planned restructuring. This gamble follows from the fact that – unlike the opposition who can appeal to monetarism and the market – the Social Democrats have no coherent policy for crisis management. But perhaps, here too, the organizational cohesion of labour and capital will bring the gamble off and so allow Swedish social democracy to survive.

## 2.3 Comparative work on housing provision and the Swedish model

The previous section has shown how several factors essentially contingent to the structures of advanced capitalism (e.g. the importance of land ownership, the organizational coherence of labour and capital, the cultural tradition of state activity) are either minimized or exaggerated in Sweden. Nevertheless, these sorts of social relations are potentially significant, as they combine with more general and structural conditions, in forming actual historical outcomes in different places. Comparison with Sweden therefore, where the effects of several such contingencies are emphasized by their relative presence or absence, can provide a pale social science shadow of the controlled experiment. Although not usually perceived in this way, this role has been a well-worn one for social science research on Sweden, and a further expansion of this real world 'contingency control' is the additional attraction Sweden holds for the liberal and reformist wing of social policy research.

How has this real world 'model' of social democratic capitalism been used in previous comparative analysis on housing provision? In thinking back to our earlier discussions of comparative study (section 1.4) and theorizing housing (section 1.3) the answer seems to be 'not very well'. This is because such analysis has not usually succeeded in avoiding the two major pitfalls we identified in those discussions. First of all, it has been assumed that comparative juxtaposition can in itself produce explanation, when it cannot. Second, housing provision has been seen as almost entirely a matter of tenure change and state distributional policy, when questions of construction, land ownership, and wider social relations – where policies and processes come from – are equally important if not more so. This is probably why comparative housing analysis, although usually greeted with initial enthusiasm, has ultimately led to some considerable disappointment. As one recent survey concludes:

> To summarise, the current state of comparative housing research . . . is not encouraging. Much of the literature is superficial – often it is simply inaccurate or misleading – and abstracts housing policy developments from their broader economic and political context, and even from the workings of the housing system as a whole.                    (Harloe and Martens 1984, 268)

This is not to say that some of this work has not been useful in presenting comparative information on housing consumption and distribution in Sweden. As far back as 1971, Greve provided a description of housing policy in Scandinavia, concentrating on the co-operative sector (Greve 1971). This study aimed to make recommendations for British housing policy and may have contributed to the emergence of the housing association sector in Britain. It also commented on the much higher Scandinavian investment levels in housing. In this way Greve's comparative study was helping to point out that what, in Britain, was taken for granted was in fact socially created. British tenure patterns and levels of investment in housing were not natural, inviolable or even normal. This is one possible role for social science comparative analysis, as identified in section 1.4. Although the least ambitious, this is often the more successful role. Unless suffocated by a priori typologies and if given sufficient room for detail, most comparative study can fulfil this function. So Kemeny's research on Sweden, Britain and Australia helps to demolish the notion that owner-occupation is the natural and inevitably superior tenure for advanced capitalism (Kemeny 1980). Popenoe's (1977) comparison of living conditions in Swedish and American suburbs, which strongly favours the former, comes to similar conclusions about public development versus private. All this work concentrates on distribution policy and consumption patterns. Our own work on housing construction in Sweden performs a similar function for production (see chapter three). In this way comparative analysis can provide a check on generalization and abstraction procedures.

The trouble, and the disappointment, comes with the remaining and more ambitious role for comparative analysis discussed in section 1.4. This is the possibility of using the relative (and uncontrolled) case study control over real world variability to work out how contingent conditions vary and how important this variance is. This possibility has not been taken up successfully just because researchers have not seen things this way (even if this has been an implicit and unexpressed ideal). Rather, it has been assumed that comparative empirical juxtaposition would itself create explanatory analysis. Unfortunately, comparative work can only provide more favourable conditions in which such analysis can take place. The analysis still has to be developed. It is this development which is missing, although – hence the disappointment – it was implicitly assumed that comparative work would somehow produce it.

One of the most known comparative studies of housing policy, which uses the Swedish, British and US cases (Heady 1978), shows this inadequacy very well.

This is quite apart from serious conceptual deficiencies, such as the neglect of production, of wider social relations, and the treatment of the state as a benevolent and essentially neutral referee (cf. the reviews by Marcuse 1982, Harloe and Martens 1984). Over and above all this, comparison becomes the quasi-analysis of juxtaposition of typologies. The USA is seen as showing a 'private enterprise approach', Sweden a 'social market' approach, and Britain a 'welfare approach'. This might be a good place to start, but the comparative part of the analysis effectively stops there; the argument boils down to the notion that different political systems produce different housing systems. Thus strongly developed social democracy in Sweden means the strong development of social housing and more egalitarian policies. But this tells us very little about how and why this happened, and what produced the observed difference from Britain and the USA. Similarly, this essentially deterministic analysis by typology cuts off more sensitive and flexible explanation. For instance, social democratic political forms can influence economic change, as well as state policy. Industrial location and concentration, the relation between industry and land ownership, the development of the building industry itself, all these are good examples. Factors like these are crucial for both the supply and demand of housing, for its socio-political importance at any one time, and for the likelihood of successfully doing anything about it. So too, changes in political consciousness change the understanding of state policy, when housing may come to have a quite different social and political meaning from what it had before. Analysis of these socio-economic and political changes and interrelationships requires much more analytically than reduction to 'the social market approach'. Typology in itself can explain very little but the expectation that the comparative typology can somehow produce analysis out of the air bolsters this failure; conceptual inadequacies are isolated from empirical testing.

This example refers directly to our general discussion of comparative analysis in section 1.4, where we pointed out that the ex-post division of a non-experimental situation (real world Britain, Sweden, USA) is by no means the same as experimental control. But this fundamental difference is not picked up, and it is assumed that the variations observed in the cases are simply and easily caused by the typology used to choose them in the first place. Even if true, this still has to be demonstrated. The strength of Heady's study remains at the useful, but limited, level of a descriptive summary of housing consumption policy. But even in this case the material would be better uncluttered by the inadequate attempt to mount a comparative analysis.

Kemeny's study of home-ownership appreciates some of the results of this traditional failure of comparative analysis. He refers to 'the narrow empiricism' of most comparative work which is unable to relate the study of housing to the wider social structure. But although recognizing some of the theoretical knock-on effects, he does not identify the contributory role of conventional comparative typology and so eventually falls into the same traps. He returns to the deterministic appeal to 'privatism' in Britain and especially Australia versus the stronger presence of 'collectivism' in Sweden. As one reviewer commented:

> Kemeny sees tenures as immutable in terms of their finance and effects. Yet tenure is only an aspect of the social relations involved in forms of housing

provision. Distinct types of finance, construction and land acquisition, for example, are found associated with different tenures and these combinations vary between countries. Moreover, the place of these tenure-related forms of provision within the wider social structure varies over time and also between countries. Surely, such developments and inter-country differences must be central to an analysis of the growth of specific tenure in different countries.

(Ball 1982, 293, quoted in Harloe and Martens 1984, 267)

Nor, as Harloe and Martens point out, and as discussed earlier, is it any advantage to replace non-Marxist functional determinism by a Marxist variant.

It is supremely ironic that the study of Swedish housing which uses comparative analysis most sensibly also has the worst (for us) theoretical apparatus for doing so. This is Popenoe's (1976) detailed comparison of two suburban experiences in Stockholm and Philadelphia (USA). The study does well in avoiding typological juxtaposition; having established differences between the two cases the analysis is taken further using the techniques of in-depth interviewing, detailed description, intuitive empathy, the construction of 'characteristic households' and so on. In other words an attempt is made to discover how differences are established and what effects these have. Our criticism here merely concerns the conceptual apparatus which informs the analysis. This consists of a voluntaristic interpretation of environmental determinism, where environment is limited to local suburban features and access to transport, so that the immediate residential environment remains as a kind of independent variable. Although political and economic relations are acknowledged as crucial, these inevitably remain quite peripheral to an analysis focusing on passive individuals in a 'community' largely cut off from politics, work, and the social order. For instance, one important – but neglected – reason for apparently higher levels of 'environmental congruence' in Vällingby as opposed to Philadelphia's Levittown is that workers in the former generally received higher wages for shorter hours and longer holidays. Similarly, Vällingby was relatively replete with public services and transport as one result of Swedish welfarism, and because housing itself could be built more cheaply – on land costing virtually nothing. (See the review by Duncan 1978c.) The theoretical apparatus removes these essential explanatory factors from the analysis.

The studies already referred to by Heady and Kemeny do better than this in theoretical terms. Heady is the weakest, where the explanatory dynamic is reduced to 'political and operational feasibility' for a rational and benevolent state which acts as neutral referee among non-social political actors (see Marcuse 1982). Kemeny recognizes these limitations, and instead propounds the need to relate housing to the wider social structure, using a political economy approach to achieve this. None the less this study, like all the others we have reviewed here (with the partial exception of Greve) remain almost entirely based on comparisons of tenure change and distributional policy. Construction and land are almost completely ignored. Similarly, rather than examining how policy is implemented, and how it is opposed, these studies have reduced the social processes of distribution and consumption to consumption *patterns* in isolation. The focus is squarely on national state housing policy, the wider social relations of providing housing are severely neglected. The implicit assumption that local states are merely scaled down reflections of national states follows from this focus. It is quite ironic that studies based on the importance of national variation hardly mention sub-national differences. Indeed, recent single country studies have been much more sensitive to this issue (e.g. Merrett 1979, Merrett with Gray 1982). These deficiencies usually find their origin in an inadequate theorization of housing provision; housing is seen as a neutral good produced by benevolent states rather than as playing a social role in maintaining and reforming capitalist societies. (See section 1.3 for expansion.) Not only do very important components of housing provision and policy remain peripheral to the analyses, but the resulting explanations are inevitably limited and lopsided, if not actually beside the point.

It is, of course, far easier to oppose than propose. It is now time to move on to our own comparative analyses of housing provision. But even if the greater ambition of using comparative analysis to work out the balance of structure and contingency cannot be totally fulfilled, at the very least we can undercut the 'taken for granted' on how housing is provided and how to study it. Housing provision is not just a question of national state policy.

## CHAPTER THREE

# The social organization of supply

## 3.1 Structure and variation: comparing house building in Britain and Sweden

Our first comparative study deals with the production of housing in Britain and Sweden. This is also, therefore, a study of how the common economic and social structures of advanced capitalism vary in practice. Why start the empirical chapter with a national level comparison of housing production? This relates to the two roles of comparative research identified in section 1.4 (and see also the discussion of previous international comparisons in section 2.3). First, comparative research can be used to undercut the taken for granted, where it acts as a check on generalization or abstraction procedures. Second, it can allow some partial and relative reduction of real world variation and complexity, and so help in estimating the causal significance of such variations and the processes that create them.

There are three reasons for beginning the empirical chapters with a comparison of *production*. First of all, as we described in the last chapter (see section 2.3) house building has nearly always been ignored in earlier international comparative work. Until recently, this has also been the case for nearly all research on housing provision, whether explicitly comparative or not. We thought it important to ram home from the very beginning the significance of production for housing provision. How many dwellings can be built at what cost is a crucial factor and any amount of consumption subsidy or tenure change cannot escape this fact. Our comparison of dwelling construction in the two countries shows up very well the limits of political determinism.

But paradoxically, although perhaps inevitably given the weakness of the traditional distribution policy approach, the research pendulum has swung rather too violently to a focus on production. At times, construction in isolation is seen as the one determinate factor, a kind of 'construction rules OK' economic determinism. This has taken several forms. Sometimes researchers have forced housing provision into a base and superstructure model; construction is the determinate economic level and political or ideological events merely timetable the inevitable (cf. Ball 1978, and the critique by Duncan 1978a).[1] Interestingly enough, although Castells's work focused explicitly on the political level of the urban question, the 'economic determinism of the last resort' of Althusserian Marxism ended up with the same result (Castells 1977, see the critique by

Duncan 1978a, 1981). At other times it is merely implicitly assumed that a study of construction is the single key to explaining how the built environment is created (e.g. Bartlett School 1980). This is partly because construction has become a sort of invariant 'real life structure'; the nature and importance of distribution policy and consumption patterns are allowed to vary, but production is seen as a rock solid determinate feature. Yet, as we shall see, it is not as simple as 'construction rules OK' because the way in which it rules can vary and this is in itself socially produced. Our comparison made this clear. It is the specific characteristics of Swedish and British society, including among other things how construction relates to other parts of the housing system, that determine how labour is to be exploited in building, and how dwellings are to be produced as a commodity.

Finally, a weaker side effect of this determinist legacy is to assume that housing construction is doomed to be the bottleneck of housing provision. Because of the special characteristics of building houses, so the argument goes – their bulk, the complex integration of multifarious tasks on site, the necessity for craft work, the complication of land development profits – building houses will always suffer from relatively low productivity levels, with relatively low degrees of mechanization and capitalization. Low output, high prices, and the inability – or lack of necessity – to restructure the labour process will result. Sometimes this is merely asserted (cf. Castells 1976, stressing the stranglehold of land ownership). More recently this has been argued more satisfactorily, using detailed empirical reference to the British case, where indeed housing construction displays just these features (e.g. Merrett 1979, chapter four). But note that much of this list of causes could just as easily be symptoms. Why is it that craft work remains so important, that so much production is unstandardized and undertaken on site, etc.?

We should not, in turn, send the pendulum swinging too far back in the other direction. It is probably the case that the special complications of building a dwelling will always produce differences from other manufacturing sectors – just as the special technical features of producing food crops, cars or software packages will continue to be important. But, as our comparison showed very clearly, there is no given need for building construction to be *so* different from other industries as it is in Britain. Nor are technical differences insulated from social change; quite the opposite. This degree of difference between building and other industries in Britain, as described by Merrett (1979) and others, is socially created – not technically determined. In Sweden the building industry is much more like other manufacturing sectors, although significant differences remain. This returns us to the 'undercutting the taken for granted' role of comparative research; housing construction has either been so much taken for granted as to have been completely ignored, or, more recently, its importance and nature has been estimated largely on the basis of analysis of the British situation. In going on from this stage – comparison as conceptual challenge – to attempt some analysis of how and why these differences exist, the 'variability reduction' role of comparison can be useful. This is one aide in extending and refining pre-existing concepts.

So much for starting off with housing production, but why choose an international comparative focus with all the practical difficulties this involves (language, institutional differences, statistical measurement, etc.)? This is dictated by the level of variation, and so the level of generality, we are interested in. Our problem is to relate variability in housing production to variability in social structure in capitalist society. On the one hand we are not concerned with the effects of differences on mode of production scale, on whether housing is produced as a commodity or not. At this high level of generality, comparisons between East and West Europe, or with pre-capitalist societies, could be instructive. But on the other hand, we are not primarily concerned in this chapter with the effect of detailed variations in social institutions. For instance, building labour has been better organized in central Scotland than elsewhere in Britain and comparing the former with say, South Wales could be instructive (note the comparison control element in choosing the second case study). Rather, we are interested in large scale social structure differences within capitalism – such as land ownership as a socio-political force or the overall relative strength of labour and capital.

Such features do vary and can be important on a sub-national level, and we follow this up in chapters five and six. But these differences often have clearest expression at the national level; certainly in the case of comparing Britain and Sweden (as discussed in section 2.2). In brief, Sweden can provide a model of social democratic forms of capitalism. This is also the case for housing production in Sweden where construction gives a relative exemplar of state-regulated efficient capitalism. This is not so in Britain even though in both countries housing is produced as a commodity. Furthermore, the 'variability reduction' role of Sweden is significant because it takes some of these differences to extremes. Large – especially aristocratic – landed interests are relatively very weak; labour – including building labour – is strong; capital – including building capital – is technically progressive; and both labour and capital remain the major social actors in Swedish society, integrated through a particularly successful 'historical compromise' (see section 2.2 for expansion).

Before we go on to make the comparison, a final word about the sort of comparison we are undertaking. We are not directly comparing economic or technical variations in house building; rather, we are comparing the nature and effects of varying social relations at the national level which create these variations. Economic and technical differences are in this sense illustrative. This is not meant to remove attention from the procedures of statistical comparison, which remain important, but rather to place them in perspective. For an adequate comparison of the building process in detail very specific case studies – for example of building firms of a certain size constructing certain products – would have to be undertaken. But this level of comparison would control the many variations we are interested in.

## 3.2 Exploitation and surplus value in housing construction

In both Britain and Sweden over 90 per cent of dwellings are produced as commodities for sale. This necessarily involves selling at prices above production costs, in turn based on the exploitation of labour. This exploitation takes three major forms. First of all, and most directly, it takes place in the building process itself, which includes site development (levelling, drainage, service provision, landscaping, and so on) as well as dwelling construction and the installation of its equipment (e.g. the sanitary and electrical systems). The value of the dwelling produced by these operations is appropriated by the firm, and the various workers who combined to build the dwelling – from unskilled labourer to designer – receive wages in exchange for their labour power. The aim is, of course, that the wage bill together with all other costs is less than the market value of the dwelling, which was created by the labour expended in producing it; in other words surplus value is to be created which can be taken over by the firm, and realized in monetary terms when the sale is made. This is the goal of the whole process, and to this extent producing a dwelling is only a means to an end. The crucial social relation determining how this appropriation works and how far it succeeds is the class relation between appropriators and producers, in this case between building firms and building labour. Appropriation of surplus value in the production process is the central mode of surplus appropriation in capitalism, both quantitatively as the basic means of exploitation and hence of economic organization. (We have no space to develop these general themes here, but see Massey and Catalano 1978, Sainte Croix 1982 for readable accounts which are all the more useful because they have specific historical circumstances in mind.)

However, the production of buildings – including dwellings – allows greater scope for two subsidiary and secondary methods of appropriating surplus value; land development profit and what we have labelled, unsatisfactorily, 'extra profit'. These are both indirect forms of labour exploitation as far as building capitalists are concerned, and both can be conceptualized as forms of rent. Labour expended outside the building process has created surplus value but construction firms, in producing and selling buildings, may be able to tap some of this surplus.

Land development profits provide the clearest case, where the value created by earlier labour inputs on the environment is only realized by the sale of buildings built subsequently. The classic example is when a builder can sell housing at higher prices because of the immense labour someone else has used in constructing an underground railway into a previously unbuilt area. The underground developer has not been able to appropriate all the value increase created by labour power under his control. This is primarily because the surrounding land is owned by others, even though it is the labour power expended on underground building which has increased its use value (e.g. it is more suitable for housing) and hence also its speculative value in exchange. This situation is usually exacerbated, in advanced capitalist societies, where infrastructure developers are very often state institutions. These expend public funds to create value increases which are usually appropriated privately. The same principle, that is a land rent relation, exists equally for all land development gains. In this case the crucial social relation, which determines how this value is distributed, is that between builder and landowner, although this is very often mediated by state planning institutions in advanced capitalist societies. The landowner, instead of the builder, may be able to appropriate surplus value created by the earlier labour expenditure. This can be taken as increased land rent or (the same thing capitalized) as profits on sale, when the landowner can realize land value increases produced in expectation of future production now possible on that site. It may even be possible to use the state machinery to pass land development profits to other groups. This is the case in Sweden, where it is consumers who benefit in the form of lower housing costs and in eventual capital gains on sale if the dwelling is privately owned. (Clearly, 'land development profit' should not be confused with the 'site development' component of construction work mentioned above. The latter involves an expenditure of labour power so as to change physically the site – levelling, drainage, services, etc. Such labour expenditure creates value directly.)

Third, and finally, builders may be able to sell the dwellings themselves at above their value. This 'extra profit' as we have termed it, is a sort of 'tax' on surplus value produced elsewhere. It is a major source of speculative profit taken from the dwellings, as opposed to the land they are built on. It can, however, be conceptualized as a form of rent, where extra profit represents capitalized building rent rather than land rent. Because of a particular resolution of class and political relations, builders are able successfully to demand prices for dwellings above their value (cf. 'absolute land rent', Massey and Catalano, 1978). This situation will reproduce itself, for there is now less incentive to invest capital, so as to increase labour productivity, technical innovation and organizational efficiency. Profits are made anyway. Consequently, dwellings will be produced below levels of productivity technically possible, more labour power will be expended, and consumers will pay above what is strictly necessary. Housing is produced at below average productivity and indeed below possible productivity and this reinforces the diversion of surplus value from other sectors into house building.

But where do these extra payments, to provide extra profit, come from and how can such payments be maintained and enforced on a large scale? In the first case this is simple enough, extra payments are made in the market from purchasers' incomes including state subsidies of various forms. The origin of both these sources of extra profit is value produced elsewhere; surplus value must be diverted into higher wages for workers (to finance their housing consumption or tax payments) or into higher taxes paid by firms.

At first sight this seems little different from any other sector of production. Surplus value equalization to and from sectors of below and above average productivity normally takes place in the market. Similarly, any capitalist is glad of 'extra profit' when it comes his way, for example when market imperfections or monopoly power give one producer an unfair advantage. However, housing production is a special case. Because of its social and economic importance, national states in advanced capitalism have created mechanisms which can maintain extra profit appropriation at a higher level than normal and with a greater degree of permanency. This happens in three major ways. First of all national states enforce minimum housing standards and housing consumption levels, both legally or directly through housing investment. Payment for housing must be made. Second, nearly all housing consumption in advanced capitalist countries is heavily subsidized in one way or another. In this sense owner-occupation is just as much 'state housing' as public housing. (At the time of writing, in Britain, it is probably more so.) Third, systems of financing housing consumption have been developed which allow consumers to pay extra profits more easily from their incomes. The housing mortgage system is an obvious example, a system which also reallocates the risk of this operation from builders to consumers,[2] although local authority borrowing to finance house building is similar. In turn, the very existence of state enforced consumption levels, state directed investment, state consumption subsidies and state supported loan systems encourages this situation to continue. Extra profits are more easily made, there is less incentive to invest capital in building production, low productivity remains and high housing costs are sustained. The British housing market is a good example of all this. So by 1983 the ratio of initial mortgage repayments to average earnings had reached 45 per cent (compared to 25 per cent in the 1960s) and certain building society economists were arguing that it was only the state supplementary benefit system which was preventing total collapse of the private housing market (*Financial Times*, 20 August 1983).

It is instructive to examine situations where extra profit is not so easy to come by, perhaps because of insecure consumer income or low state subsidy levels. For instance, in the undeveloping Atlantic Provinces of Canada[3] about half of new houses built in the 1970s lacked mortgage financing, and this meant that the consumers had to finance building out of savings or land sales or even replace the builder entirely through using his/her own 'sweat equity'. Ironically enough, there is greater security of tenure for owner-occupiers financed in these alternative ways (Rowe 1983). Similarly, in Portugal a large proportion of new dwellings have been constructed illegally, without government subsidy or 'normal' mortgage finance and often financed through the savings of expatriate workers (Lewis and Williams 1984). In both these cases a mass building industry is hardly possible and house construction has more of the nature of petty commodity production or even domestic labour. Alternative arrangements have developed which cut building capital off from a potential source of surplus value. This is an illuminating judgement on the technical progress of house building. Without state supported extra profit it would find it difficult to compete against non-capitalist forms of production.

But what happens in those cases where housing consumption *is* largely financed through long-term loans and state subsidies, as in Britain? (Inner cites have been a partial exception, e.g. Karn 1979.) Here the crucial social relation in appropriating surplus value through this extra profit will be that between state institutions and loan capital. (Local authorities must borrow in order to pay builders just as much as owner-occupiers, although in this case they may have more control over the financial system of doing so.) This is not to suggest that state bureaucracies are the ultimate social interests involved, rather they represent, in a confused and contradictory manner, the interests of both builders and consumers.

Both land development profit and extra profit are significant, even dominant, as a source of builders' profits in Britain. In this sense the British building industry is abnormal. It is able to subvert part of the usual operation of the 'law of value', the process by which capital is invested in more profitable outlets and, in doing so, pressurizes firms to reallocate the expenditure of labour power among sectors and tasks, increase labour productivity, transform labour processes and create new products. In British house building profits can be maintained in other ways and capital investment in the production process (as opposed to, say, land banking) is retarded. A concomitant is high construction costs and high housing costs for consumers.

Finally we must repeat that both land development profit and extra profit are secondary and parasitic means for house building firms to appropriate surplus value. They are parasitic because their existence depends on value production in other sectors of the economy; they are secondary because their realization depends on continuing labour exploitation in the building process. The 'tax' on surplus produced elsewhere should accrue to building firms as land development profits or extra profits, not increase the real wages of building workers and at some stage housing must be produced. Both land development profit and extra profit are forms of appropriating surplus value, not creating it. However, how the housing is produced and at what cost can be crucially affected by the relative importance of these forms of realizing value through the construction of housing.

What are the implications of this discussion of the appropriation of surplus and the exploitation of labour for our comparative work on housing production in Britain and Sweden? First of all, it allows us to conceptualize the common structures in which both building industries operate, and which they also help maintain. If one point of our comparison is to relate common structure to varying outcome, in the attempt to allocate causal significance to social features, it clearly helps to know what these structures are. Such a structural discussion also allows us to find a bench mark – the limits of any successful variation, if the structure is to be maintained, can be established in advance. (This does *not* mean that it is impossible to change the structure or even abolish it completely.) But second, and equally important, the discussion of structures has paradoxically pointed towards a major theme of the book. The outcomes of social conflicts, including class conflict, are not predetermined by the structural sources of the conflicts in the first place.

This is perhaps clearest for the case of struggle over land development profits, where it is up for grabs how far the builder or the landowner – or even the consumer – appropriate these profits. The result will reflect the changing balance of economic and political power of these groups, perhaps institutionalized in a state planning system as well as in market relations (see Backwell and Dickens 1978, Ball 1983 for the British case). But the same applies for the direct exploitation of labour in house building itself. Exactly how building capital can exploit labour may vary considerably. This may be a consequence of the differing organizational and economic strengths of the two partners. For example, within Britain building labour is apparently much better organized – and hence economically more central – in lowland Scotland than elsewhere (Ball 1983). We might expect this to have some effects on how building is carried out and what is produced. This may be one reason why a smaller proportion of housing in central Scotland has been produced speculatively, and more for tender to local authorities. However, this balance between building capital and labour will again be influenced by external factors – for example the degree to which builders can appropriate land development profits, or current state legislation on trade union rights (both are changing dramatically in Britain at the time of writing – in favour of builders). Similarly, relations between state institutions (and hence builders and consumers) and loan capital change and vary and so produce different outcomes in the appropriation of extra profit. At the time of writing, in Britain, new taxation arrangements on banks and building societies threaten to reduce the level of extra profit that can be paid to building capital.

The overall result of these conflicts is that quite different sorts of building production can be created according to how exploitation takes place. There are two dimensions to this variance – the balance between the three forms of labour exploitation in building identified above (i.e. land rent, extra profit and surplus value production in building) and also the precise methods and degree of exploitation in any one form. And, as discussed in chapter one, capitalist societies are unevenly developed; they are not in a state of simultaneous equilibrium however much traditional economies or sociology may assume otherwise. Given uneven development such differences in how houses are built and thus how profits are made by producing them can persist over the medium or long term. As the reader may have guessed by now, this is exactly what we found in comparing housing production in Britain and Sweden. And this difference has considerable social, economic and political effects – on housing costs, conditions, and access; on the cost of reproduction and hence of labour power and on economic demand; on the strength and possibility of political compromise and settlement.

## 3.3 Undercutting the taken for granted: housing output and costs

The next two sections will compare the nature and effects of housing production in Britain and Sweden, looking in turn at output levels, consumption costs, construction costs, productivity levels, and speculation versus market regulation. The aim is to undercut the taken for granted, which is based on British experience, in two ways. First of all the comparison makes it plain just how important housing production can be to the success or otherwise of housing provision. What quantity of housing can be built at what relative cost is fundamental to the housing question as a social, political and economic problem, and the comparison shows that this can vary considerably even within advanced capitalist countries. Second, in section 3.4, the comparison goes on to demonstrate that the British 'model' of housing production so ably described by Merrett (1979) and Ball (1983) – very low relative productivity, low relative levels of capitalization and industrialization, the speculative organization of production – is not a necessary condition in advanced capitalist countries nor, possibly, even a 'normal one'. Subsequent sections of the chapter will go on to examine more fully the social basis of these differences both within building itself (3.5) and in relation to wider social processes (3.6).

These discussions use statistical material of various sorts and we have found ourselves torn between providing an explication of the statistical sources, their adequacy and how they may be interpreted on the one hand, and developing our empirical and conceptual argument on the other. We have tried to do both things, but in the space available we will inevitably have failed to carry out either to everyone's satisfaction.

*Output levels*

Figure 3.1 presents three different measures of relative housing output in Britain and Sweden. For all three, Sweden shows consistently higher rates over the whole post-war period, and for substantial periods the Swedish rates are around double the British figure. For instance, expressing yearly Swedish rates as a percentage of the equivalent British figure, the differential for new dwellings per 1000 population varied from a high of 205 per cent in 1974 to a low of 135 per cent in 1961 (excluding the immediate post-war years). For newly built rooms per 1000 population equivalent figures were 207 per cent (1970) and 111 per cent (1954). Indeed, it comes as something of a shock to find that the *highest* British new building rates hardly exceed the *lowest* Swedish rates. Only for the periods 1969–74 (dwellings) and 1964–8 (rooms) do British rates exceed Sweden's low 1980 figure (although output rates continue to decline in both countries).

Crude dwelling output rates do, of course, neglect size and quality differences in new building as well as improvement to existing stock. To some extent the rooms per 1000 population index tackles the problem of dwelling size. During the 1950s and 1960s, most new dwellings built in Britain were larger than in Sweden. This was partly because builders have concentrated much more on the higher income end of the private housing market. But since then, and indicatively, the situation has been reversed. In absolute terms (m² floor space) newly built dwellings in Sweden were on average 59 per cent larger in 1980 than in 1963, although this partly reflects a shift in building type and tenure – public sector dwellings were only 28 per cent larger. But for Britain, average floor space has actually *decreased* substantially over this period, by 13 per cent for local authority dwellings and – although difficult to quantify exactly – for owner-occupied buildings since the late 1960s. Sweden reached British standards in floor space terms by the late 1960s, although – as British builders tried desperately to keep up bedroom number by minimizing room size – not until 1975 in terms of rooms per dwelling. By 1980 the average new dwelling in Britain was being built to the equivalent of Sweden's 1960 space standards. So although size variation will narrow the crude output differentials somewhat in the early post-war period, it has actually increased them since around 1970. Also significant is that dwelling size was the only measure of housing quality and cost where post-war new building in Britain could once unequivocally claim some superiority. Now even that advantage has been lost.

Quality differences are more difficult to measure. Certainly there has been a substantial improvement in Sweden in the 1970s over what was already a high level in terms of design, insulation, equipment and external environment. Most statistical measures suggest higher dwelling quality in Sweden even before this improvement. We can safely assume that this factor will not reduce the differentials illustrated in figure 3.1a – indeed, it probably widens them.

Figure 3.1b gives a better overall measure of total housing output including size and quality levels, by measuring gross fixed capital formation in housing as a

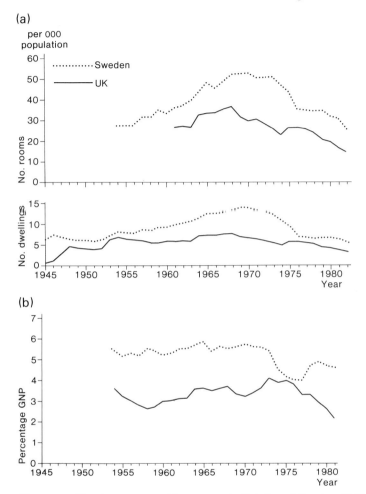

*Figure 3.1*  Housing output and investment in Britain and Sweden, 1945–80
a) New construction per 000 population
b) Gross fixed capital formation in housing as a percentage of GNP

*Sources:* Compiled from Annual Abstract of Statistics; Annual Bulletin of Housing and Building Statistics; Södersten 1968.

share of GNP. It also reflects investment in upgrading and repairs to older dwellings and the improvement booms of the mid-1970s in Britain, and the late 1970s and 1980s in Sweden. (Compare figures 3.1a and 3.1b.) By 1980 nearly 50 per cent of Swedish housing output, measured by value, was in improvement, conversion and repairs. This compares with a low of about 25 per cent in 1970 at the height of the new build 'million programme' which lasted from 1963 to 1973. (The Swedish government promised to build a million dwellings over 10 years. They succeeded – in per capita terms equivalent to a British rate, never remotely achieved, of 650,000 houses per year.) Although this measure inevitably introduces further statistical problems, for instance that of what other sectors were doing, the overall difference of degree between the two countries is repeated. As a percentage of British figures Swedish rates vary from a high of 219 per cent in 1981 (with 211 per cent in 1958) to a low of 105 per cent in 1975 at the end of the 'million programme'. The highest British figures *never* reach the lowest Swedish rates. Although any one of the measures used in figure 3.1 can only give a crude estimate of output, in combination the message is clear.

The other striking thing about figure 3.1 is the overall similarity in broad output trends, although the UK figures are less stable. Increasing output rates in the post-war boom and high rates in the 1960s 'record years' are succeeded by decline with the onset of recession after 1973. (A break magnified for Sweden with the end of the 'million programme'.) In this way the overall effect of world capitalism overrides the national differences of output level and the smaller booms and slumps created by political or policy shifts. Note, however, the increasing differences emerging in the 1980s. Sweden maintains a housing output roughly similar in gross terms to the period before the 'million programme', and appears to have recovered from the mid-1970s slump. (See figure 3.1b, although note that there have been important output switches within housing since 1973.) The British figures continue to plummet.

In summary, from a Swedish perspective, housing output in Britain has nearly always been low, sometimes very low. Similarly, size and quality differences between new housing in the two countries are increasing, so that by the 1980s new output in Britain appears well below standard in Swedish terms. (Remember, of course, that we are dealing with an aggregate picture here, not with particular housing types and still less with the overall quality of life.) However, these differences might not matter so much if housing consumption costs are stable in Britain. The next sub-section turns to this issue.

*Consumption costs*

Figure 3.2 turns to the other side of the coin: housing costs for consumers. The graph portrays absolute household expenditure on housing, that is actual monetary payments, in constant price terms standardized as a percentage of 1949 values. Here the national differences are startling. Between 1949 and 1980 real costs had risen by 8.6 per cent in Sweden, but by over 130 per cent in Britain.

This huge difference cannot be accounted for by quality and quantity differences in what is being bought, as we have suggested these have improved in Sweden as much as in Britain, if not more so. Indeed, the Swedish figures will be slightly inflated because they include repair costs and some service costs excluded from the British statistics. Similarly, the effects of consumption payment subsidies can be largely discounted (e.g. housing benefits and mortgage tax relief)[4]. The graph does not, therefore, address the issue of how far it is the state or the household which assumes the burden of increasing housing costs. Rather, the indices measure actual payments made by households in order to consume housing, irrespective of where this money comes from. They are indices of the cost of the commodity–housing.

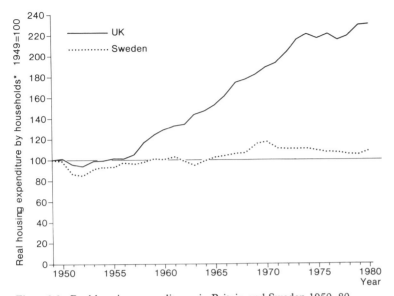

*Figure 3.2*   Real housing expenditures in Britain and Sweden 1950–80

*Note:* *Average household housing payments, property taxes and water charges, deflated by CPI. Repairs and some other service charges are included for Sweden.

*Sources:* Calculated from BBÅ 1981; CSO 1981 national income and expenditure annual reports.

In one sense, however, a 'statistical explanation' of this huge national difference does hold some validity. For by standardizing both sets of expenditure figures as percentages of 1949 values we cover up an important difference in base levels. In the early 1950s average housing costs took on average only 9 per cent of household income in Britain but around 15 per cent in Sweden, although by 1980 the British figure had doubled to 16 per cent while in Sweden there had been a slight decrease to around 13 per cent of household income (over the same period average industrial wages in Britain fell from 80 per cent to 50 per cent of Swedish levels). None the less, the significance of completely different trends remains – and other statistics tell a similar story. For example, in Britain, housing consumption costs have increased much more than the index of all other consumer prices. Taking 1970 as base year, the former exceeded the latter by 75 percentage points in 1983. But in Sweden housing costs were 53 percentage points *lower* than the index of all other consumer prices by the same date (UN Housing and Building Statistics, provided for us by J. Barlow).

How, then, has it been possible to keep real housing costs almost stable in Sweden, and why have they more than doubled in Britain since 1949? As we mentioned above, real housing cost trends have considerable impact on the relative costs of labour and this can have significant economic and social effects. Just one immediate illustration: by 1980 around 40 per cent of Swedish households used *two* dwellings, a permanent one *and* a holiday dwelling. (Over 20 per cent of households own holiday homes, the other 20 per cent have access through family ties, etc.) Others, no doubt, are able to spend income on other goods that in Britain would be absorbed by permanent housing consumption.

There are several possible answers to Sweden's relative success since 1945 in terms of both housing output and consumption costs, and Britain's relative failure. For political and economic reasons investment in housing construction may have been higher in Sweden (as figure 3.1b suggests). This was one answer suggested by Greve as long ago as 1971 (see also Duncan 1978) but however important in terms of output levels this 'social choice' cannot go far in explaining differences in costs per unit. Also important, as many observers have shown, is how the housing stock is distributed, what methods are used to purchase it, and what effects consumption subsidies have on costs (e.g. Greve 1971; Heady 1978; Kemeny 1980). There is now more 'non-profit' distribution in Sweden than in Britain, 38 per cent of stock was owned by public sector authorities and co-operatives by 1980 compared to 32 per cent in Britain. Equally important for price development, as much as 52 per cent of construction in Sweden since 1945 has been for distribution through these 'non-profit' tenures, compared to only 41 per cent in Britain. All these factors are important in understanding national differences in housing costs, not to mention access by income, social class and family type, and will be discussed in more detail in chapter four. But the remaining major candidate in explaining these large differences in output and price development is the cost of producing dwellings in the first place. We know that overall rent and price levels are significantly affected by the costs of new building (see Ball 1983, chapter four), and in any case by 1980 half the stock in Britain and as much as 70 per cent in Sweden had been built since 1945. How far do trends in construction costs differ between the two countries?

*Construction costs*

Figure 3.3 provides a quick answer to this question. Construction costs are out of control in Britain and relatively stable in Sweden. In the latter (see figure 3.3a) real production costs per unit volume increased by only 15 per cent for group built small houses (i.e. detached, semi-detached and terrace) between 1965 and 1980. For multi-dwelling construction (flats and maisonettes) the real increase amounted to 33 per cent and in both cases production costs were below 1965 values until the late 1970s. (There are no figures for individually built small houses, usually a minor part of new building.) The Swedish data also allows a breakdown into site development costs (levelling, demolition, site services, site planning, landscaping, etc.) and building costs proper. For small houses building costs proper in 1980 were still below 1965 levels, while for multi-dwellings building costs had increased by 20 per cent in real terms (although definitional changes in 1973 complicate this a little). For both dwelling types building costs were well below 1965 levels by the mid-1970s.

Contrast this situation with the British experience (figure 3.3b). Here tender costs per unit area for local authority housing in England and Wales show real increases of between 42 per cent and 57 per cent over the same period. What is more, tender costs exhibit violent swings where increases of 10 per cent or even 20 per cent in one year are not uncommon. Flats of five storeys or above give the extreme example; by 1974 they had reached 176 per cent of 1965 levels and since then have swung violently up or down no fewer than five times. The Swedish cost

(a)

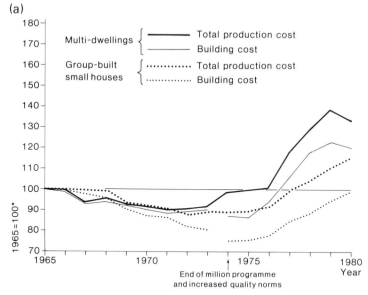

(b)

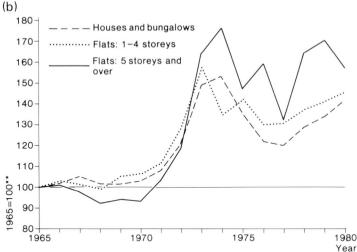

*Figure 3.3*   Production costs in Britain and Sweden, 1965–80
a) Real total production and building cost trends in Sweden
b) Real tender cost trends in England and Wales: local authority construction

*Notes:*
* Index of total dwelling production costs (kr m$^2$) deflated by CPI
** Index of tender costs (£ m$^2$) England and Wales excluding GLC deflated by RPI

*Sources:* Calculated from BO; HCS.

increases since the mid-1970s are sedate in comparison. Instability on the British scale is likely to be more damaging than steady, even if steep, increases. Figure 3.3 also shows that the national variation in construction costs is more important than the variation between different types of housing (e.g. flats versus single houses). This reinforces the view that house building should not be seen as a purely technical process.

Both sets of figures measure slightly different things, but both in essence refer to dwelling production costs including profits but excluding land acquisition costs. The British tender costs approximate a position half way between the Swedish 'building costs' and 'total production costs', where local authorities in Britain usually take care of the bulk– but not all – of site development for public sector construction as well as land acquisition. The Swedish data refers to all tenures, but here most development land is already owned by local authorities and land acquisition costs rarely exceed 2 per cent of total production costs (cf. 8 to 45 per cent in Britain). Note that in Sweden nearly all housing, of whatever tenure, is built to local authority contract, not speculatively. We will return to this important point later.

The most significant shortcoming with figure 3.3 is that comparable production cost per unit dwelling figures are not available for private sector house building in Britain. But as this is the sector where we might expect even more unfavourable construction cost trends (cf. Ball 1983), the figure if anything under-represents cost escalation and instability in Britain. However a rough surrogate is provided by the 'output indices' of construction used in the HCS statistics (figure 3.4). Some fluctuation is already removed in calculating the index, which is only available from 1970, but the same picture of rapid and unstable cost escalation emerges. More importantly, for our purposes, both

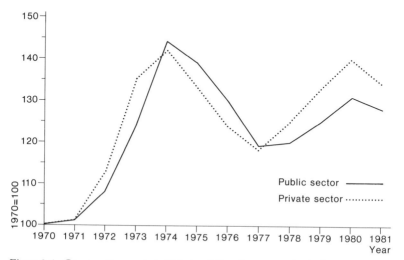

*Figure 3.4*   Construction costs in Britain: deflated output price indices, 1970–81

*Source:* Calculated from HCS.

public and private sector construction show very similar trends. Finally, the England and Wales figures in figure 3.3 exclude Greater London – where we know house building to be more expensive than elsewhere. This will again tend to reduce the British figures in comparison to the Swedish data. We can conclude that trend differences of the scale shown by figure 3.3 cannot be significantly affected by the measurement differences involved; indeed the statistical inconsistencies probably reduce national differences more than increase them.

The picture of spiralling increases in housing construction costs in Britain supports the more detailed arguments already made by Ball (1983). As he shows, these long-term cost increases are not caused by long-term changes in factor input costs, such as building material costs. Still less are they due to land acquisition costs (which the industry itself likes to blame). These merely follow construction cost trends. Rather, Ball concludes, building capital has somehow lost control over the building process itself.

We do not need to expand on this picture here, and we refer readers to Ball's excellent analysis. We will, however, spend some more time examining cost developments in Sweden. This also allows us to signpost some important factors, such as building process changes and labour productivity, which are central to later parts of the chapter.

Two things are most obvious in figure 3.3b: the sustained real cost decreases up to the mid-1970s (other evidence suggests that they began in the 1950s, if not earlier) and the cost increases since then, especially for multi-dwelling construction. Building cost decreases on this scale are remarkable in British terms, although this is of course what one expects for commodity production in capitalism over the long term and in this sense it is the British figures which are 'deviant'. As we shall see, the cost decreases in house building in Sweden are to be explained in this 'normal' way. Product innovation and productivity increases resulting from capitalization, labour process change, enterprise reorganization and economies of scale have led to reductions in the real costs of commodity production, in this case housing.

What went wrong, then, with the production cost increases in the late 1970s? (Although figure 3.3 suggests that these are now subsiding.) Minor in British terms, these are serious in the Swedish context, so much so that a government inquiry was set up to study the problem (SOU 1982: 34, 35) – although this is also a comment on the political differences between the two countries. Significantly, the inquiry concluded that little had gone wrong in the terms in which we have set the issue. Certainly there had been construction cost increases for housing, and these were disturbing. However, these were for 'good' reasons, because of increasing product quality (in effect more units of housing output per dwelling) and because of developments outside the construction industry. There had not been a significant loss of control over the construction process or over construction costs *per se*. Swedish house building had not caught the 'British disease'.

We will briefly discuss these arguments here, as they provide a useful introduction to how house building takes place in Sweden. First of all, the quality of the product had improved substantially between 1974 and 1980. Increased dwelling quality would account for *all* the real production cost increases for small houses over this period, and as much as 60 per cent for multi-dwelling building. Up to 1973 such changes had been absorbed easily enough by increasing productivity. However, most quality changes since 1973 have been bunched together over a few years, furthermore they were state enforced for all new housing and relatively costly. Government norms on environmental standards (e.g. play areas, child safety) and facilities for the handicapped (including more lifts) were increased. Improved safety standards for building workers can also be included here. Above all, insulation and heating control standards were substantially increased and these accounted for 40 per cent of norm increase costs in multi-dwelling construction and no less than 80 per cent with small house building. Indeed it was the prompt state reaction to the 1973 oil price rises that produced this 'bunching' of quality improvement. Most of Sweden's energy is produced from imported oil and domestic heating is a major energy user. Short-term increases in construction costs would be more than offset by long-term savings for the national economy – just the sort of calculation that is so difficult to act on in Britain.

This line of argument is supported by figure 3.5 on output productivity. The figure measures the cost of factor inputs in house building (for instance, the cost of insulation materials and the labour, equipment and energy necessary to use them) in relation to the final building price. If the index increases, more output is being produced for the same unit price (the purchaser gets more housing quality for the same money) and vice versa. As we would expect from the construction cost diagram (figure 3.3b), substantial gains in output productivity are recorded for both small house and multi-dwelling construction between 1968 and 1977. For small houses, output productivity has since stabilized around this level and in 1980 was still 38 per cent above the 1968 figure. In 1980 purchasers received the same amount of factor input per unit price as in 1977; it is only because there are more inputs (due to the increased quality norms for instance) that total costs have increased. This agrees with the calculations made above where all production cost increases for small housing could be attributed to quality improvement.

But for multi-dwelling construction quality improvement can only account for 60 per cent of production cost increase and figure 3.5 demonstrates this where output productivity declined substantially between 1977 and 1979 (although the

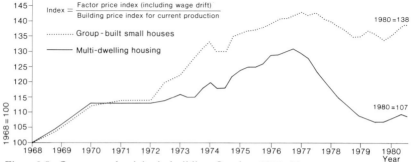

*Figure 3.5*   Output productivity in building, Sweden, 1968–80

*Source:* Adapted from SOU 1982: 34.

position seems to be stabilizing with 1980 still 7 per cent over the 1968 level). This brings us to a second major external reason for increases in production costs, one that has particularly affected multi-dwelling construction – the loss of economies of scale. For the public sector 'million programme' housing drive was overwhelmingly based on multi-dwelling construction, and this ceased in 1973/4. Consequently project sizes, and hence also economies of scale, declined substantially and quite suddenly. SOU 1982: 34 gives detailed estimates of the associated increase per dwelling in the costs of labour, materials, administration and overheads. For instance, for a multi-dwelling project of only twenty dwellings labour productivity would decrease by 28 per cent compared to a 150 unit project; as much as 60 per cent more roof area per flat would be required, and so on. In fact average project sizes nearly halved between 1967–73 and 1974–8, from 160 to 90 dwellings. This loss of scale economies would account for another 15 per cent of real construction cost increases in the multi-dwelling sector. Finally, increased 'taxation' on building, through legal, planning and service charges, also raised costs. According to SOU 1982: 34 the cost of building materials, land acquisition, labour power and finance (accepting that these increased in line with inflation) had little effect on real construction costs.

Like quality improvement, the loss of scale economies should eventually be absorbed by productivity increase and product innovation. For instance lighter and cheaper load-bearing materials, allowed by smaller flat block size, are now in common use and prefabricated component manufacturers have switched production accordingly. Similarly, even though project size has decreased, small 'product unit' sizes (i.e. the on-site construction unit) have become less common. Both developments will increase labour productivity. The same goes for product innovation and RK – the second largest co-operative developer – gives one good example. In 1973 it replaced its older 'S design' for flat blocks with an 'F design'. The latter, not technically possible with high rise, was 20 per cent cheaper to build per flat (BPA/RK 1978). It is changes like these that help explain the stabilization of output productivity and production costs by 1980 (figures 3.3b and 3.5). It is more the suddenness of the loss of economies of scale with the end of the 'million programme' that caused the cost problem. This was exacerbated by further demand downturn caused by the international slump, also beginning in 1973, and the accession to power in 1976 of a centre–right government which favoured small house building.

The considerable material presented by SOU 1982: 34 is quite persuasive. All the real production cost increases for small house building, and at least 80 per cent of them for multi-dwelling building, were attributable to external changes rather than declining building efficiency as such. Although in Britain loss of economies of scale may also have played a similar role (evidence is sparse) quality was actually decreasing over this period. Factors like these cannot explain the large differential in production costs compared to Sweden, still less the chronic instability recorded.

Nevertheless, we should remember that SOU 1982: 34 was largely staffed by representatives from Social Democratic institutions and building interests (both labour and capital). A major function of the inquiry seems to have been to present arguments for greater state expenditure on public sector house building. Evidence like that we have used here would show this to be economically sensible, as well as socially meritorious. The 'historic compromise' between capital and labour expressed in bricks and mortar (or, rather, concrete and mineral wool) could be prolonged. Any 'housing crisis' would be the result of state investment policy, rather than changes in the building industry itself. There is however an alternative argument which the 1982 Inquiry acts to deflect, that Sweden has in fact caught a version of the British building disease since 1975.

Certainly, seen from a Swedish perspective in isolation, there have been important shifts in housing construction since then (e.g. Chambert and Skoglund 1983). Reduced home demand with the end of the 'million programme' and the recession, combined with increasing costs and reductions in state investment, produced something of a crisis compared with the boom years of steady output increase in the 1960s. One response has been shifts in what is produced – from new building to upgrading, from multi-dwelling to small houses, from the home market to export. But although there have been important internal adjustments, the evidence does not suggest any significant change in industrial *structure*. (Nor has total output collapsed as in Britain, where now even repair work is declining.) This is a major point for our argument. As succeeding sections will show, the Swedish construction industry has not decapitalized, deindustrialized, or disorganized itself to British levels. If anything the demand crisis has stimulated the opposite. Similarly, there has been no return to large-scale speculative house building, largely banished from Sweden since 1942. Indeed, since the mid-1970s crisis there has been even less. The significant structural differences between house building in the two countries remain and, with them, marked differences in production cost trends. In Britain, construction costs are apparently out of control and large price increases are necessary to induce new output. Quality per unit output is also declining. Fewer houses are built, producing inflationary price increases and the resulting instability in demand compounds construction problems (cf. Ball 1983). This house construction crisis will affect the existing stock, with increases in both consumption costs and waiting lists. In short, more money (and more waiting) buys less output. In Sweden, less money buys more output, or at least (in the 1977–80 period) more money buys more output. It is one of the promises of a capitalist system of production that, whatever unfortunate social effects it may have, it can at least reduce the cost of commodities and so make an increasing range of things available to an increasing number of people. This does not seem to be happening with house building in Britain, although this deviant position has often been taken for granted. The next section will start the analysis of how and why housing production costs in Sweden and Britain differ so much.

### 3.4 Undercutting the taken for granted: the structure of housing production

There are two aspects of construction cost development in the two countries to be explained: overall trend differences and volatility differences. These can be explained in a fairly simple way if we are content to take the argument only one step further. Speculative house building as an industrial strategy gives rise to conditions which cause chronic instability in construction costs and do nothing for cost control. Management becomes focused on the speculative skills of selling the product at the right time, buying and selling land, and arranging favourable deals with sub-contractors and purchasers. This means that the problem of reorganizing the labour process so as to produce better dwellings more cheaply is neglected, as this is no longer the central means of increasing profits. To return to the terms of our theoretical discussion (section 3.2) land development profits and financial profits are more important than improving the exploitation of building labour as a means of realizing surplus value. These speculative processes may assure companies a profit – although hordes of weaker firms go bankrupt and this in itself wastes effort and resources – but do nothing to improve the efficiency of the building process. In fact, as Ball (1983) shows very well, construction costs are essentially out of control in Britain. Productivity remains low and so increasing real costs threaten profitability which comes to depend more and more on the instability of speculative booms and slumps fuelled by conditions (e.g. interest rates) essentially out of the control of the industry.

A similar situation applied in Sweden before the war. (See figure 4.4 for the notorious example of Stockholm.) But since the 1942–8 housing reforms there has been little speculative house building, only 13 per cent of new housing between 1946 and 1980 was constructed under speculative conditions, compared to 60 per cent in Britain (see figure 3.6). Also, partly as a consequence of these reforms and partly because of development land policy throughout the post-war period (see Duncan 1985) it has not usually been possible for builders to make significant land development profits in Sweden. The production process itself becomes the chief way of increasing surplus value appropriation. But building labour is well organized and highly paid in Sweden. Management skills must be squarely focused on the problem of labour productivity and product development. Innovation and labour process restructuring, so as to provide an improved product at competitive cost, become the road to profitability. This is of course the 'normal' capitalist road, which results in more and cheaper commodities. This road is not without its own problems, of overcapacity for instance. But this is better than in-capacity.

The problems of speculative house building compound the effects of low productivity levels. Low productivity increase in building compared to other sectors will increase the cost of housing in relation to other commodities over the long term. If speculative house building is a major cause of the instability of construction costs, and also contributes to a poor productivity record, it is relative productivity levels which play the major part in long-term real cost trends. The national contrasts are equally dramatic. In Britain output per unit labour in house building increased by a maximum of 50 per cent between 1950 and 1980, for Sweden the corresponding figure was nearer 200 per cent. These figures are approximate and for the moment ignore measurement problems, but the overall trend differences remain however labour productivity is defined. The British rate is well below the average for manufacturing and even the commercial economy as a whole; the Swedish figure is nearer average rates and at times (e.g. 1965–75) has exceeded them. This is a central reason explaining why the relative real increase in dwelling production costs was up to 50 per cent lower in Sweden than in Britain between 1965 and 1980 (figure 3.3). Indeed, although our data series only

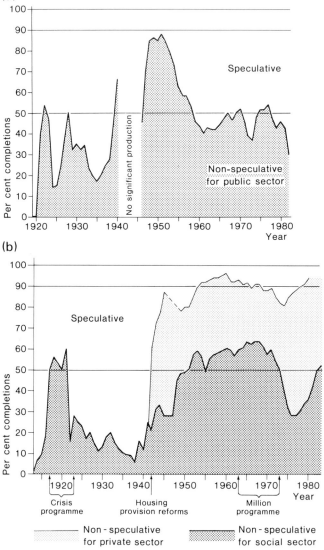

*Figure 3.6*  Speculation and regulation in housing production
a) UK 1919–82
b) Sweden 1913–83

*Sources:* (a) Compiled from HCS, Housing Returns; Merrett (1979); Merrett with Gray (1982). (b) Compiled from Ekbrant 1981, 1982; SOU 1945: 63; BBÅ.

begins in 1965, these costs have decreased in real terms for most of the post-war period in Sweden. Whatever the effects of methods of housing distribution and subsidy or of different levels of housing investment – and these can be significant – productivity in house building will have profound importance. In Sweden much more housing can be built for the same expenditure of labour. This is crucial in understanding how it is that housing quality and output levels can be so much higher, and increases in housing consumption costs so much lower, than in Britain.

We shall return to the discussion of how and why these productivity differences have emerged in the next two sections. Similarly, chapter four looks in more detail at how and why speculative house production became pushed to the sidelines in Sweden. For the rest of this section we shall establish these national contrasts more adequately. This is to extend the 'undercutting the taken for granted' role to a more explicit 'abstraction checking' role. Comparison will be used to confront arguments accepting the importance of production just as much as those ignoring it.

*Speculation versus regulation*

We can start with figure 3.6 and the relative importance of speculative production in the two countries. Looking at Britain first (figure 3.6a) it is clear that speculative house building has always been dominant, except for the 1945–60 period. (It is most useful at this point to work in percentage terms, but for absolute figures see figures 4.1 and 4.2.) In fact as much as 60 per cent of housing built from 1946 to 1980 has been produced speculatively. But turning to Sweden (figure 3.6b) a quite different picture emerges. Speculative house building was, if anything, more dominant than in Britain in the pre-war period. Since the war, however, this form of housing production becomes of quite minor significance; only 13 per cent of dwellings built between 1946 and 1980 were produced in this way. This reduction is not so much because of the expansion of the social 'non-profit' (public and co-op) sector, although clearly this has been of much greater import-ance since the war (52 per cent of total new completions, compared to 40 per cent public sector in Britain). Rather this is because of the emergence of a totally new production form which we have labelled 'non speculative for private sector'. This category accounts for 35 per cent of all new completions between 1946 and 1980. (There is actually a fourth category of production: non-commodity production carried out by self-build organizations, by individuals building for themselves, or state bodies like the Direct Labour Organizations in Britain.[5] In both countries this is insignificant in national terms and has been omitted for the sake of clarity – but in both countries non-commodity production can be ideologically challenging and important locally, as figure 5.6 shows for Sheffield.)

What do these categories imply? The dichotomy in Britain between speculative and contract building for the public sector is familiar enough (Merrett 1979). With the latter, firms build 'bespoke' for state developers (usually local auth-orities) according to tender. This is more like the normal method of selling commodities in that there is no opportunity for builders to make land develop-ment profits (the land is acquired by the state developer) and the avenues of making extra profit are also narrowed. However, although profits may be less spectacular, they are also more certain. Public sector contracts also hold the advantages of a quicker rotation of capital including some payment before completion as well as an almost certain sale.

None the less, although there is some evidence that firms specializing in this sector have responded to these conditions, by concentrating more on increasing construction profits through labour process restructuring and technical development, the features of speculative production described earlier have remained dominant. This is partly because most firms switch between public and private sectors, and indeed other construction work. Public sector housing work has been more of a handy supplement especially useful in economic downturns. (Hence the loud complaints from the construction industry with the collapse of public sector house building since 1979.) The easy route to high profits has remained in speculative production, which also accounts for the bulk of dwelling construction. This has been exacerbated by the 'sub-contracting game' so developed in the British building industry (see section 3.5 for contrasts with Sweden), essentially a means of concentrating land development and extra profits into certain hands. The actual units of production taking up sub-contracting work (medium and small firms, labour gangs) have little opportunity or incentive to specialize in public sector work. The dominance of speculative methods of making profits is well demonstrated by the spectacular price hikes in local authority tenders in 1972–3 (see figure 3.3, Merrett 1979, chapter four). Much of this rise was a simple matter of builders demanding higher profits in accordance with the rates available in private sector and commercial building. In turn, these rates were fuelled by the 'Barber boom' of low interest lending by banks and building societies. Financial profits, rather than construction profits, were the clearest route to company success and this carried over into the public sector work.

The situation in Sweden is quite different (figure 3.6b). Speculative house building on the British model is mostly confined to the upper end of the owner-occupied market; it is very much a residual form of production accounting for only 13 per cent of dwellings built between 1946 and 1980. Consequently the features of speculative production are central only to a few relatively small firms which specialize in this sector. The remainder, the bulk of new housing production in all tenures (87 per cent between 1946 and 1980) is built to local authority contract.

We have split this non-speculative sector into two categories, 'non-speculative for the social housing sector' (52 per cent completion from 1946 to 1980) and 'non-speculative for the private sector' (35 per cent). The 'social housing sector' (public housing companies[6] and co-operatives[7]) share the aims of British council housing up to 1980[8] in providing rented housing at cost price.[9] Public housing companies, effectively controlled by local authorities (communes), and housing co-operatives, one part of the labour movement, act as developers and contract out construction work to building companies (although there is some direct labour work). In the same way as in Britain, building capital's access to land development profits and extra profits will be curtailed. However, to some extent this is a secondary point because *all* developers in receipt of State Housing Loans (*Statligt*

*Bostadslån*), whatever the tenure of the dwellings involved, must build according to contracts agreed with the communes and overseen by the County Boards (*länstyrelse*). This applies to private sector developers, including building firms developing on their own account, just as much as to co-operatives and public housing companies. State Housing Loans (hereafter SHLs) which cover between 22 and 30 per cent of the mortgageable value of development (the precise proportion depends on tenure) provide a significant subsidy to developers and hence also to builders. This subsidy is not just financial, in terms of lower interest rates than would otherwise be available on the open market. It is also a matter of availability, stability and the reduction of business uncertainty. Access to development land is also much easier with an SHL backed development. It is to the considerable advantage of developers in most cases (in fact for 87 per cent of completions between 1946 and 1980) to gain this state financial support. But this subsidy is not open-ended. Developers must enter into development contracts with communes which regulate the allocation of SHLs and the building they are used for.

This is what makes the bulk of Swedish housing since the war 'non-speculative'. It is not the case that all opportunities for speculative gain are magically abolished, but that the contract form as developed in Sweden regulates and restricts the builders' access to land development and extra profits. The contracts do not only specify when, where and how the housing is to be built, but also its final price including the land acquisition element. Most SHL development has in any case used publicly owned land provided at cost price, and since the 1974 'land condition' this has become mandatory.[10] Finally, dwellings are allocated by managerial, waiting list systems as well as the market. In the owner-occupied sector these are commune lists, sometimes jointly held with savings banks in communes controlled by the right. Public rented and most new private rented dwellings are allocated by the commune housing exchanges (*bostadsförmedlingen*), and co-operative allocation is based on their membership waiting lists. Clearly, in the owner-occupied sector purchasers must also have enough cash and status for a deposit and loan. None the less, the waiting list allocation, together with price regulation and controls over when, where and how the housing is to be constructed curtail builders' access to extra profit. Similarly, the land provisions of the SHL contract severely restrict access to land development profits. For the bulk of Swedish housing production the route to increased profitability is through construction profits. SHLs make house building a subsidized and favoured way to making a profit, but to benefit in this way management must devise means of building housing more cheaply and effectively.

A brief look at relative profit levels in the two countries supports this contrasting picture. In Britain, Ball's (1983, chapter four) indices suggest a pattern of short and insecure booms followed by longer slumps over the period 1970–82 for private sector house building. (See also the discussion of the 1972–3 public sector price hikes, page 84.) Profit booms, heavily dependent on speculative sources, were constantly threatened by increasing construction costs. In Sweden the picture between 1968 and 1980 is one of smaller but relatively sustained periods of potential profitability, with shorter, much shallower periods of potential loss. (We have used relative changes in standardized final building prices and total production costs as a guide.) This picture is supported by the available evidence on yield on total capital for house building firms as reported in SIND 1977: 5 and 1978: 5, and rates of return measured in this way are not that different from private manufacturing industry as a whole. We can imagine that builders, confronted by the SHL regulations including price control and threatened by competition from other builders (the emergence of the union-owned BPA in 1967 as the second largest house builder disturbed cartel tendencies) increased their profit margins through productivity gains. Eventually contract prices reflect these gains and the process must begin again. Contrast with Britain, where state intervention since 1979 seems mainly confined to increasing builders' access to land development profits (see Duncan and Goodwin 1985, Hooper 1984). But clearly more research on the levels and sources of profits is necessary.

SHLs do not only act as a building regulator in this negative sense, through supervision over the building process and profit sources. They have also been used for more positive planning.[11] This has occurred in three major ways. First of all a degree of intervention is established over housing distribution methods. The more 'social' tenures have been encouraged by proportionally larger SHLs. At the time of writing public housing companies were eligible for SHLs of 30 per cent mortgageable value, and the least 'social', private renting, of only 22 per cent (previously 15 per cent). Co-operative developers can receive a 29 per cent loan and owner-occupation developers 25 per cent. As all housing developments are eligible for a 70 per cent 'bottom loan' from state regulated housing credit institutions (these are funded by the financial institutions) this leaves public housing companies eligible for 100 per cent development finance from state and long-term regulated sources. Similarly housing co-operatives are eligible for 99 per cent, and private sector developers for 95 per cent and 92 per cent for owner-occupation and renting respectively. The remainder, plus a 'top loan' covering excess building costs over mortgageable value and also extra items like landscaping, must be found by the developer (figure 3.7 summarizes this housing finance system). This is one reason why 'non-profit' house building is weathering the 1980s house building slump better than the private sector (cf. figures 3.6, 4.1).

Second, SHLs have allowed a degree of national planning over the amount and distribution of house building as a whole. SHLs are allocated by the National Housing Board *and* National Labour Board to County Housing Boards according to a five-year rolling programme. The County Boards then allocate to Communes. This system cannot of course produce house building out of the blue. As the 1976 to the mid-1980s (and continuing) building slump has shown all too well, this depends on developers' calculations of profits and loss (or at least costs for co-op and public developers) in producing and selling dwellings as a commodity, not to mention the level of state finance for public housing. None the less, SHLs influence these calculations, and at least regulate the temporal and spatial distribution of what developers decide to produce. This gives a useful purchase on matching housing supply to needs as well as another means of intervening in local labour markets. Finally, and perhaps most interestingly from our point of view, SHLs have been used as a means of enforcing productivity increases in house building. Developers who could ensure productivity increases had a better

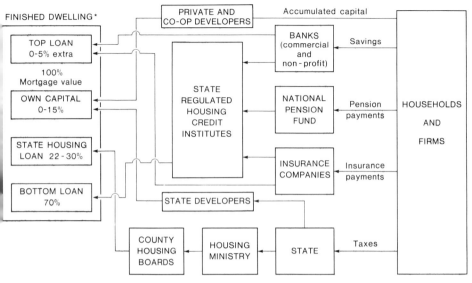

*Figure 3.7* Housing finance in Sweden

*Note:* * During construction itself housing finance is provided by 'building credit' from banks (as well as developers' own sources). This is then paid back with the final finance.

chance of receiving SHLs, and this became formally established in the 1967 Housing Act.

Before leaving this sub-section it is important to repeat that speculative sources of profit are not completely removed with the SHL/commune contract system of housing production. This particularly applies to the 'non-speculative for private sector' category, where builders will have a better chance of making extra profits, and to some extent land development profits, than in building for the social housing sector. This is particularly the case for redevelopment. The shifts towards this production category, as well as to the speculative sector in the mid-1970s (see figure 3.6b) caused some concern in Sweden because of this. In 1974 as little as 81 per cent of all completions were within the SHL system (and only 66 per cent of owner-occupied completions) with 41 per cent in the 'non-speculative for private sector' category. This shift is now partly reversed with only 5 per cent speculative production by 1983 and over 50 per cent in the non-profit sector although total output is much lower. None the less, it should be clear that this has not been a shift to speculative production on the British model. The ability of builders to appropriate surplus value through land development and extra profits is constrained and this means the accent must be on the improved exploitation of building labour in construction. As the next section (3.5) will show, this has meant, in comparison to Britain, a rapid restructuring of the labour process in building with considerable capital investment and technical inno-vation. Before that, however, we will survey the comparative evidence on one result of that process, productivity gains in house building.

*Low productivity versus high productivity*

Productivity indices essentially measure the relative efficiency in the use of labour, including here labour fixed or transformed into fixed capital and money capital. As such, they have emerged as important indicators in most versions of economics, if from different starting points. Productivity change in any activity means a change in the amount of labour (or labour as capital) necessary to produce the object or service in question. In the monetary economy, such changes will substantially affect the production costs of commodities. Indeed, over the long term productivity changes are crucial in this way.[12] Note also that this is as much a matter of relative productivity change between activities — where commodities become more or less expressive in relation to others, as absolute changes. This importance is exacerbated in the case of dwelling production, where the cost of housing has such important economic, social and political effects (section 1.3; Ball, 1978).

Clearly then, in attempting to understand why both housing production cost trends and consumption cost trends are more favourable in Sweden than in Britain, we must pay some attention to relative productivity trends in house building in the two countries. However, there are two major problems with using

*Table 3.1*   Productivity increase by sector in Britain and Sweden, 1960–81

| a  UK | % change per annum in output per person employed* | | |
|---|---|---|---|
| | *1960–73* | *1973–5* | *1975–81* |
| 1  Construction | 1.6** | −5.9 | −1.4 |
| 2  Manufacturing | 3.6 | −1.8 | 0.5 |
| 3  Total economy | 2.6 | −1.7 | 0.9 |
| | — | — | — |
| 4  Difference between 1 and 3 | −1.0 | −4.2 | −2.3 |

| b  SWEDEN | % change per annum in value added per work hour | | | |
|---|---|---|---|---|
| | *1960–5* | *1965–70* | *1970–5* | *1974–81* |
| 1  Construction | 4.5 | 3.5 | 4.9 | 3.5 |
| 2  Manufacturing† | 7.1 | 7.3 | 5.9 | 1.8 |
| 3  Total economy | 5.1 | 4.5 | 4.1 | 1.8 |
| | — | — | — | — |
| 4  Difference between 1 and 3 | −0.6 | −1.0 | +0.8 | +1.7 |

*Notes:*
  * Variations in hours worked are estimated to have negligible effect.
  ** Other sources give higher rates, of around 2–3 per cent for this period.
  † Includes mining.

*Sources:* Compiled from NIER London, NIER Stockholm, SOU 1977: 17.

productivity measures. First of all, it is very difficult to measure in any standard way over time or over different activities. Second, not unrelated, it is difficult to control exactly what is being measured. So, for instance, monetary measures will be severely affected by inflationary changes, but controlling for inflation or measuring by output volume or production time will cover up quality changes. Similarly, the costs of inputs and how they are used are difficult to separate. For example, measures of productivity in one sector (e.g. the building industry) will often record productivity change in input sectors (e.g. the building materials industry). These problems are exaggerated for house building and construction. The product is heterogeneous, there are problems of measuring output and, especially in Britain, employment. All these difficulties are compounded for international comparison, although – as with most other statistical information – there is a greater level of detail on Sweden. However, the damage caused by these problems can be minimized. Relative changes, where measurement and definition errors are constant within the statistics are easier to measure than absolute changes; even for those measures which are less reliable over time (such as monetary indices) it is still possible to make intersectoral comparisons at one time. Productivity comparisons can give us considerable information if we use them as indices of relative trends and magnitudes, and the conclusions they suggest in this case concur with the evidence on labour process changes, capitalization, etc. as well as fitting in with movements in production costs.

Information on productivity in house building is particularly sketchy in Britain; for this reason we start with relative productivity changes in construction as a whole (table 3.1). As can be seen from this table, national and sectoral differences in productivity trends are marked. In construction the British rates are considerably worse than for manufacturing industry or even the economy as a whole (which includes many service and administrative functions where mechanization has been more difficult to achieve). Productivity in construction actually decreased between 1973 and 1981.[13] This fits in with other productivity evidence. NIER figures on absolute productivity change show a decrease of 0.6 per cent for construction between 1970 and 1982, compared with increases of 21 per cent in the whole economy and 29 per cent in manufacturing. According to the survey of various estimates in Ball (1978), this picture of relatively low productivity increase in construction has been the same since 1900. We would expect built commodities, on average, to become more expensive in real terms. The Swedish figures are quite different. Not only have rates of change in productivity been healthier than in the economy as a whole, but construction rates are nearer average rates and indeed by 1970–5 had overtaken them. Built commodities would become less expensive in real terms.

Construction as a whole is not, of course, house building. We have few British productivity figures on the latter although Swedish statistics allow us to go much further (tables 3.2, 3.3, 3.4). However, we would expect *lower* productivity and rates of change in house building. Dwelling construction is one of the more complicated building tasks because of the multiple use to be made of the building, emphasized by the density of social rules and expectations over its form, in contrast to building a road or a factory, for instance. This is indeed what we find

*Table 3.2*  Productivity change in house building and other construction sectors: Sweden, 1967–79

| | % change per annum in value added per hour of work | | |
|---|---|---|---|
| | *1967–71* | *1971–5* | *1975–9* |
| All new housing | 8.3 | 5.4 | −0.8 |
| of which: small houses | 8.5 | 5.4 | 1.5 |
| multi-dwelling | 8.0 | 5.4 | −3.4 |
| Other buildings | 7.8 | 6.2 | 3.0 |
| Industrial work | 6.5 | 6.7 | 0.4 |
| Civil engineering | 4.3 | 4.3 | 3.5 |
| Total all new construction | 6.9 | 5.4 | 2.7 |
| Improvement, repairs, maintenance | 3.5 | 3.0 | 5.6 |
| Total all construction: | | | |
| including white collar | 5.6 | 3.8 | 3.0 |
| excluding white collar | 4.9 | 3.1 | 3.1 |

*Sources:* Compiled from SIND 1978: 5; SOU 1982: 34.

looking at Swedish figures (table 3.2). The table also shows up the variability of productivity estimates; because of changes in definitions and measurement categories, the figures do not correspond with table 3.1.

According to table 3.2, the increase in construction productivity has slowed during the 1967–79 period. This was accentuated during 1975–9, the crisis period for the industry with the end of the 'million programme', a slowdown in state expenditure and the world recession. Other evidence suggests recovery since then. The slowdown was particularly marked for house building, which has changed from the category with most rapid increase to that with the least. However, only multi-dwelling construction has shown any productivity decrease. As discussed earlier, multi-dwelling house building suffered particularly from external shocks in the crisis of the late 1970s and most of the ensuing productivity slowdown resulted from lost economies of scale and suddenly enforced quality increases rather than a slowdown in labour productivity *per se*. This conclusion is also supported by the government inquiry on house building costs, SOU 1982: 34. Using calculations of output per unit time, they demonstrate how labour productivity itself increased although this was swamped by the effects of lost economies of scale. In 1974 7.5 flats per month were produced in the multi-dwelling sector, but by 1978 this had been reduced to 4.2 flats per month, a decrease of 3.3 (44 per cent). However, the inquiry calculates that lower economies of scale should have produced a decrease of 3.4 flats per month (−2.3 because of lower standardization, −1.1 because of lower project size). The sector had done better than expected in view of these 'external' factors.

Increased safety standards for building workers during the 1970s will also have reduced productivity increases over construction as a whole, as will the shift to improvement, repairs and construction (37 per cent in 1980 but only 21 per cent in 1970). This type of work is more difficult to industrialize because of the difficulty of standardizing work, of achieving economies of scale, and of replacing site work by factory work. Note, however, the large increase in productivity in this category over 1975–9. This is most important for our argument. It supports the view that it is industrial structure, not production form, which is crucial to relative productivity and it suggests that the structure of the Swedish construction industry has not been fundamentally altered by a shift in output type. This is backed up by evidence on labour process change discussed in section 3.5.

Table 3.3 on building construction uses a volume measure of productivity change. This is perhaps most useful for temporal comparisons, although quality changes will not be adequately reflected and the index over-estimates productivity slowdown for this reason. The same broad pattern emerges, but note in this case the variation between 'conventional' and 'ready to erect' housing. (The latter implies completely prefabricated; the former includes considerable prefabrication and on-site industrialization, but 'conventional' in the sense of building as well as assembly occurring on site.) These detailed productivity changes reflect a number

*Table 3.3* Productivity in building construction, volume terms: Sweden, 1967–80

| | *% change per annum m³ production per work hour* | | | | |
|---|---|---|---|---|---|
| | *1967–71* | *1971–6* | *1975–8* | *1977–80* | *Whole period* |
| *Small houses* | | | | | |
| Conventional | 7.8 | 5.6 | 0.5 | −4.0 | 3.5 |
| Ready to erect | 12.3 | 2.8 | −2.7 | 6.8 | 4.9 |
| All | 10.1 | 4.0 | −1.3 | −0.7 | 3.8 |
| *Multi-Dwelling* | | | | | |
| Conventional | 8.1 | 3.8 | −7.9 | 1.3 | 1.9 |
| Ready to erect | 7.8 | 1.2 | −8.1 | −1.6 | 0.5 |
| All | 8.9 | 2.9 | −7.0 | −0.6 | 1.7 |
| | *1967–71* | *1971–8* | | | |
| Administrative building | 8.8 | 6.3 | n.a. | | |
| Industrial building | 7.9 | 9.6 | n.a. | | |
| All building | 7.8 | 6.8 | n.a. | | |

*Sources:* Compiled from SIND 1977: 5, SOU 1982: 34.

of factors, but the competitive conflict between on-site industrialization by building firms, and off-site industrialization by building material firms, seems crucial (SOU 1977: 43). For instance high productivity increases in ready to erect small housing in the late 1960s partly reflect the development of prefabricated concrete frames; by the mid-1970s builders had responded with on-site industrialization in concrete as well as expanding timber-frame building methods. By the late 1970s conventional building was suffering from decreased economies of scale while ready to erect had responded with wood-material based prefabrication. Note, however, in terms of absolute productivity 'ready to erect' has normally been higher than 'conventional' for both small house and multi-dwelling construction (for small housing $0.65/0.89m^3$ per hour in 1980, and $0.61/0.77m^3$ for multi-dwelling. In 1967 these figures were $0.35/0.33m^3$ per hour and $0.46/0.72$ respectively).

Overlying these detailed differences is the effect of the 1975–8 'housing crisis'. As discussed before, this was largely the result of external factors (economic recession, slowdown in state spending, the end of the 'million programme') which affected multi-dwelling construction especially severely. Indeed, SOU 1982: 34 calculate that almost half of the productivity decline in this sector from 1974 to 1978 was due to decreased project sizes alone. This interpretation is supported by the productivity improvement over the latest period (1977–80). As expected, productivity increase in non-residential building has held up well.

Finally, figure 3.8 shows how absolute productivity levels in house building, measured in volume terms, have changed since the 1950s. Again, the effects of the 'million programme' and the externally produced crisis in 1975–8 are clear, but this graph also allows us to put these events into perspective. Small house building, not directly involved in the 'million programme', shared equally in

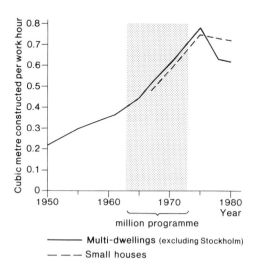

*Figure 3.8* Labour productivity for new construction, Sweden, 1950–80

*Sources:* Adapted from SIND: 1977: 5; SOU 1982: 34.

productivity increases over the 1967–74 period. This increase was common to house building as a whole, more a structural feature than a direct response to political events. Similarly, the 1974–8 crisis, although significant, is relatively minor in the context of a long-term trend towards higher productivity in house building. The most recent 1980 figures are still 200 per cent over 1950 levels even for multi-dwelling housing. It will be developments over the next decade however, that will settle the long-term significance of the 1974–8 'break'.

What can we conclude from this discussion of productivity change in house building? First of all, as far as we can tell given the paucity of British data, productivity change in Swedish house building is much nearer the economic average than in Britain. Similarly, Swedish house building shows substantial productivity increase over the long term compared to the British situation.

This returns us to our earlier discussions of sources of surplus value appropriation and industrial strategy and structure in consequence. We would expect substantial productivity increases in a house building system relying largely on construction profits, such as Sweden. The behaviour of productivity in the improvement/repairs sector, and the competitive struggle between builders and building material firms through production costs, are instructive in this respect. Equally, we would not expect similar increases in a house building system where land development profit and extra profit were major sources of surplus value appropriation and this is indeed the case in Britain. Two recent building fashions in each country illustrate this well. In Britain, timber frame construction has become widespread since the late 1970s. Potentially, this reduces building times and increases productivity levels by transferring site building to the factory, and this has been true in Sweden since the 1950s and before. However, in Britain timber frame building can actually *increase* building time. Builders amass frames on site with half-built houses waiting for the best time to make speculative land and extra profits (Cullen 1982). A similar example – but working the other way – is the recent popularity of an 'English style' in Swedish house building. This means the use of red-brick with tiling giving a fussier and more individual definition of particular dwellings. But this is created by fixing semi-fabricated cladding to pre-fabricated frames.

Second, the detailed movements of productivity within and between building types and forms, as well as the British–Swedish comparison, support the view that relative building efficiency is a social question more than a purely technical one. It is a question of sources of profit, external economic and political events, inter-firm competition and so on; relative productivity levels are not given for all time (or even for all capitalism) because of the inherent features of building dwellings.

This discussion takes us back to the 'abstraction procedure checking' role of comparative analysis. At the time of writing current understanding of house building in capitalist economies is based on recent and detailed work on the British case (DLC 1978, Merrett 1979, Merrett with Gray 1982, Ball 1983 among others). This work has advanced our knowledge considerably, and it should be clear that this chapter could only have been written with reference to the framework it provides. None the less, the comparison of Britain and Sweden in this section qualifies this framework in two important ways. First of all, the production of housing as a commodity does not necessarily mean speculative production. This can have important effects on how production occurs and hence its costs, quality and socio-economic effects. In this respect Ball (1983, 160) is quite wrong when he asserts that 'Recourse to cross country comparisons would at best bring out differences of degree as a similar structure of housing provision exists in other advanced capitalist countries'. At the very least, it is a question of how large the difference of degree is and this can have significant effects.

Second, it is not the case that house building is doomed to low productivity levels because of its inherent technical peculiarities. Merrett (1979, 86–7) claims that this will be so because of the bulk and weight of dwellings, the need for site development as well as construction, the need for complex assembly on site, and consequent low degrees of mechanization, industrialization and capitalization. How then, are we to explain the large apparent differences in productivity rates between Britain and Sweden? Indeed, in Sweden there has been a trend towards much lighter dwellings and building materials, towards simpler on-site assembly, off-site and on-site prefabrication, and significant degrees of mechanization and capitalization. Hence the favourable productivity developments in Swedish house building. It is even possible to order complete dwellings, in the style of one's choice (mid-century Swedish peasant style, Spanish ranch-house style, and so on) in mail order catalogues, which arrive by lorry ready-built. This is of course one extreme. But although it may be the case that house building will always present some obstacles to productivity increase (e.g. the need to tailor site to dwelling) there seems no inherent reason why this increase should be as weakly developed as in Britain, or why these obstacles cannot be compensated for by changes elsewhere. However, we certainly agree with Ball (1983, 161) when he states, in the same passage as that quoted above, that empirical emphasis has to be placed on how and why technical development does or does not take place in house building. We turn to this question in the next section.

### 3.5  Restructuring or retrenching in the building industry

*Restructuring and surplus value*

In 1978 the Direct Labour Collective (DLC), the pioneering modern study of the British construction industry, concluded that

> Construction is the only industry in which a revival of demand is seen as the sole solution. In other industries, reductions in the costs of production, through increases in investment and 'restructuring', are viewed as a prerequisite for survival and revival.                                    (DLC 1978, 31)

We have already pointed to some of the reasons, as well as the effects, of this 'abnormality' of the British construction industry with reference to house building. This theme is followed up in detail by Merrett (1979), Merrett with Gray (1982), Ball (1983) as well as the DLC (1978, 1980). The British construction industry, or at least parts of it, can survive and indeed make above average profits because of the possibility of making significant profits in 'abnormal' ways. Access to land development profit and extra profit allows builders to sidestep the hard and narrow road of labour process restructuring, technical innovation and product development. Management becomes focused on speculative skills, and this in itself compounds problems of demand, production costs and stability. Speculative building is actually a good way of reacting quickly to changes in demand, where low capitalization and mechanization levels allow rapid 'switching' from one market or building sector to another. Similarly, builders play the 'sub-contracting game' the aim of which is to do as little building work as possible (after all, construction costs are out of control), contract out to small firms or work gangs, and arrange favourable financial contracts for themselves with both purchasers and sub-contractors. (So some of the largest British house builders carry out very little direct building work.) This is essentially a way of concentrating profits by a form of cheating. Again, management must apply itself to the game, the production process itself almost becomes secondary. But, however successful these strategies may be at making profits – for some – the concomitant is low levels of mechanization, standardization and organization. Productivity increase will remain relatively stagnant and production costs will relatively increase. This 'abnormality' does not only depend on builders' access to land development and extra profit, however. It also depends on weak labour in production itself. Low levels of pay and job security give employers the considerable room for manoeuvre the speculative game demands.

This is because surplus value appropriation is not just a matter of the balance between various possible routes, such as land development profits, extra profit and construction value itself. It is also a question of the degree and nature of exploitation possible in any one route. Furthermore, however significant land and extra profits are in day-to-day management, these ultimately depend on success in exploiting building labour and all are subject to social conflict. We have already discussed how builders' land development profits are relatively curtailed in Sweden, and this reflects the comparative weakness there of landed interests combined with labour's high degree of access to state power (cf. section 2.2). But the same principle applies to direct capital–labour relations. Normally in advanced capitalist countries labour has had some success in resisting exploitation, partly through high levels of union organization together with its political access to state power enabled by franchise democracy. This has had fundamental effects on how surplus value is appropriated in production. Relative surplus value has been increasingly substituted for absolute surplus value in this situation. That is, instead of making workers work longer or harder for the same pay, or the same time for less pay, capitalists reorganize the labour process so that each worker produces more value per unit labour power. There is an increased co-operation of labour, an increased division of tasks, greater standardization and mechanization. The value of commodities bought by workers may also fall, so that a smaller relative share of value needs to be diverted to their wages (a process which has not happened with British housing!). Real wages can increase but exploitation levels, in the sense of surplus value appropriation, can increase even more (cf. figure 2.1 for Sweden 1870–1970).

The development of relative surplus value will also be associated with changes in the nature of the labour force and the capital employing it. More managers, and soon technicians, researchers, planners and other white-collar workers are needed to co-ordinate, maintain and develop new labour processes; old skills become less important, new skills emerge, and so workers are deskilled and reskilled. Workers will lose the capacity for day-to-day control over the labour process as their monopoly over skilled tasks is removed, but other workers may gain new skill monopolies or substitute trade union organization. Above all the work-force becomes differentiated into technical, skilled and unskilled workers, into central labour and peripheral labour. These divisions interact with pre-existing social divisions (class, gender, race, age) and become crucial elements in the conflict over levels and degree of labour exploitation (cf. Cockburn 1983). Inter-capital relations also change. To carry out effectively the relative surplus labour strategy firms need high levels of investment, research and development, and organizational capacity. Unsuccessful firms go to the wall, or are taken over as their competitors struggle for markets and new products, barriers to the entry of new firms rise considerably. Capital – the control of labour – becomes concentrated in fewer and larger units which often dominate product markets.

None the less, the trend towards relative surplus value is by no means invariant or even irreversible. It will be strongly influenced by the comparative strengths of labour and capital, in firms, sectors, in localities and in nation states. Relations to state power and other classes or interests will be important. Research has already shown that the British construction industry is a shade 'abnormal' compared to the general trend. Labour is weak in comparison to other sectors and relative surplus exploitation is more weakly developed (Merrett 1979, Ball 1983). This provides the theme for this section. Labour in Sweden is probably the most effectively organized in the capitalist world (see section 2.2) and, if anything, building labour is among the better organized within Sweden. The Swedish construction industry also shows more 'normal' advanced capitalist behaviour; relative surplus value is more developed than in Britain. We will first describe varying degrees of 'industrialization' in Sweden and Britain, looking at capitalization, organization and centralization. We will begin to answer why this national variation is so marked with reference to 'internal' labour–capital relations. This section therefore provides a transition from the 'undercutting the taken for granted' role to the 'variability reduction' role of comparison. The next and last section (3.6) will continue this theme with respect to social relations 'external' to house building.

*Capitalization and industrialization*

Sugden (1975, 4) has claimed that the average building site in Britain employed machinery 'only in the same order of value as a family motor car'. This may be somewhat exaggerated as a *statistical* average, although in 1982 the construction sector was much less capitalized in Britain than manufacturing as a whole (see table 3.4; note particularly the large differential for 'plant and machinery'). But certainly the *normal* British house building site is remarkable for the relative lack of machinery, particularly in contrast to Sweden where – among other machines

*Table 3.4* Relative capitalization in the British construction sector

| | Fixed investment by sector and asset 1982 (£ per employee) | | | |
| --- | --- | --- | --- | --- |
| | *Buildings* | *Plant and Machinery* | *Vehicles* | *Total* |
| 1 Construction | 21 | 234 | 134 | 389 |
| 2 Manufacturing | 124 | 671 | 85 | 881 |
| 3 1 as percentage of 2 | 16.9 | 34.9 | 157.6 | 44.2 |

*Sources:* Compiled and calculated from NIER (London) 1982; *Employment Gazette* (various issues).

– many sites have one or more tower-cranes employed in lifting off- or on-site pre-fabricated elements. By the late-1970s these cranes cost between £25,000 and £100,000 each. Unfortunately, we do not have access to directly comparable statistics for Sweden. However, available figures from the national accounts and business statistics (SOS:NR,F) suggest that although construction is less capitalized than Swedish manufacturing both are more capitalized than their British counterparts. More detailed figures are available, however, for the replacement of labour by capital during the 1970s, and these are shown as part of table 3.5.

One interesting feature shown by table 3.5 is that the replacement of labour by capital was clearly as much a part of the 'crisis' years (included in the 1970–7 period) as it seems to have been in the years of output expansion. The same goes for productivity in terms of the ratio between output and employment. Mechanization was as much a response to demand reduction as demand growth, and demand change has not meant structural change. (Increasing export is another response, building overseas increased from only 1 per cent of production value in building in 1973 to about 10 per cent in 1978.) The employment figures in table 3.5 will also reflect production transferred from building sites to the building

*Table 3.5* Replacing labour with capital in the Swedish building industry, 1965–77

| | % change per annum | | |
| --- | --- | --- | --- |
| | *1960–5* | *1965–70* | *1970–7* |
| 1 Hours worked | 3.0 | 0.5 | −1.8 |
| 2 Building volume | 6.0 | 3.6 | −0.6 |
| 3 Machine capital* | n.a. | n.a. | 2.4 |

*Note:* * Replacement value of building machinery in stock.

*Sources:* Compiled from SIND 1977: 5, SIND 1978: 5, NR.

materials industry. SIND 1977: 5 estimates that half of the labour time 'rationalized out' in construction is accounted for in this way, and the other half is replaced
by machinery or infrastructure. However, not only is work input reduced or
transferred, but mechanization will also increase tempo, improve work continuity, and very often allow better management control. Three procedures are at
work: 1) the building materials industry takes over and transforms some work
processes (e.g. building frames are produced in the factory); 2) product development eliminates or changes work processes (e.g. the increasing use of light wood
based wall materials; 3) work processes remain on site but are transformed by
mechanization (e.g. concrete pumps and cranes allow on-site prefabrication).
Points 1 and 2 are clearly closely linked to developments in the building materials
industry, indeed, as SIND 1977: 5 puts it 'this implies integration into the
production chain of the materials industry' (p. 283). As we shall see, this integration is not only functional but extends to organizational and ownership
linkages.

What does capitalization and mechanization mean on the ground? Swedish
construction has in fact been consistently to the fore in introducing and standardizing the use of new machines and technologies (Hoppe 1976, SIND 1977: 5,
1978: 5). A good example are mechanical methods of concrete production
(mixers, vibrators, mechanical quality control) which had become widespread by
the late 1930s and were joined by concrete pumps in the 1950s. Before this, three
or more men, even with a cement mixer, were engaged in the physically exhaust-
ing job of shifting over 30 tons of cement materials per day. Using these machines
one man can produce more cement and the pump allows centralization of the
process rather than constantly shifting it between work stations. Mobile cranes to
shift prefabricated components (timber frames, roof frames, concrete frames,
sanitary units, staircases, balconies, floors, window units, etc.) were widespread
by the 1950s. As prefabrication increased, these were joined by tower-cranes and
by hydraulic lift trucks (both Swedish developments) in the 1960s. In 1950 only
20 tower-cranes were used in building, by 1970 this had increased to 4500 while
the capacity and flexibility of both lifts and cranes had improved considerably.
Similar developments took place in other labour processes. The introduction of
water-cooled drilling and hardened metal drills in the 1940s, and the pioneering
development of internal explosions, have speeded up site clearance. Swedish
firms also pioneered innovations in earth moving, excavating and load-bearing
vehicles in the 1930s (e.g. hydraulics replacing cables) and here too capacity has
since increased dramatically. Finally, site floodlights became common in the
1950s, extending both the working day and the working year.

These technical developments are most applicable to new building. It is most
important, therefore, that the same trends are apparent in the increasingly
important repair and improvement sector (cf. the productivity measures in table
3.2). Prefabrication is this sector follows the 'Lego principle'. For instance,
instead of destroying old walls and floors to insert new pipes for improved heating
systems, etc., prefabricated elements with pipes already installed are mounted
over the existing construction. At worst part of the old wall or floor can be
removed and a prefabricated element plugged in. New machinery and materials

appropriate to repair and improvement work have also been developed, for example mobile hydraulic work platforms, improved filler, and so on.

Three points are important in comparison to the British situation. First of all, the Swedish state was actively involved in this mechanization process. A 'State Machine Loan Fund' was introduced in 1952; aimed especially at the acquisition of more expensive equipment such as tower-cranes. In the mid-1960s this fund was extended to finance capital equipment on the part of prefabricating firms. More indirectly, State Housing Loans (SHLs) were used to stimulate pro-ductivity increase and standardization, and constantly increasing state building norms enforced standardization. Only the latter has a corresponding British development (e.g. Parker Morris building standards). Even in this case, however, the effect has been different. Such standards in Britain have not been applied comprehensively, they have oscillated up and down in tune with political changes, and they have been more relevant to final output than production elements.

Second, although this technology – either pioneered or standardized in Sweden – became rapidly available worldwide, British firms did not take them up as fully. Of course, there has been some technical development in the British construction industry, but as table 3.1 suggests this lags behind the Swedish experience (see also Ive 1980, Sugden 1980). Even if technical innovations have been introduced in Britain, they have sometimes been used ineffectively from the viewpoint of labour productivity. We have already mentioned the example of timber-framed housing. Similarly, the high rise 'systems building' of the 1960s was not only more expensive to build than conventional construction (central government subsidized local authorities to use this costlier building method) but it was built to low and sometimes technically incompetent standards (Ive 1980, Dunleavy 1981). This was not just because builders infiltrated local and national state agencies. (Compare with Sweden where state institutions policed builders with building norms, local authority development contracts and SHLs.) High degrees of prefabrication, standardization and labour division also need high degrees of planning, work control and capitalization. The British building industry, under-capitalized and playing the land speculation and contracting games, was structur-ally incapable of carrying this out.

Finally, and equally important, building industrialization in Britain has very often been a matter of off-site prefabrication. Industrialization has taken place in the building materials sector or hardly at all. This has not been the case in Sweden. Although off-site prefabrication is well developed (again, Sweden took a pioneering role in the 1930s and 1950s), on-site industrialization including pre-fabrication and process integration between sites and suppliers has been just as important. So, while complete off-site prefabrication reached a peak by the early-1970s, (with 30 per cent of multi-dwelling completions and 50 per cent of small house completions) decline since then has not meant a return to traditional pre-fabrication building. The labour time saved by prefabrication (SIND 1977: 5 estimates a reduction of between 30 per cent and 70 per cent on-site labour time for complete prefabrication) has been replaced and even increased by site restruc-turing. This has used a combination of off-site prefabricated components – often

arriving ready shaped, drilled and screwed for assembly – and on-site prefabrication in 'site factories'. Site factories concentrate and rationalize operations like
concreting and carpentry, and finished elements can then be allocated to dwelling
sites by crane. This amounted to a 'site-based system building using ready to erect
material packets' according to SIND 1977: 5 (p. 270).

It is quite indicative, therefore, that whereas in Britain off-site prefabrication
has been most developed for multi-dwelling construction, in Sweden it is most
common in small house building (detached, semi-detached, etc.). Prefabrication
has in Britain followed political dictates; high-rise and systems building was seen
as a technical fix to political problems of housing the inner-city poor. Land-use
planning was incapable of overcoming outer-city resistance to providing building
land, nor could central government force recalcitrant local governments into line
(Young and Kramer 1978, Dunleavy 1981). Sheffield is a good example of this
stranglehold (see chapter five). In any case, even if inner-city local governments
and the planning system had been able to surmount this political obstacle, they
could not have escaped paying for development gains. Still less could they conjure
up cheap but good quality housing. Systems built high rise was seen as a way out
and furthermore it was only to be applied to the more powerless section of the
working class. In Sweden complete off-site prefabrication has been most used
where it is technically more appropriate, in small house building. Ironically
enough, it is at the very top end of the housing market that off-site prefabrication
is used most, for building one-off detached residences. An 'on-site factory' to
build one house is clearly inappropriate, and by 1980 70 per cent of this market
was of the 'mail order' type with complete prefabrication. Quality is usually very
high and this is one illustration that prefabrication does not necessarily mean low
standards. Again, these are socially and politically determined, not technically
given.

*Organization and concentration*

Much of this chapter has been concerned to show that increasing housing construction costs in Britain are due to the importance, for building firms, of land
development profit and extra profit. Management becomes focused on speculative skills and, with little incentive to restructure the building process itself, the
result is relatively low rates of industrialization and productivity growth. In this
section we pursue another aspect of this argument. 'Industrialization' depends on
a high level of planning and work control. It is vital to integrate, for any one
construction project, the divided and standardized tasks and outputs that now
make up the production line. The ready screwed and shaped floor units arriving
from one factory should fit precisely the prefabricated frame from another; when
these inputs arrive they should dovetail with work progress on site, and so on.
Similarly, industrialization depends on a high level of capital investment, not
only to finance mechanization itself but also the research, development and planning necessary for labour process and product innovation. It is large firms which
can undertake this most easily. Again, contrasts between Britain and Sweden
seem marked in these respects. We will concentrate here on two aspects of organizational capacity, first the relation between inter-firm organization and sub-
contracting systems, and second the nature of capital concentration in firms.

The sub-contracting system, like speculative house building, has been seen very much as the villain of the piece as far as British house building is concerned. A key way for firms to amass profit is by arranging suitable contracts with both purchasers and other firms, while avoiding the dirty process of production itself. Although only about 25 per cent (by value) of construction work as a whole is carried out by sub-contractors, this proportion is undoubtedly much higher for house building, especially in the private sector. Ball (1983) even found that some of Britain's largest private sector 'house builders' in fact build very little housing at all. Rather, they assemble land, sell the finished product and arrange for others to do the building. The focus is squarely on speculative land development profit, extra profit, and contract 'cheating'. Sub-contractors, however, often follow the same path and sometimes a chain of sub-contracting develops. Furthermore, it is not only production that is sub-contracted in this way, labour inputs are subject to the same fragmenting system. Ball (1983) estimates that about one half of the labour inputs in private-sector house building is organized in this way, and that this is increasing. The final production unit may well be a number of small and medium firms heavily dependent on labour only sub-contractors.

Yet again, this sets up a vicious circle with low productivity as one result. A high level of organization, project control and planning is difficult to achieve when both management and labour is so fragmented in this way. Management and process innovation are also less likely, for at the end of each project or even part project the production team is broken up and the store of socially developed learning is dissipated. Nor is it in the immediate interests of either the employers or providers of sub-contracted labour to 'waste' time learning something new. However, the sub-contracting system does have considerable advantages for both firms and workers in coping with turbulent demand changes. Both can switch sites and sectors with a minimum of friction. This of course, by consolidating speculative practice and militating against industrialization and productivity growth, does nothing to control construction costs and so contributes to demand problems.

The situation in Sweden is quite different (see Merrett 1979; Bartlett School 1980; Ball 1983 for further details on Britain). Project sub-contracting is not so pervasive; when it is used it is much more a matter of work specialization than financial manoeuvre, and labour only sub-contracting is virtually unknown. We will look at these in turn.

First of all, the contract form between developer and contractor in Sweden is not always conducive to sub-contracting, and contract forms on the British private sector model are in fact quite rare. There are four major contract forms. In 'total contracting' (*totalentreprenad*) the developer contracts out the project to a single (total) contractor who is to carry out the great bulk of the work. Sub-contracting should be limited to particular specialized tasks only. 'Split contracting' (*deladentreprenad*) has little room for any sub-contracting as such. The developer organizes contracts with a 'major' contractor to carry out the bulk of the work and also any 'side contractors' necessary for specialized tasks. These two development contract forms, inimical to the sub-contracting system as developed in Britain, accounted for over 60 per cent of multi-dwelling contracts and at least half small house contracts by the late 1970s. Furthermore, these contract forms were most common for the larger projects (SIND 1977: 5). 'General contracting' (*generalentreprenad*) was responsible for the remaining multi-dwelling contracts and almost all the remaining small house production. This is more like the British system, where the developer arranges a contract for the whole project with one firm which then in turn sub-contracts particular tasks. However, even here the 'general contractor' carries out much of the building work. The SIND 1977: 5 report quotes a 1974 survey showing that 57 per cent of project work on average, by value, was carried out by the general contractor for multi-dwelling housing using six contractors. For small houses this was 54 per cent of project value with eight contractors. Non-residential building had similar figures, although more sub-contractors were used, while civil engineering projects had very low rates of sub-contracting value (usually below 20 per cent with only two or three sub-contractors). Finally, the developed British system, where the major contractor in fact arranged for a number of sub-contractors to carry out the actual building work, is in Sweden a relative rarity confined to private sector small house construction. This is referred to as 'sub-contracted general contracting' (*delupphandlad generalentrepenad*). However, SIND 1977: 5 claims that the general contractor always carried out some work with its own resources. At the other extreme, only 4.3 per cent of building firms and 8 per cent of building craft firms were classified as sub-contractors only in 1976 (SOS BO).

In other words, the developer-builder contract form is not often conducive to the 'sub-contracting system' in Sweden, indeed over half the time split contracting or total contracting will militate against it. Again, these contract forms have been directly encouraged by both national state and union action. The allocation of SHLs, in the search for rationalized production, was more readily available for contract forms of this type.

The building unions have also favoured contracts of these sorts and, furthermore, have established a degree of control over the degree of sub-contracting in any contract form. Building labour in Sweden is almost totally unionized (the majority in the Building Union with the remainder in craft or white-collar unions). They are able to demand agreements from employers on the exact use and amount of sub-contracting work before allowing workers to be employed. This is strengthened by the 'joint decision law' (*medbestämmandelagen*) whereby unions have representatives on firm boards and SIND 1977: 5 even claims that unions in fact exercise a 'veto-right' over sub-contracting. As in Britain, unions are circumspect about sub-contracting where such forms may not be covered by collective agreements on pay and conditions and may compete unfairly against those who do. But in Sweden they can do a lot more about it. Finally, the union-owned building firm BPA, the second largest house builder, does not sub-contract at all but uses its own specialist sections which often have their origins in workers' co-operatives.

This is not to say that sub-contracting is unimportant. Rather, it is undertaken for good 'technical division of labour' reasons rather than for speculative and financial manoeuvre, and it is quite heavily policed. It is most commonly used for traditional craft work (e.g. painting, electrical) or newer specialized work (e.g. diamond boring in concrete construction) where major contractors are limited in

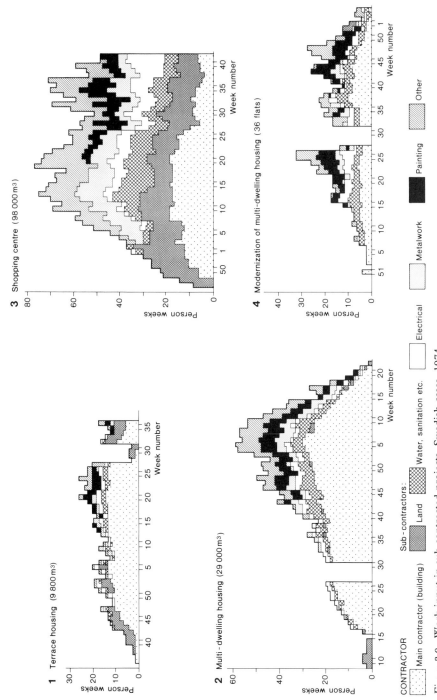

**1** Terrace housing (9 800 m³)

**2** Multi-dwelling housing (29 000 m³)

**3** Shopping centre (98 000 m³)

**4** Modernization of multi-dwelling housing (36 flats)

CONTRACTOR

Main contractor (building)

Sub-contractors:

Land  Water, sanitation etc.  Electrical

Metalwork  Painting  Other

*Figure 3.9* Work input in sub-contracted projects, Swedish cases, 1974

*Source:* Calculated from SIND 1977: 5.

competence, labour skills and equipment and therefore have no cost incentive to cover such work. But, where land profit and extra profit is severely curtailed, they do have a very good reason to get involved in as much construction as possible. Different degrees of sub-contracting will of course also be necessary for different types of building projects. Thus a 1974 survey (SIND 1977: 5) of construction projects using sub-contracting found that 38 per cent of work time in small house building was accounted for by sub-contractors, rising to 79 per cent for the building of a neighbourhood shopping centre. Figure 3.9 shows this variation quite well – and also the relative importance of major contractors in house building.

Finally, we have not been able to find any mention of labour only sub-contracting in the Swedish sources. British building unions generally oppose labour sub-contracting, especially when it takes the form of illegal contract forms ('the Lump', see Ball 1983). Labour sub-contracting will stimulate the use of casual labour, and so reduce union strength directly as well as encourage unfavourable working conditions and reduce job security. But again, in Sweden unions are able to do much more about such situations while state authorities are both more willing and able to intervene. If for no other reason, the sometimes oppressive power of the tax collection system in Sweden would make the Lump virtually impossible.

In conclusion then, sub-contracting in Sweden will usually act to increase production efficiency. It is a means of allowing specialization in certain construction tasks rather than as a means of speculative manoeuvre. Similar contrasts emerge when we move to the organization of production in terms of concentration and firm size. House building in Sweden has been dominated by a few large firms since the 1950s and even before. Although concentration of production has significantly increased in Britain over the 1975–80 period, this concentration is often different to the Swedish case. Concentration in Britain has more of a financial than a production rationale, and in production terms is constantly undermined by the sub-contracting system. We will first establish some of these contrasts.

Tables 3.6 and 3.7 present information on output concentration by size of firm and sector in the two countries. As always, greater detail is available for Sweden. In broad cross-national terms production is more concentrated in Sweden (note that most firms with over 500 employees in fact employ over 1000). This is the case with every category of work. The contrast is most established for housing production, however, especially for the private/small house sectors. In Sweden firms with over 100 employees built over 68 per cent of multi-dwelling housing in 1976, and 58 per cent of small houses.[14] In Britain equivalent 1978 figures were 57 per cent public sector and only 39 per cent private sector. Large firms in Sweden also had a significant stake in repairs, whereas this was dominated by small firms in Britain.

Of course these figures provide us with only one snapshot of a developing pattern. The British figures show some considerable concentration since 1970 when the top 1 per cent of firms accounted for only 24 per cent of construction output. This can be compared with only 0.2 per cent of firms accounting for over 50 per cent of construction output in Sweden at this date. One firm alone, Skånska

*Table 3.6* Concentration by project type and size of firm: UK, 1978

| Size of Firm (by number of employees) | % of value | | | | |
|---|---|---|---|---|---|
| | *0–24* | *25–114* | *115–599* | *600+* | *Total* |
| Private housing | 40 | 21 | 21 | 18 | 100 |
| Public housing | 17 | 26 | 30 | 27 | 100 |
| Other new work | 14 | 17 | 30 | 37 | 100 |
| Repair and maintenance | 50 | 24 | 15 | 11 | 100 |

*Source:* Adapted from Ball 1983: 46.

Cementgjuteriet, the largest construction firm in Europe and Sweden's eleventh biggest in terms of turnover, accounted for 15 per cent of construction output in 1970. Ball (1983) claims that concentration in Britain is still increasing. In Sweden this has also been the case, although the smallest firms had marginally improved their position by 1980 with the shift to repair work, while medium sized firms had suffered considerably in the crisis years. (They were most dependent on multi-dwelling work.) The long-term winners were the largest firms especially the fourteen dominant firms with over 1000 employees, and these bought out at least 200 medium sized firms during 1970–80. The Swedish data also provides information on regional concentration (SOU 1982: 34). At this level, as we might expect, large firms are often even more dominant especially outside the metropolitan regions. Available information also shows that the

*Table 3.7* Concentration by project type and size of firm: Sweden, 1976

| Firm size (by number of employees) | % of production value | | | |
|---|---|---|---|---|
| | *2–19* | *20–99* | *100–499* | *500+* |
| *Housing* | | | | |
| Multi-dwelling | 10.7 | 21.6 | 11.7 | 56.0 |
| Small houses including | | | | |
|   holiday housing | 25.7 | 16.3 | 9.1 | 49.0 |
| Total housing | 20.5 | 18.1 | 10.0 | 51.4 |
|   % of which repairs | 48.7 | 18.1 | 3.9 | 20.0 |
| *Other building* | | | | |
| Total | 7.9 | 17.6 | 13.9 | 61.1 |
|   % of which repairs | 31.5 | 33.0 | 11.5 | 30.5 |
| *Infrastructure* | 10.5 | 10.9 | 7.2 | 71.3 |
| Total construction | 13.2 | 16.3 | 11.1 | 59.6 |
| Per cent employees | 17.5 | 18.2 | 10.6 | 53.3 |
| No. of firms | 4302 | 653 | 65 | 17 |

*Source:* Calculated from BO 1978: 6.

largest firms have greater productivity levels (up to double the smallest firms), higher wages and a larger proportion of white-collar workers (BO).

So although the concentration of building capital is more developed in Sweden, the British construction industry shows signs of catching up. However, like sub-contracting, this is also a question of the *nature* of concentration and here important differences emerge. First of all, evidence for Britain suggests that mergers and conglomerate links are not so much part of the process of organizing (and dominating) production in one sector, or even (as has occurred frequently in Sweden) increasing vertical integration through mergers with building materials and building craft firms. Rather, concentration through conglomerate linkage is more a means of profit acquisition, not profit development. The Trafalgar House Group, which includes New Ideal Homes and Willett Homes as well as a whole range of property, transport and leisure interests, provides the clearest example. It has been described as 'an unwieldy conglomerate, whose profits owe more to its accounting policies and its success in buying and selling assets than to its skill in running a business day to day' (Stern 1981, 13).

Contrast this to Skånska Cementgjuteriet (SC), the second biggest house builder. It is part of a multi-national conglomerate which is centred around Sweden's monopoly cement firm, the country's second largest building materials firm and the leading chain of department stores. Overall Swedish building firms are more and more linked, functionally and by ownership, to the building materials sector and this is one part of the manufacturing–finance empires we described in chapter two. (Thus Swedish Match, part of the 'Wallenberg empire' portrayed in figure 2.2, has considerable building technology, research and production interests.) This linkage extends to the 'alternative' ownership structure, the union and co-operative movement. BPA, the union owned and second largest house builder, has strong (non-ownership) links with the housing co-operatives and through them to leading building materials and household goods suppliers.

This difference between the nature of concentration extends also to how the house building work itself is organized in production units. In Britain this is largely carried out by fragmented sub-contracting units, and these will often be small and quite temporary irrespective of overall financial or product ownership. As we have seen, this is less likely to be the case in Sweden. However, as the building market is very often a regional one, the largest firms in Sweden often have a high degree of decentralization and internal autonomy by district production units. In one sense, this combines the advantages of concentration (for R & D, investment, planning, etc.) with those of sub-contracting (flexibility, specialization). Information is available on output concentration by 'production unit' (SOU 1982: 34), that is the unit in which any building project is organized. As we would expect, concentration levels are lower than with the firm level data summarized in table 3.7. None the less, the trend is towards larger production units and in 1978 the 7 per cent of units with over 50 employees completely dominated group small house and multi-dwelling production. In contrast to Sweden, concentration in the British building industry is 'shadow concentration': it is more a legal centralization of ownership, rather than a functional concentration of work organization.

*Labour relations*

Different degrees of industrialization, embodying different profit-making strategies, will create – and in part depend on – different labour management relations. If building work in Sweden is much more like large-scale factory work
than in Britain – it is more intense, standardized and continuous – then so are
labour relations. Building labour is well paid, well organized and holds considerable influence over management practice. Exactly the opposite is usually the case
in Britain, where a weakly unionized and low paid work-force is organized through
a casual labour system.

Perhaps the key starting point is unionization. In Britain the major unions
(UCATT, TGWU, GMWU, FTAT) account for no more than a third of the
work-force, although some craft unions are far better organized. The result is that
unions have only rarely had much influence on how labour is employed, and only
in central Scotland and perhaps London and Liverpool has such influence been
maintained (Ball 1983). In any case, union organization and action is far more
difficult with largely small scale workplaces and a constantly shifting work-force.
In Sweden the situation is quite different. Here there is virtually complete unionization. Over 70 per cent of the work-force are members of the Building Union,
the remainder are members of craft unions and white-collar unions. The Building
Union is a powerful element of a pervasive labour movement which has had
considerable and almost continual access to state power since the 1930s. It is one
part of the 'labour movement housing coalition' (with the Tenants' Union, the
housing co-operatives, the large urban authorities) which has had a key part in
producing state housing, building and land policy. It even owns the second largest
construction firm and has effective veto rights over the use of sub-contracting.
Supporting all this, union rights are more assured than in Britain – the 'joint
decision law' is just one recent example. The result of this national difference
becomes apparent when we examine how labour is employed, how much it is paid
and how it is controlled.

A crucial difference is in how labour is employed. In Britain housing construction is still essentially a casual labour system. This was a common form of
employment (in both Britain and Sweden) in the nineteenth century for those
trades with an excess labour supply, low skill levels and low capitalization levels
(see Stedman-Jones 1971 for a classic account). Its great advantages for employers
were the ability to fine tune labour supply to demand, to reduce real wages and to
increase control over individual workers. This is not to say that all labour need be
casual – key workers including some skilled craftsmen are often permanently
employed, while a considerable number of workers are less peripheral. But this
too is one aspect of the system, enabling more sensitive control as well as dividing
the work-force. Increasing unionization has minimized the ability to casualize
labour, while increasing capitalization has made a casual system less profitable.
Neither is advanced in the British building industry, and employers have been
able to maintain a casual labour system. This, indeed, is perhaps one of their
greatest achievements and the use of labour only sub-contracting and the Lump
has enabled them to maintain a casual labour system – even though, at least up to

the 1970s, there has been a labour shortage since the war. Furthermore, given this situation, labourers can find individual advantages in accepting casual employment (see Ball 1983, chapter four). In Sweden the role of casual labour in building is quite peripheral, most building workers are permanent employees. Of course, this permanence is subject to overall profitability and redundancies can occur – but labour is not organized on a casual basis and there is little scope for labour only sub-contracting or the Lump.

Following directly from the degrees of casualization and industrialization is the way control is exercised over labour. In Britain this takes the form of hiring and firing within the casual system. Workers can be laid off immediately if the order book suddenly looks bad, if work should stop in accordance with speculative downturns or even if the weather is inclement. Little capital equipment is lying unused for lack of workers, and key workers like foremen will acquiesce in this situation. The payment of a lump sum and the adoption of incentive schemes and bonus payments maintains tempo when quick work is required. In Sweden the more permanent work-force is managed and paid according to employer-union collective agreements made under the umbrella of LO–SAF agreements for all industrial sectors at the national level. The struggle becomes more like the Taylorist model. Management attempts to increase the tempo of work either through controlling the labour process or directly. Work studies and the nature of joint piece rates are the terrain for this conflict.

If in Sweden the work-force bear costs in terms of an increased tempo and stress of work, in Britain they bear it through low wages and unemployment. Ball (1983, chapter three) shows how construction wages have usually been 5 to 10 per cent below the manufacturing average since the war, and workers have had to work about 5 to 10 per cent longer even to achieve this lower rate. Although individual per unit time wages may be higher with the Lump system, the employer's wage bill per project will still be lower. For casual labour is not employed any longer than necessary and the considerable extra cost of permanent employees – holiday pay, sickness pay, wet time, administrative staff, etc. – can be avoided. Discontinuities of work are borne by the labour-force. In the intense downturn of 1982 as many as 45 per cent of building workers were estimated to be unemployed (Carter 1982). In Sweden, also at a time of historically high unemployment, the corresponding figure was only 7 per cent and this was after a decade in which building employment as a whole had declined by 12 per cent. Furthermore, Swedish building workers have always received higher wages, for shorter hours, than in manufacturing, although this had declined from 30 per cent above the average in the 1960s to 13 per cent in 1980. Over 1971–80 manufacturing wages (for adult men) had increased by 13.3 per cent per annum compared to only 12.7 per cent per annum in construction.

The reasons for this decline in Swedish construction workers' differential are unclear. Two factors are probably most important. One is the 'solidarity wage policy' adopted at national level. Wages should be equalized for the same work across different sectors and regions. Another, however, is deskilling and here some Swedish workers may bear costs less prevalent in Britain. Bricklaying and plastering are dying trades in Sweden, while architects are increasingly replaced by management's own building technicians. (In Britain displaced architects sometimes turn to land and property speculation.) None the less, deskilling also involves reskilling and management does not always establish the whip hand. There are probably more building technicians than the architects they replaced, heating engineers may make up for the decline in plasterers, and so on.

These contrasting management–labour relations feed into builders' profit strategies and hence how effectively and cheaply housing is constructed. The employer's response in Sweden, given the severe constraints over access to land development and extra profit, must be to increase relative exploitation of building labour through productivity increase. The response is different in Britain. Here enough direct control has been established over the labour-force to allow speculative pursuit of land development and extra profits. When times get bad the wages bill can be substantially decreased. But this sort of control over labour, however successful, is only one part of the capitalist use of labour. Control also extends to increasing the division and co-operation of labour. This is weakly developed in Britain and in this sense labour control remains shadow control.

### 3.6  Enforcing normality and external social relations in Sweden

A major theme of this chapter has been that the differential cost, quality and output developments in British and Swedish housing are crucially affected by the way in which building capital exploits labour. In Britain the path of indirect exploitation through land development and extra profits is very significant and, with less incentive to industrialize building processes so as to increase labour productivity, relative surplus exploitation is more weakly developed. In this way the British house building industry is 'abnormal' by the standards of advanced capitalism and so too, as has long been recognized (e.g. Bowley 1945, DLC 1978), is the way it produces commodities. In Sweden speculative avenues to building profitability are much more closed off and – given strong labour – industrialization and increased labour productivity remain as a way out. This has the happy side-effect of producing more housing per unit labour, more output at less relative cost, than in Britain. As we have begun to see, social relations between classes are crucial in this resolution, for example those between building labour and capital. Similarly important, as reflected in state intervention in house building (state housing loans, state machine loan fund, building norms and so on) are relations between these groups and other interests. Referring back to chapter two, the result is typical for social democratic class compromise – higher wages at work, higher consumption levels, state regulation, and higher profitability for big capital. In this last section we will briefly examine house building with respect to two 'external' social relations: land ownership and class compromise as reflected in state policy. We will end with some brief comments on the political implication of this.

*Land ownership and house building*

Access by builders to land development profits has been relatively constrained in Sweden since the war. This has been an important theme in the last two sections, as one means of explaining why builders must concentrate on the direct exploitation of building labour. In this section we will go a little further into explaining how and why this occurs, how – in this respect – 'normality' has been socially enforced in house-building. We find the by now familiar duo, a specific structure of class relations reinforced by a particular state intervention which reflects this structure, taking prime place in such an explanation. We will not, however, attempt to give a full survey of this issue, where the land question in Britain and Sweden could fairly easily fill another book. For further details readers are referred to Massey and Catalano (1978) on land ownership in Britain; Ball (1983, chapters seven and eight) on development land, the planning system and house building in Britain; and Duncan (1985) on state intervention and development land in Sweden. This section is largely based on the latter.

There are two groups in advanced capitalist societies who usually make the running in appropriating land development gains, landowners and developers including builders. A third group, conventionally represented as the 'public interest' but actually reflecting a more complex balance of power between landed interests, industrial and finance capital, labour and housing consumers, has attempted to intervene in order to regulate private ownership rights over both the use of land and the acquisition of land gains. This intervention proceeds through the state machinery, very often through a planning monopoly over land use planning. This monopoly remains, of course, negative in the sense that it can only – at best – prevent or influence development. There is little ability to control development because there is no positive control over land ownership or development itself. At worst – and this is not uncommon – land-use planning is almost completely subordinate to development and landed interests (see Ambrose and Colenutt 1975; Wates 1976 for British cases). In this respect Ball (1983) sees the British planning system as very much a battleground between builders and landowners. Who will get the development gains?

The situation in Sweden is different. This is not just a matter of degree, where state intervention into development land supply is more thorough, wide-ranging and pervasive. It is also a difference of kind. If the British land use planning system is eventually negative, the Swedish system has a strong prescriptive side with positive powers over land ownership and urban development. Planning, in a wider sense, extends to state regulation of land supply and, as we have seen, housing production (other public services are included). This has three major results. First, land ownership is separated from land development in housing, in such a way that neither builders *nor* landowners can expect to make significant development gains. (There are of course some exceptions, especially for re-development, see Duncan 1985.) The cost of acquiring building land only amounts to a very small proportion of final housing production costs (less than 2 per cent on average), while builders can do little more than pass these costs on and so are unable to gain where landowners have lost out. This brings us to the second result – who does gain? The substantial part of land development profits are in effect socialized in the form of cheaper and better quality housing, better planned and equipped environments, or taken by owner-occupiers and co-op tenants in capital gains. Finally, a major source of unearned income for landowners and builders is substantially reduced. This encourages more properly capitalist behaviour where financial reward follows the efficient investment of capital in commodity production, rather than rewarding unproductive political influence or speculative skill. Witness, of course, house-building.

How is this situation produced? First of all, the state dominates development land ownership. By 1980 about 80 per cent of new housing was built on land released from local authority (commune) land banks. This land has very often been acquired by communes at stable or declining real costs under legislative and

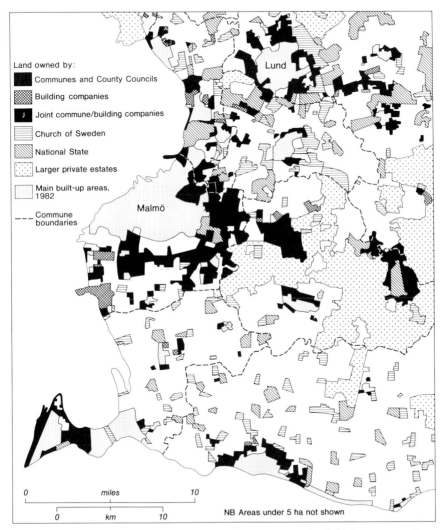

*Figure 3.10*   Land ownership and the control of development land, Malmö metropolitan region, 1982

*Source:* Adapted from SSK, 1983.

financial conditions which favour local authorities rather than private land-owners. Communes have a statutory duty to amass land banks sufficient for seven to ten years of urban development. To help them to do this they have access to subsidized state land loans and strong expropriation rights. The latter are much stronger than British compulsory purchase both in scope and effect. Any land thought likely to be used for urban development in the next ten years or more can be expropriated by the commune, possession can take place before appeal and compensation is set at land prices current ten years *before* expropriation. In addition, all land sellers must inform the relevant commune of their intentions, and land registration is both efficient, detailed and public. Information, as the inner-London story shows, is a good part of power (cf. Wates 1976). Furthermore, developers will only receive SHLs if they build on land from commune land banks (the 'Land Condition') although redevelopment is now excluded. As a consequence of these measures, communes are the dominant development land-owners and there is often little chance of finding anyone else to sell to. In any case, faced with rarely used but very threatening expropriation rights, landowners often prefer to sell to communes even at the low prices set by past expropriation cases. Landowners, including builders acting as landowners, are frozen out of land development gains. (See figure 3.10 for one regional case. Note the extensive commune land banks surrounding major urban areas and the virtual absence of building company landholding.)

How is the developer also frozen out? This is largely a function of the State Housing Loan (SHL) system discussed in section 3.4. Over 90 per cent of new housing is built according to commune contracts which, among other things, regulate final prices including the land component. Indeed, quite apart from the financial advantages of SHLs – they effectively provide a state prop for construction profits if production norms are met – this is the chief way of actually gaining access to building land.

Finally, we should note that not all these provisions were introduced at one go. This is a description of the 1980 situation where major reforms took place in 1947, 1966–8 and 1974. Three periods, representing different forms of state intervention can be distinguished. In the first period, up to the 1940s, the problem of land ownership was solved by default coupled with energetic municipal land assembly. The problem of 'former landed property' had been solved long ago and there were no large scale or concerted aristocratic landed interests, while financial and industrial ownership of agricultural land was already regulated following peasant agitation at the end of the nineteenth century. Building capital was still small scale, and most of the larger urban authorities had amassed significant land banks long before national state policy changes in this direction. For instance, much of Stockholm's expansion in the 1950s and early 1960s was built on commune-owned land bought very cheaply in the agricultural depression of the 1930s.

The second period, between the 1942 housing reforms and the late 1960s, can be seen as transitional. Landowners' access to development land profits was still muted and this position was consolidated by the 1947 planning and housing legislation which gave communes responsibility for planning housing supply as well as a monopoly over land use planning. This was supplemented by as yet weak expropriation rights in 1949. Together with the SHL system, these measures also seemed adequate to control builders' access to land development profits, even though building capital was now concentrating rapidly. However, during the 1960s the development land question re-emerged. Strong suburban expansion in the major urban areas was accompanied by electoral pressure on the Social Democrats over the housing question. At the same time the evidence was that the larger building firms were beginning to amass large land banks in suburban areas, and this was seen as a threat to the ruling party's ability to deliver adequate amounts of cheap, high quality housing. This evidence was confirmed by a number of government inquiries (e.g. SOU 1966: 23, 1972: 42) and, where elements of the labour movement were also becoming more radical, the result was legislation for ten-year revision on public leasehold (1966), statutory commune land banking and state land loans (1967), stronger expropriation rights (1966 and 1971), public information over land transactions (1968), and the 'land condition' for SHLs in 1974. In this third period, then, state regulation over builders' access to land development profit has been extended considerably. Building companies now own very little greenfield land and have disposed of most of their land stocks; there is little point any more in them owning land (cf. figure 3.10).

Before going on to look at those economic and political relations which have allowed state power to be used in this way, we will first examine the cost effects produced by the separation of land ownership from land development. We will deal in turn with the cost of purchasing development land and then with the proportional share of housing production costs accounted for by land acquisition.

A first diagnostic is to compare development land costs in the 'state sector' to those outside. This is conveniently measured by costs for small housing, within the state sector, and those for recreation housing – often of very similar size and construction – outside. In the late 1970s real prices per unit building land were declining for the small house sector (minus 1.3 per cent kr m$^2$ constant prices 1976–9); in the recreation house sector they were increasing strongly (plus 17.3 per cent). The situation has now been reached where rural land, with little agricultural value, costs more than suburban land. In fact real plot prices, per unit area, only increased by an average of 0.9 per cent per year in the small house sector between 1957 and 1980. Contrast to Britain, where private sector land prices increased by 82 per cent in real terms between 1969 and 1979 (in Sweden this was 9 per cent). Like housing construction costs, development land cost trends are also far more stable in Sweden. 'Extremes' of plus or minus 3 per cent contrast with British rates of plus 105 per cent (1973) and minus 139 per cent (1975). These figures are reflected in the land acquisition cost share of final costs. In Sweden these average at between 1 and 1.4 per cent in the small house sector between 1965 and 1980, although regional variations are larger with extremes of 0.7 and 3.5 per cent in 1980 (Norrland and Greater Stockholm). But again, compare with Britain where these costs ranged between 15 and 27 per cent in the 1970s, with regional variations between 8 per cent and as much as 43 per cent (Wales and the Outer South East, both in 1973). These figures are a tribute to the landowner's ability, in Britain, to gain land development profits in line with the builder's speculative profits. Finally, in Britain builders have a chance of taking over some of these gains through land banking, (through, effectively, becoming landowners) or by using the planning system to circumvent the original landowners. Neither option is easy in Sweden, except sometimes in redevelopment.

One corollary of this is cheaper housing construction costs directly – land development profits are largely removed. Second, as we have seen, builders are pushed onto the path of realizing profits through improving the productivity of labour, or product innovation, in the building process. This will also cheapen housing construction costs. Finally, and this provides a physical illustration of what is implied, builders can use more and better land and do more with it. Dwelling sizes and plot sizes have increased substantially in Sweden and, over and above that, considerable effort can be put into site development. This is a matter of employing capital and labour to make real physical changes, such as the construction of play areas, landscaping, parking areas, on a scale almost unknown in Britain. The costs of doing this are now fairly stable at around 7–8 per cent of total production costs, that is little more than the lowest share apparently passed on, without producing any physical change whatsoever, to landowners in Britain. A similar advance is established for land use planning. This is no longer in the forefront of the battle to control land development gains; a battle it is ill-equipped to fight, as the British experience makes plain. Planners can concentrate on just that – planning – and in relative freedom from land supply constraints.

The reasons why this separation of land ownership from land development has taken place take us back to the concerns of section 2.2. Aristocratic landed interests in Sweden have been weak – economically, politically and culturally – since the seventeenth century. The major 'landed interest' has been that of small farmers, interested more in production issues (e.g. food prices) and their own survival in the face of big business rather than rent or development gain. Landed interests have not held any political or ownership stranglehold over development land policy and indeed the farmers, opposed to big business and big landowning, were responsible for the first state interventions to control industrial and financial land ownership in the 1880–1920 period. Labour – organized in unions, co-ops and politically – has had influential access to state policy since the 1930s, where the 'labour movement housing coalition' has been fundamental to formulating the housing and land policies described in this chapter. Right-wing political parties are weak, while the Farmers' and Liberal party often supported the Social Democrats before 1960, and since the 1930s big business has taken the 'progressive' path of compromise with big labour. In any case, the weight of loan capital lies in domestic manufacturing rather than separate financial and property interests.

All this is in obvious contrast to Britain. And, following this, attempts to control land development profits have been simultaneously less ambitious and less successful. The 1947 Town and Country Planning Act (see chapter four) is essentially negative in effect and has been increasingly subverted into a means by which development gains can be made by larger house builders (Rydin 1983). Other attempted interventions, like the 1967 Land Commission and the 1975

Land Community Act have been short-lived. Even if they had lasted they were underfinanced, very often diluted following landowning pressure, and partly aimed at the wrong target. So the 1975 Act would perhaps have been most effective in attacking landowners' development gain, rather than developers, while the state would have used the windfall as more of a taxation device than a means of reducing consumers' housing costs. More recently builders have been easing themselves further towards the centre of the planning system with the establishment of what Hooper (1984) calls the 'Manchester Model' (HBF/DOE 1979). Builders themselves advise planners on which land should be released for development. In the Brighton area, for instance, two planners are assisted by ten representatives from the house building industry (ESCC/HBF 1980).

*Class relations, state power and housing reform*

The questions of labour relations and land ownership have brought us back to the concerns of chapter two. Capitalism is unevenly developed and in Sweden this has meant producing housing commodities in a way different from that in Britain. This is because the structure of Swedish society has allowed organized labour and big capital to emerge as the major social actors. Housing provision is a key area, for both sides, in their 'historic compromise'. Gains for consumers and building workers are matched by support for big capital's profitability; less well established interests – like those of land ownership, small capital or speculative interests – have been frozen out. However, just as the structure of Swedish society is not given for all time neither is this compromise. As we described in chapter two, both were under strain by the mid-1970s and the 'housing crisis' of falling output and shifts in demand reflected this just as much as world recession or changes in the housing market. Symptomatically, the rise of housing construction costs in the late 1970s was felt as an important political problem – one result is the government inquiry (SOU 1982: 34, 35) which we have found useful.

It is important to start off on this note because one important difference between housing production in the two countries is the much higher level of state intervention in Sweden – State Housing Loans, State Machine Loans, State Land Loans, commune land banks, the 'Land Condition', etc. This is not, however, the result of a rational and benevolent state somehow incorporating the idea of reform better than anyone else. It is due to a specific resolution of class and other social interests and, hence, the way state power is used. 'The State' is not a social actor. Hence, also, the importance to how housing is produced of class relations articulated as much outside state institutions as inside; those between building labour and building capital, and the position of land ownership, being crucial.

This being said, the importance of the agency of state institutions cannot be denied. So far, we have considered three major intervention roles which have both reflected and supported trends already produced by the overall structure of Swedish society. First, the SHL system among other measures helped push speculative production into the background; builders' access to extra profits was considerably reduced. Second, land ownership was separated from land development, the SHL system was also important here although so too was a range of direct land policies. Access by builders and landowners to land development profits was severely curtailed. Finally, state power was used directly to support industrialization in the building process itself. Here again, SHLs were important as well as other measures and the result was to stimulate improved labour exploitation while maintaining high wage levels.

In part, then, state intervention in housing production has reinforced those pressures enforcing labour process restructuring in the Swedish building industry. But this has not only been a question of restricting builders' access to land development profits and speculative extra profits, or even of the direct support for industrialization in building. State power has also been used to support builders' profits. This is almost like compensation for having to take the hard path of labour process restructuring. It has certainly been essential to the compromise worked out in housing.

This has happened in two major ways. First of all, the intervention closing off speculative profits and supporting industrialization has also provided subsidies for building capital. Sometimes this is fairly direct, for instance SHLs provide developers (and hence builders) with a stable source of long-term, subsidized finance. Other measures are less direct, but probably still appreciable in their effect. For example, given that land gains are curtailed, state activity in actually assembling and enabling the planned release of development land will save building firms from considerable administrative and infrastructural costs. Compare with Britain, where it has been estimated that as much as two thirds of the money capital employed in building a private sector dwelling is taken up by land banking (House of Commons, 1980, Appendix 2). And as with housing finance, a stable and ensured supply of building land will contribute to market and business stability.

This shades into the second major profit support role played by state intervention, that of regulating demand so as to further industrial stability. The failures of the British building industry are very much associated with market instabilities and discontinuities.[15] In this situation, sub-contracting, the piecemeal use of land banks and low capitalization are sensible precautions. In Sweden the SHL system, combined with a longer lasting commitment to public sector provision (e.g. the 'million programme') has reduced this problem. Firms who could bring off their side of the bargain were virtually ensured a steady market. It was the strong disturbance of this market regulation with the end of the 'million programme' in 1973 that was partly responsible for the mid-1970s housing crisis. Since then attempts have been made to re-establish demand stability through the improvement drive (often against tenants' wishes – their 'demand' is enforced via state policy). Similarly, public sector house building has been stable since the late-1970s and is actually increasing as a proportion of completions (figures 3.6, 4.1). However, this support for building capital is not open ended. There *is* a compromise, with socially desirable results for labour in the form of cheaper and better housing, higher and less insecure building wages, and a building industry which can produce houses efficiently.

It is instructive in this respect to look at one of the latest emissions of this housing compromise. These are the proposals for a large scale research and development programme for the building sector, supported by state finance and institutions, that were gaining ground by the early 1980s (e.g. SCBR, 1983). The building sector is seen as taking in the whole of the building industry, the building materials industry, building management, urban planning and housing provision. The starting point is unambiguously seen as the sector's crucial importance in the Swedish economy. Counting everything, the building sector accounts for about 50 per cent of total investment, 25 per cent of GNP, and 20 per cent of employment. The building stock was the biggest element of fixed capital and – including transport to and from buildings – accounted for 60 per cent of oil consumption. Building sector exports were of increasing importance, while construction was an important economic and employment regulator. However, and this was also important to the calculation, it was also much more possible to achieve changes through state regulation than in other sectors, because of the importance of state investment and intervention mechanisms built up over a long period. Finally, the building sector was seen as vital for the central reform programmes in housing, social policy, energy, the labour market and the environment. For all these reasons a long-term R & D programme on building construction, energy use, administration, etc. was vital, based around the bench mark of maintaining international competitiveness.

A key moment in the formulation of this 'building sector' compromise was the realization that a speculative house building industry was congenitally incapable of mass-producing relatively cheap and high quality housing. It is ironic that this realization was established by the 'Stockholm School' of applied economists by the 1930s, for in Britain the intellectual breakthrough was not fully demonstrated until the wave of housing production work in the late 1970s (e.g. DLC 1978, Bartlett School 1978). The Stockholm technocrats were also in a position to do more about it. They were an influential part of the dominant political party, and this party desperately needed means to deliver the promises of social democratic electoral ideology – full employment and a better quality of life. Having already tried, and to their mind failed, with housing consumption subsidies of various sorts, the Stockholm School could present housing production reforms as a central social and economic lever (see chapter four).

In this way housing provision provides a set piece of the differences between British and Swedish reformism as a whole. Not only has it been possible to take the latter version further, but because of this it has been more successful in delivering its promises and has therefore been better able to sustain legitimacy. There are also important strategic differences. First, Swedish reformism has been aimed at production as well as distribution, this is especially the case for housing but in the economy as a whole state regulation of labour, capital and information markets is more advanced than in Britain. As we have seen for housing, action in the production sphere is vital even for distributive reformism to work. In turn, this has important implications for political legitimacy as we have learnt by bitter experience in Britain since 1979. Second, Swedish reformism – especially in production – has often been effected through a 'commanding the heights' strategy, rather than attempting direct socialization. This is not only a politically easier route, but is probably a more effective one. It is more possible to sustain a flexible intervention which can both better deal with changing political and economic circumstances and be extended to cover new areas of reform. The SHL system is a good example. It has enabled a degree of state management over housing production for over forty years but at the same time could be used to extend intervention into the building process itself and into the supply of development land. Contrast the unsustained and essentially failing attempt in Britain to socialize housing provision through consumption with the post-war concentration on council housing. This contrast is, of course, a mirror image of economic intervention as a whole in the two countries. There is far less direct state ownership of productive enterprises in Sweden but, with more effective state intervention over capital, labour, land and information markets, arguably greater potential for socialist transformation.

The same sort of comparison can be drawn with current research-based proposals for solving the British house building disaster. To a considerable extent, these rely on nationalization of land and parts of construction (e.g. Merrett 1979, Ball 1982, 1983). This is not just to argue for an eternal middle way, and in any case Britain and Sweden are rather different places to begin within. Nationalization may be the only means to confront Britain's politically stronger and more backward capital, nor do these proposals argue that nationalization is any simple solution. None the less, our comparison gives some food for thought. If social reform is to be measured by the extent to which it weakens or removes capitalist power over everyday life, then the 'commanding the heights' strategy may have more to offer. This is not just a matter of what reforms are meant to establish; to be established and even more important, sustained, it is necessary for people at large to want to carry them through. This is partly why nationalization can so easily become a state capitalism (e.g. British Steel) largely bereft of socialist potential and indeed – as sometimes with council housing – often quite negative in this respect. Similarly, what is nationalized is sometimes just what capitalists would like to be nationalized. It would be ironic but possible that low income house building, shorn of land gains, could be exchanged for compensation payments to be invested in R & D and building materials where (like drug companies and the health service) profitability and control are more easily sustained.

There are of course substantial penalties possible with any reform of housing production in Britain. Not only may reforms not go far enough, but a 'middle way' strategy which supports efficient capitalism on the Swedish model can reproduce the very problems it is supposed to alleviate. Deskilling, increased work stress and labour-force reduction are all possible for building workers, for instance. Increased capitalist efficiency in one place means market loss elsewhere. (By the early 1980s the Swedish building materials industry had established a significant import penetration in Britain, Swedish building firms had begun to export complete house kits and even set up subsidiaries in Britain.) None the less, there can hardly be any convincing intellectual defence of the present structure of house building in Britain, even from the point of view of many house builders. Not only this, but transformation from this structure would necessitate social changes that in themselves would challenge capitalist power.

## CHAPTER FOUR

# The social organization of demand

## 4.1 Introduction: decommodification, recommodification and the regulation of class relations

In the last chapter our focus was on the supply of housing, but we finished by emphasizing the social organization of supply. This meant exploring political and economic struggles and alliances over housing; particularly the relations between labour and capital, but also the relations within labour and capital that favour, or perhaps militate against, restructuring how dwellings are produced. This progressive widening out of the analysis helped in our task of explaining the variability of housing production costs between Sweden and Britain. In this chapter on the demand for housing a similar procedure is adopted; starting with the important but relatively limited question of variability in consumer costs but, in attempting to explain these differences, again moving outwards towards the wider social factors determining these costs.

This chapter is also, however, addressed to a series of current debates on housing under capitalism. A recurrent theme in much of the Marxist work on housing, and particularly that concerning state intervention over housing, is that this is one way in which the class relations necessary for the reproduction of capitalism are maintained. It is, in other words, one way in which social order is reproduced. Now, in terms of gaining an understanding of the role of housing under capitalism this is clearly an improvement, as for example Harloe and Martens (1984) have recently stressed, on work which simply focuses on housing policies themselves. However, there remain some serious problems within the literature even if housing policies are seen in relation to what Harloe and Martens call the 'contextual factors which structure housing policies'. One is an overemphasis on class relations which insists on seeing state intervention over housing as straightforwardly a victory for working-class political pressure.

Byrne and Damer (1980), for example, give great emphasis to the demands made in Glasgow and elsewhere in Britain during the First World War, in explaining the emergence of rent control and the first national state housing policies. The problem here is not that it is wrong in itself, but that the approach does not give sufficient attention to those other interests (particularly those capitalist interests such as finance and large-scale industrial capital) *also* supporting rent restrictions and the supply of new dwellings. As the last chapter on production indicates, it is more useful for explanatory purposes to think in terms of the alliances forged over housing between capitals and labours which will of course vary not just between societies, but between sub-national localities and over time.

This last point brings us to our second concern with housing studies from a Marxist viewpoint, particularly with French structuralist accounts. For example, Lefebvre (1976) and Castells (1977) also identify housing as a means by which class relations are regulated. Our argument here is similar to that made in the last chapter. How, when, where (perhaps even whether) the social relations of production are reproduced through housing and other forms of state intervention cannot be simply assumed, and again can be expected to vary considerably over time and space and under different versions of capitalism. Furthermore, the effects of regulating the social relations of production (in terms of, for example, the costs that particular people have to pay) may vary considerably according to precisely how these relations are reproduced.

A similar point can be made regarding two other broad processes affecting housing under advanced capitalism; decommodification and recommodification. As outlined in more detail later, Britain and Sweden, like many other West European governments, forty years ago exercised considerable control over the demand for housing. 'Decommodification' measures (such as government subsidies, rent control, welfare benefits, control over housing finance and land prices) were, in varying combinations, the order of the day. But, though these forms of state intervention might be generally classified as 'decommodification' and may appear broadly similar, the important thing for someone trying to buy or rent a house is not simply state control in itself, but which interests are being controlled, which are thriving and the effects that this has on costs, access and conditions.

The same applies to 'recommodification'. Again in Sweden and Britain and in many other European countries, the structure of demand is now changing in a number of important, and apparently similar, ways. Perhaps the most important general tendency has been increased levels of owner-occupation and a broad return to the commodity form of distribution, at the expense of socialized or partially socialized forms (Harloe 1981). But, though there might have been a general recent tendency for capital to penetrate the form of distribution, the point must again be made that the ways in which it is allowed to happen and the consequent results on people's lives may well vary considerably and need to be carefully monitored. How, then, decommodification or recommodification actually works out whether in Sweden or Britain, in Sheffield or in Norfolk, is just as important as these general processes in themselves. Perhaps, in the end, the two words 'decommodification' and 'recommodification' are misleading; both of them in fact refer to relationships between states and markets. There never was a time when housing was truly 'decommodified' and it is difficult to imagine a housing system which is totally free of state intervention.

Finally, and bringing together the two themes of recommodification and the regulation of class relations through housing, it might well be asked whether they are in conflict with one another. Does, in other words, a return to a more market-oriented form of distribution threaten to undermine the kind of corporate class compromise over the production and consumption of housing that has, so far at least, been successfully achieved in Sweden? Once more, there is no necessary reason why increasing levels of owner-occupation should either undermine or sustain such a compromise. This again depends more on the particular forms of owner-occupation and class compromise involved. The answer is again an empirical one, one which we attempt to answer here; again using Sweden as a 'purer' form of capitalism which helps us better understand Britain's more complex, even deviant, form.

## 4.2 Variability in consumption costs: towards an explanation

We now come to the empirical starting-point of this chapter; the costs that consumers have to pay. The point of emphasizing variability under capitalism becomes clear if we look back to figure 3.2 (p. 73) showing trends in consumers' housing expenditure in Britain and Sweden between 1950 and 1980. After a fall in the early 1950s in both countries, costs in Britain have increased by nearly two and a half times whereas those in Sweden have remained relatively stable.

Here we will be concentrating particularly on the Swedish case; again using it as a foil against which to compare Britain. As noted in chapter three, there are problems with direct statistical comparisons between the two countries. However, here we are more interested in broad trends and the reasons for them.

The percentage of an average manual worker's disposable income (i.e. after tax) needed to rent a two-room flat in Sweden (this flat including kitchen and bathroom) has dropped from an astronomic 40 per cent in 1933 to 28 per cent in 1945 and 24 per cent in 1980, with a low of 18 per cent in 1975 (BPA/RK 1978, Boberg *et al.* 1974). As regards the costs (after housing allowances) for particular kinds of tenure, those for the predominantly rented/co-op 'multi dwellings' varied in 1980 between 10 and 14 per cent of income for most types of household and levels of household income (BBÅ 1981). Costs for the predominantly owner-occupied 'small houses' are, if we compare equivalent groups in the two categories, around 2 per cent higher. Only a few, relatively small, groups (for example low income, single parent families) have housing costs over 20 per cent of household income.

The relative stability in consumption costs in Sweden since the war could of course have been achieved through a reduction of standards or an improvement in some people's standards at the expense of others. This has not, however, occurred; indeed this stability in costs has occurred around a general improvement in quality levels. In 1945 for example, 51 per cent of households were 'overcrowded' (using a definition of two persons per room excluding kitchen and one living room) and by 1980 this had decreased to 4 per cent. Similarly, the number of rooms per person had increased from 1.0 to 1.8 over this period. As regards quality, 54 per cent of households were without central heating in 1945, compared with 1 per cent in 1980. Similarly, 64 per cent did not have exclusive use of a w.c. in 1945, compared with only 2 per cent in 1980. An aggregate measure of 'low' space and quality standards shows that 37 per cent lived in this quality of accommodation in 1960, compared with 3 per cent in 1980 (BS 1983, BBÅ 1981).

*Table 4.1*   Housing conditions in Sweden, 1968–81

| Inequality index for housing space | Difference from the average of all other groups | |
|---|---|---|
| | 1968 | 1981 |
| a *Family type* | | |
| 1  Single without children | +19 | +12 |
| 2  Couples without children | +16 | +14 |
| 3  Single with 1 child | +10 | +15 |
| 4  Single with 2+ children | −19 | −17 |
| 5  Couples with 1 child | −18 | −9 |
| 6  Couples with 2 children | −21 | −17 |
| 7  Couples with 3+ children | −28 | −38 |
| b *Social group* | | |
| Workers | −22 | −19 |
| White-collar | −4 | +2 |
| Social group I | +32 | +27 |
| Small firm owners/self-employed | +17 | +15 |
| Farmers | +19 | +18 |
| Students | −35 | −35 |
| Pensioners II (i.e. ex-white collar) | +29 | +21 |
| Pensioners III (i.e. ex-workers) | +11 | +9 |

*Source:* Adapted from unpublished Swedish government statistics.

As regards the distribution of these increasing standards, the general trend appears to be one of equalization. As table 4.1a shows, only couples with more than three children have seen their standards deteriorate relative to the average for all family types. And, as regards the distribution to social groups, table 4.1b again shows a general equalization of housing space standards.

In summary, therefore, the relative stability in Swedish consumption costs has taken place in the context of considerable increases in quality and space standards and a tendency towards the equalization of distribution. The next question is, of course, why should this be? The stability of costs is partly a result of the high levels of productivity and cost reductions achieved by the Swedish building industry; a point covered in the last chapter and referred to again shortly. But cost-reductions and equalization across households and social groups are also a reflection of the relationships between the supplier and the consumer. Is the consumer's access to housing determined mainly by the capacity to pay? Or is housing consumption predominantly socialized, with allocation based primarily on some measure of need?

At this point we return to the question of decommodification, recommodification and the differential impact of these processes over time as well as over space. Both societies have seen a post-war period when non-profit tenures were for a time dominant in terms of the production of new housing. In Sweden this lasted for thirty years after 1945 and in Britain for only seven. Both societies too have seen periods when owner-occupation as a form of distribution has become dominant and non-profit tenures have become secondary; from the early 1950s in Britain to around 1976 in Britain and from the mid-1970s to 1982 in Sweden. Britain, however, has seen since the mid-1970s non-profit state housing becoming what is often now called a 'residual' tenure; a process which, so far at least, has not happened on a large scale in Sweden. Indeed, non-profit tenures in Sweden for new house construction are now becoming increasingly important. In the early 1980s they were back to about 50 per cent of production.

And, as we have suggested earlier, the ways in which these general processes have occurred vary enormously. Consumers in Britain have to a much greater extent been exposed to market forces in the form of the land market, finance for housing production and the construction industry. In Sweden, on the other hand, the state has retained (despite, as we will see, a considerable recent growth in owner-occupation) crucial control over the costs of development land, finance and housing production, with the latter including control over the prices of new houses. We need, then, to carefully 'unpack' these concepts. Sweden's 'recommodified' system is still actually quite close to the 'decommodified' system established in 1945, despite a considerable boom in owner-occupation. Britain's 'decommodified' system, on the other hand, was always limited; never involving, for example, significant state control over the building industry.

How do we account for these differences in both the extents and the forms of penetration of market relations into the distribution process? We must in particular continue to bear in mind the alliances in Sweden over housing between strong blocs of capital and labour. This alliance started to be formed in the 1920s and was established as early as the 1930s. Crucially, it has been retained and even strengthened up to the present day.

The maintenance and reinforcement of this coalition, formed in Sweden's 'historic compromise', was developed in the immediate post-war years. It has, in combination with historically weak landed interests and the different structures of labour and capital in the two societies (involving, for example, the integration of finance and industry in Sweden), prevented recommodification along British lines (see chapter two). But this prevention has involved struggle and constant renegotiation. To understand adequately how it is that people in Sweden are now relatively well housed, and at fairly stable costs, it is essential to take an historical view; looking at particular forms of state intervention and seeing them as both a product of and a means of maintaining a class society. We can then also begin to understand why, when Swedish housing conditions were generally much worse than those in Britain in 1930, they are now considerably better.

## 4.3 Early alliances and forms of intervention

### Housing and social crisis

On 21 April 1917 the Stockholm police were secretly armed as 20,000 people besieged the Swedish Royal Palace and Parliament demanding 'bread, freedom

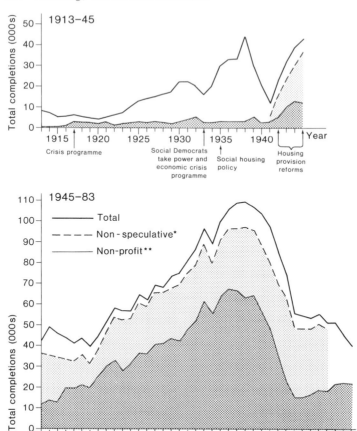

*Figure 4.1* Commodification and decommodification: new dwellings completed in Sweden, 1913–83

*Notes:*
 \* Controlled through public contract and state housing loan
\*\* Produced for public housing companies, co-operatives of state authorities

*Sources:* Compiled from Ekbrant 1981, 1982; Södersten 1968; BBÅ, SOU 1945: 63.

and laws against housing profiteers'. Housing conditions were one of the central issues in this proto-revolutionary upheaval as tenants' unions linked up with trade union organizations and the Social Democrat Party. This Party had a long-standing commitment to revolutionary reform and the public appropriation of the means of production and (while not yet in control of central government) had gained control of many important city councils, starting with Malmö in 1908. In Sweden, as in Britain at the same time (Clarke and Ginsburg 1975, Dickens 1978,

Melling 1980) rent strikes and housing blockades were being linked to demands for higher wages.

And, again as in Britain, this combination of housing and workplace struggle forced state intervention over housing on to the political agenda. A 'Crisis Programme' was introduced (see figure 4.1 with 4.2 for the British comparison). This consisted of rent controls, an investment programme with state credit for housing

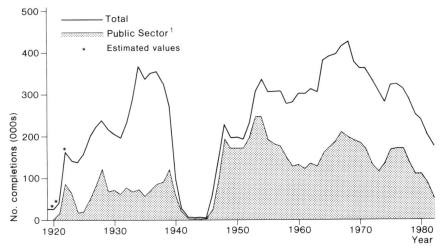

*Figure 4.2* Commodification and decommodification: new dwellings completed in UK, 1919–82

*Note:* [1] Public Sector–Local Authorities before 1945 and Local Authorities, new towns, housing associations and government departments after 1945

*Sources:* Compiled from HCS, Housing Returns; Merrett (1979); Merrett with Gray (1982).

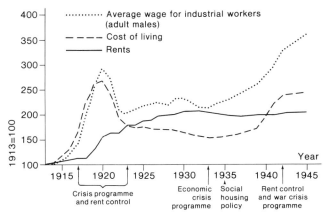

*Figure 4.3* Wages, rents and living costs, Sweden, 1913–45

*Source:* Adapted from SOU 1945: 63.

construction and loans to compensate for rises in building material costs during the war. Furthermore, a system of housing exchanges was set up, modelled on labour exchanges. The measures were in fact insufficient to hold production to 1917 levels and they were progressively diluted as the crisis eased. By the early 1920s wages were rapidly falling but rents escalating (see figure 4.3). Indeed, the crisis measures were finally axed in 1923, with a Conservative government replacing the Liberals in April of that year.

But the importance of the measures lay less in their absolute results and more in the establishment of the precedent of central state intervention. The idea of rent control was now established, even if the landlords felt themselves unfairly penalized and (for a while) successfully fought back. The programme had also introduced controlled public housing companies, providing non-profit housing for rent and with the companies working closely with (and in practice almost always controlled by) the local authorities. But this should still not be seen as a form of radical state intervention replacing the market organization of housing; indeed the objective was to support the market and make it work better. The Social Democrat Party strongly supported state intervention over housing but this cause still had little political and ideological backing from those in power. Contemporary developments in Britain (perhaps seen through rose-coloured spectacles) continued to serve as a model for the Social Democrats, even during the time of defeat over housing in 1923.

> In England the state took the lead in housing supply, and struggled to plan the base for production and its consequences – a housing policy which aimed to supply those in need of housing with decent dwellings in line with their income.                                                                        (SOU 1945: 63, 69)

The Crisis Programme (as figure 4.1 indicates) did not achieve a great deal in quantitative terms, despite over half the completions being in non-profit tenures. Furthermore, the already bad housing situation was rapidly worsening. The International Labour Organization reported in 1924 that Sweden had the highest rents for the worst conditions in any European country (ILO 1924) and Stockholm was commonly supposed to have even worse housing conditions than the internationally notorious city of Berlin (Hultén 1973). And Sweden was now suffering from what was popularly known as 'the Berlin sickness' whereby there was no production until there was a housing shortage, production increasing only when rents increased. But when production went up demand came down, bringing rents with it. Waves of supply and demand were consistently out of phase and the situation seemed, as figure 4.4 indicates, to be getting out of control. Here then, was a spectacular and politically significant example of the failures of speculative housing production.

Meanwhile, the tenants' associations were reorganizing after their 1923 defeat. A much strengthened labour movement housing coalition was now emerging and this was to be crucially important in later establishing housing as a central part of Sweden's 'historic compromise'. A national tenants' union (HGR) was established with stronger links to the Social Democratic Party and to LO, the confederation of manual trade unions. Their programme for reform included

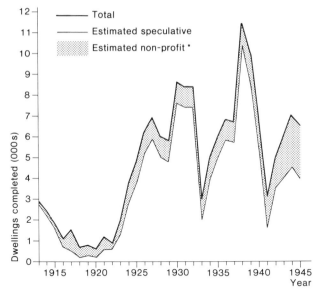

*Figure 4.4*  The 'Berlin sickness': speculative housing production in Stockholm, 1913–45

*Note:* * Public housing companies, co-operatives and state authorities

*Source:* Calculated from Ekbrant 1981.

commune-controlled and supported housing provision, direct housing provision for the poor and special help for the evicted and homeless. These alliances were not, however, being made without pain. The labour movement itself was split after 1917 between those pursuing the 'parliamentary road' to reform and those taking a radical, 'direct action' line. And the splits between those directly confronting capitalism and the bourgeoisie and those attempting amelioration within the existing order were reflected in divisions in the housing organizations. The radical line, emphasized by *Hyregästen* (*The Tenant*, the paper of the Tenants' Union) was particularly inspired by 'the Scottish Rent Strike'. This was seen as a precedent for mass working-class action over housing:

> The movement for proletarian rent strikes had already begun in England (sic) during the War. In Clydebank, the workers' town for Glasgow, an important tenants' strike has recently been underway. It was followed with great interest by working class and bourgeoisie alike, for this shows what can be achieved by a united proletarian front.                                          (Hultén 1973, 46)

And, in terms of explaining the key role that housing was later to play in official policy-making, it is particularly important to mention at this early stage a group of intellectuals. This was the 'Stockholm School' of economists and social scientists. This group included Gunnar Myrdal, (later to become the internationally known economist) who, with his wife Alvia, was in the 1920s and 1930s working on questions of population and family policy and its links with housing.

The group also included Alf Johansson, the Stockholm School's housing expert who from 1942 to 1960 was to become head of the National Housing Board, a key instrument of state policy. The point about this group is that it was later to provide the technocratic basis for the coalition between the labour movement and big capital over housing; indeed we could say that the Stockholm Group used the Social Democrats, when they came into power, to put their ideas into effect. Similarly, the intellectuals were used by the Social Democrats when they took control at central government level, the Stockholm group being asked to develop a housing programme to solve Sweden's problems of a declining population.

*Housing and the 'historic compromise'*

Between 1928 and 1932 labour and capital had been reaching their 'historic compromise' and this was, as we have discussed in chapter two, cemented by the election of the Social Democrats to power (see table 4.2). In essence, this guaranteed the continuation of capitalist industry in return for trade union influence and rewards. It is difficult to over-emphasize the importance of this compromise between classes in attempting to explain why decent housing is such a key feature of Swedish society. A central element of these rewards was a welfare state, of which housing was a key feature. Swedish and British housing policies had already begun to diverge at this stage. As a comparison between figures 4.1 and 4.2 shows, significant levels of local authority building had been undertaken in Britain since 1919 whereas in Sweden there had been little non-profit building before 1930, and, indeed as figure 4.1 shows, there was little move until 1942. But in the 1930s Swedish and British state policies towards housing started to differ in

*Table 4.2*   The rise of the Social Democratic Workers' Party in national government, 1911–32

| Election | % of votes and political grouping | | | |
|---|---|---|---|---|
| | Social Democrats (SD) | Communist Party (CP) | Centre and right (Liberals, Farmers, Conservatives) | Governments |
| 1911 | 28.5 | — | 71.5 | Liberal |
| 1914 (1) | 30.1 | — | 69.9 | Liberal |
| (2) | 36.4 | — | 63.6 | Conservative |
| 1917 | 39.2 | — | 60.8 | Liberal-SD, Lib. |
| 1920 | 36.1 | — | 63.9 | SD |
| 1921 | 39.4 | 4.6 | 56.0 | Con-Lib. |
| 1924 | 41.1 | 5.1 | 53.8 | Cons, SD, Lib. |
| 1928 | 37.0 | 6.4 | 56.6 | Cons, Lib. |
| 1932 | 41.7 | 8.3 | 50.0 | SD up to 1976 |

*Source:* Adapted from Levnadsundersökningen (1968); unpublished report, SOS.

ways which were to recur in the post-war period. The slump in Britain during the 1930s became a reason for the National Government's drastic halting of new built state housing to add to the existing stock. 'City' interests called for a slowdown in public spending and the building societies, bursting with money, pressured governments into concentrating on slum-clearance and allowing the private sector its head in supplying predominantly speculative construction for owner-occupation (Dickens 1978, Merrett 1979). The dramatic results are shown in figure 4.2.

In Sweden, by contrast, state-directed house building was specifically seen as the *way out* of the recession, with the Social Democrats' policy being a simple 'pre-Keynes Keynesianism'; attempting to solve unemployment and economic depression through state spending. As figure 4.1 indicates, a new 'Crisis Programme' was inaugurated with construction generally, and house construction in particular, greatly benefiting. Later this purely 'economic' intervention was to become (under the influence of the Stockholm intellectuals) more 'social'. From 1935 support was given to the construction of large family dwellings and family allowances; the object being, in line with the thinking first put forward by the Myrdals and now being more widely accepted, to use improved housing conditions as a means of encouraging people to have children and thereby overcoming what their controversial best-seller called the 'Crisis in the Population Question' (*Kris i befokningsfrågen*). As well as consumption subsidies, the intervention also took the form of subsidies to builders, an additional 20 per cent being added to the loans which could be raised on the market with a limit of 90 per cent of the cost of building.

Again, the importance of these early interventions lies less with their quantitative effects and rather more with the establishment of forms of intervention (particularly the subsidies direct to production) and the formation of strong coalitions around housing. The Social Democrat Party, closely connected to a strong labour movement, was now concentrating on redistribution in *consumption* and was committed to the principle of providing housing on social, as distinct from purely economic, grounds. By the 1930s the Swedish state had acquired the key symbolic responsibility for the regulation of social conflict and social reproduction via housing.

Nevertheless, by the outbreak of the war, the Social Democrat Party's intellectuals were concluding that the 1933–40 period had been one of relative failure as regards housing policy, and that greatly extended state intervention was necessary. High costs for new flats meant that 'for the majority of households with low incomes it was still beyond that ability to realize an adequate housing standard through the payment of an acceptable proportion of their income' (SOU 1945: 63, 169). State control over rents, housing prices and land costs (that is control over *production* as well as distribution) was now urgently needed 'A state loan facility should, as is obvious, necessitate complementary control over land prices, company profits and rent levels, especially in a situation of greatly increased demand on the housing market as in the late 1930s' (SOU 1945: 63, 61). Moreover, for a number of reasons it was now becoming possible to put the intellectuals' ideas into practice; ideas that were in effect to become the basis of post-war intervention. Not only had a working-class movement established the Social Democrats in power and forged a strong labour movement housing coalition, but state intervention had acquired a key Keynesian role and the specific circumstances of war were now providing the circumstances for the kind of strong comprehensive intervention which the intellectuals wanted.

It was in the context of a major collapse in house production during the war that the 'post-war' system was in effect introduced. In 1941 only 12,000 units were constructed, compared with 44,000 in 1939; mainly a result of a switch of capital out of housing into the much more profitable armaments sectors. Legislation in 1942 (see figure 4.1) now greatly expanded the pre-war SHL system, providing a stable availability of finance to builders but (to stop these loans simply resulting in higher rents and production costs) controls over builders' profits and rents. This was effected by a contract with the communes over building methods, quality-levels and the costs of production and land. An 'historic compromise' was established with the building workers. Their rates of pay were decreased, but this was compensated by the more secure and continuous work resulting from slumps and booms being ironed out.

By 1942, therefore, the Swedish state, reflecting the demands of the labour movement, the Social Democrat Party and the Stockholm intellectuals had introduced a system of state control and management of house production and provision. And, crucially, these reforms also actively supported Sweden's capitalist economy. The alliance over housing was complete, even if some people (particularly the interests in speculative housing production and exchange) had suffered in the process. On the other hand, the larger building firms, the building workers and the consumers had benefited.

## 4.4  Post-war settlements and forms of decommodification

*Changes in national class relations*

A popular shift to the left and widespread demands for social reform were features of the wartime and immediate post-war years in Sweden, Britain and many other European countries. Sweden was not directly engaged in hostilities but was actively engaged in the production of materials for the countries at war, especially Germany. Some of the main reasons underlying new and concerted demands for an organized welfare state were present in both societies; full employment combined with worsening social conditions, the latter exacerbated by the virtual halt of new building during the war. In Britain, of course, the hardships of the blitz added to the already miserable conditions of many inner-urban areas (Calder 1969). And in Sweden all the efforts of the 1930s and the early 1940s emergency housing programme had still failed to make a substantial impression on the problem. One commentator wrote in 1945 that 'Stockholm has gained the unenviable reputation of having the highest rents in the world for the most congested dwellings.' (Sandström 1945). Again, Britain's large scale engagement in what Calder calls 'The People's War' added to the demands (recognized by many politicians of the day) that there should be no return to the social conditions of the 1930s when the war was over and the troops returned. As Ernest Bevin, Minister of Labour in the wartime Coalition Government, stressed to his Cabinet colleagues as early as 1942

> The demand for homes on the scale we may anticipate raises social problems of the first order and it is highly important to the morale of the troops, the munitions workers and indeed all prospective householders, that the Government should demonstrate at the earliest possible moment how it intends to meet their need for a home. (PRO CAB 87/2)

There were, then, some important underlying similarities in the reasons for a widespread popular demand in Sweden and Britain for decent housing and social conditions after the war. And there were also some broad similarities in the forms of state intervention which, as a result of these pressures, took place in the two societies. These might be broadly characterized as 'decommodification'; the partial suspension of the market in certain areas of consumption and its replacement by a rational or bureaucratic form of distribution (Cawson and Saunders 1983). Thus both Britain and Sweden saw a major extension, during and immediately after the war, of state-financed housing and welfare programmes, combined with strong central intervention over the control of land use.

But though widespread demands for a welfare state were now being forcefully articulated in both countries and although somewhat similar forms of state intervention took place, it is crucial to recognize the differences both in how these demands were being articulated and the specific forms which state decommodification took. At this point we need to turn from general conditions affecting both countries and back to their particular characteristics and earlier histories.

It is particularly important to remember the alliances and forms of state intervention already established before the war. In Sweden, as described earlier, housing was already established as a central element in the 'historic compromise' between labour and capital, and house building was a crucial element around which the economy was organized. The strengthened social and political demands being made during and after the war for a large-scale state-orchestrated housing drive continued to be channelled through the powerful labour movement housing coalition which we have discussed in chapters two and three. This included not only the National Tenants' Union, the housing co-operatives, the larger local authorities and the building unions, but also the Social Democrat intellectuals and technocrats who had by now become part of the state apparatus and had formed their own state institutions such as the Housing Board.

Extremely important again was the over-arching political alliance between the Social Democrat Party and LO, the federation of blue-collar unions. The Social Democrats were particularly conscious of the political costs of dividing the housing market into state-supported and non-state sectors; the pre-war period having shown that 'child rich' families had particularly benefited; gaining cheaper access to relatively superior dwellings. A continuation of this process could have fractured the electoral support given to the Social Democrats by unskilled workers, agricultural workers, skilled workers and many lower income white-collar groups.

By comparison with Sweden, it is difficult to find in Britain the same kind of concerted and centralized alliances on the left over housing. If, for example, we look at the demands made by the 1945 TUC Congress we find that it was only under the 'Miscellaneous' heading on the conference agenda that the TUC was pressing for a government-led housing drive and state control over the land market. And significantly, it was a member of the Association of Building Technicians who raised the subject. Of course we need to be very careful here about simply attributing this to an 'economistic' British labour movement, supposedly loath to widen the struggle out from the workplace.

A member of a building union in Britain was (and still is) in a very different position from the equivalent worker in Sweden; being in one of the weaker sectors of the economy and, indeed, of the labour movement. Certainly, a building worker is not in a strong position to be making political demands. This raises the more important and indeed central point that, with building already a key part of the economy, the demands of the Swedish labour movement coalition coincided very closely with the demands of capital's housing coalition; the construction and materials firms linked to the banks and financial institutions (see chapters two and three).

Consequently, the leaders of the Social Democrats, unlike the leaders of the British Labour Party, were, in calling for social reforms, also calling for state support for capital accumulation by one of Sweden's main blocs of economic power. This provides a powerful contrast with the situation in Britain where some of the strongest sources of political leverage (the City and landed interests in particular) were, and indeed remain, at best lukewarm and at worst hostile to state intervention in the form of, for example, public housing programmes. This situation was to be reflected in the particular kinds of decommodification which the British government undertook. So whereas the Swedish government was able to construct an impressive machine for assisting the consumption and production of houses, this proved impossible in the British case.

*Decommodification in Sweden and Britain: restructuring versus rationing*

Though it was recognized in Sweden in the late 1930s that full-scale intervention over housing (involving control over production) was both needed and feasible, and though the wartime intervention had *de facto* been using such a form of intervention from 1942, it was not until after the war that such a system was fully established.

Between 1946 and 1948 the Social Democrat Party, now with a simple majority in Parliament, enthusiastically implemented the findings of a key postwar government inquiry on construction and housing (SOU 1945: 63). It firmly endorsed the idea of construction (a sector with about 15 per cent of employment and an important multiplier) as a prime means of counteracting an anticipated economic depression:

> It seems clear that the stabilization of housing production, over a period stretching over that of the expected high risk after the immediate post-war years, becomes important not only from the point of view of housing supply,

but also with regard to the general development of the economy and the labour market. The question is more how the demand for newly built dwellings, and thus for continuing housing production, can be maintained.

(SOU 1945: 63, 359)

But housing was also now being used counter-cyclically in another sense; and one which in effect made the Myrdals' earlier *Crisis in the Population Question* into policy. It was now widely feared that low levels of baby production in the 1920s and 1930s would result in low levels of household formation and, therefore, low economic demand in the 1940s and 1950s. House building was seen by the inquiry as a way of both stimulating the economy directly and through improving social conditions, encouraging people to have more children and thereby to increase what they saw as a national demand.

In the future this 'automatic' growth in demand (i.e. population growth) cannot be counted on. Any crisis which occurs will be much more difficult to correct because the opportunity for self-correction will be much less. The risk would then arise that the flow of housing construction would come to be marked by the occurrence of altogether worse crises, if the decrease in the crucial factor of household formation is not replaced by something else.

(SOU 1945: 63, 357–8)

The upshot of the 1945 inquiries was to recommend greater power for central and local governments for securing the necessary conditions for meeting housing needs. And this included improving space standards and abolishing overcrowding, improving conditions of hygiene and housing quality, managing price levels and changing the dominant ownership of housing from private to social. One reason for the active endorsement of these proposals by the Social Democrats was that the political stakes were high. The party had been elected to power on the basis of a full employment, high wages and high profits programme. A 1950s economic crisis, which they expected, would have threatened their relationships with their electorate and with the key power blocs of Swedish society.

The existing system of family housing allowances was now extended to include all families with two or more children and any families whose rents were above 20 per cent of income. The subsidies were based on particular living standards; the norm being that a family was to occupy at least two rooms plus kitchen but less than five rooms plus kitchen (or six rooms plus kitchen in the case of owner-occupiers). And these subsidies could be applied to all tenures, thereby avoiding the problems of supporting particular types of family or housing, as had happened in the 1930s. The system of subsidies was also improved for pensioners, the elimination of poverty for this group being another key element in the Social Democrats' welfare reform programme. In addition to a national pensions scheme, a system of housing allowances was introduced which recognized local variations in costs of living, and particularly housing, over the country. Communes themselves were to judge the sizes of these allowances and rules for their allocation, and this soon became an important political issue at the local level. We might, in passing, note the relative precision of these post-war recommendations compared with their equivalent in Britain. Official 'overcrowding' under

Britain's post-war housing system stayed at the 1935 level of two persons per room; where, incidentally, it still stays (Merrett 1979). And local authorities continued to set their own rent levels, so long as they were 'reasonable' (Murie *et al.* 1976).

However, measures on the production side are where the contrasts between Sweden's and Britain's decommodification become most evident. And it is here that British governments' attempts to direct the economy towards the construction of a welfare state were much less effective, this being less a product of British governments' failures of nerve and more a reflection of the particular strengths and weaknesses of the interests affected. First of all we should examine the Swedish form of intervention in some detail.

A comprehensive system of financing the costs of construction was introduced, further developing the wartime system. Now housing was no longer a matter of isolated distributional reforms to clear up particular problems. The system included supplementary loans to reduce the costs of construction and thus the costs of housing. And these supplementary loans were indeed a substantial subsidy. Interest and mortgage repayments were not payable for ten years and recommended levels were 4000 kr. to builders constructing houses for rural owner-occupiers, 2000 kr. to those building for urban owner-occupiers and 3 kr. per square metre to public housing companies. The size of the loan also varied according to the locality where construction was taking place, being larger in those areas with the lowest wages. Incidentally, this is another example of the kind of social democratic compromise typical of Sweden; bringing about cheaper building by concentrating on low-wage areas, but at the same time improving on employment levels.

Another way of sustaining production was the continuation of the SHL System whereby developers received loans covering 15–30 per cent of capital needed to finance the building. This was necessary to make the consumption subsidies and supplementary loans effective, as well as to give the state management over the whole house construction sector. The Swedish state could now plan where, when and to some extent how house building occurred; the loans being allocated to developers to pay builders, with a range of attached conditions. These included controls over production, costs of dwellings and the final selling prices of owner-occupied houses. Again, and this is most important, there were controls over land costs and housing quality, as well as the technical details of construction and land use planning. The central idea was that private capital could not supply the riskiest part of the finance necessary for the production of social housing, nor could speculative housing supported by open market finance provide a stable supply of high quality, low cost housing. It was central government that should take the economic risk, with the communes' role being mainly that of planning and administering housing schemes. But this risk subsidy also meant replacing a system of speculative housing production with a tendered system.

The SHL system also now enabled the state to favour non-profit tenures. All housing was given a mortgage value of 100 per cent; the value at which it was estimated the dwelling could be sold. Of this, 70 per cent was from a so-called 'bottom loan' (see figure 3.7) and the remainder either from an SHL or from the finance market directly. Even the bottom loan was not, however, directly open market finance; being supplied by quasi-government organizations such as housing credit bodies and (after 1957) from the National Pension Fund via state regulated housing credit institutes. Whereas the Public Housing Companies had the whole of the remaining 30 per cent paid by the SHL, private firms producing for renting received only 15 per cent SHL (with 15 per cent of their own capital), housing co-ops 25 per cent SHL and developers (or self-builders) producing for owner-occupied construction 20 per cent. The state undertook to subsidize interest payments on loans as they increased over 3 per cent for bottom loans and 3.5 per cent for the SHLs, this later involving a substantial subsidy as interest rates crept up above these levels during the period of the Korean War.

These measures provided for public domination over the development process and a high degree of public management over the building process; particularly over rented flats, which formed the greater part of the supply. Building itself, however, was left in private hands. The overall objective was that the bulk of production should be transferred to the 'non-profit making' public housing companies under the direction of the communes, supplemented by the housing co-operatives. This would 'replace speculative profit seeking interests' (SOU 1945: 63) while allowing the increased rationalization of construction and planning. However, this did not mean direct building by the communes. The public housing companies were the developers and landlords, not the builders, and this left open (another case of the social democratic compromise) 'free competition' between different building companies. These latter could in theory include local authority direct labour, though in practice only the largest urban authorities and some production by the co-operatives actually used much direct labour.

The new system established in this immediate post-war period also established new commune responsibilities and relations between housing institutions. Restrictive '*ultra vires*' laws over local authorities were dropped, now allowing them the responsibility for administering the SHL system and planning local supply. Communes with populations over 10,000 thereby gained autonomy over assessing housing need and requirements for housing units of different sizes, types and tenures. The public housing companies became the favoured instruments for positively effecting these plans (although nominally separate organizations they were, and remain, effectively commune instruments) and from 1946 to 1949 their purchase of total production increased from 11 to 33 per cent. Co-operative housing began to acquire a subsidiary role (although RK, the building workers' co-op, was particularly favoured in some areas) and production for private tenures, both rental and owner-occupation, now started to acquire a more residual status. 1949 was the last year before 1975 when dwellings for owner occupation were over 50 per cent of production.

These measures meant that access to accommodation was now more distributed according to need rather than income and status. Furthermore, state intervention in Sweden was no longer *ad hoc* crisis management and resolution of anomalies but a comprehensive system of production and distribution. Before going on to describe how this decommodified system was later used and modified we can now take the opportunity of comparing it with the equivalent British version established at the same time. However, rather than giving a detailed account of the British model (see, for example, Merrett 1979 for details) here, the relatively efficient and far-reaching Swedish system is used as a point of reference and comparison.

The strategy of the wartime Coalition and post-war Labour governments in Britain was to adopt a bureaucratic rationing system, regulating the domestic economy (Gilliatt 1983 provides full details). The key difference with Sweden is that no concerted attempts were made to replace, seriously interfere with or render more efficient the economy itself. Rather, different types of economic activity were given different levels of priority, the intention being to ration or limit the availability of labour and materials towards specified priorities. This was a fairly primitive instrument of control but the effect was to allow housing, as one of the sectors of production with high priority, to be relatively insulated from market forces. A great deal of interdepartmental haggling took place about the relative priorities of housing industry, agriculture, education and other areas of investment. As an example of the processes at work we can quote an increasingly agitated President of the Board of Trade writing to his Cabinet colleagues in April 1944. Representing industry (though not the house building industry) he was clear how the rationing system was being used.

> In many cases, industrial building – e.g. the building of bombed factories, the conversion of factories to peacetime purposes and the erection of new factories – will be no less urgent than the building of new houses. Homes for workers will be of little use unless there are factories for them to work in.
>
> (PRO CAB 124/585)

By the end of the war a system of priorities for building had been hammered out. Two-thirds of the total building force was to be allocated to post-war reconstruction (with a priority to housing) and one-third to new building (of which two-thirds went to housing and one-third to other forms of construction). And the mechanisms, priorities and indeed the housing programmes developed by the (mainly Tory) wartime Coalition governments were substantially adopted by the incoming Labour government. It is crucial to note that at a very early stage in these discussions the possibility of intervening more assertively over construction itself was dismissed. Bevin may have recognized at an early date the political need for a large-scale housing programme, but as early as 1942 he stressed that there was 'no question of taking works over or hampering initiative and enterprise' (PRO CAB 87/2).

One crucial result of British governments' failure to hamper initiative or enterprise was a big slump in productivity, and at the very time when high productivity levels were needed. The three Girdwood reports (1948, 1950, 1952) show that productivity declined by 31 per cent between 1939 and 1947 and, though incentive schemes had by 1949 increased productivity, it was still below pre-war levels. Indeed, even by 1954 productivity was still below that achieved during the pre-war period (Barr 1958).

State engagement in housing production was, then, in the form of simple financial subsidies to construction. The new system was, as in Sweden, established during the war itself, the objective being to avoid the situation encountered by many local authorities after the First World War; many being forced on to the open money-markets. As a consequence, the 'Homes Fit for Heroes' programme had been seriously restricted. Instead, centralized control of the release of capital from a Treasury fund provided a much more stable and predictable source of finance for local authorities. This form of state intervention was, then, quite similar to that established in Sweden at the same time; it meant that housing loans were available largely as required in the immediate post-war period and at low interest rates (Merrett 1979, 242).

But the corollary of not restructuring the building industry was now that the British state had to guarantee a high level of finance to this relatively backward industrial sector. This was managed, but it left the housing programme in a weak position. And it was only managed for a time.

The second area of intervention with similarities to that in Sweden was that over land. In both societies monopolistic controls over land use changes were established in post-war planning legislation, although it was not until the 1960s and 1970s that really effective control was established in Sweden (see chapter three and Duncan 1984). In the words of the 1967 Housing Bill, commune authorities were to pursue 'a strong active land policy' so as to 'allow society the possibility of gaining the major part of the capital value of land'. The 1947 Town and Country Planning Act provided in Britain this kind of state control over land; local authorities being given the power to acquire land at existing use value 'so that tenants did not have to bear through their rents the burden of the development value of sites' (Merrett 1979, 69).

This similarity between Britain and Sweden might at first seem to undermine one of our main themes; that British capitalism is characterized, at least in contrast with Sweden, by particularly strong and resistant landed interests. The main point is, however, that intervention in Britain was only possible in the exceptional circumstances of the war. Scapegoating of landlords and property interests (as visible forms of exploitation) in times of social crisis often takes place in many capitalist societies. It occurred, as we have seen in both Sweden and Britain during the First World War, and the intervention in Sweden in the 1960s occurred at a time of intensifying social conflict.

The blitz in Britain weakened an already weak set of landed interests; the small-scale urban landlord. At the same time, property developers were cashing in on the blitz (Marriott 1967) and making what appeared to many people (including representatives of industrial capital) undeserved gains while the rest of society was suffering and pulling its weight. So, for a limited period of time what *The Economist* (1 February 1941) called 'the pirates' cashing in on inner-urban land, as well as 'the leeches' (15 November 1941), speculating in agricultural land, generated alliances against them. And these alliances between labour and capital against landed interests, combined with the wartime Coalition and post-war Labour Governments coming under popular pressure to carry out visible social change, led to landed interests becoming relatively easy targets for state intervention (Backwell and Dickens 1978). So for a period of approximately ten years a series of reports and pieces of legislation emerged which were detrimental to landed interests in Britain.

On the other hand, although land nationalization was considered by the 1942 Uthwatt Committee Report on Compensation and Betterment and although this was part of Labour Party policy, it did not actually occur. Pressure from landed interests prevented this more extreme step (Backwell and Dickens 1978, Ward 1975) and continuing pressure from the same groups, particularly through the Conservative Party, meant the abolition of the main provisions of this intervention by the mid-1950s. The upshot as regards state intervention over land was similar to that over construction itself. The radical intervention necessary to stop development gains being made by builders or landowners and to make a productive house construction industry was transformed into a system for the bureaucratic rationing of land use.

We will return to British recommodification shortly, but here we can summarize the different forms of decommodification in the two countries, bearing in mind our concern with the costs consumers have to pay. While there are some similarities (particularly over finance and land) the differences are crucial. Particularly important was the active reorganization of production in the Swedish case compared with the bureaucratic non-interference in Britain. And this meant that British subsidies to housing were being absorbed into an area of industry which had peculiarly low, and even worsening, levels of productivity. Furthermore, not only was the Swedish industry more efficient but it was also a central, and partially protected, part of the Swedish economy. These differences became particularly important when we look at the post-war crises that started to affect British and Swedish policies shortly after they were introduced.

*Decommodification and crisis*

The acid test of a decommodified housing system is what happens when the circumstances under which it was originally established change. What happens when, for example, a balance of payments crisis calls for cuts in public spending? And what happens when renewed demands are made for even more cheap and decent housing? Is the decommodified system retained or is it weakened in favour of a return to a system which further exposes tenants to market forces?

Since the construction of the decommodified system in the mid-1940s Sweden's governments have had to face a number of such crises; often pulling in opposite directions. On the one hand, there have been recurring 'fiscal crises' and growing concerns that an open-ended commitment to high levels of public spending on housing and other welfare state items might well exacerbate these crises. Crucial, however, to the Social Democrats' hegemony has been the electoral support of skilled and unskilled blue-collar workers and the lower strata of white-collar workers; a support that might be lost by increasing land and housing costs and decreasing housing standards.

The central economic compromise between the unions and big capital also had to be maintained and the growing radicalization of the labour movement during the 1960s posed a threat to this compromise. It led them not only to stop building companies acquiring a stranglehold over communes' access to land (see chapter three) but to intervene even further over consumption issues, and particularly over housing. Furthermore, the Social Democrats were being forced to intervene by the very fact of Sweden's economic success exacerbating the housing crisis. Big population and industrial movements took place in the 1950s and 1960s, especially to the three metropolitan regions of Stockholm, Malmö and Gothenburg.

How were these crises dealt with? Housing has remained a favoured area for expenditure and public investment, but some modifications were made. Some of the more generous terms of the post-war system were scaled down and, eventually, withdrawn. For example in 1955, a 'loan ceiling' was introduced, limiting the total amount of state expenditure for house production. But, as well as being something of a casualty, housing (as an important economic generator and, with connections to many of the central sectors of the Swedish economy) has also been used as an ideal Keynesian regulator, again offering a *way out* of crisis. The SHL system was still retained and, as a means of managing housing production, it provided the Swedish state with an important means of managing crises.

This brings us to the political crisis and, beneath that, a deeper social crisis, of the 1960s. The increased demands from the labour movement and an election reverse in 1963 led in 1964 to the inauguration of the 'million programme'; a promise to build one million housing units over ten years (see figure 4.1), a promise that was fulfilled.

The crucial way in which these contradictory pressures on government housing policy was largely resolved was, as we have outlined in the last chapter, through rationalization and increased productivity in the construction industry. This meant that the costs of increasing dwelling quality and state subsidies to the housing sector could be absorbed through the reorganization of the production process.

We must not, however, leave the impression of a totally unproblematic smooth-running housing machine. One particular, and continuing, problem has been that of rents. After the early post-war years of new house production pressures for higher rents led to rent increases being allowed (SOU 1955: 35) and, by 1956, rent restrictions were in principle withdrawn. In practice they were not completely withdrawn until 1972, the big cities coming last. While rent levels are partially determined by the production costs of public housing companies (together with tenant union–landlord negotiations) rents are only loosely controlled in districts of high demand such as Stockholm. As a result, tenants often only gain access through the illegal payment of 'key money' in these areas. Rents remain, therefore, a serious problem. And this problem has led, since 1978, to the National Renters Union (a Social Democratic institution modelled on the industrial unions, but representing only 30 per cent of tenants) being challenged by new, more combative, tenants' organizations.

If the Swedish decommodified system has, under conditions of crisis been broadly maintained (albeit in a modified form and with some serious problems remaining) what has happened in Britain? Faced by similar balance of payments problems (Jessop 1980, Gamble 1981) the British housing system has undergone a much more substantial reversion to market principles.

By the mid-1950s many of the gains made during the 1940s had been lost. These particularly include legislation giving local authorities privileged access to the land market and, through 'The People's House' a considerable reduction of space standards. Details of the processes underlying the beginning of the end for the dominance of non-profit housing are available in a number of sources (for example Pritt 1963, Coates 1975, Merrett 1979, Merrett with Gray 1982) and we need only sketch in here the broad outlines necessary for comparative purposes. Merrett refers to 'the Labour government's unwillingness to expand the public ownership of the means of production and its determination to pursue an imperial and world-power role for Britain. These were the maggots in the social democratic apple' (Merrett with Gray 1982, 25). Other maggots (of a peculiarly British breed and inside a peculiarly British variety of apple) were also at work. On the one hand, with a return in 1951 of the Tory Party to central government, landed interests started pressurizing for the dropping of the provisions giving local authority tenants protection from the development value of sites. By 1959 the pressure had proved successful (Merrett 1979). On the other hand, British governments were under constant pressure to reduce public expenditure. The administrators of Marshall Aid demanded, for example, that loans to help Britain's balance of payment problems would involve cutbacks in public housing (Pritt 1963). And further pressure came from speculative runs on the pound (a product of the City of London still attempting to remain the focus of the international financial community) and an insistence from the Federation of British Industry (not heard from their Swedish equivalents!) that: 'we must accept the need for curtailing capital expenditure on long-term capital projects – housing, schools, hospitals' (quoted in Merrett 1979, 244).

Post-war British governments facing fiscal crises were thus being both pushed and pulled out of non-profit housing; the end result, particularly for a Conservative government, being the line of least resistance. The combined attractions in this critical period of simultaneously relieving pressure on the public purse, giving way to pressure from the builders, promoting owner-occupation and dishing socialism were neatly expressed in 1952 by Lord Woolton in a memorandum to his Cabinet colleagues:

### A Property Owning Democracy

Having regard to our general endorsement of the idea of a property owning democracy, I ask my colleagues to consider whether it would be possible for us to advance this excellent principle into practice. We are in my submission concentrating unduly on the provision of Council houses which make a considerable drain on the resources of the Exchequer.

The adoption of such a policy would not make any large drain on our material resources: it would encourage the small builder, who now occupies himself with repairs and could be at least as well occupied in building some new houses; it would remove in some measure the herding of more people into these huge County Council housing areas which become predominantly Socialist in political outlook.　　　　　　　　　　(PRO CAB 1952 C(52), 207)

## 4.5 Forms of recommodification

Our emphasis has so far stressed the content, as distinct from the form, of the Swedish and British states' attempts at decommodifying the distribution and production of housing. The same emphasis applies to our treatment of the increasing privatization of housing consumption and production. Again, the point is not the purely 'academic' one of simply registering the differences themselves. It is part of an attempt to explain why it is that people in Britain seem, by comparison with Sweden, to be paying rapidly increasing proportions of their incomes on housing.

Since about 1973 there have been a number of significant changes in Sweden's housing system. The importance of construction in the Swedish economy has, as we have seen in chapter three, declined since its 1965–70 high. Furthermore, finance for the production costs of housing has decreased as a percentage of Gross National Investment and as a percentage of construction investment. Investment in new house construction and in improvements has declined by 3 per cent in constant prices between 1970 and 1980; a figure we might contrast with Britain's 37 per cent decline between 1972 and 1980.

There has also been a marked shift towards owner-occupation in Sweden, with the large-scale production of the predominantly owner-occupied 'small houses' (as distinct from multi-dwelling units) developed by private firms and investors, as distinct from public housing companies, co-ops and state institutions. In 1973 54 per cent of new dwellings were 'small houses', the first year since the 1940s when the completion of owner-occupied units outnumbered that of other tenures (BBA 1981). By 1978 Sweden's 'triumph of owner-occupation' was at its most triumphant; 71 per cent of production being 'small houses'. But, perhaps significantly, by 1983 the figure had dropped below 50 per cent. Since then a slight shift has occurred back to non-profit tenures – these recent changes being largely a result of changing forms of consumer demand with, for example, a growing emphasis on small units built for single people and with higher levels of collective services.

However, it is important to put these developments in perspective and to look at them in more detail. First, there is some evidence that the position of construction in general is improving and returning to pre-1960 levels. Housing too continues to hold a very high importance and appears to be returning to pre-'million programme' levels. Also very important are changes, since about 1970, *within* investment in housing. These include the marked shift to the improvement and modernization of existing dwellings. Furthermore, construction of new housing has been at higher space standards and with considerably improved energy-saving levels.

But, perhaps most important of all in terms of our comparison with Britain, the general recent shift towards owner-occupation (or 'privatization of consumption') should still be seen within the context of essentially *un*changed relationships in the production of housing. Houses and flats always were, and remain, predominantly produced as a commodity by private builders. But, and this is the most crucial point, the development process is still subject to the SHL control system

*Table 4.3*  Tenure by percentage of housing stock: Sweden, 1945–80

|  | *1945* | *1960* | *1970* | *1975* | *1980* |
|---|---|---|---|---|---|
| State, Communes etc. | 5 | 4 | 4 | 4 | 4 |
| Public Housing cos. | 2 | 9 | 17 | 20 | 20 |
| Co-operative | 4 | 11 | 14 | 14 | 14 |
| Private rented (including private tied, etc.) | 51 | 40 | 30 | 23 | 21 |
| Owner-occupied | 38 | 36 | 35 | 39 | 41 |
| Total | 100 | 100 | 100 | 100 | 100 |
| of which non-profit tenures | 12 | 24 | 35 | 38 | 38 |
| private tenures | 88 | 76 | 65 | 62 | 62 |

*Source:* Compiled from national censuses.

established in the 1940s. And state control over land supply has been made if anything more thorough than that in the 1940s to 1960s (Duncan 1984). It is true that a lower percentage of small houses than multi-dwelling units is subject to the SHL system, but this is in the order of 85–90 per cent rather than 90–9 per cent. It is also true that the union-owned builders and direct labour have been largely excluded from the production of small dwellings and such production gives renewed opportunities to the less productive smaller builders. But these changes are changes in the margins of what we now might term 'state capitalism in production'. This does not mean East European style state capitalism (the spectre so feared by representatives of British capital!) but state support and management of capitalist enterprises.

The result in Sweden (see table 4.3) has been an expansion of the total stock occupied by owner occupiers since 1970, this being preceded by a decline between 1945 and 1970. As a proportion of the total, however, the expansion has slowed somewhat since the mid-1970s and now ceased; partly due to the slight recovery by non-profit building and, more importantly, due to lower building rates.

In summary, then, recommodification has certainly occurred in Sweden, but it has been severely constrained within state policies which continue to be based on the growth of public investment and full employment, on severe limitations to the penetration of loan capital into housing finance and land development and control over production itself. Sweden's recommodification, in other words, is taking place within a continuing social democratic compromise between extremely strong blocs of labour and capital.

What has distinctly not occurred in Sweden is recommodification along British lines where the house building system has been predominantly speculative except for a short period following 1945 (Ball 1983). So the apparent similarity of a recent boom in privatized consumption is misleading. For, whereas in Sweden the owner-occupiers' dwellings are tender-based and predominantly controlled by the SHL system (producing high quality products at controlled prices and with the almost complete exclusion of land development gains), in Britain the land-owners and speculative builders have, at the expense of tenants and owner-occupiers, been positively encouraged to siphon off considerable development gains.

Since the dismantlement of the land acquisition provisions of the 1947 Town and Country Planning Act there have been few sustained attempts to control land development gains or to give local authorities privileged access to land (Massey and Catalano 1978, Ball 1983). And what attempts have been made have again been systematically watered down by the powerful vested interests involved. For example, the 1967 Land Commission introduced by a Labour Government (in the context of an attempt to introduce a wages policy, Miliband 1973) did not change the outlays local authorities had to make to acquire sites (Merrett 1979). And it was rapidly unscrambled by the Tory Government in 1970. Similarly, the 1975 Community Land Act (introduced to assuage widespread criticism of property speculators' politics, Massey and Catalano 1978) was intended to skim off development values for the public benefit. But in fact it received a low level of funding and was couched in a way that meant 'the community' was hardly in fact the housing consumer at all; or indeed the capital gains to be made by the consumer. Of the profits on land dealings made under the Community Land Act, 40 per cent was to go direct to the Treasury, 30 per cent to the 'home' local authority and 30 per cent to a local authority 'pool'. Local authorities were specifically directed to use the profit not for new building programmes but to reduce their borrowing requirements (Ambrose 1976). As Ambrose notes, in any event the legislation was repealed, following pressure from the property lobby, landed interests and insurance companies threatening to invest elsewhere than in Britain.

The main point is, then, that Sweden's recommodification has *not* meant the kind of wholehearted embrace of market principles experienced by the British consumer. There has been no retreat back to the speculative system of housing provision.

### 4.6  Residualization: one nation versus two nation projects

What are the main lessons to be learnt from this chapter on the social organization of demand? A comparison of two forms of housing provision can, at the very least, help to show that some apparently enduring features of a housing system should not, in fact, be considered as inevitable.

For example, the Swedish case demonstrates particularly well that there is no necessary reason for a remorseless rise of owner-occupation and that speculative house building is by no means a God-given feature of a capitalist building industry. These apparently inevitable features have in fact been socially constructed and can be made to change.

The second (and related) main point concerns structure and variability. On the one hand, housing in both Sweden and Britain is a way in which the class relations and the labour power necessary for the reproduction of capitalist society is reproduced. But, on the other hand, the forms and extents of these 'structural' processes vary considerably over time and space. And this variability is important not least because of the effects it has on the people living in these societies; effects such as the quantity and quality of housing available and the costs that must be paid. And to understand this variability means attributing as much importance to the specific 'local' features of the societies themselves as to the shared structural processes. It is, then, the combination of both 'structure' and 'contingency' (for example the particular *kinds* of class relations in Sweden or Britain) which explains an outcome such as, for example, housing costs in Sweden or Britain in the mid-1980s.

So far, we have been using this approach to examine the management of national class relations and the processes of decommodification and recommodification in Sweden and Britain. We will be using it again in the next chapter to examine sub-national localities. But, staying at the national level, we can conclude here by showing how an emphasis on structure and variability can help us understand the recent problem of the 'residualization' of non-profit housing.

What has not so far happened in Sweden is the widespread relegation of non-profit housing to 'dump' status, along the lines now rapidly developing in Britain. In Sweden, as table 4.3 shows, the various forms of non-profit housing remain a large percentage of the total stock. And co-operative housing remains of high to medium social status, even if in some areas public housing has begun to acquire a 'dump' or 'problem' tag. In Britain since the mid-1970s, on the other hand, state housing has generally acquired (though not in all localities) an ideologically, politically and economically weak status; a status again socially constructed and with the active encouragement of central state policies.

Residualized public sector housing has been constructed firstly by the way in which the post-1976 economic and social crisis has been managed in Britain. The drastic monetarist form of intervention has ensured that the effects (in terms of manufacturing decline, unemployment and under-employment) are considerably worse in Britain than in most other west European countries (Dunford 1983). At the same time, the related general tendency for capital to penetrate housing consumption relations has also been managed in Britain in a highly specific way. Owner-occupation has been very deliberately promoted through a series of measures such as the 1980 Housing Act, giving (albeit with discounts of up to 50 per cent) local authority tenants the 'right to buy' their council house. And in 1983 the already regressive system of tax relief on mortgage interest was further improved in favour of the owner-occupier (Crook and Darke 1983).

The combination of these socially constructed central state policies means that state housing provision in Britain is now not simply a question of reproducing a working class in the residual sector of public housing, but containing a possibly threatening 'reserve army of labour' (Friend and Metcalf 1981) or 'surplus reserve army' (Byrne and Parson 1983). Class relations and labour power are still being reproduced through state intervention over housing, but now in new, possibly more coercive, forms. As Byrne and Parson (1983, 150) write of a 'residualized' North Tyneside estate: 'for those without work, common spatial location in reproduction is serving as the basis for collective action. That is why the ghetto, a mechanism for division, is contradictorily a source of class action.'

How has 'residualization' worked out in Sweden? Here also, as we have mentioned, there is some evidence of the same processes occurring; although on nothing like the same scale. And the point is that the factors contingent to Swedish society have prevented this process going to the same lengths. For example, until 1983 opportunities for wealth accumulation through the tax system were also available to Swedish owner-occupiers. These opportunities (again through the deduction of interest payments from taxable income) were a considerable advantage, given high owner-occupiers' marginal tax rates. In 1983, however, the Social Democrats (again acutely conscious of the effects of residualization on its electoral support) acted to hinder the development of political divisions between tenures. Tax relief on mortgages was reduced as part of a set of complicated tax changes, one factor underlying a fall in house prices. This, combined with interest rate subsidies for those living in rented properties (available since the 1960s as a *quid pro quo* for reducing rent control) was intended to equalize the treatment of the two tenures. How successful these measures will be and whether Sweden's residualization becomes so thorough-going as that in Britain is, then, a matter of continuing contest. But the direction in which the changes are being made is the important point here. Again, the key contingent factor to bear in mind is the persistent and considerable pressure by Sweden's Labour Movement Housing Coalition, with the Tenants' Union and the Co-ops (linked to the powerful union movement) continually pressing for equal tax treatment.

Both societies, then, have recently experienced similar structural processes, but the ways in which they have been dealt with represent radically different strategies for managing people's lives. Housing in Sweden remains, so far at least, part of what Jessop (1982) calls a 'one nation' project. In Britain, on the other hand (and with owner-occupation now reaching a significant proportion of the better-paid and securely employed working class (Merrett 1979)), housing-provision has been made an integral component of a 'two nation project'.

> 'One nation' strategies aim at an expansive hegemony in which the support of the entire population is mobilised through material concessions and symbolic rewards (as in 'social imperialism' or the 'Keynesian-welfare state' projects). In contrast 'two nations' strategies aim at a more limited hegemony concerned to mobilise the support of strategically significant sectors of the population and to pass the costs of the project to other sectors (as in fascism and monetarism). (Jessop 1982, 244)

In section 6.8 we will be further developing the theme of variations in the social divisions generated by housing tenure. Meanwhile, however, we turn from national social relations and central government policies to their combination with local processes resulting in different levels of housing provision at the subnational level.

## CHAPTER FIVE

# Housing provision and the locality

## 5.1 Introduction: the twin themes of variation and locality

The previous two chapters have shown the importance of national variations within the international structures and mechanisms of capitalism. In the twin areas of housing supply and demand they highlighted the significance of specific variations within more general social structures. This chapter continues the theme, but shifts the scale of analysis to the sub-national level by examining the local provision of council housing in Britain. This shift allows us to return, in more detail, to one of the key starting points of our research: an awareness of spatial variations in housing provision. For just as, say, the construction industry and state policy vary between Britain and Sweden, so they vary between different areas within the same country. Indeed one of our major concerns is that national figures for housing provision only aggregate and average out local variations. If this is so, then the recognition, and consideration, of local variations is important, because they may well reveal social processes which usually remain masked by aggregated national statistics.

Section 5.2 of this chapter, a county by county examination of housing provision from 1919–82, is designed to indicate the scale of these local variations and the ways in which they change over time. Following a critical review of existing work on state intervention in housing provision (section 5.3), the revelation of hidden, or rather unrecognized, local social processes is then tackled with the aid of two detailed case studies (section 5.4). The analyses of local housing provision in Sheffield and rural Norfolk also serve to illustrate a number of our general points regarding the locality, local social processes and local–central relations (see section 1.3). They enable us to flesh out the abstract distinction already made between local variations and local causal processes. As noted earlier, local variation in housing provision may well be just that; local deviations to a nationally produced policy. Increased council house provision could result from national policies to increase building in, say, inner cities, or rural areas. On the other hand, it could arise largely from local social processes, which might, for example, result in increased building in particular places during times of a national slump. This difference has important consequences for understanding the significance of the locality, although it has tended to be neglected by those who have previously looked at local variations.

The switch to the local level, and the illustrative use of the case studies also focuses our attention on the actions of the local, as well as the national state. This has recently become a major area of debate both within social science in general (e.g. Cockburn 1977) and urban and regional studies in particular (e.g. Saunders 1979). The case studies illustrate both the importance of the local state as a concept, and the futility of using a unitary theory of the capitalist state (except at the most general and abstract level). Examining particular cases in detail also allows us to examine the linkages which exist between the locality and wider structural forces, a prerequisite to understanding how change occurs in any given locale. The uneven development of social relations, and hence social processes, mediates those processes generated in wider structural systems in different ways in different places. This chapter will attempt to illustrate this through reference to the local provision of council housing as one facet of these local social processes.

## 5.2  Local variations in local authority housing provision

*Pre-1919*

Although very little data is available the studies that do exist indicate the widespread nature of local variations in early public housing provision. Despite his stress on national level processes Merrett recognizes that although

> in aggregate the council sector was of minimal size before the first world war . . . I suspect that future research will demonstrate that in specific cities and towns . . . at particular times municipal house building formed a substantial part of total local construction for the working class.      (Merrett 1979, 27)

Gauldie (1974, 298–302) provides us with more detailed information on several towns, and concludes that it was local pressure which translated national legislation into actual housing provision. Moreover, this local pressure was extremely important at this time, since bourgeois democracy was being extended into mass democracy, and, especially after the extension of the franchise in 1884, local politics became the focus for the newly emerging political wing of the labour movement. Byrne and Damer conclude that this

> is the context for housing struggle and, as we shall see, the politics of the local state were to be the framework for the politics of housing . . . independent socialist intervention in elections at this level well predates its national equivalent.      (Byrne and Damer, 66–7)

Housing issues were important for the new political groups. As such, housing struggles were localized and different results emerged in different places, as the collection of papers edited by Melling (1980) illustrates. Byrne shows that in North Shields, despite terrible housing conditions, the dominance of the 'urban bourgeoisie' (housing landlords, builders, estate agents, solicitors) prevented slum clearance on any large scale until the 1930s. A few miles away in Newcastle a different balance of class forces produced a different result in housing provision.

This was more similar to that in Glasgow (Damer 1980) or Manchester, Liverpool and Sheffield (Gauldie 1974) where slum clearance occurred under the nineteenth-century acts.

The importance of the locality in these formative days was heightened by the nature of the legislation, in that it was enabling rather than directive. Local authorities were given the power to clear unfit areas and build housing, without being ordered or instructed to do so.[1] Thus 'what actually happened was determined at the local level, in the local state, and was a result of the local balance of class forces' (Byrne and Damer 1980, 67). But there were also national and international level processes helping to shape housing policy and provision, and we must be careful not to isolate the locality as a causal factor. The rise of financial institutions offering a higher return on capital than could be gained by renting out housing is one which readily springs to mind, as are the various effects of the First World War. The point is not to reduce housing provision either to the national or to the local level, but to seek its explanation in the interrelationships between the two.

*1919–40*

The passing of national legislation in 1919 which gave subsidies to local authorities in order to make up losses incurred in providing council houses, helped to negate the special effects of any given locality – although as we shall see below local social processes were important in determining the shape and form of such provision. Despite succeeding legislation which limited the role of public housing, by 1940 council housing was a familiar sight in all but a very few areas. Figure 5.1 shows the extent to which council housing had become established during the inter-war years.[2] In England and Wales as a whole more than one in four of all new dwellings were built for local authorities. This early establishment of council housing as a significant tenure was however followed by a decline in its fortunes, as its role during the thirties was limited largely to slum clearance. This switch from general purpose building to relieving overcrowding and clearing slums is usually explained in terms of the National Government's conservative ideology responding to the call for a 'property owning democracy'. Thus Merrett (1979, 281) writes that 'the switch to clearance and redevelopment in the early 1930s reflected Conservative thinking that private building, filtering and public redevelopment together could solve the housing problem'. Whilst Conservative thinking was undoubtedly important, since presumably a Labour government would have acted differently as indicated by the experience of the 1924 and 1930 Acts, it does not give us the whole picture. It may seem attractive in order to explain a shift at the national level, but how does it account for localities in which council housing continued to play a major, or even a majority, role?

As figure 5.1 illustrates, local provision of housing throughout England and Wales was extremely uneven in the inter-war period. Figure 5.1a indicates that in certain areas over half of all new dwellings were built for the local authority, hardly the sort of results one would expect from a government so heavily committed to private enterprise. Cumberland (53.5 per cent), West Suffolk (55.1 per cent) and London (57.5 per cent) all built over half their new housing through

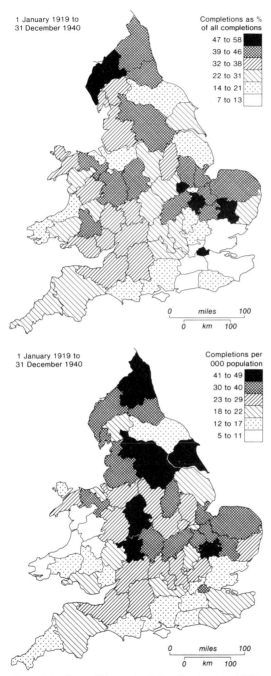

*Figure 5.1* Council house building England and Wales, 1919–40
a) Council house completions as a percentage of all completions
b) Council house completions per 000 population

local authorities. It is not without significance that one of those was a mining county (over 10 per cent of the male work-force engaged in mining and quarrying) one an agricultural county (over 25 per cent of the male work-force in agriculture) and the other the nation's capital and most populous city. It might be said that two of these were relatively low builders, but the case of London is supported by Durham, whose local authorities built 45.3 per cent of its 121,000 dwellings and West Yorkshire where 40.8 per cent out of 335,000 new houses were erected for the local councils. Moreover, these trends are confirmed by figure 5.1b which shows the same areas also building among the largest amounts per 1000 population.

Another marked trend apparent in both diagrams is the sharp increase in the amount and percentage of private housing towards the South-east of the country. Each one of the bottom 10 per cent of counties on figure 5.1a, those building less than 1 in 7 of their new houses through local authorities, lies in a ring around London from Essex to the Isle of Wight. From 1935 to 1939, at the height of the slum clearance programmes, in the South-east region (excluding London) only 35,629 council houses were built compared to over 400,000 private homes, a percentage of only eight. Yet at the same time 47 per cent of London's new homes were public, as were 35 per cent of those being built in Wales and 33 per cent of those constructed in the North and the East (Ministry of Health, Annual Reports). As we indicate below this pattern of spatial concentration did not arise by accident and cannot be explained purely through whim of government either – but nor can it be explained by reference to solely local factors. Our studies show that the answer indeed lies in how these interact with larger scale forces.

At this time, these national and international processes were leading to a wholesale restructuring of Britain's space-economy. New industries developed, old ones declined and new industrial centres arose. This in turn led to a vast change in the location of the population. In June 1923 the four Southern divisions of the Ministry of Labour contained 46.6 per cent of the insured population, and the rest of the UK 53.4 per cent. Fifteen years later in June 1938 the position was reversed, the South now having 53.9 per cent of the insured population (Pollard 1959, 127). This great shift in people was due to the establishment of new and light industries in the South, around the fringes of towns and cities. Their housing need was largely met by unshackled private enterprise, revelling in the policies of the National Government of the 1930s.

But these policies must be seen against the background of industrial restructuring, which was also responsible for the appalling poverty and depression found in many parts of the country. In 1934, when recovery was under way, the majority of towns in the Welsh valleys, and many in Durham and on the Tyne had unemployment rates of over 50 per cent, and some over 70 per cent, of the insured population (Pollard 1959, 245). In such cases it is not difficult to appreciate that lack of money to rent or buy a house privately was the norm rather than the exception, and one can readily understand why the local authority provided almost one out of every two new houses built in Durham from 1919 to 1940.

We have already noted how a similar picture was apparent in West Suffolk, where the local authority provided the majority of houses from 1919 to 1940 (see figures 5.1a, 5.1b). Other rural areas, especially those in East Anglia and the East Midlands stand out as high providers of council housing on both diagrams. This housing was provided in the face of strong opposition by the National Farmers' Union and the Country Landowners' Association, who as the principal ratepayers and the dominant faction of rural councils, actively pursued a low rate flow expenditure policy (Newby 1980, 183). In order to shift this stubborn resistance, central government provided a clause in the 1935 Act offering rural councils up to 80 per cent of the construction costs of housing built for agricultural workers. This discussion is taken further in section 5.4, when one of our case studies will be used to illustrate the types of particular social processes operating in these areas. For the present, it is sufficient to note the widespread nature of these local variations, and stress again that they are often lost, along with causal explanation, amongst aggregated national statistics.

However these variations should not be thought of as a ready made process, with a simple one-to-one correlation between unemployment or low pay, or rural regions and council housing. Such local deviation would simply be the result of a passive mapping of national policy onto existing unevenly developed areas. However the indications are that we are considering the results of a much more active interaction between national and local processes, as the social relations of specific locales produce different mediations of the same overall policy. For instance both Devon and North Yorkshire were rural areas, the same in that sense as Norfolk or West Suffolk. Yet figure 5.1 shows both to be amongst the lowest providers of council housing in both percentage terms and the amount per 1000. We can point, in a tentative manner at this stage, to the fact that there are different types of rural area with different forms of farming – in terms of production relations, land ownership relations and political formations – in other words, different sets of social relations. These differences may help us account for the variation in housing provision, differences which we will draw on and illustrate further with the aid of our case studies.

### 1945–82

We shall divide the post-war era into three separate periods, partly because of administrative boundary changes, partly because of the overall timespan involved, and partly to highlight different local and national processes. During the first period from 1945 to 1951, a fairly uniform picture of housing provision emerged as indicated by the values represented in figure 5.2. Under immediate post-war conditions, coupled with Bevan's strong legislation (see chapter four for a more detailed description of this period), most areas built a very high percentage of local authority housing. The Labour Government tried to limit private completions to one fifth of total output in any one area, and figure 5.2a shows that this worked to a certain extent. The lowest percentage figure for local authority completions was 69.1 in Lincolnshire Holland, whilst the average for England and Wales was 83.2 per cent. In a similar manner, the range of output per 1000 was more than halved in comparison to the inter-war period.

The diagrams do show, however, that variations within this uniformity did

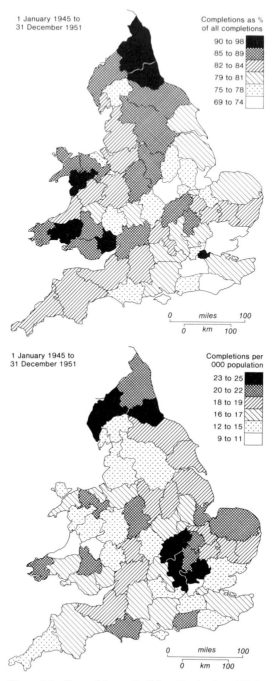

1 January 1945 to
31 December 1951

Completions as %
of all completions

90 to 98
85 to 89
82 to 84
79 to 81
75 to 78
69 to 74

0          miles          100
0          km          100

1 January 1945 to
31 December 1951

Completions per
000 population

23 to 25
20 to 22
18 to 19
16 to 17
12 to 15
9 to 11

0          miles          100
0          km          100

*Figure 5.2*   Council house building England and Wales, 1945–51
a) Council house completions as a percentage of all completions
b) Council house completions per 000 population

exist. Again the most striking differences are to be found between the South-east and the North-east, the latter building over nine out of every ten new houses for local authorities. London also reappears at the top of the council house building list, but this time accompanied mainly by South Wales and not East Anglia and the East Midlands, as in the inter-war period. The position of South Wales as a high builder of public housing, as indicated by figure 5.2a is in contrast to its low performance during the inter-war years. From 1945 to 1951 Brecknock built 88 per cent of its new houses for local councils, Glamorgan 89 per cent, Monmouth 92 per cent and Camarthen 93 per cent. The social processes lying behind this increased provision may well have been linked to changes in the social relations of the coal industry, with the decline of the private mines, and associated changes in the structure of housing ownership. (See Francis and Smith 1980 and Cooke 1983 a and b for accounts of changing local social processes in South Wales.)

Although South Wales did build a high percentage of public housing, this was not duplicated per 1000 population. The areas building the biggest volume by population can be seen in figure 5.2b, and are grouped in the counties to the north of London, especially Hertfordshire, Buckinghamshire and Northamptonshire. These all built over 23 council dwellings per 1000 population, compared to a national average of 15.8. Also prominent, once again, are the northern counties of Durham, Cumberland and Northumberland. This trend is continued throughout the next period, from 1952 to 1973 but within much wider overall variations between the counties. This is indicated by the values represented in figure 5.3. In percentage terms they range from below 20 (Isle of Wight) to over 80 (London County Council area), and in the amount built per 1000 vary from 16 (Surrey) to over 100 (West Suffolk and Huntingdonshire). These can be compared to figures in the immediate post-war period of 69–98 and 9–25. The discrepancy represents the use of much less directive legislation than that passed by the Labour Government during the era of post-war reconstruction. It also shows the way in which the more uniform social processes operating during the 1945–51 period were gradually broken down, as particular localities once again began to produce their distinctive forms of housing provision.

Within these large variations the shape of housing provision which began to emerge after the war was consolidated, in the sense that London, South Wales and the North continued to build the highest percentages of council housing, whilst the ring of counties to the north of London again stood out in terms of the amount built per 1000 (figure 5.3). If anything, this picture is even more marked than in the immediate war period, especially in the case of the counties around London. This is probably due to the expansion of overspill and new towns in this area. This would explain their high levels of building in terms of population, and also their relatively low percentage, since private building would have grown just as fast, if not faster. The effects of such expansion are also noticeable in other parts of the South-east, which begins to lose its unanimity in terms of low council building. Figure 5.3b shows that even counties such as West Sussex, Oxfordshire, Hampshire and Berkshire were among the top half of counties for council house building with regard to their population, again showing that both public and private building were increasing in these areas.

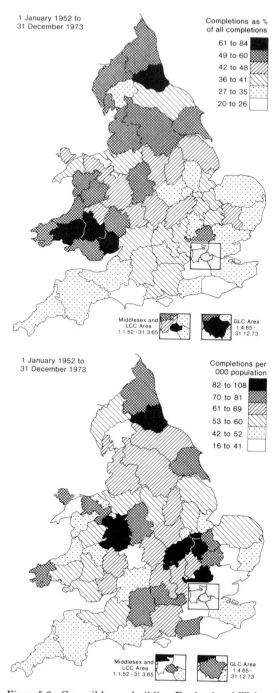

*Figure 5.3* Council house building England and Wales, 1952–73
a) Council house completions as a percentage of all completions
b) Council house completions per 000 population

In opposition to this, the northern counties, excluding rural ones such as West-morland and North Yorkshire, stand out on figure 5.3a but not on figure 5.3b. This shows that their total levels of building per 1000 population were low but that they built a high percentage of council dwellings, which in turn means that their amount of private building was very low indeed. The marked difference between the North and the South, which declined to a certain extent in the previous period has now re-emerged, as the processes of housing provision shake off the effects of the special post-war conditions. One area of little change, how-ever, is the rural South-west from the Seven estuary down to Cornwall. These counties have continually built both a low volume and a low percentage of public housing, both before and after the Second World War (see figures 5.1–5.3). They showed a slight increase in their percentage building immediately after the war, but once this small upturn in provision had been met they settled down again to low levels of council building. A similar performance in terms of public housing provision is also evident during the last period examined, from 1974 to 1982. The South-western counties stand out on figure 5.4 as low builders of council dwellings, as do the North-eastern counties as high builders. The effects of local government re-organization can also be clearly seen in figure 5.4a, as the highest percentages of council dwellings are regularly found in the newly created Metropolitan Counties. Figure 5.4b again shows that the highest amount of council building, relative to population, was concentrated in a ring of counties to the north of London. This once more reflects a shift of both population and production as in the inter-war period, but this time these shifts are largely within, and not between, regions. In this case the move has been from London to 'greenfield' sites in such places as Milton Keynes, Peterborough and Northampton, resulting in Buckinghamshire, Cambridgeshire and Northamptonshire being the three lead-ing counties in terms of building per 1000 population. Aside from these general trends figure 5.4 shows that the picture of housing provision during the period 1974–8 was extremely varied.

*Conclusions*

Probably the one clear sign, and the most important conclusion, to emerge from this brief description of local housing provision is the very fact that such vari-ations exist on the scale that they do. National figures for council house provision only serve to hide a multitude of local variations. More importantly from our point of view they may also hide significant causal processes operating on the sub-national level. To understand the actual provision of housing in any given locality we need to examine the social relations operating around the issue of housing in that area and then see how these interrelate with wider scale social processes. Even this brief examination has shown that it is impossible to reduce local level processes to those happening nationally, and likewise it becomes invalid to equate local housing provision with that occurring nationally. Explanations pitched at the macro-scale level will almost invariably miss the local element and often lead into a structuralist theory and methodology (see section 1.3).

This is not to leave the argument resting on the simple basis that 'all areas are different'. Indeed to raise the question of local variations brings us back to several

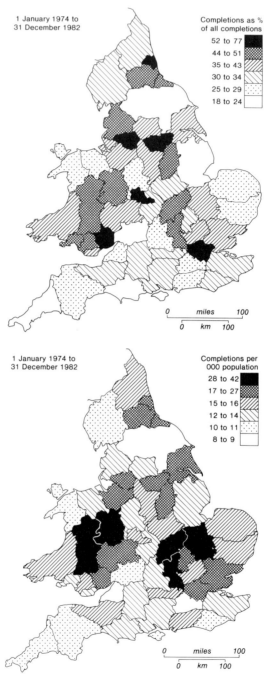

1 January 1974 to
31 December 1982

Completions as %
of all completions

52 to 77
44 to 51
35 to 43
30 to 34
25 to 29
18 to 24

0        miles        100
0        km        100

1 January 1974 to
31 December 1982

Completions per
000 population

28 to 42
17 to 27
15 to 16
12 to 14
10 to 11
8 to 9

0        miles        100
0        km        100

*Figure 5.4*  Council house building England and Wales, 1974–82
a)  Council house completions as a percentage of all completions
b)  Council house completions per 000 population

of our major concerns identified in chapter one. Why and how have specific variations emerged in relation to more general social structures? Are we justified in speaking of locally specific social processes? Can social science profitably make use of the concept of locality? How does the local state relate to the national state within capitalist social democracies? Before illustrating and developing these discussions further with the aid of our local studies, section 5.3 examines the ways others have treated local variation in housing provision.[3] This allows us to draw out some of the major points of issue and also helps to clarify our own position in relation to the more general debates.

## 5.3  Explanation and themes

Although there have been few concerted attempts to explain local variations in housing provision, several authors recognize the existence of these differences and refer, at least in passing, to their importance. These explanations are usually bound up within a wider framework of social theory utilized by the author. This normally includes a distinctive theory of the state, which is applied to the locality in the same manner as it is to the central state. Despite obvious differences the actions of local government, including housing provision, are often explained as those of the centre writ small.

### *Housing policy as social experiments*

One of the earliest, and most influential, works on state involvement in housing provision is *Housing and the State 1919–1944* by Marion Bowley (1945). It gives a very detailed account of inter-war housing policy, which it characterizes in terms of three 'experiments'. Each experiment represents a distinct phase of housing policy between the wars – the initial programmes, the expansion for general needs, and the switch to slum clearance.

Within these phases Bowley recognized the importance of local differences in provision. Despite admitting to an 'extremely cursory' examination (of the 'Third experiment – Sanitary Policy in Practice'), Bowley (1945, 159) notes that 'it has been sufficient to show the persistence of serious variations in the behaviour of local authorities'. She explained low building in terms of 'recalcitrant authorities able to abstain from slum clearance' and high building by referring to 'the more energetic or willing authorities'. The general conclusion was that 'the five-year slum clearance programme was inefficient', thus allowing the differences to occur.

A similar conclusion is reached regarding the 'second experiment'. Again Bowley (1945, 106) notes that 'The second experiment worked out very differently in different areas', and again she puts this down to 'differences in energy and efficiency in carrying out housing policy' (1945, 113). Explanations of national policy are couched in similar terms. Failure of the second experiment to provide sufficient working-class dwellings 'was due to the fact that the purpose of policy was not defined and that subsidies were offered . . . without any clear instructions about how they were to be used' (1945, 133). With little analysis of the rather fundamental conditions of the housing market, or the building industry, Bowley advocates administrative reform as the answer.

This also applies to the local level, where the replacement of 'recalcitrance' by 'energy' and 'inefficiency' by 'efficiency', would presumably lead to more rational experts and administrators and hence more houses. Such a view of the local, as well as the national state, restricts policy formulation to the state itself. A number of reformers respond to a perceived housing 'need', through a series of experiments. The state is effectively cut off from its real context – the developing processes of social relations and class forces – whether viewed nationally or locally. Thus, although she recognizes the importance of local variations in council housing provision, Bowley is unable to explain them because of her inadequate theory of state action.

*Local variations and the systems approach*

The systems approach to housing policy also recognizes the importance of local variations. Indeed the whole approach is founded upon a comparative study of these differences, and attempts to relate different policy outputs to a broad range of political, socio-economic and environmental variables. The approach does this through a complicated series of statistical manoeuvres, based around correlation and regression. The variables used differ from study to study, but include such factors as political control of councils, level of voting in local elections, social composition of an area, rateable value, population levels, condition of housing stock, administrative structure of the local government and subsidies from central government. These are then fed into the statistical machine, along with details of housing provision, and those which produce the best 'fit' are assumed to be the key factors in explaining housing output. Not surprisingly, the results appear ambiguous. In an early study Alt (1971) concluded that 'party control is by far the most important contributor to an explanation of variance in housing expenditure', although a few years later in a general review he wrote that 'the search for the impact of politics on expenditures is going to be a long and hard one' (1977, 91). Pinch (1978) used a similar approach in a study of different levels of housing provision by London boroughs. He concluded that the political variable of Labour Party control was more important than those of need or resources. This directly contradicts an earlier finding by Minns (1974) which stated that in the London context political variables were relatively unimportant.

Whilst we would not deny the right to contradict, in this case the different results are directly affected by the way in which the variables are measured and then fed into the equations, and by the way in which they are chosen in the first place. The level of political control is usually found somewhere in the analysis, but distinctly lacking as a variable is, say, the level of profitability of the local construction industry or the size of a local council's land bank. The actual social processes involved in housing provision are ignored in favour of correlating necessarily isolated variables.

*Local housing provision and housing managers*

In contrast to system analysis, 'managerialism' emphasized the processes which occurred between the inputs and the outputs. Termed 'managerialism' because of the stress it laid on the actions of 'urban managers', this approach looked at variations in local housing provision in terms of those who allocated and controlled such provision. These included public housing officials, estate agents, local government officers, property developers, building society managers and councillors, and most of them were the focus of some sort of study (see Bassett and Short 1980 for summaries). However, to explain why one area built more or less houses than another in these terms raises a set of related problems. Most obviously, by isolating specific institutions for study, and attributing certain social processes to them, the research ignores wider political and economic themes, at both local and national scales. Local authorities are part of capitalist states, and building societies are part of loan capital, and both institutions change and develop as part of a wider context. They cannot be adequately examined in isolation. Moreover, questions of state policy, land ownership and housing construction tended to be ignored, and instead explanation was confined to the sphere of consumption. Whilst research cannot study the whole world in an attempt to analyse these wider links, and must emphasize certain events, it can hope to isolate crucial relationships and processes in its attempt to make sense of society (see section 7.3). Certainly, there seems little rationale in paring down the urban to local consumption, and 'urban managers' to those who allocate housing.

Managerialist work on local authority housing, by concentrating on local government officers and councillors came to view the local political sphere as autonomous – both from local social and political pressures and from wider constraints. Thus Mellor (1977, 14) writes of such work on Sunderland, 'the professionals arbitrating over the future of the inner districts of the town were made to seem whimsically arbitrary and personally culpable'. Although this type of research served an invaluable function in shifting the area of study towards processes rather than outcomes, its neglect of these processes beyond local consumption effectively limits its capability to explain housing variations. A fuller explanation of local housing provision must be set firmly in the wider context of capitalist social relations – relations of power, ownership and control.

*Housing provision within capitalist society*

In recent years a framework has been developed which attempts to set local housing provision in this wider context, and we will briefly consider two approaches. Byrne and Damer see housing policy in terms of working-class power, arguing that the 1919 and 1924 legislation was the result of a working class that 'forced its ideas about housing onto a reluctant state' (1980, 66). They portray a highly aware group of working-class leaders, conscious of the political importance of housing, able to translate this into political action, and through this action able to force the state to implement legislation. The same sorts of processes are assumed to be happening locally. They conclude that

> The point is; the differences between practice at central and local levels is the direct outcome of the relative strength and representation locally of (i) the

'urban bourgeoisie' and the industrial bourgeoisie, and (ii) an organised working class informed by marxist analysis.                    (Byrne and Damer 1980, 69)

Although this importantly raises the role of the locality, it perhaps overstresses it.
Policy output in Glasgow, or North Shields, or presumably any other area, is seen
in terms of local class struggle alone. The wider context is allowed in the case of
national legislation, but forgotten when local provision is considered. This somewhat replicates the previous approach, only instead of a narrow focus on urban
managers we have a concentration on local class struggle. This is indeed a great
improvement, but the way in which struggle is linked to, and mediated through,
wider structural processes is still largely ignored. This may have been excusable
when one considered localized struggles in Glasgow at the turn of the century, but
gives us no purchase on later events when both political power and struggles have
become increasingly centralized (see the following section for examples of this in
the case of Sheffield).

Another recent work by Dunleavy (1981) has tried to cover both local and
national housing provision. He attempts to explain the growth of industrialized
high-rise housing in terms of national policy and local implementation. Although
three case studies of major cities take up a sizeable part of the book, Dunleavy
concludes that local factors were of minimum importance. This is not surprising,
given his explanation for the growth of high-rise on a national scale largely in
terms of the influence of large-scale construction companies facilitated by both
national and local government. He tends to dismiss both local and national
politics, although his own case studies show clearly the result of such politics on a
local scale. Bristol built significantly less high-rise than either Newham or Birmingham, a choice made within a definite local political and economic context. And
as we shall see in the next section, Sheffield's use of industrialized high-rise was
largely determined by local political influences. Having plumped for an explanation of national policy in terms of large-scale industrial influence, Dunleavy
goes on to assume that this should merely be scaled down for application at the
local level. Again explanation of local variations is hampered by an inadequate
view of the national state, and the way in which its actions are translated at the
local level.

*Local housing provision and social relations*

In the first part of this chapter we charted the local variations which have
occurred in implementing national legislation, and in the second section noted
how various studies have tried to explain these differences. We are now in a
position to develop these explanations and to draw some tentative conclusions.
Our developments do not spring from some abstract level of discussion, but rather
arise directly from the empirical work detailed elsewhere in the book. Put simply,
the existing accounts of state housing provision could not adequately explain the
processes which we found at work, both in Britain and Sweden. We were forced to
develop existing explanations in order to understand the social processes that we
studied.

In chapter one we discussed ways in which the local variability of social processes might be developed. This chapter has so far shown the importance of subnational variations with regard to local housing provision. These differences have shown the need for explanations to develop more adequate accounts of the linkages between local social processes and those operating on a wider scale. This is especially true with reference to the actions of the capitalist state, including public housing provision. All too often theories of the national state are applied to the local level, and the processes involved are assumed to operate in the same manner in each case. Yet our studies of local variations have indicated that in many cases the local state will be acting in a contrary manner to its national counterpart and we need a theory which can encompass these distinctions between different levels of the state and the ways in which they act. For an exploration of this see Duncan and Goodwin (1982b). Here we provide an analysis which explores in depth the processes which lie behind the housing provision in any locality, and one which allows us to seek the generative mechanisms which produce these events. This ought to enable us to escape the twin pitfalls of becoming stuck either at the level of the events themselves or at the level of abstract theoretical tendencies. In the next section we undertake this type of analysis, by studying in depth the provision of council dwellings in two different localities. In this way we hope to understand how national policy is translated into a very varied local provision.

### 5.4 Capital and class in the locality: Sheffield and rural Norfolk compared

The two localities have been chosen as case studies partly because of their own merits and partly because of the contrast they afford with each other. Sheffield gives us an example of what have become known as 'Red Islands' (Jäggi *et al.* 1977, Macintyre 1980). The results of over fifty years of Labour rule inside the council chamber, coupled with a very strong trade union movement, and a strong labourist political culture in the city generally, have earned Sheffield a description as the capital of the 'Socialist Republic of South Yorkshire' (see *The Guardian*, 10 January 1982). This section explores the notion of a 'red island' further by examining in what ways half a century of Labour local government has affected public housing provision.

The other locality studied is part of rural Norfolk, that area bounded by Smallburgh Rural District Council.[4] This area was also chosen partly for its political culture, which has long been dominated by rural conservative landowning interests – both before and after the introduction of the local franchise at the end of the nineteenth century. In this sense it affords a fascinating contrast with Sheffield, the city of the Left. But rural Norfolk was also chosen because at certain times, it too built high levels of council housing (see figure 5.1), and this in an area lacking the urban industrial working-class traditions usually associated with high levels of public housing provision.

Our study of housing provision in these two areas must however be placed in a wider context, and the areas must not be examined as if they exist in isolation.

This section therefore also examines the constraints operating on the respective councils and explores the ways in which these have affected the provision of housing. The overall task is one of examining the historical variations in council house building in Sheffield and rural Norfolk, and identifying the social processes which determined its shape and form. In this manner the case studies can illustrate our more general remarks about uneven development, local social processes and the links between the locality and the centre (see chapter one).

### Council house provision in Sheffield: local consciousness and oppositional culture

We noted in chapter one how the way in which localities relate to, and interact with, their wider environment has recently become a topic of heightened interest amongst social scientists. From these recent studies the indications are that the nature and level of local social consciousness is affected, for instance, by experience at work, by local political and cultural organizations, by the existing level of welfare provision and by the sexual division of paid and unpaid labour – amongst others.

In Sheffield these factors have combined to give a long history of oppositional culture. The 'Socialist Republic of South Yorkshire' may be a relatively recent media term, but the notion of a radical Sheffield is not new. E. P. Thompson (1963, 521) cites Sheffield as one of the country's leading centres of 'Jacobinism', a diverse creed of republicanism and reform operating at the beginning of the nineteenth century. Although probably not significant in a wider perspective, the events surrounding this movement help to indicate a very particular social structure in Sheffield, and by the 1840s a large number of Chartist councillors were elected. The nature of the city's industries at this time was almost unique, Sheffield being the centre of the nation's skilled metal crafts, paralleled only by certain workshop quarters of Birmingham and London. The city's social structure was dominated by these skilled craftsmen, the so-called 'Little Mester'. And because the craftsman's security, wages and social position rested on these skills they were jealously guarded through the formation of trade societies.

These were the early forerunners of the trades unions (see Pollard 1959), and were composed of widespread secret organizations centred on Sheffield (Thompson 1963, 546). Not surprisingly the nascent trades unions were also based in the city and a forerunner of the TUC was organized and administered from Sheffield. The city's industrial and social structures had thus made Sheffield an early centre for radical politics. After the coming of elected local government these early trades unions, based around the skilled craftsmen of the small workshops, contributed to the large Liberal influence on the city council. This movement helped to place issues of social welfare on the political agenda, including public housing, at an earlier stage than occurred nationally.

Also important was the shift in the centre of the city's industry to the heavy steel and engineering works of the Don Valley. By the end of the First World War these new industries had become the basis of Sheffield's political activity, bringing with them a more radical socialist outlook, which replaced the more liberal views of the older, lighter skilled trades. This led to the early hegemony of the Labour Party, and in 1926 resulted in Sheffield becoming the first major city in the country to have a Labour City Council. The new Labour council was committed to public enterprise, and placed municipal housing high on its priorities.

The place of Sheffield as a centre of radical opposition was nurtured, fostered and maintained by its skilled craftsmen and engineers and has lasted to this day, although high levels of unemployment have recently affected Sheffield and caused changes in the labour movement and its policies. The city has also become a focus of local goverments' attempts to defy the monetarist policies of the Conservative government. By using control of the city council, the local labour movement has undertaken a series of initiatives designed to 'build a confident, local working-class movement . . . committed to develop genuine, Socialist alternatives' (Sheffield City Council 1981). According to Pollard (1959, 265) Sheffield's labour movement has derived its strength from its 'foundation in class, not doctrine'. This class-based tradition has helped give Sheffield a particular blend of radical politics, and has fostered a spirit of oppositional culture for nearly three hundred years. The particular form and content of Sheffield's housing provision may well owe much to the radical culture briefly outlined above, but it is also firmly subject to determinants, contradictions and constraints operating on a wider scale. The task is now to identify how these tensions have been balanced by providing a chronological sketch of Sheffield's council-house provision.

Like most large industrial centres, at the outbreak of war in 1914 Sheffield suffered from appalling housing conditions. Seventeen thousand people were still housed in dark, damp, back-to-back terraces and another 8000 were living in dwellings even then classed as unfit for human habitation (Pollard 1959, 188; Gauldie 1974, 299). The position had, however, been gradually changing throughout the latter part of the nineteenth century, and early ideas of slum clearance and town planning had been put into practice which together 'owed much to Sheffield's working-class spokesmen' (Pollard 1959, 186).

As early as 1894 these spokesmen had played a major role in persuading the council to sanction the city's first slum clearance scheme, through which 700 people were housed on a cleared site, under the 1890 Act. Altogether nearly 900 dwellings were built under this Act, one of the largest totals in the country. In 1900 the council acquired 60 acres of land in order to build a working-class garden suburb, at High Wincobank, with housing arranged around traffic free squares. In 1907 this estate was the site of a national model cottage estate exhibition. According to Gauldie (1974, 299) 'Sheffield was in the forefront of council housing . . . [and] . . . showed more enthusiasm for housing reform among the voters than almost any other town.' The labour movement had formed the 'Sheffield Association for the Better Housing of the Poor' following a meeting in 1889, a pressure group which pushed the council towards housing provision.

To further this provision a sub-committee of the council was set up in 1911 to prepare redevelopment plans, and the local elections of that year were largely fought around the issue of municipal housing, as had been those of 1908. In both cases Conservatives were arguing for low cost centrally sited flats, whilst the Lib–Labs were pushing for an expanded scheme of country cottages. Although the First World War was to intervene, the remainder of the dwellings constructed under the 1890 Act were put up on the suburban estate. It is interesting to note that the political argument was over what type of public housing, not over whether it should be built. It was also laid out with the involvement of town planning schemes drawn up by the council, and not constructed arbitrarily at the whim of a private builder. Of the nineteen Town Planning Schemes submitted to the Ministry of Health by 1912, three had come from Sheffield.

By 1919 then, public housing had become established as a principle in Sheffield, before the national government first gave subsidies for the local provision of state housing. The local political structure in Sheffield, and the early involvement of working-class organizations in the issue of housing together established a compromise over public housing which pre-dates its national equivalent.

Sheffield continued its commitment to public housing after the First World War, but vastly increased its scale of building under the more permissive legislation of the 1920s. This increase was facilitated when Labour gained control of the council in 1926, but even prior to this date the Conservatives had continued the pre-war tradition. A large influx of munition workers during the war had increased pressure on the city's housing stock. Moreover, the rise of the heavy steel and engineering industries had led to a more socialist labour movement in Sheffield, and the breaking up of the old Lib–Lab coalition. Prior to 1919 the city had two separate trades councils, one representing the heavy sector and the other the lighter metal-working crafts. After the war this split was resolved in favour of the heavy trades, which dominated the new Trades and Labour Council formed in 1919. This led to the early strength of the Labour Party in Sheffield, in contrast to most industrial cities where more Liberal politics were still dominant, and they quickly organized themselves into an efficient local electoral force (see Pollard 1959).

This, coupled with increased post-war demand led to the Conservative council building nearly 2500 homes, all on suburban estates, under the 1919 Act.[5] However, once this immediate demand had been addressed (rather than met) there was a lull in provision. Most of these homes were completed by 1922, and although this lull partly reflects the national picture where a financial crisis had forced the lowering of subsidies, Sheffield had to wait until a Labour council was in power in 1926 before provision again increased. Of the 11,500 homes built in the city under the Chamberlain (1923) and Wheatley (1924) Acts, well over 10,000 were constructed after 1926, and of these only 450 were for sale.

This position is directly attributable to the early ascendancy of the local Labour Party. Within six months of coming to power in November 1926, the new Labour council had set up a public works department which employed over 400 people by 1930 (Green 1981). In November 1926 *Sheffield Forward*, the paper of the Trades and Labour Council, celebrated the fact that Sheffield was the first major city in the country to be governed by the Labour Party:

> *In our columns we prove by official figures that Sheffield can benefit by the elimination of profit-mongers and the substitution of Municipal enterprise based on a realisation of social consciousness.* Houses can be built better and cheaper by direct labour. Money can be obtained at a cheaper rate by the establishment of a Municipal Bank. Useful schemes of work at Trade Union rates of pay can be promoted.                                                                 (original emphasis)

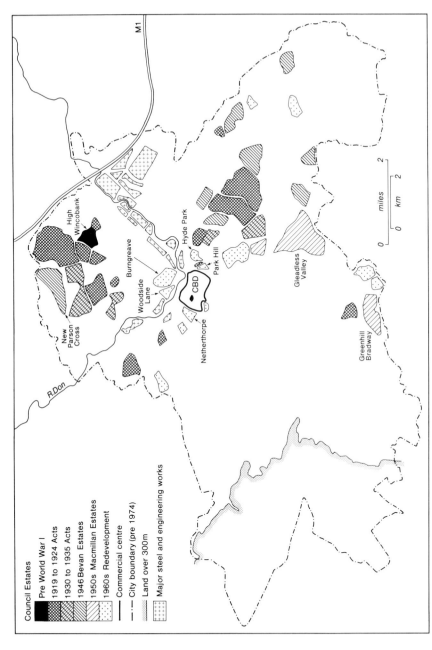

Council Estates

Pre World War I
1919 to 1924 Acts
1930 to 1935 Acts
1946 Bevan Estates
1950s Macmillan Estates
1960s Redevelopment
Commercial centre
City boundary (pre 1974)
Land over 300m
Major steel and engineering works

R.Don

M1

New Parson Cross

High Wincobank

Burngreave

Woodside Lane

CBD

Netherthorpe

Hyde Park

Park Hill

Gleadless Valley

Greenhill Bradway

miles
km
0    2

*Figure 5.5*   The location of council housing in Sheffield

The new council was committed to municipal enterprise and had placed housing at the head of its priorities. The result was a massive expansion of greenfield suburban estates, well away from the grime of the city centre (see figure 5.5). Although the 1930 Act switched the emphasis to slum clearance, Sheffield managed to maintain both the level and standard of its council dwellings. The rows of city centre tenement flats, so common in other large cities, are conspicuously absent from Sheffield. Of the 13,000 dwellings built under the 1930 Act, less than 1000 are flats – and half of these are on a suburban estate. There was also a switch from building three- to two-bedroom non-parlour houses. The former accounted for two-thirds of all dwellings built under the 1923 and 1924 Acts. The slum clearance Acts of 1930 and 1935 exactly reversed this proportion. This was a definite response to national pressure in the form of a lowering of subsidies, but the resultant provision in Sheffield was still largely suburban houses. In nearby Manchester there was a 'major change in policy, from providing . . . suburban estates . . . to building blocks of flats' (Dale 1980, 218) and this seems to have been the more general experience (see Merrett 1979).

In the inter-war period over 28,000 dwellings were built in Sheffield for the City Council, compared to 24,000 built within the city as private dwellings. This means that 53.8 per cent of Sheffield's inter-war homes were public, compared to a national percentage of 27.6 (Ministry of Health figures). In terms of houses per 1000 population Sheffield built 52.25 compared to an average of 29.98 for England as a whole. When compared to nearby cities, the commitment of Sheffield to municipal housing is also evident. The combined total of Chamberlain and Wheatley houses built in the city was 11,576, equivalent to 22.4 per 1000 of Sheffield's 1931 population. The figures for Leeds are 6191 houses at 12.8 per 1000 and for Bradford 5836 at 19.6 per 1000. The national average was 14.5 per 1000 (see Jennings 1971, 132).[6] A similar exercise for the 1930 and 1935 slum clearance Acts gives a comparable result. Sheffield built 13,055 houses, equivalent to 25.3 per 1000. Leeds built 10,941 at 22.7 per 1000 and Bradford only 1,735 at 5.8 per 1000, even less than the average of 7.2 for England and Wales.

Whichever standards of measurement are used Sheffield consistently stands out as a city in which large amounts of public housing were built during the inter-war period. In addition to these absolute figures, we should also point to the extra quality of Sheffield's dwellings, largely constructed as suburban houses when other city councils were building city centre flats. We have suggested that this was the result of the interaction of local and national forces. The national governments determined the boundaries within which Sheffield could operate through various national Acts, but the way these were interpreted and used owed much to local processes. The quality and quantity of Sheffield's council houses was also the result of a vigorous pursuance of municipal ideals by a strong labour movement, with a Labour Council. It was this spirit which largely shaped the construction of over 28,000 council dwellings in Sheffield during the inter-war period.

Despite its inter-war record of house building the city of Sheffield was still faced with severe housing problems when the Second World War ended. Like the rest of the country, building had virtually ceased throughout the war, but in addition, unlike other areas, the city's population had actually increased due to an influx of steel and munition workers. As one of the country's major steel producing areas, this growth continued after the war in the light of rationalization around a post-war reconstruction plan. To meet this influx of population, the council immediately began to construct large well-built council houses on suburban estates. Encouraged by the 1946 legislation, Sheffield had built over 3000 public dwellings by March 1950, and in the next five years almost 9000 more were put up, largely on the sprawling suburban estates.

Over the next few years the city council began to move away from constructing large semi-detached houses with gardens, and included a greater proportion of flats and maisonettes in their new developments. The reasons behind this move will be explored in the next section, but the national legislation of 1956 which abolished subsidies for dwellings having two or more bedrooms unless they were for slum clearance and encouraged high blocks by paying an increased subsidy for each storey, undoubtedly played a part. However, although nationally public housing completions reached a peak during the mid-fifties, as quality was sacrificed for quantity, this was not so in Sheffield. The years from 1952 to 1955 did see reasonably large completion rates in Sheffield, but they were easily surpassed in the 1960s and had even been bettered in the 1930s. Peak output nationally did not coincide with peak output locally in Sheffield.

In Sheffield this was achieved in the 1960s, as industrialized methods were used to build both low and high rise dwellings. In the year ending 31 March 1966 over 3400 local authority dwellings were completed, and in that ending 31 March 1968, over 3300 were built. However, as the faults in industrialized building methods became clear, their contribution to Sheffield's housing provision declined. From being 43 per cent of all completions in 1968, industrialized housing fell to 21 per cent in 1969, 7.5 per cent in 1970 and nil in 1971 and 1972. This fall was partly responsible for a general decline in the amount of houses built per year. From the beginning of the 1970s Sheffield has once more followed general trends, in switching its resources to smaller-scale developments and relying on rehabilitation rather than redevelopment. It has however continued to build a high proportion of council dwellings, remaining one of the largest builders of public housing in the country.

By the end of 1978 over 55,000 dwellings had been built for Sheffield Council since the war, in three distinct phases. Initially, the city continued its inter-war policy of building large suburban estates composed largely of semi-detached houses. From the end of the 1950s Sheffield was mainly engaged in redevelopment, replacing the remaining inner-city terraces with new estates, some suburban and some inner-city. These contained an increasing number of flats and maisonettes and also discernible was the trend towards the use of industrialized and systems building techniques. As these methods declined, at the beginning of the 1970s, the third phase of smaller-scale 'infill' redevelopments began using mainly traditional techniques.

One of our crucial tasks is to identify the processes which lie behind the local provision of public housing. In order to do this we now focus on one of the phases identified above, that which ran from the end of the 1950s to the beginning of the

1970s. This enables us to examine in more detail the processes which led to, and sustained this phase of building. In particular, it illustrates well the tensions taking place in the locality over the provision of public housing, and their relationship with wider social forces. As we saw in section 5.2, local variations were minimal in the immediate post-war years. Sheffield acted in a similar manner to the rest of the country by building large amounts of public housing under Bevan's legislation of 1946. By the mid-1950s this system of central control had begun to be revised (see chapter four for more detail). Bureaucratic licensing restrictions over building were withdrawn by 1954, and two years earlier the 1947 Town and Country Planning Act's financial provisions had been removed, enabling private builders to appropriate the development value of land. In 1955 local authorities were forced onto the money market, when the government decided that borrowing from the Public Works Loan Board should only be as a last resort. These measures represented a move away from the 'directive' form of central government towards an 'indicative' mode, producing 'enabling' rather than 'directing' legislation.

At first however, the effects continued to be very direct indeed. As money became dearer, local authorities were forced to charge economic rents, and building standards fell. Sheffield switched its emphasis towards smaller flats and maisonettes, away from houses with gardens. The 1956 Housing Act continued these trends; it abolished subsidies for dwellings having two or more bedrooms unless they were for slum clearance, and provided increased subsidies for higher buildings. The reaction to this in Sheffield was neatly summed up by the council's housing manager, when he wrote that 'This legislation caused a general re-arrangement of administration and future planning' (Hughes 1959, 19). And not unexpectedly, in view of the subsidy arrangements he concluded that 'Having taken all factors into consideration it was decided that flats should be the order of the day' (Hughes 1959, 22). But before going on to examine the results of these decisions, and pursue the ingredients which made flats the 'order of the day', it is first useful to place these events in their wider local context.

During the war the working population of Sheffield increased from 240,000 to 252,000 as the city's munition and steel workers contributed to the 'war effort'. After the war sustained demand for steel products meant that the council came under renewed pressures to replace or add to an already inadequate housing stock. Despite the inter-war efforts of the Local Authority, which we described above, the city was still full of rows of old, damp, grimy back-to-back terrace cottages. A flavour of housing conditions at the outbreak of war can be gained by examining the Sheffield County Borough Inspectors' Reports (HLG 47/863) which were made prior to establishing slum-clearance areas. For one central area (Powell Street and Weston Street) a medical officer reported that 'the density was 68 houses per acre, that the properties were some 80 years old, and that with the exception of six houses they were of the back-to-back type'.

In the immediate post-war years under Bevan's 1946 Act, the council had concentrated on providing large suburban estates of solid three-bedroom semis with gardens. New Parson Cross is a typical example, containing 2924 dwellings of which over 2000 are three-bedroom houses and only 210 flats (see figure 5.5).

But this type of building had two important effects. First the majority of back-to-back terraces were still uncleared, since greenfield suburban sites were preferred to city centre redevelopments. Second, it meant that by the mid-1950s the city's supply of available suburban land was beginning to dry up. Indeed Greenhill-Bradway started in 1954 and Gleadless, begun in 1955 were the last major suburban estates provided by the council. They both showed the direct effects of the 1955 and 1956 central legislation. Greenhill provides typical examples of Macmillan's 'People's Houses' which sacrificed quality for quantity, and of its 3278 dwellings over half are one and two-bedroom flats. On the even bigger Gleadless estate over 2000 of its 4440 homes were flats, the vast majority of these being one and two-bedroomed.

By the time these two estates had been planned, and started, in the mid-1950s, the city's shortage of land had become acute. Sheffield council had been aware of this looming problem for some time and had already made attempts to increase its stock of building land – although the council was hampered by a commitment to restrict development within Sheffield's green belt (see Dickens and Goodwin 1981). As early as 1951 a Bill granting Sheffield permission to extend its boundaries was only defeated by a Select Committee in the House of Lords, despite being supported by both Labour and Conservative councillors. One of the major reasons why it failed was that those resisting expansion were able to point to areas of open land inside the city's boundaries (House of Lords 1951; House of Commons 1951). This however was only an apparent availability since much of these areas was owned by two large-scale hereditary landlords, the Duke of Norfolk and Earl Fitswilliam. Although 'Sheffield Re-planned', the council's post-war development plan, had made much of this land it was written in 1946, when the draft details of the 1947 Planning Act were optimistic regarding the possibility of local authorities confronting local landowners.

In the end however, this Act worked against the council, for in order to evade its provisions regarding selling land at present use value, 'the great hereditary landlords decided that there was no more land to be sold in Sheffield, that for the future it was all to be leasehold' (House of Commons, 1951). Shortage of land was undoubtedly a factor in helping to commit the council to high-rise building (see Cooney 1974 and Merrett 1979, for a similar argument on the national level) and this experience agrees with the argument put forward by Drewett (1973) regarding the containment of urban England. It is confirmed by the council's housing manager, who when considering the size of schemes wrote that 'the position is of course largely governed by the availability of suitable building land' (Hughes 1959, 21). In Sheffield, however, the position was not due to any absolute shortage, but was rather the result of a particular local pattern of local land ownership.

Sheffield in the early-1950s was a 'boomtown'. The steel industry was amongst the first to rationalize its national post-war development plans, around major new investments in established steel making areas. In Sheffield this created a special demand for skilled workers living in the area, but in 1952 a shortage of skilled labour was reported to be threatening the growth of the industry (*Sheffield Telegraph*, 26 April 1952). As we have seen, the boomtown was also being threatened in other ways, namely by bad housing conditions and a lack of available building land. As a background to this, post-war economy and society both in Sheffield and nationally, were undergoing severe changes. The rise of 'corporate capitalism' began in earnest after the Second World War (see Middlemas 1977; Cawson 1982; Cawson and Saunders 1983). It took the form of increased involvement by, and collaboration between labour, capital and the state; the underlying theme being one of national interest. This was one way in which working-class opposition (such as that generated in Sheffield) could be channelled and contained. (See also chapter four.) These general developments had important ramifications in Sheffield. Local trade unions became incorporated much more closely into national bodies, and discussions over pay, conditions and the bigger issues of nationalization and workers' control were increasingly becoming centralized. Local militancy was to an increasing extent being diverted and incorporated into national structures, and at the local level trade unionism began to fragment from local politics over issues such as housing.

In Sheffield this led to a clear divide between the industrial and political wings of the labour movement. The fragmentation between work and 'non-work' politics such as housing became undeniable. It is aptly summed up in a quote from Sir Ron Ironmonger, who said to the District Secretary of the Engineering Union (AUEW) 'As leader of the council, I'll look after the water and rates, you look after the piece work prices' (George Caborn in *Sheffield Forward* October 1981). These general processes were symptomized by the defeat of the rent strike in 1968 (see Hampton 1970), and can be contrasted to the impact of the labour movement during the early years of municipal housing described above. The results of these processes in Sheffield left housing matters almost wholly in the hands of the Labour Party and its councillors. In practice, in the Sheffield of the 1950s, this meant in the hands of the committee chairmen and their officers. This extreme concentration of decision-making and power, was only really shaken after the defeat of 1968, when the Conservatives gained office for a year, and by the subsequent rise of the new Labour Party left during the 1970s. The concentration of power had important implications for the nature of Sheffield's council housing during the 1950s. The labour movement supplied a commitment to public housing, but within this broad brief officers were largely given a free rein.

In the mid-1950s the city council set out on a path which was eventually to achieve, in the words of Lord Esher, a former president of RIBA 'The first benign urban transformation – a transformation both dramatic and humane – on the scale of a city of over half a million people that we had ever seen in this country' (Esher 1983, 201). The wheels had already been set in motion during the previous few years, firstly by the appointment of J. L. Womersley as city architect and then with two trips to the continent in 1949 and 1954. In the first of these, members of the Housing Committee visited Denmark and Sweden to inspect high-rise housing estates. Despite some local protests as to the need for this visit, the council had by the following year committed itself to two main categories of flats – low blocks, three-storeys high without lifts and high blocks, over five storeys, with lifts (*Sheffield Telegraph* 22 June 1950). The second trip, five years later was a more publicized and extended tour, visiting Copenhagen, Hamburg, the

Netherlands, Antwerp, Paris, Strasbourg and Zurich. This seems largely to have been a sales exercise, aimed at convincing any doubters; by this time high-rise schemes were already coming off the architects' drawing boards (Dickens and Goodwin 1981, 36–7). In their report on the visit (Sheffield Corporation 1955) the deputation pronounced themselves impressed by the 'comprehensive nature of the schemes' they saw, and by the potential of high-rise housing for providing more open space, cutting down journey times for steel workers and providing large-scale communal facilities. It was argued that these latter would make the new flats an altogether more palatable alternative than those built in the 1930s.

Almost immediately these ideas were put into practice. Gleadless, the last of the large suburban estates was a mixed development of high and low-rise dwellings, and the whole of its site is crowned by three multi-storey blocks standing at the entrance to the valley. Gleadless gave the city architects the first opportunity to stamp their particular mark on the city. In terms of innovative planning and design it was the low-rise counterpart to Park Hill, which was being designed at the same time. The central theme of the Gleadless estate was an attempt to place a large scale development (which in the end contained 4444 dwellings) around groups of small 'villages'. Each of these was designed by a special team of architects, some responsible for old people's houses, others for two-storey dwellings, others for maisonettes. This was not only an attempt to democratize the design process, but also to harmonize the housing with the changing contours of the valley site. It was felt that one or two types of dwellings would have been inappropriate for such a varied site.

This was also planned to relate the estate to the structure of the city itself, for Sheffield is traditionally a city built and grouped around very definite industrial village sites (see Hampton 1970, 31–4). Another innovation was the extensive use of public open space, incorporating large areas of footpaths, woodland and play space for children. This can be contrasted with the contemporary private development at Knab Farm along Bannerdale Road, where almost all the open space is contained within private individual plots. The architects were attempting to provide a public housing environment and landscape different to that envisaged by the private sector, one with definite roots and links with the city of Sheffield. They did not accept standardized Ministry designs or those of the private sector, but tried to stamp their output with a definite 'Sheffield flavour'. (In contrast to many other large authorities which accepted without protest standardized designs – see Dunleavy 1981.) Gleadless was the first result of their particular role in the construction process, a role which was to be distinctively confirmed in the Park Hill development a few years later.

The ideas of mixed developments were continued when the city centre areas were cleared. From 1958 onwards a number of sites were redeveloped with mixed low-rise and high-rise dwellings, including those at Netherthorpe, Burngreave and Woodside Lane, in a ring around the city centre (see figure 5.5). The use of industrialized systems building increased as the developments grew larger. Sheffield became a pioneer in this area in 1961, when it joined with Leeds and Hull to form the Yorkshire Design Group. According to the Minutes of the Housing Development Committee (23 November 1961) the joint venture was 'seeking methods of speeding up the construction, including joint activity with regard to research into new building methods, and the exchange of information and the development and joint use of new type plans.' *Sheffield Forward* (January 1962) commented that

> Building is changing from a craft industry using hand tools and small units to a mechanical industry using large plant and factory made components . . . need demands we take advantage of all that modernisation can offer.

The city council certainly tried to follow this advice. In 1962 they collaborated with the Ministry of Housing to produce the 5M house, a light industrialized type initially built in Sheffield before being promoted around the country by Ministry brochures. Sheffield went on to complete almost 1000 of these 5M houses. It also entered into partnership with Vic Hallam Ltd, a private company with which Womersley designed another type of industrialized dwelling. Hallam eventually built over 2000 of these for the council, which the *Homemaker* magazine termed 'the finest council houses in Britain' (*Sheffield Telegraph*, 11 October 1963). Thus, whether in partnership with other local authorities, with central government or with private industry Sheffield pioneered and promoted the use of industrialized building.

In addition to land shortages, the people of Sheffield were given a number of factors to account for the city council's expansive use of high-rise and industrialized dwellings. Among those cited in various articles and press reports were: a need to build quickly to shorten the waiting list; the need to ensure continuity of production; the lack of building labour; and the fact that Sheffield's Public Works Department was 'geared up' to produce high flats.[7] This 'official' list of local factors is not complete. As we have indicated, pressure from national government, the building industry and the ideology of architects all played a role. (Cooney 1974; Merrett 1979; Dunleavy 1981.) These operated on both a national and a local level but as we shall see they had specific effects in the particular locale of Sheffield. The shortage of suitable labour tended to be stressed in relation to industrialized housing generally, whereas the land shortage argument surfaced most often in conjunction with high-rise developments. In 1962 the city's Chief Architect cited a lack of building labour as Sheffield's major housing problem on a Granada TV Documentary (*Sheffield Star*, 4 October 1962), and Clive Betts, at the time of writing the chairman of the Housing Committee, tells of builders being offered inducements such as washing machines to leave jobs in Hull and come to Sheffield (interview). Harold Lambert, the Chairman of the Housing Development Committee at the time, put it in the following manner when speaking of factory built houses: 'there is no shortage of labour in the factories whereas the building site has traditionally been hampered by lack of men' (*Sheffield Star*, 16 September 1966).

Another favourite justification for the use of industrialized techniques was the speed of building. Often the two reasons were intermingled as in this quote from Lambert's successor, Albert Wood:

If Sheffield wants to keep on building about 2,500 new homes a year it has to continue using industrialised methods . . . traditional building can only produce about 1,700 houses a year. The numbers of traditional houses in the pipeline will stretch the capacities of the building labour force available in the Sheffield area.                    (*Sheffield Morning Telegraph*, 12 August 1967)

Shortage of land, speed of construction and shortage of labour were the most often quoted reasons for Sheffield's increasing use of industrialized building. Of course these were not peculiar to Sheffield, they occurred in many urban areas during the Sixties (Cooney 1974; Merrett 1979; Dunleavy 1981). They were, however, mixed with and related to a host of factors which were specific to Sheffield. One of these, although rarely mentioned directly, is implicit in almost all the literature of the period. This was the fact that the development of industrialized building tailored perfectly with the image of Sheffield as a radical, go-ahead city, keen to develop municipal socialism, anxious to harness technological improvements for public benefit. This was certainly the image held by the councillors themselves, and the one they wanted to project. The council correspondent of *Sheffield Forward* toured the redevelopment sites in 1965. He concluded that Sheffield

> is unrivalled anywhere in Britain for its imagination and achievement. This is the new Sheffield, which sweeps aside the residue of the industrial revolution and replaces anew areas destroyed by war. This is the city of the innovators, of the imaginative planners, and skilled builders, directed by a Party who are building the future along lines commensurate with a new society, whose values are completely different from those which went before.
>
> (*Sheffield Forward*, August 1965)

The statements equating modernization, technological advancement and progress with new forms of housing were given a particular hue in Sheffield by the involvement of the Public Works Department (PWD) (see figure 5.6). Authors have documented how building companies were at the forefront of the national drive for sytems building (e.g. Cooney 1974; Dunleavy 1981; Merrett 1979). This was not so in Sheffield, for apart from some early involvement by Wimpeys and Tersons in point block building, much of the industrialized construction was undertaken by the council's own PWD. The simple explanation that high-rise redevelopment was the result of pressure from building companies does not apply in Sheffield.

As figure 5.6 shows, the PWD built over one-fifth of all new dwellings in Sheffield from 1948 to 1980. In some years one in three of all new buildings were erected by the council's own PWD. These figures are very high indeed, and compare to a national rate of less than one in twenty even in peak years. They are even more impressive if we only consider public sector housing. On average from 1948 to 1980 29 per cent of all new council dwellings were built by the PWD, and in peak years the figure reaches over 50 per cent. But it should be stressed that we are not dealing with numbers alone; the figures are the outcomes of particular processes and relations in the production process.

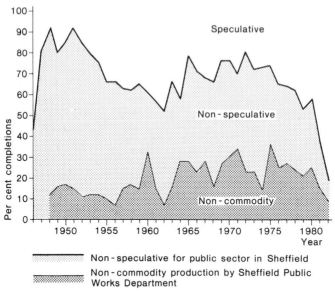

*Figure 5.6* Speculation, regulation and non-commodity house building, Sheffield, 1945–82

*Sources:* Compiled from local housing statistics and Sheffield City Council Planning Department projects co-ordination file.

Thus nationally more than 95 per cent of all new housing is built by private enterprise to be sold as commodities. In post-war Sheffield the average amount has been only 80 per cent, and in some years this has dropped to less than 70 per cent. In terms of public sector housing, the figures mean that almost one in three of the city's post-war council dwellings was built by public, not private, enterprise in non-commodity production. In some years this reached more than one in two of council dwellings. Behind these bare statistics, then, lies a city determined to municipalize its council building programmes. The council wanted to replace private capitalist relations of production as much as possible with those of a more planned, more socialized, less market orientated, less profit conscious Public Works Department. Political considerations therefore governed the use of the PWD. As Harold Lambert said in discussing its use:

> This strikes at the very root of the politics of housing. It is the dilemma. Do the electorate support a Tory dominated society where the money lender and speculator take the pickings or are the public entitled to social justice. The choice for the future is as simple as that.
>
> (*Sheffield Forward*, February 1962)

On its first big industrialized scheme, at Park Hill the PWD tendered a price £170,000 lower than any private contractor, and saved another £100,000 by finishing early. This helped it gain the contract for the second phase of this scheme, the taller blocks of Hyde Park. This time the PWD saved £385,000. The works department was held up by the council as public enterprise successfully at work, and councillors never lost an opportunity to remind the public that money saved by the PWD represented 'the profit margin creamed off by private speculators', and helped keep their rents and rates down. According to *Sheffield Forward* (July 1965) the saving on Hyde Park was 'as remarkable an achievement as any ever achieved by public enterprise'. From 1955 to 1972 the works department built 10,730 dwellings, over one-third of all those built for the council in this period. The use of the PWD was a conscious decision by the council, to promote municipal enterprise at the expense of private industry. It resulted in a particular type, and amount, of public housing determined not by the private building firms but by a Labour council, and a labour movement.

The wide use of the public works department helped give industrialized housing a particular municipal tinge in Sheffield. In the words of one article on redevelopment,

> perhaps the electorate might begin to appreciate that local government can be exciting. That it is something which they can mould to change their everyday lives, that it is creative, is considerate and provides a heritage for the rising generation and those which come after.     (*Sheffield Forward*, June 1960)

The vision of local government as something able to shape the future for the benefits of local people was very dominant in Sheffield. As the councillors recognized, it could be most easily realized in the field of housing. Public housing served as a reminder to any who entered the city, as well as to those who grew up in the cramped terraces of the thirties, that Sheffield was at the forefront of municipal enterprise. Nearly all sections of Sheffield's local government seem to have accepted the notion of forward looking high-rise housing, spurred on by scientific demographic evidence from the architects themselves (*Sheffield Telegraph*, 28 October 1955) indicating that decreases in family size, increasing proportions of elderly people and growing female employment participation all meant that the time was ripe for high-rise housing.

Municipal socialism became converted into a kind of competitive municipal progressivism, with advance being measured in terms of building speed and the import of continental housing styles. Unfortunately, these latter were often divorced from the cultures and social relations which originally underlay their development. (Many of the continental flats were financed by co-operatives and trade unions – see chapter four.) Some present councillors, who first entered the labour movement during the 1960s confirm that the feeling at the time was one of loss of direction. As one of them said to us: in trying to follow the 'municipal pioneers and visionaries' of the 1920s and 1930s, the Labour Group of the 1950s and 1960s 'lost their way. They had no clear-cut idea of what they were doing or where they were going'. All they had essentially was public housing, which represented for them a new Sheffield rising from the slums of the nineteenth century. (Interview, 4 November 1983.)

The peak of this vision was reached in the early 1960s with the development of Park Hill and Hyde Park flats, which according to the council's housing manager were 'a masterpiece of Town Planning and Housing Development rolled into one' (*Sheffield Telegraph*, 29 October 1963). Park Hill, completed in 1961, was the council's first large industrialized scheme and has quite literally gained the city a world-wide reputation. It manages to combine most of the factors we have so far discussed, in an estate which dominates the skyline of the city. It was designed by Womersley's assistants Jack Lynn and Ivor Smith. Both were sensitive to working-class culture, although tending to romanticize it, and wanted to recreate patterns of a community lost when the small terrace houses were redeveloped. Lynn especially, talked of pigeon lofts on the top of Park Hill and wanted the 'street decks' to be wide enough to replace the traditional terrace street as a meeting place and 'social centre'. As he wrote in 1962,

> In our zeal to erase the evils arising out of a lack of proper water supply, sanitation and ventilation, we had torn down streets of houses which, despite their sanitary shortcomings, harboured a social structure of friendliness and mutual aid. We had thrown the baby out with the bathwater.
>
> (*RIBA Journal*, December 1962)

In an effort to recreate this social structure Park Hill was built on deck access principles, with wide street decks leading to the front doors on every level supposedly to act as a point of contact for the residents. Similarly, communal facilities for laundry and refuse were provided, along with shops, a pub and recreational space within the complex itself. The architects tried to enhance the terrace feeling by building the scheme on a steep slope in such a manner that tenants were able to walk on at the south end, and find themselves fourteen storeys up at the north end. They could walk straight from the street to their door, whatever level they lived on. Walkways linked the flats directly to the city centre's nearest shopping complex, and they were deliberately sited as close as possible to the steel works of the Don Valley. The two schemes contained nearly 2500 flats between them, and were both built by the council's own public works department.

They provided evidence of municipal socialism at work, able to produce in the case of Park Hill 1000 dwellings in two years as part of the most modern housing scheme in Europe. As Hugh Gaitskell, then leader of the Labour Party said when he opened the development 'The speed of construction on this project is without parallel either in this country or any other country in Europe' (*Sheffield Forward*, July 1962). In a like manner the work of the PWD on Hyde Park the second phase of the scheme,[8] was supposedly 'the fastest building of flats of their kind in the country or possibly in Europe' (*Sheffield Telegraph*, 29 October 1963). The Hyde Park phase was different in style to Park Hill. The street decks were largely absent, and the monolithic blocks reached up to eighteen storeys in contrast to the longer decks of the first phase, which reach twelve storeys at the lowest ground level, although the average height is less. In a sense this represented a retreat from the innovative design and planning of Park Hill, and the results have been felt over the past few years. Hyde Park is now the most deprived area of the city (1981 Census data) whilst Park Hill still retains the community feeling and appreciation which have been evident from the 1960s. Somewhat prophetically, the construction of Hyde Park heralded the last years of this type of building in Sheffield.

The vision of municipal progressivism through high-rise housing began to collapse towards the end of the 1960s. There was a very large, and public, debate within the Labour Council over the commitment to industrialized housing during the latter part of 1966. True to Sheffield style of the time, the battle was largely fought out between Alderman Dyson, Chairman of the Housing Management Committee, and Alderman Lambert, Chairman of the Housing Development Committee. As one committee was responsible for managing the dwellings which the other one ordered to be built, the potential for conflict was obvious. It reached a head when the industrialized dwellings began to show faults, and thus 'the apparent calm with which the building revolution in Sheffield had been accepted was shattered' (*Sheffield Star*, 16 September 1966). Dyson claimed that Sheffield would face huge increases in maintenance costs, 'making the introduction of reasonable rents impossible' (*Sheffield Star*, 16 September 1966). He also thought the city had been too willing to dispense with traditional building methods, stating that 'I think industrialised building can be exploited by advertising. We should not throw traditional techniques out of the window on the basis of somebody selling us a brochure' (*Sheffield Telegraph*, 7 April 1966). Moreover, he considered the houses to be unsuitable even when they didn't need repairing, claiming that they 'reduce the estate down to something that is meaningless. We are not going to reduce people to a tin can mentality' (*Sheffield Star*, 16 September 1966).

Lambert countered by pointing to the 9000 strong waiting list, and asserting that by this method houses were going up twice as fast as traditional homes. He concluded that 'There is a future for industrialized building and Sheffield in my opinion will be sensible enough to take its share of it in order to meet its commitments' (*Sheffield Star*, 8 September 1966). The outcome seems to have been something of a stalemate, with no reduction, but no expansion. Initially, contracts were not renewed. Then in January 1968 a contract worth £14 million, entered into with the Yorkshire Design Group, was cancelled, due to difficulties with the flats. The halting of this contract, at that time the biggest in Europe for industrialized dwellings, marked the beginning of the end of this era of building. The peak year had been reached in 1965, when 3500 dwellings were completed, 44 per cent of which were built using industrialized systems. From 1968 onwards, they showed a steady decline in Sheffield. This was mirrored by events at the national level, where central government began to switch resources into rehabilitation rather than redevelopment, through the 1969 Housing Act (see Merrett 1979). The 1967 Housing Subsidies Act had already terminated subsidy increments above six storeys, and the Ronan Point disaster in 1968, when a tower block collapsed, served to symbolize the end of high-rise building. These national events did, of course, play a role in Sheffield's change of emphasis. From the beginning of the 1970s the city switched to small-scale rehabilitation and infill schemes. The days of massive redevelopments composed of industrialized and high-rise buildings have disappeared from Sheffield, as elsewhere, and the likes of Park Hill and Hyde Park now represent an outmoded and discredited past. The new estates of the 1950s and 1960s were, however, an integral part of the rebuilding of Sheffield. In the words of Lord Esher,

> Nothing can detract from the triumph that clean air and brave architecture have wrought in Sheffield, so that what was a generation ago a blackened and impenetrable urban wilderness is now . . . one of the small company of British cities which can be seen in its totality, in its uniqueness and taken pride in.                                                              (Esher 1983, 216)

*Public housing provision in rural Norfolk*

The second local case to be studied in more detail lies in the north-eastern part of Norfolk, and is bounded by Smallburgh Rural District Council (RDC). As with Sheffield, the study area is delineated by administrative boundaries; it was the rural districts that were the statutory bodies for the provision of public housing. This area affords a fascinating contrast to Sheffield, for local politics and the local social culture has always been dominated by the landowning gentry and their tenant farmers. Even today the area is predominantly rural, although not dominated by agriculture to the same extent as in the past. The area also has its own merits as a case study. Most interestingly, and most importantly, Smallburgh RDC built a high proportion of council houses during the inter-war period. From 1919 to 1939 it built 48.9 council houses per 1000 population, compared to a national figure of 30.0. (The figure for Sheffield was only 52.2.) The comparable figure for all the rural districts in Norfolk was 31.4 (see figure 5.1) so we are dealing with a particularly high rate of building for a rural area. A similar picture emerges if we only consider the 1930s, a time when public housing at a national level was being drastically curtailed. From 1930 to 1938 only 20 per cent of all new completions in England and Wales were built for local authorities (Cullingworth 1966, 28) whilst in this part of rural Norfolk the figure was over 40 per cent.

This rate of council house building did not continue after the Second World War. Between 1945 and the end of 1968, five years before it disappeared under local government re-organization, Smallburgh RDC had only built 704 homes. This is almost exactly the same as the 685 which were built during the inter-war period. As a contrast, the county of Norfolk had built over one and a half times as many post-war dwellings, compared to the inter-war period, and Britain as a whole over twice as many. Smallburgh thus built a high rate of public homes at a time when the national rate was in decline, and lagged behind the rest of the country when council building was on the upturn. This reversal of the national trend suggests the importance of local social processes in providing housing; in this sense we might define Smallburgh RDC as representing a locality. For the rest of this section we will focus on the inter-war period – a time when this rural, conservative area was constructing well above the national average rate of public housing.

During the inter-war years, this corner of north-east Norfolk was heavily dominated by agriculture. At the beginning of the period over half of the male workforce (50.6 per cent) were employed in agriculture, a figure higher than the average for Norfolk rural districts of 49.3 per cent (1921 census). We are therefore dealing with a highly agricultural area, within a predominantly agricultural county. Moreover, the agriculture in this area was of a particular nature. To quote from one description of Norfolk agriculture in 1910:

> Speaking roughly and generally, the finest land, famous for the all round excellence of its root crops, occurs in the east of the county, within reach of the Broads. . . . The Agricultural Statistics show that in Norfolk 73% of the total acreage under crops is arable land . . . and the typical Norfolk farm will possess only one or two grass fields.                           (Hall 1914, 79)

Smallburgh was a major part of this most fertile area. This had important conse-quences for the political and social culture of the locality. First, this intensive arable agriculture demanded a relatively high labour input, and hence a large local labour force. Secondly, unlike the situation in areas dominated by stock manage-ment, this labour force was relatively undifferentiated, labourers were field hands in an 'outdoor factory system' rather than agricultural craftsmen. Of course some cleavages between the work-force did exist (for example, ploughmen versus the totally unskilled, men versus women). However, these differences were mini-mized by a second feature of the area; the labour force lived in large villages. (Note that this is itself a result of sub-national variations in the development of medieval rural society and later agrarian capitalism.) This spatial concentration contributed to class identification and organization, and this fact was clearly recognized by the 1893 Royal Commission on Labour. Comparing Norfolk and Suffolk with North-umberland, Cumberland and Lancashire, it wrote,

> In Norfolk and Suffolk the labourers chiefly live in villages . . . one conse-quence of which . . . is the facility for organisation by means of unions. . . . In the two eastern counties Trades Unions exist, and have a good many adherents amongst the agricultural labourers. . . . In the three northern districts there are no unions, the reason being the existence of cordial relations between employers and employed, engendered by the system of the labourers living in the farmhouses or in close proximity to them, another being the difficulty of promoting and maintaining organisations owing to the scarcity of villages.       (Reported in *East Anglian Daily Times*, 15 June 1893)

One major result of the spatial organization of farming in Norfolk was the facility for unionization afforded by village, rather than farmstead, communities. The particular history of class domination in the area gave the formation of working-class organizations even more scope. For villages or, more precisely, parishes as the local unit of government, were most often 'open' rather than 'closed'. That is, they were dominated by several manors – and later landowners – rather than one. (In turn partly a consequence of the Danish settlement of the area before the Conquest.) Class domination was never so successful in open villages where several ruling class families were competing for status, influence and labour; nor could the social organization of the village revolve around one family. Most villages in the area, therefore, were more socially 'open' than the conventional picture of the traditional English village.

For all these reasons then – the size and skills of the agricultural labour force, its relations to farmers, its socio-spatial cohesiveness, the organization of village society – working-class identification and organization was more likely. Norfolk was certainly at the forefront in the growth of agricultural unionism, being prominent in the very first Agricultural Labourers Union, 'The National', founded in the early 1870s. (See Edwards 1922; Groves 1949; Selley 1919; Springall 1936.) Although this declined during the last quarter of the century, mainly due to agricultural depression, unionization helped to bring the living conditions of the labourer onto the political agenda. This included housing: 'The housing question was brought prominently to the front' (Selley 1919, 89).

Similarly, the revival of the agricultural unions following the depression began in Norfolk. In 1906 the Eastern Counties Agricultural Labourers and Small-holders Union was formed, after an initial conference at North Walsham the market town that served much of the locality under study; 'by 1908 there were 5000 members, drawn chiefly from Norfolk' (Springall 1936, 128). The first large strike of the union started in the village of Trunch, near North Walsham in the centre of Smallburgh RDC, in March 1911. It soon spread to surrounding districts of Norfolk and did not end in some villages until January 1912, after almost a year of struggle. Later in that year the name was changed to the National Agricultural Labourers' and Rural Workers' Union, as membership began to expand outside Norfolk. By the end of 1913 there were branches in twenty-six counties, numbering nearly 12,000 members, and these were to grow into the National Union of Agricultural and Allied Workers.

The Union remained strong in its birthplace of Norfolk. The next large strike took place in 1923 and was also centred on Norfolk. It had ramifications outside the county as Groves (1949, 149) pointed out 'Both sides now saw the importance of the struggle, not just for Norfolk, but for the whole country . . . "What Norfolk does will probably determine what is to happen in adjoining counties" declared *The Times*.' We are therefore dealing with a locality in which there was both a long tradition, and a current occasion, of agricultural unionization. This was fuelled by the conditions under which the labourers had to work. Howkins (1977) in an article on Norfolk which questions Newby's view of the 'deferential worker' (Newby 1979), charts some of the structural causes of the conflict between labourer and farmer which was inherent in farm work. Disputes occurred regularly over the length of the working day (which in some places only ended when you could see two stars with one eye – although no mention is made of what happened when it was cloudy), job definitions, winter and summer wage differentials, and over pay for piecework, which was paid for hoeing, drilling, muck-spreading, threshing and the harvest. According to Howkins (1977, 223) 'these considerations, working from both sides, created a situation of tension which could easily erupt into argument, a walk off or a strike.' In some cases the union supported such actions, whilst in others it remained quiet. But beneath the history of union-backed actions lay a constant tension between masters and men, a tension particularly strong in Norfolk. Howkins (1977, 228) writes that his paper, specifically concerned with this county, had 'sought to show a certain kind of conflict on the farm which goes on beneath the apparently calm and ordered relationship of what is categorised as a paternalistic and deferential society'.

These conditions need to be borne in mind when considering the provision of public housing in Norfolk – especially considering the appalling housing conditions suffered by the labourers and the fact that nearly all the councillors were agricultural employers, concerned as much about their work-force as with the electorate.

The system and organization of farming in this part of Norfolk also had other consequences. The area had a higher than average amount of small tenant farmers. As we have seen, it was less dominated than other areas by the large land-owner. According to Springall (1936, 102–3) 'Norfolk swarmed with tenant farmers who had risen from labouring life by way of the cattle trade' – which was centred around the marshes of the Broads. Another, perhaps contradictory, result of the relative scarcity of 'closed' villages, in this part of Norfolk, was that housing conditions tended to be worse. If there was no one dominant landowner, the social source of paternalism would also be missing. The Royal Commission of 1893 noted that

> The worst and the best cottages are to be found in Norfolk and Suffolk, the worst being chiefly in open villages, where impernicious owners, or small and greedy speculators are frequently the landlords . . . The best are nearly always situated on farms, or in 'close' villages belonging to landed pro-prietors. (*East Anglia Daily Times*, 15 June 1893)

The wages of the agricultural workers occupied a similarly low position on any national table. In 1910 the average weekly wage of agricultural labourers was 12s. 4d. in Norfolk, the second lowest in the whole country. This compared to an average for the Eastern counties of 14s., for the South-east of 15s. 1d. and for the North of 18s. Going round the villages of Norfolk prior to the strike of 1923, the correspondent of the ultra Tory *Morning Post* was moved to writing 'It is impossible to write without emotion of the agricultural distress prevailing in Norfolk . . . the labourer is worse off than he has been in the memory of living man' (Groves 1949, 177).

One of the chief causes of this distress was the appalling housing conditions suffered by the rural working class. The Land Enquiry Committee, set up by Lloyd George in 1912, reached the same conclusion, and spoke of 'the urgent need in every county for more labourers' cottages' since 'the condition of many of the existing cottages is most unsatisfactory, a considerable number being entirely unfit for human habitation'. Moreover it found that 'large numbers of cottages unfit for human habitation are not closed, owing to the lack of alternative accom-modation' (Selley 1919, 113). Poor housing prevailed amongst agricultural labourers across the whole country, but conditions were especially acute in Norfolk. The Royal Commission of Labour found that the labourers in the North were in 'much better' conditions than those in Norfolk and Suffolk, and that first on the list of requirements for labourers of the Eastern counties were 'Better

Cottages'. Writing of Norfolk around the time of the First World War, Springall (1936, 123) notes that

> Rowntree's researchers revealed that most agricultural labourers were living below the standard necessary for the maintenance of health and efficiency. Housing was still inadequate and unhygienic, for almost forty years there had been little incentive to improvement.

Many reformers pinned their hopes on the newly formed District and Parish Councils, created in 1894. Selley (1919, 91) summed up their feelings when he wrote that 'they have placed in his hands (the labourer's) a powerful instrument which, if rightly used, may in the near future, make rural democracy a possibility'. Unfortunately for the labourer, the Rural District councils became the statutory housing authorities – 'unfortunately' for as Springall (1936, 119) wrote

> The Rural District Council became from the first the 'rural House of Lords', mainly composed of smaller farmers and clergy who were more obstinate and conservative in their outlook than their brethren on the county council; occasionally a radical joined them, but he had a hard fight to carry anything against such opposition.

As ever, material reasons lay behind this obstinacy and conservatism. Smallburgh was no exception. In its early days the council was chaired by the Earl of Kimberley, who owned a few thousand acres at Witton Park, near North Walsham, and during the inter war period each village was represented either by farmer, landowner, clergyman or small businessman. As such, the councillors themselves were the principal ratepayers in the area, even after the de-rating of agricultural land in 1927, and were reluctant to raise any expenditure which placed a burden on the rates. The following observation, made in neighbouring Suffolk in 1927, can be generalized without too much fear of contradiction:

> The Rural District Councils have power to build cottages, but take very good care not to exercise their prerogative. The fear of the smallest increase in rates weighs heavily upon the councillors, and as many of them will neglect their obvious duty in dealing with such primitive matters as village sanitation and water supply, it is hardly to be expected that they will reconcile themselves to outlay on cottages particularly when they realise that the agricultural labourer cannot pay an economic rent.                 (Bensusan 1928, 38–9)

We are thus faced with several unresolved and contradictory tensions operating around the sphere of rural council housing, during the inter-war period. First, there were the main protagonists, on the one hand the rural worker backed by an emerging labour movement, and on the other the farmer and landowner seeking to retain control of the social and political culture of the district. Then there were the real material conditions of low wages, abject poverty and poor housing provision suffered by the majority of the labourers, and the equal desire of farmers and landowners to keep low wages and low rates. (Remember this was also a time of relative agricultural depression, when both agricultural prices and rents were being squeezed.) At the turn of the century a new institutional force was pitched into this landscape – the rural councils, with both a power and a duty to remedy the housing situation. As we have seen, however, they were controlled by the very people who pursued a low rate and low expenditure policy. None the less, a considerable amount of council housing was eventually built. The problem lies in untangling these tensions and tracing the reasons behind this apparently perverse result. Before attempting this however, we must briefly consider the national context within which this corner of Norfolk should be placed.

The national governments during the inter-war years were well aware of the housing problems and shortages which existed in rural areas. The First World War had brought particular problems to add to those already present. An early suggestion was to use the combined powers of the Ministry of Health, and the Board of Agriculture and Fisheries in the rural areas. The following proposal went to the Cabinet in November 1919:

> That the Board of Agriculture and Fisheries should co-operate with the Ministry of Health in carrying out building schemes in local areas. . . . The Board could use its special experience to stimulate the very inadequate provision of houses in rural Districts, which was discouraging the farmers and creating great unrest amongst ex-servicemen to many of whom undertakings had been given that houses would be built.
>
> (PRO CAB 23/18/14 November 1919)

As the quote suggests, the housing question is foremost a political one; housing conditions themselves are necessary but not sufficient. None the less, another remedy saw the problem, and solution, in purely technical terms. According to a memorandum presented to the same Cabinet

> The failure of Rural District Councils to rise to the duty of providing houses is easily understood. The councils have little vision; they distrust, because they do not understand, the government's system of loan and subsidy, and in any case they cannot build in an economical and seemly way because they do not employ skilled architects to design and superintend the work.
>
> (PRO CAB 24/93)

The solution here was seen in terms of using the larger resources, and greater technical expertise, of the county councils in order to build cottages on behalf of the rural district councils. The President of the Local Government Board had previously drafted a Bill which 'gave power to the Board to put County Councils in motion where the smaller authorities were inert' (PRO CAB 63/5/12 March 1918). As we have seen, given the social and political nature of county councils this trust in purely technical arguments may well have been misplaced. However, this Cabinet, like succeeding ones, decided that 'subject to the financial situation, the right principle was that of local need', and it was thought better for the housing powers to remain with the district authorities.

It was recognized that rural areas needed special assistance, yet governments were unwilling to consider measures beyond these technical and administrative changes until 1924. In that year the Wheatley Act of the first Labour Government established generous subsidies for the provision of public housing. It also differentiated between urban and rural areas, the subsidy being £9 per dwelling for forty years in urban parishes and £12 10s. per dwelling in rural parishes. For the first time a government had backed its recognition of the rural housing problem with extra money from the exchequer. Even when these subsidies were lowered in 1927 the differential remained, £11 per house in rural areas compared to £7 10s. in urban areas.

This rural–urban differential was also retained when the emphasis was switched from general building to slum clearance. The Greenwood Act of 1930 paid annual subsidies per person rehoused through slum clearance schemes, again for forty years; £2 5s. in urban parishes and £2 10s. in agricultural parishes. Further-more, in the case of houses provided by rural district councils for the agricultural population, the county council were obliged to pay the district council £1 per house per year for forty years. A Special Act was passed in July 1931, the Housing (Rural Authorities) Act, enabling extra exchequer subsidy to be paid on the recommendation of an advisory committee, to those rural authorities in financial difficulty. Earlier Acts had also tackled the problem of private rented cottages in agricultural areas ('tied cottages'). The Housing (Rural Workers) Acts of 1926 and 1931 provided an exchequer subsidy of half the annual cost incurred by local authorities in reconditioning private cottages. Again, if the farmer or landowner would not act unaided the government would pay him to do so.

The 1935 Housing Act continued to favour rural areas. The Act was aimed at the relief of overcrowding and where new houses were provided to reduce over-crowding amongst agricultural workers a subsidy of £2 to £8 per dwelling per year for forty years could be given. The only other cases available for subsidy were for the building of flats, and this was restricted to a maximum of £5 per house per year to those municipalities unable to bear the rates burden. If the maximum amount was taken for the housing of agricultural workers, it amounted to no less than 80 per cent of the cost of the dwelling. The rural housing question must have been quite pressing, considering that a government supposedly committed to private enterprise and private sector house building was prepared to give an 80 per cent subsidy to Conservative local authorities to provide council houses. Governments of all political shades therefore intervened in both the public and the private sector, in an effort to relieve the rural housing problem. The extra subsidies given to rural areas, and for rehousing agricultural labourers, are testi-mony to the appalling housing conditions faced by the rural worker – and to the political problems these presented. We will now turn more directly back to our case study, to see how these national directives interacted with the local tensions described earlier. In building a relatively large number of council houses, was Smallburgh RDC merely reflecting national legislation, or can we see local pro-cesses at work?

We have already seen that, for an area of its size and population, this part of rural Norfolk built a large number of council houses between the wars. The fact that this area was amongst the most prolific builders of all rural districts is confirmed by an examination of its pre-First World War record. On the eve of the war in 1914 the Medical Officer of Health for the area noted that 'practically every parish in the district requires more and better cottages' (Smallburgh RDC,

Medical Officer of Health Annual Reports). He had stated in 1907 and 1908 that many cottages would be condemned 'but for lack of an alternative', and in 1909 that because of this labourers were forced to live in 'cottages almost unfit for human habitation'. A particularly local factor contributing to this situation was the emergence at this time of the Norfolk Broads as a holiday centre for the rich. Thus the Medical Officer of Health wrote in 1910 of the

> scarcity of suitable dwellings for large families in some parishes of the District, particularly in those parishes situated in and near the locality of the Broads, where in recent years a number of cottages previously occupied by the working class are now used as summer residences.

The advent of tourism on and around the Broads only added to the housing problems of an already deficient area. The council was, however, to take steps to ameliorate these conditions before the war even started. In 1911 twelve cottages were built in two villages, followed by six more in 1912 and 1913, under the measures contained in the 1890 Act. At the time the Medical Officer of Health commented that

> If only blocks like these could be erected in every village where wanted, and let at £5 to £5 10s. per annum, the labourer would have little case for complaint as to his housing accommodation. But I fear this wish is Utopian.

This wish is still Utopian today, but none the less Smallburgh had taken some minor steps in this direction as early as 1911. Where did this Utopianism come from? Complaints over housing were at this time being strongly voiced by the Eastern Counties Agricultural Labourers' Union. Every one of their Annual General Meetings contained a resolution on housing. For instance in 1911 the following recommendations were made:

> That the Executive use their influence with the Farmers Federation, to secure for agricultural labourers the following improvements in their con-
> dition of life (1) half holiday on Saturday and a general raise in wages (2) Better Housing Conditions.                    (ECU, Minutes of AGM 1911)

Housing was high on their list of priorities and to some extent they succeeded in forcing the RDC to build the pre-First World War cottages. Very few dwellings were built under the 1890 Act even by large towns and cities. For its provisions to be used by a rural district council was almost unheard of. As the Medical Officer of Health stated in 1911, 'It was gratifying for me to be able to prepare the plans . . . especially as I believe my council were the first in any Rural District to build under the new Housing Act'. We are considering an area in which the conditions were so bad, and the protests so loud, that action was taken by the local authority which predates public housing provision in any other rural part of the country.

These few houses, however significant as a social indicator, made little impact on the scale of the housing problem in the area, and this was soon to be worsened by the return of ex-servicemen to an area with virtually no wartime building. In 1917 the District had received a circular from the Local Government Board enquiring about the likely post-war housing needs. After receiving replies from most parishes it was decided that 'about 100 houses would be required in the whole district' (Smallburgh RDC Minutes, 2 October 1917), but rather uncommittedly the council decided this 'depended upon what financial assistance would be given by the government'. After more correspondence in which the Local Government Board informed the council it could not wait until after the January 1919 election, because 'there was an urgent need for working-class houses in the district' (Smallburgh RDC Minutes, 21 January 1919), the council decided it needed 142 houses to meet the demand. By the end of 1919, after visits by the Sanitary Inspector to most parishes this number had risen to '250 homes at least' (Inspector's Report 1919). To meet this need the 'Council propose to build 230 and estimate that 20 will be built by private persons', an indication of the relative importance attached to each sector. Interestingly, the Inspector wrote separately to those parishes 'practically all owned by one landowner' to enquire whether they would meet the housing needs in their parishes. One such landowner present at the Housing Committee stated 'that no extra houses were needed at Westwick (almost all owned by him), one cottage being empty at the present time' (Housing Committee Minutes, 4 November 1919). Although we might perhaps expect landowners to play down the housing problem (and note that this one stressed quantity rather than quality, rents or eligibility), this does suggest that the contrast between the more numerous open villages – where landlords were profit maximizers rather than paternalists – and the closed villages persisted.

Thus after some pressure from the Local Government Board, coupled with visits to each parish and pleas from individual parish councils and local voluntary bodies (such as the Women's Institute), the council decided to more than double its original estimate of public housing needs (Smallburgh RDC Minutes, 21 January 1919, 10 June 1919). When it came to put these plans into operation the Housing Commissioners in Whitehall were as forceful as the Local Government Board, but not as helpful. Parishes for the initial schemes were chosen partly on housing need criteria but also partly on the availability of suitable land at a suitable price. Several times the Housing Commissioners forced a change of site onto the council (Smallburgh RDC Minutes, 7 October 1919). They also asked the council for the number of schemes proposed for the next two years, and their expected completion dates. The council replied

> that it is impossible to fix a date for completion of the scheme, or even to state definitely the number of houses to be erected this year, as the results attained would largely depend upon whether the necessary materials were available as required, and there was also the labour question to consider.
>
> (Smallburgh RDC Minutes, 11 May 1920)

They nevertheless decided about twenty houses could be erected under favourable conditions. The council was extremely worried about 'shortage' of labour, although clearly this must partly have resulted from an inability, or unwillingness, to pay higher than the very low agricultural rates. None the less, they continued to attempt to build. In June 1920 they even went so far as to borrow money privately to enable a scheme to be started on time (permission to borrow a public loan having been delayed). This was because the builders 'were very anxious to commence work as early as possible and delay might result in the builders seeking other work' (Smallburgh RDC Minutes, 8 June 1920). Despite this somewhat unusual step, the Housing Commissioners were not satisfied that twenty houses represented a reasonable target, telling the council instead that eighty would be more adequate. In the end local factors prevailed, and the supposed scarcity of labour meant that only twelve new houses were erected in 1920, with a further thirty-two under construction. This still left an estimated shortage of 200 (Inspector's Report 1920). Trouble obtaining loan sanction continued, and at one stage in 1920 the council wrote letters to 'prominent residents in the District with a view to obtaining amounts required' (Smallburgh RDC Minutes, 8 June 1920) and also approached various friendly societies. It would seem from these efforts as if the council did genuinely try to raise the money to finance housing schemes. 'Scarcity of labour', although perhaps unreal in economic terms, was not just an excuse to maintain a low expenditure/low rate policy. But low wages were to continue.

This is also borne out by the fact that Smallburgh had endless arguments over the rents which they charged, with the Ministry of Health constantly trying to raise the rents and Smallburgh trying to lower them. This meant a heavier burden on the rates, but also lower pressure on wages. They also applied a rent differential between agricultural labourers and other workers, the rents for the initial houses being 5s. per week for the former and 6s. 6d. per week for the latter. Again, the Housing Commissioners questioned this policy, asking for 6s. 6d. for all houses. This was after they had written to the council calling for evidence of wages paid in the district. Once more however, Smallburgh succeeded in over-ruling their objections and continued to let at differential rents. However, the council was not as philanthropic as this might seem. Often there were far more applicants in any one village than there were houses available and in almost every case those who could pay 6s. 6d. were given the tenancy rather than agricultural labourers who could only afford 5s.

The council was not always able to disregard the wishes of the Ministry. In June 1923 Smallburgh had asked parishes for an estimation of their housing needs. The replies indicated that about seventy houses were needed (Smallburgh RDC Minutes, 3 July 1923) and the Housing Committee agreed that this was a 'real need' and authorized the drawing up of plans and tenders for several parishes. However, in September 1923 the council 'decided not to recommend acceptance of any tenders at present, but to first ascertain what houses were likely to be erected by private enterprise with the aid of a subsidy' (Smallburgh RDC Minutes, 25 September 1923). The following month the council authorized the Housing Committee to sell any portion of the sites it had bought 'for the express purpose of erection of houses thereon by private enterprise' (Smallburgh RDC Minutes, 23 October 1923). This switch of emphasis was the direct result of the 1923 Housing Act, which permitted local authorities to build houses only if they could prove that this was preferable to private enterprise. Private enterprise builders received the same subsidy as local authorities under the Act and the Ministry asked for information 'particularly on the question of whether the council are satisfied that the amount of assistance approved is still the minimum required to induce builders to proceed with the erection of houses'. In other words if more subsidy was needed to 'induce' private enterprise to build houses, the government would provide it.

Less than a year later the Sanitary Inspector was being requested 'to go very carefully into the housing requirements in various parishes and submit a statement as early as possible' (Smallburgh RDC Minutes, 23 September 1924) and by February 1925 the council had submitted a scheme for fifty council houses to the Ministry. The switch was once more engineered by a change of central policy, this time in the form of the 1924 Wheatley Act which encouraged council building. The Ministry approved forty-six of these houses and building began in the summer of that year in parishes where the council already owned land. Again we can see how local factors, such as the ownership of land, intermeshed with national changes to produce the actual form of housing provision in the locality. The availability of land for public sector building, a result of previous pressures on the council to answer the housing problem, was to be crucial for future output.

The Wheatley Act was to be the mainspring of the council's housing programme. Of the 685 houses constructed during the inter-war period, over 60 per cent, 412, were built under this Act. At first the going was slow, due to labour shortages and by the end of 1926 'only 28 (houses) have been completed, owing to the various contractors having a lot of work in hand' (Sanitary Inspector's Report 1926). Although this was overcome in subsequent years, and building levels reached the hundred mark, the processes of construction were never very smooth, and sometimes seem almost haphazard. These were especially affected by considerations regarding land. Quite often the houses would be put up wherever there was land available at the right price, regardless of need in that village (Smallburgh RDC Minutes, 3 May 1927). Even if the site remained in the village originally identified for house building on need criteria, the number of houses built was often dependent upon the size of land purchased. Rather than fixing the number of houses and then looking for a suitable site, the council preferred to build on existing sites, whatever their size and situation.

Despite these methods, the council did seem to be gradually overcoming the housing problem. At the end of 1928 the Sanitary Inspector was able to report that the 'housing question is not in my opinion as acute as in previous years'. However, at the beginning of the 1930s the depression began to bite. By the end of 1930 many farm workers were being laid off and rents were being lowered to 3s. a week in an effort to meet needs. In his report for 1932 the Inspector wrote that

> the past year has been a very serious one for this agricultural district. Many of the skilled agricultural workers have been unemployed and forced to apply to the council for relief. It is difficult to get repairs carried out, rents being roughly 2s. 6d. a week.

By 1935 the picture had not changed. The report noted that 'the housing situation is still very acute' and pertinently pointed out that 'it does not appear that any help can be expected from the government to erect cottages, other than that to replace existing cottages'. By the next year the situation had become so bad, that the council were considering the erection of non-subsidized cottages despite 'knowing as they do that the rental to be expected from these will not cover working expenses' (Sanitary Inspector's Report 1936). The situation had not arisen for lack of trying for in the same report the Inspector was able to congratulate the council for reconstructing more cottages under the Rural Workers Act than any other authority in Norfolk. National figures show the district to be not only at the top of the Norfolk table, but also to be amongst the highest users of these powers in the country. (Ministry of Health, Annual Report 1936.)

The council was even to build seventy-seven houses without subsidy in the last few years of the 1930s, more than it built with subsidy under either the 1919 Addison Act, the 1923 Chamberlain Act, or the slum clearance Acts. Severe local conditions were forcing the council into providing public housing, even when the government nationally was refusing to switch resources to public housing. In an effort to change central government's stance Smallburgh RDC sent the following resolution to the Ministry of Health:

> It is resolved that this council, having considered the question of the provision of houses at an economic rent is of the opinion that such houses cannot be provided for the agricultural community at an inclusive rental within the means of the lower paid wage earners.
>
> In order to assist the rural Authorities to adequately meet the housing needs in their districts, this council strongly urges the Ministry of Health to strongly consider the reintroduction of the Exchequer contributions payable under the 1924 Housing Act, which would result in the necessary houses being provided at inclusive rentals within the means of the workers concerned.                    (Housing Committee Minutes, 31 March 1936)

Not unexpectedly, this proposal made no apparent impact upon national government. None the less, it indicates the type of problems faced by a particular rural locality trying to meet its housing needs during a time of agricultural depression. These were illustrated further in the following year, 1937, when the council received a petition from the labourers of one village demanding 'the erection of council houses' (Housing Committee Minutes, 2 March 1937). The next year some houses were built in their village, indicating that the council could be pushed into action, against central government's wishes, by specific local demands and local circumstances.

As we have noted, these demands and circumstances led to the building of a high proportion of council dwellings in Smallburgh RDC during the inter-war years. This achievement took place in a rural area dominated socially and politically by its landowners and farmers. Yet in several senses, the results reached represented a good compromise between the different groups of social forces operating in the area. It was hard for the rural bourgeoisie to ignore the issues of poverty and poor housing, especially when faced with a discontented, sullen and hungry labour force. Moreover, this labour force was organized in trade union terms, and was beginning to vote Labour. Given this, the farmers were not too adverse to the building of council houses, since the agricultural labourers could never have afforded private dwellings on their low wages. This also meant that the cost of reproducing labour power was now being met partly by the social wage, rather than wholly by the work wage. For the owners and managers it was far better that higher housing standards were paid for by the ratepayers in general, and by the taxpayer nationally, than for these to have been met by direct wage increases. The farmer may have lost some social control over the labourers if they moved out of tied accommodation, but the most valuable members of his work-force, such as the foreman and stockman, still tended to live close to the farm often remaining in tied cottages. These conclusions seem to match those of the landowners in charge of this particular District Council, as is indicated by their willingness to provide council homes, even unsubsidized, during the inter-war period.

### Conclusions: centre and locality in Sheffield and Norfolk

Our two case studies have served to illustrate some of the more general themes we identified in the opening chapter. In particular they have shown the importance of those local social processes which operate around the provision of public housing, and we can begin to appreciate how the variations identified in section 5.2 are reached in any given area. For instance in Sheffield the strength and traditions of the labour movement, coupled with its early and continued occu-pation of the council chamber, led to a sustained commitment to build council housing. Yet this commitment was shaped and fashioned by a number of other local processes. These included the nature of land ownership in Sheffield, which largely determined available building land and thus helped determine also the type and density of dwellings. The continued growth of the local economy played a role in causing the council to adopt faster building techniques in an effort to meet sustained need. We were also able to appreciate the effect of the councils' officers, especially its architects, upon the nature of the city's housing stock. Their influence enabled the council to continue to build high levels of public housing even when the sector was in decline nationally.

In Norfolk the particular nature of farming in this part of East Anglia contri-buted to a certain type of housing conditions. It also contributed to the early unionization of the farm labourer, which in turn promoted poor rural housing conditions as a political issue. As in Sheffield local land ownership helped deter-mine public housing provision, and lack of land often caused the council to postpone or even abandon its planned schemes. Again, social relations in the local workplace – the level of wages as well as unionization – were important. But it is not enough for us to provide a litany of local factors. The two local studies also indicated the way in which these interlink with, and are constrained by, wider social forces.

National housing policy, for instance, provided the limits within which both localities had to work. In Sheffield the beginning and end of its industrialized high-rise programme can be traced to national government Acts, which in 1956 increased subsidies and in 1967 decreased them for this type of building. Norfolk also shows the importance of central parameters. Its council house building only began in earnest after 1924 when the Wheatley Act introduced higher subsidies for rural areas, and the year before it had been forced to halt its planned pro-gramme when the Chamberlain Act switched resources to the private sector.

None the less, national policy was not wholly determinant. Similarly, the *way* in which the opportunities and limits of national policy were interpreted locally was vital. Smallburgh used the 1924 Act to build many houses, other – ostensibly similar – areas did not.

We are also able to appreciate the way in which wider economic factors helped shape the localities' housing provision. The restructuring and nationalization of the post-war British steel industry directly affected Sheffield's housing needs, as did the severe agricultural depression of the 1930s in Norfolk. But the aim has not been to assert the primacy of either the local, or the national, in an explanation of public housing provision in the two localities. Rather, we have tried to show how a causal explanation must link the local forms of social relations with those operating on a wider scale. In this manner through the illustrations provided by our two case studies, we can begin to gain a leverage on those processes lying behind the local provision, and the local variation, of council housing.

## 5.5  Concluding comments: variability, social processes and the locality

This chapter has switched the focus of study from the national to the local level. This switch should not imply that we see a sharp break between the two. Indeed, on the contrary, we have been arguing for a greater linkage between the two levels of analysis, and this chapter has served to reinforce this need. Chapters three and four demonstrated the importance of variations between ostensibly similar national states. This chapter has shown the variability of social processes within a national state. In the early sections we showed the scale, and importance, of these variations, and that national averages only serve to hide a multitude of local differences. To concentrate on the national level of housing provision only provides us with an aggregated picture which may fail to correspond to any of its constituent parts. Existing accounts of these local differences (section 5.3) tend to stress either the national or the local level, and rarely attempt to link the two. This stems largely from the way in which such accounts use an inadequate theoretical view of the state, which either sees the local state as autonomous or as an arm of the central state. This in turn calls into question existing theories of the state and the local state. In order to help explain the local provision of council housing, we need an adequate conceptual understanding of the relation between the central and the local state. The local case studies of Norfolk and Sheffield illustrate the complexity of social forces operating in and around the local state. Some of these forces are institutionalized through the organs of local government, others are not (see also chapter six). In any case existing accounts are unable to give us any leverage on how they connect with those social processes operating in and around the national state. The development of this connection is crucial in understanding any state service, including local housing provision.

The local case studies also demonstrate the importance of specifically local social processes. As the discussion in chapter one indicated, it is quite possible for local variation to be caused by a passive mapping of national processes onto an already unevenly developed surface. Yet our two studies show that in these localities there were very definite local processes operating which helped shape their provision of housing. The particular nature of class relations in both Sheffield and rural Norfolk is the most obvious process which mediated national policy, and helped translate it into actual local provision. As we saw in section 5.4, a whole number of contingent factors were operating in these localities, and these mixed with structural forces, at both the local and the national level, to determine the shape and form of local council housing. Our case studies serve to illustrate the importance of this interlinkage between the two levels of analysis, in explaining the specific outcome of local housing provision.

But these outcomes in terms of housing provision are themselves important to future change. The people affected do not suddenly become passive; the interaction between already created structure and agency continues. In other words, the existing form of housing provision helps determine future practices around the same issue. We saw this clearly in the case of both Norfolk and Sheffield. The next chapter shows how such local processes continue to operate around the specific area of protest over access, costs, and conditions of housing already provided.

## CHAPTER SIX

# Housing consumption, state and the locality

## 6.1 Introduction

This chapter is about housing consumption. It is appropriate that it should be the final substantial empirical chapter in the book because the process of housing consumption – how housing is occupied and used by those people who live in it – is the end point of the various aspects of the housing question examined in the preceding chapters. Put another way, the activities of all the parties and organizations involved in the design, production, finance and allocation of housing are, of course, pointless without housing consumption.

Marx (1973, 91) expresses the importance of consumption for production very well indeed. He writes

> Consumption produces production . . . because a product becomes a real product only by being consumed. For example, a garment becomes a real garment only in the act of being worn; a house where no one lives is in fact not a real house; thus the product, unlike a mere natural object, proves itself to be, *becomes*, a product only through consumption. Only by decomposing the product does consumption give the product the finishing touch.

Since Marx wrote this, and increasingly during the present century, the nature of housing consumption – how people live in houses – has evolved to become increasingly complex. For reasons already discussed in chapter one, in countries such as Britain and Sweden a house is no longer simply used by those who live in it as shelter and as a place to eat, sleep and raise children. Instead, housing consumption is a complex and multi-faceted process. As Merrett says, 'for working people the dwelling should be understood as an activity centre required to meet an extremely diverse range of cultural needs.' (Merrett with Gray 1982, 58). It has social, economic and political significance, and is an essential component in social reproduction and the reproduction of labour in advanced capitalist countries. People's identities and status as individuals and members of social groups are, in part, conferred and maintained in the home and in the process of housing consumption.

Housing consumption is, therefore, of crucial significance for individuals, governments and societies. But as the following section points out we have an inadequate understanding of the relations and patterns of cause and effect involved. Much of the literature suggests, for example, that housing form (and in particular tenure) has a simple causal influence on patterns of housing consumption and the social relations of housing consumers. Such deterministic views are rejected, and section 6.3 consequently turns the focus to housing consumers and the actions they may take to preserve or enhance their housing conditions and experiences.

The argument is extended in the subsequent section (6.4) to an examination of the wider significance of housing consumption actions – particularly for state intervention and the evolution of the housing question. In this, stress is placed on the crucial role of the locality, for it is the nature of specific localities – and in particular local social relations and local state institutions – which go a long way to determining the form of a housing action and in turn its influence.

The subsequent three sections (6.5 to 6.7) exemplify this theme through an examination of housing consumption issues and collective action in two specific localities in Britain – Brighton and Crawley. Here the aim is to portray something of the complex processes underlying housing actions and the tangled relations which exist between local and national, and housing consumers and state institutions in the real world. The final section (6.8) returns more directly to the national and conceptual levels. It attempts, in particular, to isolate some of the factors which limit and influence state intervention in housing consumption in countries such as Britain and Sweden.

## 6.2  Housing form and consumption process

As the way housing is used has developed, so the broader significance of housing consumption for people has increased. In turn, government, housing institutions and academic commentators have sought to understand the relationships between type of housing, form of housing consumption and the social relations and everyday lives of people. It is widely accepted that particular forms of housing consumption are tied to specific types of dwelling, and in turn confer upon people varying potentialities and limitations on their everyday lives. However, over a long period of time there has been considerable and often contradictory debate on the precise nature of these relationships. We might include here ideas that slum conditions breed slum dwellers;[1] closely packed, inner-city terrace housing fosters the development of close-knit working-class communities (see, for example, Young and Willmott 1962); the sprawl of single-tenure, suburban estates creates single-class, family-centred suburban households (Thorns 1972); owner-occupation enforces a possessive individualism (Pawley 1978); local authority housing splits the working class into competing groups (Gray 1976); and so on.

Merrett has perhaps gone furthest in detailing the significance of the dwelling for housing consumption and the opportunities the dwelling *itself* may allow those people who occupy it. He argues (Merrett with Gray 1982, 58) that every dwelling can be described in terms of six major predicates or attributes 'enjoyed by the house itself or associated with its possession': the dwelling's physical character; the control exercised over its use by the occupier; the environmental locus (i.e. the quality and nature of the neighbourhood); the relative locus (the availability of alternative transport modes to points in space beyond the neighbourhood, and the costs in time and money of such journeys); the housing mobility a dwelling offers; and, the dwelling's financial attractiveness.

With a somewhat different perspective, Saunders (1982) highlights housing tenure, and in particular the rights enjoyed by people in particular tenures. He argues that owner-occupation endows the rights of control, benefit and disposal to the occupier, whereas local authority housing allows only the right of benefit (and this may be severely constrained) and not those of control and disposal. This emphasis on tenure echoes a concern in much other British literature which also stresses the relationship between housing tenure and patterns of housing consumption. Although it is not appropriate to review this literature in any depth (but see Merrett with Gray 1982) it is useful to explore briefly two alternative perspectives which tend to emerge. In what might best be termed the 'status quo' tradition, literature originating in government or private sector housing institutions tends to emphasize the advantages of owner-occupation over other tenure forms (and particularly local authority renting) for individual, family and general societal well-being. In this view owner-occupation creates beneficial forms of housing consumption and in turn 'positive' social relations.

For example, in one of the more recent of a long line of pro-home ownership statements from central government, the then Environment Minister, Michael Heseltine, said in 1980

> There is in this country a deeply ingrained desire for home ownership. The Government believe that this spirit should be fostered. It reflects the wishes of the people, ensures the widest spread of wealth through society, encourages a personal desire to improve and modernise one's home, enables people to accrue wealth for their children, and stimulates the attitudes of independence and self-reliance that are the bedrock of a free society.
>
> (*Hansard*, 15 January 1980, column 1445)

Similarly during the Second Reading of the Housing and Building Control Bill in 1983, Ian Gow, Minister for Housing argued

> a proper sense of humility requires that our whole housing policy needs to be based on a recognition that we should give every assistance and encouragement to the preferred choice of the people. That preferred choice is, overwhelmingly, for the pride and independence which go hand in hand with home ownership.               (*Hansard*, 5 July 1983, column 161)

Private housing institutions, and particularly building societies, have been prone to echo these sentiments. In the mid-1960s the chairman of the Building Societies' Association (Lee 1964, 11) asserted that owner-occupation

> is an essential part of one's life. It satisfies a basic human need to surround onself with something that is absolutely personal and private between members of one's family.

When one talks about it becoming the background of family life one thinks of it as an anchorage or harbour from which one emerges each day. Night after night one returns and becomes part of the family again.

Again in 1980, but in less sentimental fashion, one authority (Gilchrist 1980, 16) discussed the reasons for people to buy their own homes: 'Motivations are not purely financial. People want to buy because buying gives them freedom, choice, security, mobility, pride, maybe extra status, and extra borrowing power.'

The other side of the same coin tends to be adopted in certain literature following a 'radical' perspective. However, rather than being viewed as beneficial and positive, owner-occupation and its concomitant patterns of housing consumption are viewed as having a depressing effect on social relations. For instance, apart from acting 'to legitimate private property by reference to its socially useful character' it also functions 'both in fragmenting the working class and giving the individual workers a "stake in the system"' (Clarke and Ginsburg 1975, 25). A similar argument is that by Boddy (1980, 21) that 'the structure of housing tenure has a particular social impact and definite political and ideological implications'. He continues that owner-occupation in particular 'anaesthetises' social conflict in housing. In political struggle, 'home owners have no obvious opponent against which to struggle.' This theme of housing tenure and consumption depoliticizing social relations is echoed in some radical literature which discusses public sector housing (Gray 1976).

There are clearly strong common features shared by both status-quo and radical perspectives outlined above. Specific tenures are tied to specific patterns of housing consumption and, in turn, produce clearly identifiable and homogeneous social relations. The phrase 'social relations' as used here is meant to capture the range of relations undertaken and experienced by people in their daily lives as individuals and members of social groups.

Both perspectives are open to very similar criticisms. One is the tendency to give tenure an independent causal primacy over both consumption and social relations. Following on from this, much existing work has tended towards very deterministic and functional assumptions of how tenure form relates to social relations. Patterns of cause and effect are generally asserted rather than demonstrated either empirically or conceptually. Moreover, such perspectives appear not to produce a very close fit to reality. In practice, for example, tenure is not a homogeneous, static and unchanging phenomenon (Merrett with Gray 1982). Accepting this casts some doubt on the cause and effect arguments that are central to both radical and status quo perspectives. But, apart from missing historical and geographical variation in the relationships between tenure, consumption and social relations, such perspectives also, as Ball (1983) argues, tend to ignore or dismiss other central determinants of housing consumption. Indeed, one theme of the previous chapters of this book has been the attempt to show tenure as a consequence of a wide range of social processes.

Another often implicit but none the less important related assumption also tends to be carried along with much of this literature. This is that the consumers of housing are essentially passive and submissive creatures. With a number of exceptions, such is the general impression to be gained from the available literature about housing consumption, whatever its orientation and theoretical perspective. Individuals and social groups are usually seen as simply soaking up the patterns of housing consumption tied to particular types of housing, and as accepting the housing system presented to them and already created by some hidden hand generator. This generator might be, for instance, 'market mechanisms', central government, housing institutions or 'capitalism'. Whatever the case, both housing consumption and housing system are generally argued to be outside the control and influence, and sometimes indeed the identification, of housing consumers themselves. It is as though people living in houses make no important contribution in determining housing consumption and the nature of the housing problem.

Implicit throughout this book has been the rejection of the neo-classical paradigm for its economism and generally grossly inadequate representations of the relations between individual, economy and society. None the less, in a perverse way it is perhaps this very literature about housing supply and demand which gets nearest to a general acceptance of the idea that the consumers of housing (albeit as individuals in the market place attempting to maximize their 'place utility' or responding to external 'threats' or 'stimuli') do, indeed, have some role in determining their own housing consumption experiences, and that such actions have a much wider impact as well. To this extent neo-classical economics can be argued to twist the dominant perspective described above on its head. Rather than the housing system determining housing consumption, and in turn social relations, instead housing consumers determine the housing system. A central theme of this chapter is to explore this latter notion, although this is in relation to the structure of social relations rather than (as falsely expressed in neo-classical work) in terms of atomistic and sovereign consumers. What role do housing consumers have in addressing and determining the nature of housing consumption and, in turn, what if any are the implications of this for how the housing question has evolved over time and space?

## 6.3 Housing consumers and housing action

In examining this general issue – of the role and importance of housing consumers and housing consumption – a central area concerns the responses of people to their housing consumption experiences. A starting point is to note that consuming a dwelling is neither a passive nor an independent act. Not only does it involve decisions and choices about what use is to be made of a dwelling, but, apart from perhaps Robinson Crusoe, housing consumption is bound up with social relations between people. Of course, even for Crusoe social relations took place with Man Friday, and this ideal relationship was eventually disrupted when the serenity of his island home was challenged by other people. Housing consumption is, ultimately, a question of the social relations which exist in, over and around housing. Without these relations the physical dwelling structure, the neighbourhood and other dwelling attributes have little if any meaning. It is the social relations of housing consumers (not the publicity machines of building firms) which can turn a house into a home.

Saunders's 'tenure rights' (see p. 195) are rights of the occupier over other people. Status quo notions of 'independence' and 'self-reliance', 'something that is absolutely personal and private between members of one's family', and 'freedom, choice, security, mobility, pride, maybe extra status' are meaningless unless understood as social relations between people. The same point is also true of those notions central to the radical perspective.

All of Merrett's six sets of dwelling attributes also encapsulate acts of social relations which either existed in the past or occur in the present. For example, the first predicate, the dwelling's physical character, expresses the past social relations of production involved in its production and construction. Clearly, the physical dwelling structure also has an effect on the current social relations of those who occupy it. The second predicate, the control exercised over a dwelling's use by the occupier, hinges on a range of present social relations. Here social relations of the workplace are crucially important in determining the income and time available fully to use a dwelling as the consumer wishes. But perhaps more central, and certainly more difficult to assess, are the social relations associated with the particular tenure of a specific dwelling.

A council house is a council house for the occupier because of the specific relations between her or him as a tenant and the local authority as landlord. Similarly, owner-occupation also carries with it sets of social relations. The occupier as owner of private property has legally defined rights, obligations and duties. Although tenure forms also suggest and imply more subtle connotations about the social relations to be enjoyed (or endured) by the occupier, legal definitions and rules underpin most of what is understood by tenure. Legal definitions and rules are, of course, societal creations. Law is one of the principal means through which governments attempt to achieve, maintain and legitimate their intervention in housing consumption. But to be successful the use of law has, ultimately, to be socially accepted and both feasible and practical. As such the mere existence of legal rules and definitions cannot guarantee that a particular housing consumption relationship will, in fact, occur. This strikes at the heart of the tenure, consumption and social relations debate. Despite frequent recourse to the power and sanction of law to determine tenure form and its consequences on people, in practice law has often been an unsuccessful means of achieving the aims of state intervention in housing consumption.

A number of examples help illustrate the point. Many of the difficulties and tensions which exist in the British private rented sector reflect either the failure of the social relations between tenant and landlord which occur in practice to match up to legal expectations, or the inability of legal definitions to be easily imposed on the real world if the parties to the relationship fundamentally disagree and conflict with each other. Similarly, Saunders' three rights associated with home ownership may in Britain be sanctioned by law (although this is not always the case) but may also be unobtainable in practice. For instance a badly maintained owner-occupied house in a depressed area with little demand for house purchase may be impossible to dispose of. In the case of British public sector housing, legal definitions and rules have tended to err on the side of the landlord rather than tenant or potential tenant. Local authorities have been relatively free to impose their own quasi-legal definitions of the landlord–tenant relationship. As a result, there has been considerable geographical and historical variation in these re-lations (for example, tenants being allowed more say in some places than others, Merrett 1979, chapter eight) and, concomitantly, considerable differences in how tenants have responded to the relations local authorities attempt to impose on them.

These illustrations point to the importance of both law and, concomitantly, state intervention in housing consumption – both themes which are woven into the fabric of this chapter. For the moment, however, if we accept that housing consumption is a social act with social implications and consequences it appears likely that housing consumers will not always passively accept or conform with legal definitions and rules – particularly when they are disadvantageous – of what their social relations with others should be.

The more general point to arise out of this specific instance is that we should expect housing consumers in countries such as Britain and Sweden to attempt to enhance and improve or at least to maintain their existing pattern of housing consumption. In this context what Willis argues of commodities in general may be true of housing (and, for instance, tenure) in particular:

> Though the whole commodity form provides powerful implications for the manner of its consumption it by no means enforces them. Commodities can be taken out of context, clarified in a particular way, developed and repos-sessed to express something deeply and thereby to change somehow the feelings which are their product. And all this can happen under the very nose of the dominant class – and with their products.
>
> (Willis 1978, quoted in Thrift 1983, 39)

In addition, action over housing consumption also involves social relations between the consumer as an individual or a member of a group and other individ-uals, social groups and institutions. In so far as these relations revolve around questions of power and control and access to and use of scarce resources they will be relations which are latently if not manifestly conflicting.

This suggests the very broad range of *issues* that may occur in, over and around housing consumption. For those consuming housing, dissatisfaction with one or more aspects of the consumption process can take a wide variety of forms. At one extreme there may be conflict between members of a single household which perhaps ultimately leads to household dissolution and ritual conflict in the courts over who retains which material possession and legal rights over the home. At another extreme, groups of consuming households may form and conflict with other sets of consumers or with, for instance, government, courts or housing insti-tutions.

As housing consumption issues arise, so different sorts of response and *action* by housing consumers occur. In most situations it appears that housing consumption actions are reactive and defensive: that is, responses to some present or future event or set of activities which is perceived to threaten, challenge or harm the

*Table 6.1*   Local actions over housing consumption issues in Britain

| Housing consumption situation | Individual action | Collective action |
|---|---|---|
| All | (I)<br>Requests/pressure for state action/aid<br>Voting in elections<br>Membership of political parties<br>Membership of housing interest groups<br>Use of law<br>Lawlessness<br>Use of media<br>Direct action/physical demonstrations, etc. | (II)<br>As for (I) except:<br>Formation (rather than membership) of housing interest groups<br>Political representation (rather than voting in elections), e.g. rate-payer councillors |
| Homelessness | (III)<br>Homeless Persons/waiting list application<br>Pressure on local authority officials/councillors<br>Squatting<br>Taking local authority to court<br>Membership of squatting group, etc.<br>Increasing eligibility (e.g. move to worse accommodation) | (IV)<br>Interest group campaigning/lobbying/collective pressure on, e.g. housing institutions, the local authority<br>Organized squatting<br>'Test' legal cases in the courts |
| Public sector tenants | (V)<br>Vandalism<br>Moving: a) moonlighting, b) applying for transfer or exchange, c) legitimately moving to another tenure<br>Pressure on officers/councillors for change (e.g. repairs, 'bad' neighbours)<br>Membership of tenants' association<br>Withholding rent<br>Taking local authority to court | (VI)<br>Vandalism<br>Petitions on rent levels, repairs, etc.<br>Tenants' association demonstrations<br>Rent strikes, work-based strikes<br>Taking local authority to court in test case |
| Owner-occupiers | (VII)<br>Moving<br>Mortgage defaulting/arrears<br>Membership of residents'/ratepayers' association<br>Taking exchange professionals to court | (VIII)<br>Vigilante groups<br>Mortgage strikes<br>Taking building society, builder, etc. to court<br>Requests to local authority for environmental action (e.g. lobbying by residents' groups)<br>Withholding of rates<br>Ratepayers' association activities |

*(continued)*

*Table 6.1—continued*

| Housing consumption situation | Individual action | Collective action |
|---|---|---|
| Private sector tenants | (IX)<br>Moving: a) moonlighting,<br> b) legitimately moving to other<br>  accommodation/tenure<br>Withholding rent<br>Taking landlord to court<br>Application to rent officer for<br> rent reduction | (X)<br>Rent strikes, work-based<br> strikes<br>Demands for local authority<br> intervention (e.g. repairs,<br> municipalization)<br>Taking landlord to court |

consumers' consumption experiences. It is useful to look in a little more detail at some of the range of actions which may be undertaken by housing consumers attempting to defend or improve their housing consumption experiences. One important distinction to be made is that between individual and collective action. Table 6.1 takes this division and uses it in a listing of housing actions in a range of housing situations typical of Britain. The attempt is made to describe differences in housing actions by people in the three main British tenures and by the homeless.

A number of points should be made about table 6.1. The actions mentioned are illustrative rather than a comprehensive list. Boxes I and II are general descriptions of actions which may occur in most if not all housing situations, whereas boxes III to X give examples for particular housing situations. Some sets of action over housing consumption are not tenure based. As the work of Lambert *et al.* (1978) demonstrates, people in a particular locality, whatever their tenure may share common interests and take common action on this basis. Conversely, people within a single tenure in a specific locality may have dissimilar interests and work towards different goals. For example, some private tenants may want their homes municipalized while others may not.

Many housing consumption responses will be actions of last resort. Some issues may be resolved without housing consumption action *per se.* For example, a rent or mortgage increase may be paralleled by a rise in wages or state benefit. Indeed, in Britain this has generally been true in the two major tenures for much of the post-war period with owner-occupiers especially often experiencing income levels pushing ahead of housing costs.

When housing actions *are* taken, more extreme or visible responses may occur only after other measures have failed. For example, people may only resort to illegal actions, such as withholding rent or squatting, after 'legitimate' or legal remedies have proved ineffectual. Clearly not all housing consumers will have all forms of action open to them – council tenants may resort to lawlessness more often than owner-occupiers simply because they have few legally defined 'rights'.

This sort of variation may change over time. For example, before the Housing (Homeless Persons) Act of 1976 local authorities had complete discretionary power over which of the homeless they housed – homeless people had no legal redress if they were refused accommodation. Today the Act allows some opportunity of forcing a local authority to provide housing by action through the courts.

One important issue concerns how best to conceptualize the social groups that emerge in housing consumption actions. This will partly hinge on the specific housing issue, but also on the 'vertical' and 'horizontal' organization of the specific capitalist society and the particular locality (see chapter one for a more detailed discussion of the anatomy of capitalist societies). On some occasions housing consumption actions are probably best analysed as class actions (cf. Corrigan and Ginsburg 1975). Class struggle and housing struggle have merged as one in a range of localities with different tenure forms (both public and private) and local state institutions. On other occasions housing consumption actions are not, in a direct sense, class actions between capital and labour – which become relatively crude analytical terms in such a context. For example, individuals may fight individuals and groups of housing consumers may conflict with other groups over dwelling 'rights' and consumption practices. Such conflict between housing consumers is relatively well documented by authors such as Kramer and Young (1978) and Saunders (1979) and may be on the basis of any of a variety of schisms. Much will depend on social differentiation and social practices in 'civil society' (again see chapter one). In Britain, for instance, middle-class consumers may conflict with working-class consumers, home owners with tenants, the 'respectable' with the 'rough', the homeless with the housed, and so on.

Forms of housing action may also be spatially specific. This will hinge, in part, on the particular housing forms, local state institutions and local social relations found from place to place. For instance, there may be more reason for housing action in some places, and the nature of local social relations (for example, a strong degree of unity and consciousness of the issue) may allow a collective rather than individual response. Conversely, in other places, whatever the issue, responses may be very muted and ineffectual and collective action over housing non-existent. In some situations disorganized and poorly developed local social relations may preclude the possibility of collective action. In other cases, social relations, although well developed, may be inimical to collective action over housing and lead, instead, to fascism, racism or some other reactionary response hitting at disadvantaged or scapegoated social groups rather than the individuals, groups, institutions or processes creating specific housing problems.

Historical and geographical variation is, then, an important aspect of housing consumption issues and action. In particular, since housing consumption takes place in space, the locality, or rather the *specific* locality, becomes a crucial concern. It is the arena within which housing consumption issues manifest themselves and where most forms of action will occur. This point may be taken as one instance of the general argument detailed in chapters one and two, about the specificity of the locality. Thrift makes an essentially similar point:

> part of the reason why some people do certain things at certain places in

certain periods while other people at other places in other or the same periods do not, or why different forms of protest and patterns of organisation arise in apparently similar conditions, is quite specific to particular contexts, to particular *places*.                                                         (Thrift 1983, 36)

The general thrust of this section has been that housing consumers are not always passive receivers of the housing consumption experiences imposed upon them. Instead, housing consumers appear capable of addressing housing consumption issues and problems in a wide variety of ways. The major question that remains concerns the significance of the resultant housing consumption actions.

## 6.4 The significance of housing action

Enough has been said to suggest that in Britain housing consumers have at times been successful – although sometimes only after considerable struggle – in achieving the immediate aims of their consumption actions. Indeed, national measures showing changes in housing quality, costs, security of tenure, and so on might, at least in part, be taken as an indication of the success of housing consumers in defending or enhancing their housing conditions and experiences. In a similar fashion, housing consumption differentials between social groups say something about the success or failure of different groups in pushing for and achieving housing consumption gains.

Against this, in practice housing consumption social relations and actions often appear insignificant – that is without any wider implication – although they may be of overbearing interest and concern to the people involved. Disputes over the boundaries of suburban gardens might be treated as a case in point. However, even this illustration might be taken as symptomatic of much more than an argument between two individual households, involving as it does definitions of property rights and a struggle over housing consumption. If such a dispute continues it will probably be channelled into the courts and resolved through the use of law. The apparatus of the state will be brought to bear on what appear as very personal, immediate and insignificant housing consumption issues and actions. This illustration re-emphasizes the point that housing consumption has, over a long period of time, attracted considerable state intervention and attempted management and regulation.

At this level the important issue appears to become one concerning the relationship between housing consumers and national states such as those of Britain and Sweden. Can housing consumers sway a national state? To what extent can a national state dominate and regulate housing assumption? It is clear that many housing consumption actions will have no scope or opportunity to move away from immediate and local issues. Most will have no wider impact on state intervention and action, and will remain as local level issues, as individual concerns, and within 'legitimate' channels of protest and action. The expectation might be that, of the range of actions, only those taken collectively and outside legitimate channels will have any wider significance.

Unfortunately Saunders (1981) seems to dash any hopes in this direction. Although writing of 'urban struggles' generally, what he says appears to pertain to collective actions over housing consumption issues. He argues that such struggles develop around questions of social consumption; that they are typically isolated from the labour movement and strategically limited in their objectives; that they are generally orientated towards competitive rather than corporate spheres of politics; that they are typically fragmented between themselves; that they are mainly locally based; and, that they tend to be both issue-specific and locality-specific. 'In short, urban struggles are typically fragmented, localized, strategically limited, and politically isolated.' (Saunders 1981, 276).

There are, however, shafts of light which suggest that this is not perhaps the complete story. Saunders's characterization does not seem to hold true of a number of housing actions which had a demonstrable effect on a national state, and the evolution of the housing question. Chapter four (section 4.3) discussed the role of housing consumption in the proto-revolutionary upheaval in Sweden during 1917. The Clydeside rent strikes during the same period are often quoted as an influential British housing struggle leading to the heightened decline of the private-rented sector and the large-scale introduction of council housing. Indeed, this episode is worth examining in a little detail because it allows further consideration of some of the problems involved in tracing the relations between housing consumption issues and actions and the evolution of state intervention and the housing question nationally. The Glasgow area during this period was the scene of an intensive housing consumption struggle (for descriptions see Dickens 1978; Byrne and Damer 1980; and particularly Melling 1983). At issue were appalling and worsening housing conditions, high rents forced higher as workers flocked into the city to work in the expanding wartime industries, and the power and 'rights' of private landlords to do as they pleased with their property and the people occupying it. The Corporation of Glasgow, despite efforts to the contrary, failed to ease working-class housing conditions because of the power of property owners and landlords on the council. Landlords attempted to enforce rent increases by resort to law and the use of physical coercion – evicting tenants who failed to pay. Local people responded in a variety of ways. A range of home- and work-based and political organizations became more active and militant over the housing issue. Mass meetings, demonstrations and rent strikes took place and a general strike in the workplace was threatened.

An initial problem is that of simply identifying and describing in sufficient depth the form and content of the housing issue, the resultant action and the social relations which surrounded it. For the Glasgow episode, for instance, the role of trade unions and the importance of women as organizers around housing is still hotly debated. In part this is because reconstructing past housing consumption struggles such as the one in Clydeside generally lacks comprehensive and balanced source materials. 'Official' accounts and statistics and orthodox descriptions and histories, particularly those for public consumption, may be of little value. State institutions and housing institutions generally have little interest in making the most of protest, and will tell us little about the nature or extent of housing consumption struggles. Similarly, individuals and social groups involved in struggles will rarely record *their* history of events. Instead, the struggle and its consequences for local people will become embedded in the particular heritage of social relations in that locality. It may or may not be made available for general consumption depending on the particular folk memory and consciousness.

Housing consumption struggles are, then, likely to be hidden from history. The task of rescuing them, even at the level of describing events and actions, is considerable. Identifying that it is locality-based is a first step which suggests the importance of local social relations and local state institutions as factors determining the potentialities and limitations of housing consumption issues and actions. In Glasgow social relations amongst the working class were extremely influential: a high degree of consciousness and militancy spanning and eventually uniting both home and work and a variety of social groups, a local culture positively fostering working-class action, an important role for both women and men, and so on. Other local social relations were also important: a powerful urban bourgeoisie with a stranglehold over housing and local state institutions, harming both working class and at least some local employers who, as Byrne and Damer (1980, 67) argue 'had an eye to the importance of the politics of reproduction of their labour force.' Local state institutions were perhaps most influential in a negative sense. The working class (and employers) seemingly had little effective power over these institutions. As such, a major avenue whereby housing consumption issues *might* have been resolved or at least ameliorated was closed to local people.

Even assuming an adequate description of the varied relations lying behind a particular housing consumption issue and action, other perhaps more difficult problems of analysis and assessment remain. How is an analysis to be made of who wins and who loses? How should we measure and assess the significance of a particular struggle? Would subsequent events have been substantially different if a specific housing consumption episode had not occurred?

Clydeside well illustrates these sorts of problems. Following the housing struggle central government passed legislation to hold down rents nationally. After the war, more positive legislation resulted in the state taking responsibility for the provision of working-class housing. But was Glasgow important in these central policy changes? Some commentators seem able to analyse the development of state involvement in working-class housing at the time with little or no reference to local housing consumption struggles, or Glasgow in particular (Wilding 1972). Others suggest that Clydeside was part of a much wider and longer-term struggle, spanning localities in both Scotland and England, which forced the British state to intervene (Melling 1980; Englander 1982). Yet others argue that state intervention was the result, but that this was far from a working-class victory since housing provision was still under capitalist economic and political domination (Dickens 1978). In this view Clydeside was, at least in part, a struggle between fractions of capital – industrialists versus landlords (although whether landlords can strictly be considered capitalists is a debatable issue) – with the winning fraction perhaps not being able to foresee, but certainly being able to adapt successfully to working-class pressure. More radical commentators use a very different interpretative brush. For them Glasgow was a key instance of conscious class struggle forcing the state to intervene at the national level, altering the balance of class forces and resulting in a substantial evolution of the nature of the housing question (Byrne and Damer 1980).

It is clearly inappropriate to analyse such differences of interpretation at a purely empirical level. Much will depend on the theoretical perspective of the researcher involved. None the less, the balance of evidence is that Clydeside (and related local actions) was of crucial significance in determining changes in state intervention and housing consumption in Britain. But however the impact of Glasgow might be theorized, how exceptional was it as a local action producing a national evolution in the housing question? There are other episodes where specific housing struggles have produced national change. Perhaps the most well documented recent instance of local social pressures ultimately contributing to central policy change is the local opposition to the 1972 Housing Finance Act (Sklair 1975, Beirne 1977) out of which Clay Cross (Skinner and Langdon 1974) emerged as the sacrificial lamb.

None the less, such episodes still appear to be relatively rare, although a number of factors could account for this. First, where struggles over housing consumption have indeed been important in creating change in the housing system, it is far better for state institutions, building societies or whatever to re-write history. Housing change then becomes the result of acts of benevolence and foresight by politicians, administrators or managers on behalf of people. Or perhaps some 'natural' (and hence classless) process reflecting the 'deep-seated desires' of individuals. Or as a logical or evolutionary policy development, perhaps as a response to a particular problem such as some variant of unmet housing need versus the ability of new and existing consumers to pay more for housing. Good examples of such views are to be found in many of the most dominant explanations of the evolution of housing tenures in Britain. Much of the literature may, therefore, underplay the extent of housing struggles, and indeed this suggestion is supported by the results of our case study research in Brighton and Crawley.

Another reason why consumption actions so rarely appear to be significant in any clearly demonstrable empirical way may be that in most cases either consumers, or state institutions, concede before a pitched battle is reached. In this way the exceptional housing consumption struggles that do produce central and national change appear as major watersheds, which subsequently channel other housing consumption issues and action in new directions – the battlelines and limits of action by both consumers and national state being drawn anew. This appears to be the case for housing struggles in both Sweden and Britain during the First World War. A yet further explanation might be that despite the supposed insignificance of housing consumption actions, even of a collective nature, they do have a cumulative effect on state intervention; taken singularly they may usually be unimportant, but taken together they may constitute a formative context and pressure on a national state.

These are issues returned to in the final section of this chapter where the focus is on the state and state action *vis-à-vis* housing consumption. At present however the chapter presents three separate instances of housing consumption actions in two of our British case study areas: Brighton and Crawley. All three examples are of collective action; each of which was challenging to patterns of housing consumption both locally and nationally, and also to state intervention in housing consumption.

It is worth noting that at the outset of the research we had no idea that housing struggles in any meaningful form had taken place in either Brighton or Crawley. The localities were chosen for the other reasons discussed in chapters one and two. If anything our expectation was that both localities would be barren ground for consumption actions – Brighton because of the dominance of local institutions by a relatively repressive status quo and Crawley because of non-electoral local state institutions imposed by central government.

A common aim in all three examples is to examine the processes which resulted in collective action. Another aim is to demonstrate the fruits of undertaking *intensive* local studies with housing consumption and its attendant social relations the prime focus, rather than the more usual extensive housing studies which stress, for example, tenure, stock or institutions rather than social relations. A further objective is to provide more material on which to base an examination of the consequences of housing actions on state intervention and the evolution of the housing question nationally. This theme is discussed in the concluding section of the chapter.

## 6.5 Homelessness and squatting in Brighton

The geographical and historical focus of this case study is Brighton immediately after the Second World War. During this period homelessness existed as a major housing consumption issue for many people in the locality. The particular concern here is the resultant vigorous and ultimately influential squatting campaign.

Clearly the circumstances surrounding the housing question nationally during this period provide an essential background to the situation in Brighton. We might include here the restructuring of social relations and state power and activity in wartime, and the immense national housing problem combined with new and greater housing consumption expectations and demands (Backwell and Dickens 1978). However, the housing question in Brighton had specific local features, and the resultant action by housing consumers was, at the time, very unusual in national terms. Brighton, as a specific locality, contained its own mix of relations which – to a greater or lesser extent – were unique to the area (see chapters one and two). Thus, while no locality exists in isolation, we need to look to the specific locality to understand what was happening in Brighton at the time. In addition, as we shall see, homelessness and squatting in Brighton had more than local significance, ultimately contributing to more widespread housing action and national state response.

Two particularly important dimensions of the locality are local social relations and local state institutions. In considering housing consumption actions, the influence of these can be either positive or negative: they may either help or hinder housing consumers in their response to housing consumption issues. In

Brighton, paradoxically, the dominant status quo social relations and unproductive local state institutions both functioned to push the responses of housing
consumers in a particular direction, barring some forms of action and leaving only
illegal actions as a worthwhile tactic.

Since its establishment as a resort in the eighteenth century, local class relations
in Brighton have been dominated by status quo interests favouring a range of
groups including, at different times, property and landowners and speculators,
landlords, estate agents, hoteliers and wealthy home owners (Gilbert 1954).
These local social relations have been reflected in the control and actions of local
state institutions. For example, electoral politics have generally put conservative
and right-wing politicians in control of the town council. To this extent Brighton
conforms to the image of a bourgeois, complacent and reactionary seaside resort
town. Were this image to be wholly accurate, however, we might expect very little
scope for the least privileged housing consumers to address their housing problems except through the dead-end channels managed by the status quo.

In fact this domination of local social relations and state institutions has been
neither total nor unchallenged. Throughout the modern history of the locality,
radical oppositional social relations, sometimes relatively weakly but sometimes
very strongly, have countered the imposition of status quo ideas and actions. This
working-class culture and opposition has expressed itself in many ways. For
example: electoral politics in the town have long contained a strong (if subsidiary)
radical left-wing element with sometimes considerable popular support (Durr
1980a); a multi-faceted co-operative movement emerged very early in the locality
(Durr 1980b and 1983); after the First World War servicemen directed a variety
of actions at the town council over unemployment (including attacks on the
police, a march to the town hall in January 1919 by 7000 soldiers awaiting
demobilization, and large public demonstrations) (Dickens and Gilbert 1981);
and the 1926 General Strike was widely supported in the locality and included a
violent, pitched battle against police and special constables outside the tram depot
(Trory 1975).

However these and other episodes are not best analysed as an expression of
united working-class action with common and agreed objectives. It is, instead,
more appropriate to view local working-class social relations as fragmentary and
disjointed. For a long period the oppositional politics and culture was centred
around various élite working-class groups. Particularly influential were
locomotive and railway workers – relatively well paid, skilled, unionized, collectively conscious and powerful (Langley 1976). Such groups appear to have been
relatively advantaged in their housing consumption experiences, often occupying
good private sector dwellings, and, after the First World War, some of the best
public sector dwellings (Dickens and Gilbert 1981). In contrast to these groups,
many other people in the town were employed servicing the resort industries and
wealthy residents. Conditions of work, pay and union strength all tended to be
poor, and these people occupied often appalling dwellings (Gray and Lowerson
1979; Farrant *et al.* 1981, chapter six). None the less, it is clear that at times the
politics and actions of the more powerful working-class groups rubbed off on
others in a variety of ways.

The national origins of housing consumption problems were, in Brighton, aggravated by a series of local factors. The large, low-waged and generally unorganized section of the working class worked and lived in a town where land was expensive and in short supply: the rich and wealthy dominated in the housing market being able to reserve much of the Brighton residential space for their own use; land and property speculation was generally unbridled; private landlords were a powerful and influential group; and local state institutions typically failed to respond to working-class needs without considerable pressure and struggle on the part of the working class themselves. Indeed, although the details have altered, this state of affairs remains relatively unchanged today (Queenspark Rates Book Group 1983).

In this situation after the Second World War homelessness existed as the major housing consumption issue for many people. Other courses of legitimate action were either ineffective or non-existent (particularly given the control of local state institutions) and in consequence the homeless responded by moving outside the law. But why was collective (rather than individual) action undertaken, and why was squatting (rather than some other action) so central an activity?

In part, what happened in Brighton during this period was a consequence of the *previous* social relations and housing consumption actions in the locality. In particular, the very similar issues and actions immediately following the First World War provided a rich heritage on which to draw. In 1919 the town's pioneering medical officer – representing a professional group partly at least autonomous from political pressure – estimated that 3052 houses were needed over the coming three years (Dickens and Gilbert 1981). Some 30,000 people had come to live in the Brighton area during the war. In consequence, as Musgrave (1970) notes there was 'a boom in property and household investments during and immediately after the War, lodgings were at a premium, and the trains became so crowded with London commuters that the issue of season tickets was restricted.' Against this at least 270 houses in the central area of the town were empty. In part this appears a consequence of a national crisis of profitability in the private rented sector, but also the high cost of repairs, the 'servant problem' leading to many larger houses being left vacant and – perhaps most importantly – high and rapidly rising house values leading to dwellings being speculatively left empty in the hope of an easy sale and profit. The particular patterns of property and social relations in the town at the time were, in turn, reflected in the make-up of the city council. In the 1920s approximately two-thirds had been elected on platforms of civic thrift and the minimization of rates. In addition, the majority of the twenty-five Guardians favoured the case of the local ratepayers.

During the early inter-war years then, it was in the context of an unresponsive set of local state institutions and empty houses but high rents that many local people experienced either appalling housing conditions or homelessness. In part because of the tradition of oppositional social relations in the town, their response was collective. But this form of action was facilitated by the fact that many of the homeless shared a common identity, being unemployed and also ex-servicemen. Also important appears to be their idiosyncratic leader, Harry Cowley, an ex-chimney-sweep and market trader.

As 'vigilantes' the group was not only concerned with housing but with a range of local social conditions. Cowley and the vigilantes became involved for example, in violent street fights with the police over the protection of market traders against established commercial interests and engaged in repeated vilification of the reactionary Board of Guardians (which one unemployed vigilante threatened 'to strangle with my own hands' if local rates of unemployment pay were not increased). Similarly, the group broke up a civic banquet, forcing a berobed Lord Mayor to release an unemployed man from jail while the festivities proceeded. Food problems were occasionally resolved by expropriating sheep off the Sussex Downs.

With hindsight, it is the vigilantes' action over housing which proved most significant. Servicemen and other homeless people were moved into sixty-four of the empty properties in the town. Property interests seemed surprisingly muted in their response. For example, although one house was deliberately damaged in attempting to evict an elderly woman squatter, the situation was successfully retrieved for the vigilantes when Cowley threatened the estate agent managing the property with two dummy bombs if the house was not quickly repaired. The group also submitted house building schemes to the council as a means of dealing with both the local housing and unemployment problems. None the less, the squatting element of this diverse campaign was most important, being the first recorded instance of collective squatting used as a form of housing consumption action in modern Britain.

It is important to point out that this movement was populist and to this degree apolitical. The available evidence indicates the vigilantes denied any 'political' motives and distanced themselves from political parties. Cowley[2] summed up his particular combination of anarchism and deference by later saying 'We only did what Christ would have done if he had been on earth'. Similarly:

> I honestly believe I have been guided by a Supreme Being. I think God gave us a mind, and if your mind tells you to do wrong you won't do it. But if you are right there's nothing on earth will stop you – not the King of England or the Prime Minister will stop you.

Consequently, despite its popular support in the locality, the linking of widely different forms of protest, and the *potentially* far-reaching implications of squatting in the erosion of private property rights, Cowley's view of natural justice was not, in fact, a *radical* attack on established patterns of authority, ownership and control (although we do not know how far this view was shared by others of the group). Some sense of the degree of threat posed by the campaign at this stage is suggested by the fact that, relative to the scale of the problem, only a small number of people were housed. Subsequently, Brighton's local authority housing programme resulted in only 556 houses being built under Addison's 1919 Housing Act and they contained (as in other areas of the country) not the homeless but the local labour aristocracy who could afford the high rents resulting from the high building costs and interest rates (Dickens and Gilbert 1981). A demand by a local Labour Party councillor to bring empty houses into local authority control was not implemented – despite the vigilantes' activities and the fact that it was permitted under government legislation.

A squatting campaign centred on the vigilantes (still led by Cowley) again emerged in Brighton immediately after the Second World War. On this occasion, however, it developed and spread to become far more threatening to established social relations, particularly those in and around the state. As it spread to London and elsewhere it became explicitly 'political' and, on the basis of documentary evidence, of considerable concern to central government.

Nationally, immediately after the Second World War, returning servicemen occupied over 1000 service camps. By late 1946 approximately 40,000 people were involved in England and Wales and 7000 in Scotland. These squatters received considerable public support, partly because of the 'homes fit for heroes' promises made by government during the war itself. Moreover, squatting on 'public' property represented little threat to the principle of private property. However, by April 1945 the Brighton vigilantes had begun squatting in privately owned houses in the locality, and subsequently this spread, on the basis of local initiatives, to Portsmouth, parts of South London, Birmingham and Liverpool.

At an early stage the then Coalition government became extremely concerned over the prospects of the squatting movement. In part activists were difficult to attack because of public support and obvious housing need which existed. More-over, during the war central government had demonstrated itself capable of over-riding private property interests in the public good and indeed in blitz conditions, particularly those of 1940–1, temporary use of empty accommodation by private citizens without homes could hardly be deemed illegal by those in authority. In consequence, immediately after the war the *principle* of private property rights, whatever the circumstances, was less than easy to defend: there appeared no logical reason why, if dwellings were unused, property rights could not be over-ridden. Shortly the government's position on this issue became clear. While individuals should not take the law into their own hands, the government, in the 'national interest', could overturn existing property rights. (As we shall see in the subsequent section, this was done vigorously in the new towns.) Effectively, then, the British state was attempting to control the social relations of housing con-sumption and the form of housing action and to reassert the dominance of national social relations.

On 6 July 1945 the Cabinet (PRO CAB CM(45), 11th Conclusion) discussed newspaper reports about

> the illegal occupation of empty houses in Brighton by homeless families. . . .
> There was general agreement that the Home Office and Ministry of Health should act quickly in order to prevent any further lawless actions. It should be possible for the local police to shadow the person who had broken into the houses and so make sure that he did not break into any further houses.

At the same meeting the Cabinet began to discuss powers to undertake the direct requisitioning of privately owned empty premises: a measure that was eventually implemented and widely used throughout the country (Dickens 1977, 761). The new powers were greeted with enthusiasm by the *News Chronicle* (24 July 1945) as 'the first instance of really successful pressure by public opinion in relation to a major domestic issue. Dissatisfaction with Government policy has forced these major concessions'.

Nine days later Churchill himself became still more agitated about the continuation and expansion of the vigilantes' activities. Intensified legal proceedings and control over newspaper coverage were his preferred solutions to the issue (PRO CAB 66/67):

> THE VIGILANTES
> Note by the Prime Minister
> I deeply regret to see the continued prominence of the vigilantes, as reported in the newspapers. This is a matter of considerable importance, and lawlessness should not be allowed. The law officers and the police should consider all means of putting an end to these pranks; and the newspapers should be induced as far as possible by the Minister of Information to curtail their publicity. I thought we decided at the last cabinet at which I was present that all possible steps be taken.
> Pray let me have a report.                                                    WSC

However, Churchill's Cabinet colleagues were not willing to undertake press censorship so directly, although the Minister of Information did express himself 'glad to consult with the Minister (of Health) with regard to the possibility of giving some guidance to friendly editors' (PRO CAB 66/67).

In fact we might still argue that the squatting movement at this stage, as after the First World War, was not a major and *fundamental* challenge either to existing patterns of housing consumption or to the state itself. The movement was still largely populist, spontaneous and opportunist, containing little in the way of an explicit political programme. Given the legislative concessions, Churchill's repressive threats were not needed during 1945 for the campaign appears to have gradually subsided. None the less, by September of the following year the seeds laid in Brighton flowered in other localities and, significantly, squatting became an explicit political issue.

By this date the Labour Government had taken office and made a number of service camps available to the homeless. (This means of housing the homeless continued well into the 1950s. In 1954, for example, over 23,000 families were still occupying 1168 camps in England and Wales.) But at the same time there were widespread outbreaks of squatting in private property in Glasgow and London (Hill 1946).[3] More important than these actions in themselves was that the Communist Party became directly involved. The Party co-ordinated the takeover by 1500 people of ten blocks of hotels and empty houses in the West End owned by Lord Ilchester and other peers. The tone of the new squatting was set by the leader of the Communist Party, Harry Pollitt, in addressing a demonstration in London in September 1946:

> All this talk about 'the liberty of the individual', about the sacred rights of private property, about the forces of anarchy which have been let loose, is all done to help preserve the system of rich and poor, homeless and those who

are not content to live in one house, but have special ones to run for their long week-ends in the country.[4]

The government responded to this linking of housing consumption action with radical politics by attempting to reassert its own authority and presumed dominance of social relations.[5] One route was via the law. For example, on one concessional legal hand local authorities were given additional powers of requisitioning, while on the other repressive legal hand (aided by physical coercion) the High Court (despite the vagueness of the legal position) granted an interim injunction restraining the squatters against further trespass and five Party members were arrested, charged with 'conspiring together with other people to trespass on property', found guilty and bound over. In addition, in the late summer of 1946 the Cabinet instructed the Home Office to revise the vague legal position relating to squatting by drafting a law to make it a criminal offence (Friend 1980, 119). A Bill never came before Parliament because of the rapid collapse of the campaign.

Another route was the attempt to impose the state's own values and assumptions on the issue. This was done largely by publicity stressing the 'unfairness' of squatting. For example, at a Cabinet meeting on 12 September 1946 (PRO CAB 128/6) it was agreed that upon the basis of police intelligence 'there was a risk of these activities spreading throughout the country' and

> Ministers considered that further steps should be taken to bring it home to the public that the squatters were overriding the claims of many people who had been waiting a long time for houses, and that the effect of their activities would be to delay the completion of the rehousing programme.

Five days later the Cabinet agreed (PRO CAB 128/6)

> that proceedings for possession and damages might be commenced against all who remained in illegal occupation of premises in this way, but that the government should offer to discontinue such proceedings against any squatters who left voluntarily and to recommend to local authorities that their claims to priority in the allocation of housing should not be prejudiced.

The *News Chronicle* (12 September 1946) carried the following Cabinet statement, which well sums up how squatting was to be regarded and counter 'steps' taken:

> A very serious view is taken by the Cabinet of the forcible seizure and occupation by unauthorised persons of private premises in London. This action has been instigated and organised by the Communist Party and must result in hindering rather than in helping the arrangements made for the orderly rehousing of those in need of accommodation. The Government is advised that the civil and criminal laws have been violated. Unless steps are taken to check lawless measures of this sort the rights of the ordinary law-abiding citizens are endangered and anarchy may result.

Whether or not because of government intervention, the squatting campaign subsided during the following months.[6] As suggested above, there is no certain empirical means of demonstrating the full impact of the campaign on the state and housing consumption. At the conceptual level, however, what happened in Brighton and other localities may be viewed as one instance of action by housing consumers exerting pressure on the state to positively reform housing consumption. Certainly, the subsequent post-war period experienced a startling revolution in housing consumption. In many respects the cornerstone and beacon of this revolution became the new towns programme although, in turn, the impact on the social relations of housing consumers was not always anticipated or foreseen.

## 6.6  Private property rights and legal action in Crawley

As the Brighton squatting campaign withered, the residents of Crawley, twenty-five miles to the north, learnt that their locality was to be the location of one of the first government new towns. The origins of the British new towns programme are well documented elsewhere (Aldridge 1979; Cullingworth 1979; Schaffer 1970). The following widely quoted terms of reference of the Advisory Committee under Lord Reith appointed by Lewis Silkin (the Minister of Town and Country Planning) suggest something of the assumptions and broad objectives of the programme. The New Towns Committee (1946, 2) was

> to consider the general questions of the establishment, development, organis-ation and administration that will arise in the promotion of New Towns in furtherance of the policy of planned decentralisation from congested urban areas; and in accordance therewith to suggest guiding principles on which such Towns should be established and developed as self-contained and balanced communities for work and living.

As many politicians and professionals suggested at the time, the new towns were in part aimed at resolving locality-based housing consumption problems; essentially the very issues which squatters in Brighton, London and elsewhere attempted to overcome through direct action. Lord Beveridge (1952) for example, argued that 'the new towns are in intention the most complete of all attacks' on the so called 'Goliath Squalor'. Squalor meant

> the conditions under which so many of our people are forced to live – in houses too small and inconvenient and ill-equipped, impossible to keep clean by any reasonable amount of labour, too thick upon the ground, too far from work or country air.

The programme was to involve the restructuring of social relations in and around housing consumption and related aspects of social life. Silkin, for instance, argued

> Our aim must be to combine in the new town the friendly spirit of the former slum with the vastly improved health conditions of the new estate but it must be a broadened spirit, embracing all classes of society. . . . We may produce in the new towns a new type of citizen, a healthy, self-respecting dignified person with a sense of beauty, culture and civic pride.
>
> (Quoted in Aldridge 1979, 36)

In retrospect the radical, all-embracing and far-reaching scope of the new town proposals stand out as perhaps the most complete example of central government in Britain attempting to control and restructure local social relations at home, work and in other spheres. In turn, this activity we see as reflecting radical changes in economy, society and the balance of social forces, and concomitantly in state social relations. New towns at the early stage were both products and local versions of the corporatist compromise attempted nationally during the 1940s. Aldridge (1979, 29) sums up the situation as follows:

> The British new towns programme has been arguably the most striking example yet seen of an attempt at comprehensive social and physical (and by implication economic) planning in this country or in most of the West. It is doubtful whether such a grandiose vision could have been contemplated at any other time than 1945–7 when socialism, optimism and national enterprise made the project seem attainable.

As social relations exist in space, their restructuring has to take account of space. In the new towns programme, *physical* and *land-use* planning, sanctioned by the rule of parliament and use of law, was a prime tool used by the government in this direction. Moreover, clearly the new towns had to exist in space, in specific localities. However, the chosen policies and the necessarily locality-specific nature of their objectives contained a series of difficulties hindering the easy implementation of state power. For instance, perhaps even more so than in the use of tenure and law, physical and land-use planning, cornerstones of the new town policy, were clumsy and blunt instruments for central government to attempt to control local social relations.

In essence the British state was attempting to impose new rules on how the use of space in the locality was to be determined, and this in many spheres (such as 'middle-class' housing consumption) and localities previously largely untouched by explicit state activity. As the quote above from Silkin suggests, one policy objective was to move away from the situation where localities and local social relations were dominated by a single 'class' to one 'embracing all classes of society'. However, the determinants of local social relations, perhaps particularly class-based ones, lay largely outside the scope of essentially non-social policies. Consequently, there is no guarantee that state power – whatever policy tools are used – will successfully be able to dominate in all localities. As the subsequent section makes clear, this is the root of the housing consumption issue and actions which emerged in Crawley following the establishment of the new town.

Another difficulty may be in successfully overriding the *existing* social relations in a specific locality in order to implement government policy. In some new towns this was especially problematic because of the radical objectives of the policy. The government was intervening in spheres previously left untouched and controlled either individually or by social groups. Housing consumption of the type dominant in Crawley was just this. State activity, concomitantly, also involved a realignment in the position and power of different social groups and (in Silkin's terms) classes in the locality and local social relations.

In the particular case of Crawley, established social relations in the locality vigorously fought against the imposition of a new town on the area by central government. Rightly they saw the designation and development of a new town as a radical threat to their existing pattern of housing consumption, their current control and use of the primarily 'residential' area, and their domination of local state institutions. Many local people were being asked (or told) to sacrifice their individual rights and privileges, particularly those associated with housing consumption, in the 'national interest'.

Central government was clearly aware that individuals and social groups in Crawley and other designated areas might not concede without struggle. Law, in particular, was used to push through government policy. In the new towns programme the use of law had a number of dimensions. First, although existing local state institutions were allowed to continue (the Crawley designated area was administered by four parish councils, three rural district councils and three county councils) the fundamental control of the new town was taken by central government itself. Local electoral politics, as such, had no part to play in any major aspect of the development, building, planning or administration of the new town. Instead (and after considerable debate), a development corporation directly responsible to central government was set up to guide and control growth of the new town. Interestingly, new town development corporations, the institutional ancestors of urban development corporations in inner cities, may be taken as one extreme of forms of local state institutions. In theory at least they were and are accountable only to central government and a means of government dominating the locality and local social relations. In practice, as section 6.7 indicates, in Crawley this imposition of non-electoral local government institutions from above resulted in unforeseen tensions and difficulties.

A second dimension of the use of law was the passing of legislation allowing private land and property rights to be taken into public ownership. This refutation or seizing of existing rights clearly implied that some residents at least were no longer to exert any control over important aspects of their housing consumption experiences. Indeed, the property of many individuals in Crawley was compulsorily purchased and the occupiers forced to move elsewhere. In Saunders' terms, the rights of benefit, control and disposal of owner-occupied property were all removed.

The use of law had other effects on the housing consumption experiences of existing residents. For instance, as the enabling legislation was applied in the building of the new town, so the physical environment and social relations in the area changed. As, for example, the quality and nature of the neighbourhood altered, existing residents had no redress through local state institutions (which previously functioned to maintain the dominance of the local status quo) or legal means of combating what they saw as disadvantageous. Again, the rights of owners to obtain the 'market value' of their property was legally withdrawn and substituted by compensation at statutorily agreed levels.

In essence then the battle over the coming of the new town to the Crawley area was a struggle between British state and locality. The British state was requisitioning a specific locality in order to restructure the social relations existing in other places. This involved overriding established local social relations and local state institutions neither of which were likely to facilitate the implementation of national policy in the locality. Government actions were of potentially wide significance in that they included the denial of established and enshrined property rights and patterns of housing consumption. Residents, in a majority of cases as housing consumers, reacted with considerable anger and fury. A collective response was made although, perhaps because they were attempting to protect existing rights (unlike the squatters who were trying to gain new rights for themselves), this was within the framework of law.

When Crawley was proposed as a new town location in 1946 the area, like most of the other first London new towns, was far from being a rural greenfield site – although the phrase 'new town' suggests just that. Rather than being dominated by landed or agricultural interests (altough the latter were of some importance) middle-class property owners were pre-eminent. Most of these owner-occupiers had moved into the area (Crawley itself, Ifield and Three Bridges) during the inter-war period following the disintegration of landed estates and considerable speculative house-building. The locality was emerging as a high status, 'discontinuous' residential suburb closely linked to London (Gray 1983).

In part these newcomers were lured by a set of images – stressing the history and healthy nature of the environment and the freedom bound to living in and owning a house in the area – extolled by estate developers and estate agents. The dwelling designs, drawing on and combining a variety of styles of rural vernacular architecture, often typified in the mock Tudor, partially tile-hung, detached house (with adjacent garage), tell much about this attempt to draw on the presumed power of an image of a half-remembered, idyllic rural past. Perhaps ironically, given the later sweeping away of many individual land ownership and property rights, the promoters of the Ifield estate (in the west of the designated area) had claimed in the 1930s

> there will be no fear of Balham or Tooting being planted on this sylvan spot. . . . Fortunately Ifield will never be doomed to administration by the exploiter who is willing to destroy natural beauty in order to cram every available inch of ground with every variety of habitation.[7]

Given such expectations, the concern of property owners at the new town plan is of no surprise. Within a month of the announcement of the new town (July 1946) proposals emerged to form a local branch of the National Federation of Property Owners. The aim as reported in the *Crawley and District Observer* (CDO) 30 August 1946, was to form 'a protection association to safeguard the interests of owner-occupiers in the area affected by the new town'. At first the prime concern of home owners, as reported in the press, was with the levels of compensation for compulsory purchase – limited to 1939 values plus no more than 60 per cent. The general secretary of the NFPO lent his support to the idea of setting up a Crawley branch, arguing

> The residents cannot fight as individuals and no association of them, however strong, can fight alone. Experience is accumulative. Weight of numbers and national backing is what counts with this and any other Government.
>
> (*CDO*, 6 September 1946)

Within a few weeks the Worth, Crawley and Ifield Property Owners' Association had been formed, and, through the National Federation, had briefed Erskine Symers KC to represent their case.

Ultimately the POA claimed a local membership of some 800 and 'represented property to the value of £250,000'. At the time the designated area contained a population of about 9500 people. Even assuming the 800 members of the association represented households, rather than individuals alone, clearly many local people held alternative views on the new town proposal, although these were rarely the most publicized. However, one parish councillor argued that every time the new town came up for discussion people who owned a house or a small portion of land objected. In his view, 'The new town is for the working classes in a big way. The people who are objecting are all persons of one class. The new town is a good idea and is sticking up for the working classes.' (*CDO*, 18 October 1946). The Three Bridges Labour Party made the most sustained response to the property owners, unanimously carrying the following resolution:

> The executive council of the Three Bridges Labour Party welcomes the proposed new town of Crawley–Three Bridges and pledges its wholehearted support to the project. It recognizes that this is a great opportunity for this area to emerge from haphazard development towards a properly planned and balanced community . . . [the scheme] . . . will not only bring happier and more prosperous times to our local community, but will also create conditions which will provide employment, good housing and proper amenities for 50,000 people – many of whom at the moment are living in deplorable conditions as a result of the war. It regrets that the larger issues and undoubted benefits of this proposal are being clouded by intensive propaganda on the part of those who are bent on placing their own selfish interests before the welfare of the community as a whole. (*CDO*, 25 October 1946)

Despite such opinions in favour of the new town, the public inquiry in the November was packed by those opposing the scheme. The inquiry, both then and now, does appear little more than a quasi-legal means of allowing people to vent their feelings rather than a mechanism that might seriously challenge what the government wanted to do. The first draft of the New Towns Bill in 1946 made no provision for either consultation with the inhabitants of designated areas or for a public inquiry. This was changed, following debate in parliament and elsewhere, by an opposition amendment providing for a local inquiry to be held if there were objections. None the less, central government was clear that the locality was to have no significant say. In Stevenage, the first government new town, Silkin had declared well before the inquiry 'It is no use jibbing, it's going to be done' (Quoted in Benny 1947, 48). The Crawley inquiry inspector, R. T. Russell, was a civil servant in the Ministry of Town and County Planning – hardly an impartial background. Russell pointed out the narrow purpose of the proceedings, arguing that most objections concerned levels of compensation and the loss of freeholds –

both matters 'regulated by existing legislation and thus outside the scope of the inquiry' (*CDO*, 8 November 1946).[8]

The inquiry lasted a mere two and a half days. In retrospect, and in comparison with present-day planning inquiries, it is a fascinating instance of a crude and blunt yet effective instrument for implementing government policies. With it the government was able to impose its own legally sanctioned rules and wishes on the locality, rule out of order basic and underlying complaints and draw clear boundaries around what it considered legitimate arguments. Thus the 'legitimate' battleground, much to the dismay of the objectors (who interrupted Russell's opening address with 'cries of "nonsense and absolute tosh" ') was defined in terms of essentially technical issues such as the feasibility of the site for a new town, likely water supply and drainage problems, the loss of agricultural land and milk supply to the nation, and so on.

Property owners and other opponents, once they accepted that their actions should be within the law, could do little about this situation apart from verbally venting their protests. For example, one legal representative argued that 'Industry would ruin the new town and prevent it from being a pleasant place to live in'. He continued, 'This is not an inquiry. It is not a judicial inquiry or a quasi-judicial inquiry. It is an act of deliberate administrative lawlessness.' Similarly, Erskine Symes for the property owners pointed out that the scheme was well under way before the inquiry, Silkin having appointed a Local Advisory Committee and Ministry staff having begun survey work. This suggested

> either the Minister has decided he is going to designate this area no matter what is said at this inquiry, or he is running the risk of incurring considerable expense of public money, which is going to be wasted if the area is not confirmed. I should hate to think that your Minister would incur a waste of public money, and one is left to the unfortunate alternative.

A Mrs Hawksley-Hill, after vehemently complaining about compensation levels, continued to applause, 'I also maintain that all English people have equal rights under Magna Carta and that no section should be exploited for the good of any other section whatever. I have a right to own a house and a little piece of land. It is a very small house, but it is my house, and that is the point, and I defy anybody to take it from me'. Another individual, in anguish at the possible loss of his home, asked: 'What are we in – England or Russia?' Perhaps the most individual objection involving housing consumption came from 84-year old W. F. Noaks, who proclaimed

> At the top of my house in Horley I can have the advantage of sea breezes. When the wind is in the south I can feel the ozone. I think I have some advantage in mentioning that because I was Mayor of Islington for a year, which has a population of 330,000, and when we go to 50,000 I know something of what the exhalations will be. Therefore, I know the air will be vitiated by the people living in the area, and the opportunity I have to enjoy the sea breezes in Horley will cease.

Apart from the inquiry, a series of public meetings was used to organize and listen to protests over the proposals. For example, a speaker at a Liberal Liberty League meeting argued for more direct action:

> What the people really wanted to know was: Is the new town going to affect my house or my land? Make no mistake about it, if our people would rise against the tyrannies which are now being imposed upon us now, this satellite town, just as one instance, could be prevented from taking shape.
>
> (*CDO*, 29 November 1946)

Similarly, at the same gathering it was argued that legal proceedings were ineffective but that political action could bring about the desired effect: 'The Government are taking political action, and the only way that you can stand up against it is by taking political action yourselves.' Unfortunately neither speaker illustrated what form such political action might take in the property owners' case. Crawley opponents might, however, have drawn on the example of Stevenage (Orlans 1952, Benny 1947), where the railway station signs were changed from Stevenage to Silkingrad, the Minister himself on a visit to the locality was heckled with cries of 'Gestapo!' and 'Dictator' and gravel was thrown into the engine of his car. In Crawley one protester declared his willingness to go to gaol, but such opinions did not receive any support. Popular political action outside the law was not a realistic option given the social relations dominant in both Crawley and Stevenage.

A little after two months later, in January 1947, Silkin announced that 'after considering all the objections to the scheme' he had decided to make the appropriate designation order (*CDO*, 10 January 1947). The plan was to go ahead as far as the government was concerned. However, the local Member of Parliament, Earl Winterton, continued to oppose the scheme. At a public meeting in February he endorsed the property owners' case: 'Should a new town be built in this area it will affect prejudicially by depriving them of their freehold interests, hundreds of households, mostly not rich people, who are constituents of mine' (*CDO*, 21 February 1947). Discussing the emergent economic crisis, he added that what was needed was a 'property-owning democracy that would work hard because it had a stake in the country'.

In the same month two local residents (Percy J. Watkin of The Priors Farm and the Hon. Mrs C. E. Rollo of The Spindle) decided to resume the legal battle with the support of the Property Owners' Association. Drawing on the parallel Stevenage case, where an appeal had initially been successful (this was later reversed in a higher court), Mr Watkins, a London import and export merchant, argued in the press that if property owners 'want to protect their rights they must be prepared to fight. We all want to see new houses erected quickly for people who are in urgent need, but it cannot be done by riding rough-shod over property owners' (*CDO*, 28 February 1947). The Hon. Mrs Rollo added:

> We are out to help the small man, because we feel he is not getting a fair deal at all. We also want to see the law of England upheld, and cannot agree that it has been in our case. The inquiry was not held in proper judicial fashion.

In May, two months before the High Court hearing, Silkin sought to appease property owners in Crawley and elsewhere by announcing that compensation levels were to be improved. Rather than being based on the New Town Act, 1946 – 1939 values plus up to 60 per cent – the Minister announced in Bletchley that he would introduce an amendment to the Town and Country Planning Bill then going through parliament so that owners would receive the 'ordinary market value when the community needs to purchase this property compulsorily' (*CDO*, 9 May 1947, see also Schaffer 1970).

With this concession, undoubtedly due in part to the continuous action by property owners in various new town areas and the delay in starting serious planning and development created by the legal battle, Silkin was able to subdue the opposition somewhat. In any event, the legal battle was on ground chosen by the government itself. The High Court appeal was not over whether the government could override established property interests (which it legally could) but over whether the Minister gave proper information to the objectors about the proposed order and consulted with the local authorities concerned. In the event, the appeal was dismissed, the court finding that the Minister had complied with the legislation. Three weeks later Silkin himself visited the locality, making a conciliatory speech: 'In this country we have our battle, the thing is settled in the proper way, and once it is settled we sit down and make a job of it, and it is in that spirit that I come to you' (*CDO* 22 August 1947).

Mr Watkins was, however, undaunted, arguing

> If Mr Silkin thinks the battle is over, he is very much mistaken. In fact it is only just begun. He will find there are people still prepared to fight for their homes and freeholds in which many have invested their life savings.
>
> (*CDO*, 29 August 1947)

The Property Owners' Association was less optimistic, withdrawing its financial support. Subsequently, although a further appeal was made to the Court of Appeal, this too was dismissed. Leave was refused to take the case to the House of Lords on the grounds that 'this has really become an extremely academic matter' – even if the House of Lords decided in favour of the appellants, the Minister would go through the whole process again, but in a more formal manner. Consequently, 'the only achievement . . . would be to further delay the coming of the new town and to create further uncertainty and to incur further cost'.[9]

Schaffer (1970, 48–9) well sums up the results of the Crawley litigation and that about other London new towns:

> The Court decisions had firmly established that the Minister was entitled – and indeed had a duty under the Act – to satisfy himself *before* designation that the project was a sound one. Provided he supplied the local authorities with sufficient information and gave them sufficient opportunity to state their views and provided he listened to objections and properly considered them, it was no part of the Court's duty to say whether his decision was right or wrong.

In essence, through its own legislative machinery, government was able to determine the rules of the legal battle over the new town. Property owners had little chance of winning once the battlefield had been chosen and they had implicitly accepted it. Through their actions, however, the new town programme was delayed for perhaps two years. In addition, the improved compensation levels meant that property owners were able to retreat from Crawley during the following years to buy homes in other localities in the South-east – localities where local social relations continued to favour property owners. In any event, the changing balance of social forces in society during the post-war period resulted in a withdrawal of state interference with private property rights. Property owners may have lost the Crawley battle, but the war itself swung decisively in their favour in the subsequent decades. But immediately after the legislative battles the Minister of Town and Country Planning was at last able to begin in earnest the 'great and far-reaching social experiment'.[10] As we shall see, however, despite the belief in the benefits of a radical restructuring of social relations, housing consumption issues and actions were to re-emerge in Crawley in new and unforeseen forms.

## 6.7 Rent increases and collective action in Crawley

By the mid-1950s the building of Crawley New Town was well under way. The built environment and economic and social fabric of the area had been revolutionized. For example, by April 1956[11] 47 new factories were in production covering 1,642,000 square feet and employing 7380 people. Almost a hundred new shops, and handfuls of schools, community centres and churches had been built. Five of the eight planned neighbourhoods had been completed and 5651 development corporation and 328 private sector dwellings constructed. Work was proceeding apace to complete the new town. In six years the population had increased from 10,000 to 30,000 people, and by the mid-1950s was growing at a rate of 5000 people per year towards the initial target population of 50,000.

These changes in the built environment and influx of people and jobs were the physical and statistical symbols of the restructuring of the locality. However, although the locality was now an urban area, an industrial and service centre with a large resident population, it had very atypical local state institutions. It retained the pre-new town mix of local state institutions of parish, rural district and county councils until 1956 when the former two of these three were abolished and Crawley Urban District Council was formed. But, despite the existence of the UDC, even at this stage local state institutions in Crawley (and other new towns) remained anomalous for the government and administration of the locality continued to be dominated by the development corporation. As noted above, this non-elected body, responsible not to the local population but directly to central government, had immense powers in the spheres of consumption and (unusually for local state institutions) production. It was, for example, influential in determining which employers moved into the locality and also the landlord for all business and commercial property and for the vast majority of new (and for a significant proportion of pre-new town) residential property. Theoretically, and to a large degree in practice, the corporation determined who lived and worked in the new town. Turning more directly to housing consumption, the corporation was responsible for the planning, design, building, finance, administration, allocation and maintenance and repair of the majority of dwellings in Crawley.

The principal reason for the power and autonomy of the development corporation was that it was seen by central government as the most suitable institutional means for implementing new town policy. If only by implication, the view was that the great economic and social experiment would succeed only if it were distanced from existing forms of local state institutions and from the possibly detrimental influence of local social relations. But perhaps somewhat contradictorily, the development corporation, while being designed to be independent of the locality and local social relations, also had the task of restructuring these very social relations. Amongst the objectives of the first new towns were such things as attaining social balance and social mixing, an end to class antagonism, and, perhaps most ambitious and nebulous of all, the creation of a new community. Precisely how this was to be done, with what policy tools and using what measures of success was never really clearly spelt out by those in authority, although planning and architectural determinism does appear as a popular line of argument. In this view controlling how space was used could influence social relations. Building neighbourhoods of a particular size and careful attention to the layout of streets were thought to facilitate social encounters between, for example, young mothers taking their children to the neighbourhood primary school or visiting the neighbourhood shops. Similarly, mixing different social groups as housing was allocated was thought to encourage 'community leadership' by the middle class.[12] Such plans, of course, hinge on a number of assumptions about gender, family and class relations which were essentially status-quo in character. Despite these original aims, as Crawley was developed such ideals and assumptions seem to have been mentioned less and less, perhaps in part because their attainment was never very likely but also because the 1950s was a period when material objectives rapidly transcended the more nebulous and idealist social ones dominant immediately after the war.

None the less, social relations in the locality *were* radically altered. For the first time the working class replaced the middle class as the dominant political force in the town. The newcomers were mostly skilled and semi-skilled workers in families with children, who moved to Crawley with their existing employers from South London boroughs. Although denied any significant input into local state institutions (particularly before the creation of the UDC in 1956), the newcomers at work had active and strong trade unions. Party politics was increasingly dominated by the Labour Party with the Communist Party also being active, while a majority of corporation tenants joined Crawley Tenants' Association. Indeed, the absence or weakness of more usual democratic local state institutions helped activate and strengthen these other organizations.

In many respects corporation tenants had excellent housing consumption experiences, particularly when compared with their previous London housing (Gray 1983). New town dwellings were built to very high standards (although these lessened during the 1950s with increasing building costs and decreased government finance for the new towns). Densities were low, houses were the norm, gardens were large, materials were of high quality, designs were modern, and so on. The early neighbourhoods were built within easy cycling time of the industrial estate and many workers returned home for lunch each day. Each neighbourhood was also relatively well served with shops, schools and other communal facilities. The publicly available official view was that despite obvious settling-in problems, the revolutionary change for newcomers was proceeding smoothly. For example, Margaret Wragg the Crawley housing manager, described 'starting life in a new town' as the

> opening chapter of a great undertaking. A complete cross-section of London society is on the move to Crawley: industrialists, technicians, administrative and clerical staffs, skilled and unskilled tradesmen, etc., most of whom have wives and children. . . .
>
> It will readily be understood that this move has meant a great change in the way of living for many of these families. For those living in some of the more overcrowded areas, cinemas, dance halls, and 'pubs' were the main source of entertainment. As one tenant put it the other day: 'We relied on synthetic pleasures, now our life is simpler but much more fun.' . . . Families are becoming closer knit. Father now comes home at mid-day. . . .
>
> Money spent on these 'synthetic' pleasures is now going into the home. There is a great pride taken in the house and the garden and much budget scheming is going on in order to provide the best for both.
>
> (Wragg 1951, 249–50)

But this rosy housing consumption picture was beset, for most families, by one considerable thorn, that of costs. There were a number of elements to this problem: wages were lower than London rates; food and consumer goods bought locally were relatively expensive; moving to a new house, particularly for those people who did not previously have a home of their own, often meant that families had to make considerable hire-purchase payments; and corporation rents were high, tending to be greater than either private sector or local authority rents. New town corporations were required to balance their housing accounts, making neither a profit nor loss. Significantly, then, the option of subsidizing rents from the rates available to local authorities was not available in new towns.

Both corporation and tenants had been aware of the potential rents problem for a number of years. As early as 1949 the Corporation Research Section, in a paper entitled 'Social implications of high building costs', noted that rent pooling, a solution available to local authorities, 'is not applicable to a Development Corporation' (having no older dwellings available amongst which to spread the cost of new construction). It continued

> It appears that, without an increased Exchequer Subsidy, the burden of higher costs in New Towns must fall on the tenant. Since the bulk of houses in this country are pegged to the pre-war level and in many cases are related to the 1914 level, and since also the level of wages in the country is determined in part by the level of rents, then the inhabitants of new towns will be paying, on the average, a rent higher than the normal rent and somewhat out of proportion to the national wage-price structure. In view of the situation, and of

its possible harmful social effects, it is desirable to investigate more closely the difference in rent levels and the proportion of income spent on rent by families of various income groups.

A variety of evidence was used to show that average London rents for similar houses were 4 to 7 shillings lower than 'the economic rent of currently constructed houses in Crawley', and that over 60 per cent of all London households paid rents below (often substantially below) Crawley New Town rents. The question was raised

> Can these households be attracted to the New Towns and will the high rents, by taking an undue proportion of their income, have a harmful effect on their health and standard of living? The penalties of failure are an unbalanced population and an insufficient labour supply or a population which has to concentrate on the payment of its rent and necessities to the exclusion of more ample living.

In a later amended version of the report a number of possible 'solutions' were discussed. Noting that a rent problem, although less severe, also existed in many local authorities, it was suggested that 'it may, therefore, occur that the increasingly wide importance of the problem will demand national attention and that the Crawley problem will be tackled as part of a wider problem'. An alternative possibility was that a continuing long-term rise in wages and prices would decrease the proportion of income being paid in rent. Failing either of these eventualities the 'central authorities' might give new towns separate attention because of their special difficulties, although the likely unpopularity of such a course of action with local authorities was noted. In this situation, 'each New Town may have to seek salvation in its own way', options including 'simplicity and economy of lay-out and design and continuous experimentation both in building and engineering technique'.

In the event, the worst fears of the authors of the report did not materialize during the early 1950s. Although rents were relatively high, the issue simmered rather than boiled over. A number of new town organizations became actively involved in the matter. For example, in 1952 the Joint Shop Stewards' Committee of APV, one of the largest employers, wrote to the corporation about the fact that rents for new houses were increasing although standards were falling. They pointed out the disadvantageous differentials between London and Crawley rents and wages. In 1952 and 1953 Crawley Tenants' Association, in part led by Communist Party members, became increasingly vocal about rents, linking the problem to the structure of the building industry, interest rates and central government subsidy levels for new town housing. In September 1953, for instance, Crawley Tenants' Association *Newsletter* reported that a diverse range of organizations in the town, ranging from Crawley Co-operative Women's Guild to Crawley Communist Party, and from the Trades Council, to the Transport and General Workers' Union, had agreed about the seriousness of the rents situation and on 1) the need to secure a reduction in the rate of interest charged on borrowed capital for house construction; 2) the need to increase state subsidy for new towns; and 3) the need to improve the existing organization of the building industry. During this period senior officials in the corporation increasingly reacted against the 'political' nature of the association. Indeed, although the association had been formally recognized by the corporation in May 1952, relationships rapidly worsened and regular contact ceased in the following year.

By 1954 the Crawley rent problem reached the pages of *Town and Country Planning*. In January the journal published a letter from the Secretary of Crawley and District Trades Council, who argued

> I would say that high rents is one of our main problems. The average worker in Crawley is having a hard task to make ends meet. Mothers are going out to work when they should be at home looking after their families.

Albert Poyton, Secretary of Crawley Communist Party, made a similar point in the same issue:

> It is almost impossible for a man to keep a wife, apart from any children, and a house when the rent is £2 or more and his wage £8 or less. I consider that a reduction in rent is essential to new town prosperity. If residents can pay their way decently, then we shall all enjoy to the full this healthy, clean, and fresh new life, away from smog.

In passing, both quotations say a good deal about the gender and family assumptions held by many male workers in the town. But despite the obvious existence of the problem, the issue did not at first result in any significant actions on the part of tenants. There were a number of reasons for this. As *Town and Country Planning* itself noted in January 1954, in playing down the existence of a 'special new towns rent problem', 'no tenant has taken a house without prior knowledge of what he would pay. . . . No rents have been increased since occupation.' During this period, then, the housing consumption status quo did not alter for tenants – rents were high from occupation, but they did not increase. In addition, during the early 1950s a combination of low interest rates, continued high government subsidies for new town housing, full employment and over-time in the town, and the fact that the lowest paid London workers did not move to the locality, all meant that rent levels did not become a *fundamental* problem. Moreover, during this early stage in the restructuring of the locality, local social relations were in a state of ferment. Tenant organizations might flex their muscles but were not perhaps strong enough to mount any sustained action.

By 1955 this changed as a consequence of a combination of local and national factors. The rent problem emerged as a major significant issue and resulted in a wide-ranging collective action. Nationally the balance of social forces swung away from the working class. Concomitantly, state social relations altered. At the level of housing policy support for the public sector declined. The Conservative government altered central support for new town housing in a number of ways. Following the Housing Rents and Repairs Act of 1954 corporations were no longer bound by the Rent Restrictions Acts which had prevented them from raising rents once dwellings were occupied. Consequently, an increase in the already high rents was now a possibility. Rises in interest rates followed government attempts to respond to the emergent economic problems of the mid-1950s. This substantially increased building costs, loan charges and the rent levels of new dwellings. At the same time, the government announced that subsidies for new town housing were to be reduced by £6 4s. 0d. to £29 8s. 0d. per house. Locally, lay-offs and short-time working made it less possible for tenants to meet high rents by increasing wages. In addition, local social relations were fully geared up to defend existing housing consumption experiences, and were, in any event, on the offensive over the non-democratic nature of the major local state institutions. Many people were aware that the formation of Crawley Urban District Council in the following April would allow new attacks to be made in this direction.

It is against this background that in late October 1955 Crawley Development Corporation announced that rents were to be increased by 2s. 3d. per week, and by 3s. 3d. per week for the 739 earliest dwellings. A letter sent to all tenants included the following:

> Since March, further increases in the interest rate on public loans, and a decrease in the rate of housing subsidies have compelled the Corporation to make a further review of its housing rents, which have continued at the same general level since April, 1952.
>
> The Corporation is reluctantly forced to increase the rents of its subsidized dwellings. . . .
>
> When the terms or conditions of a tenancy are revised, the law requires that the present tenancy must be determined and a new tenancy offered. The necessary legal notice is therefore enclosed, for your completion and return to the rent collector or Housing Office. (*CDO*, October 1955)

The executive committee of Crawley Tenants' Association immediately responded by deciding to deliver a protest to the Housing Office, requesting a meeting with the corporation, and by advising all tenants to sign the acceptance form, adding the words 'under protest' and to hand them to tenants' stewards, committee members or factory shop stewards until the matter was resolved. Throughout the episode the links with trade unions – a relatively unusual feature of housing consumption actions – were particularly strong. Early on an emergency committee was formed made up of two members of each of the CTA's neighbourhood committees and ten delegates from the industrial estate. Within a few days of the increases being announced the Crawley branch of the AEU, the largest union in the locality, 'unanimously decided that trade unionists should close their ranks and unite against the increases' (*CDO*, 21 October 1955). The AEU linked the issue directly to central government policy, calling for a reduction in interest rates for public sector house building loans, and special housing subsidies for the new town. The movement against the increases also received Labour Party support.

The extent of popular support for collective action soon became apparent. The corporation estimated that within a week of the announcement about 25 per cent of tenants had returned the forms accepting the new tenancy with rent increases.

Against this, there were extremely crowded neighbourhood meetings of many hundreds of tenants. In one neighbourhood a 'resolution calling for every man, woman and child in Crawley to go to the Houses of Parliament and tackle the Minister of Housing about the building subsidies was unanimously adopted' (*CDO*, 28 October 1955).

The significant links between workplace and homeplace action continued to be maintained. The meetings were addressed not only by CTA committee members but also by trade unionists. At some meetings it was argued that 'this rent increase would be met with a wage claim for the same amount, accompanied with the threat of strike action'.

From an early stage, the leaders of the collective action were clear about their objectives. The government rather than CDC was seen as the main culprit, and frequently tenant action was viewed as part of a longer-term struggle to increase government financial support, reduce interest rates, raise subsidy levels and so on. The aim, therefore, 'was to fight the increase and, even if it had to be accepted, to make things so hot that it would be the last'. Similarly, 'The CDC is not to blame. It is a Government body. . . . It has got to increase the rents.' A subsidiary theme was the attack against the development corporation as an undemocratic local state institution. 'The trouble is that we have no elected authority to which to appeal. If we had, this would not have come out of the blue.'

The action as it evolved was based on popular mass support. As such, it was able to disregard and nullify the sanctions of law and physical coercion on which the corporation might have drawn. For example, when questions were raised about the possibility of the corporation evicting tenants, 'an immediate assurance was given by all the shop stewards present that in the unlikely event of such tactics being employed immediate physical assistance would be forthcoming from the Manor Royal factories'.

Within a week of the increase announcement a huge demonstration took place, estimated by the local press to include 5000 people and by *The Times* to be 'several thousand workers'. A march of women and children around the neighbourhoods was joined by workers from the factory estate (which closed for the morning) and building sites, to eventually conclude in a large meeting in the town centre. The *Crawley and District Observer* (28 October 1955) described the scene graphically

> For three hours on Wednesday, Crawley looked like the set of a Hollywood film epic as 5,000 factory workers and housewives joined in a huge demonstration without parallel in the history of the New Town. . . .
>
> 'One! two! three! four! We won't pay more!' The huge army of men and women chanted as they marched in a mile-long column from Manor Royal.
>
> 'Five! six! seven! eight! Take it off the interest rate!' They chorused as they packed the Broad Walk shopping centre for half-an-hour of fiery speech-making.

More than a quarter of a century later a long-standing Labour Party member recalled the event as follows

It was quite an experience. I have been on quite a few demonstrations in my time but that was the one that brought a lump to my throat as I saw the women and children from Pound Hill (a neighbourhood) and the factory people at Manor Royal walking the entire route.

(Quoted in Gray 1983, 78)

Following the demonstration, neighbourhood meetings decided to start an immediate rent strike, withholding the increase and refusing to return the new tenancy agreement forms. At first the strike received the widespread backing of a majority of tenants. The tenants' association sought to maintain support with a series of activities, including the use of pickets to accompany rent collectors. Mass meetings continued, at which women were often particularly vocal. For example, at a town centre meeting of 2000 tenants one woman argued

If we don't fight this increase we shall go back to the days of the depression. We must make the New Town fit for our children to live in. Otherwise their only thought when they grow up will be to get out of the place.

(*CDO*, 11 November 1955)

The initial success of this illegal action reflected the social relations in the locality. Even the built environment and economic and social structures of the new town contributed to the collective action. For example, the vast majority of people worked on the one industrial estate. Most workers in the same factory lived near each other – often in the same neighbourhood and sometimes in the same street. Indeed, the architectural and planning determinism of the original plans probably had the unforeseen consequence of fostering the action. People could meet and discuss the issue readily. Moreover, organization of the protest was considerably facilitated by the strong work, home and political groups which had built up partly in response to the nature of the dominant local state institutions.

Although even now it is impossible to know fully how central government responded to the action, within two weeks of the protest developing, Duncan Sandys, the Minister of Housing and Local Government, announced a slight increase in government subsidies for new town housing and gave an undertaking that subsidies would not be reduced in the future. On this basis one might argue that the collective action did quickly succeed in securing a promise of longer-term support for new town housing.

The corporation reacted to the tenants' activities by keeping a low profile. It argued, for example, that

The Corporation has great sympathy with the anxiety felt by its tenants about the amount they have to pay in rents. . . . The present increased rents have only been imposed after most exhaustive examination of the whole financial position and are essential. (*CDO*, 4 November 1955)

Although the corporation had initially said it would refuse payment of the old rent without the increase, its opinion on this tactic rapidly changed given the scale of the protest. Sir Thomas Bennett, chairman of the development corporation, put a brave face on the retreat, saying 'We thought it much kinder to the tenants to let them run on in arrears than to refuse their rent' (*CDO*, 11 November 1955) and adding that payment of rent on account was taken by the corporation to mean that tenants had, in fact, accepted the new rent. Throughout the strike the corporation made no move to institute legal proceedings or evict tenants. This softly-softly approach also included meeting CTA representatives but essentially stonewalling in discussions – expressing sympathy and offering little but promises of future consultations and every effort to maintain present rent levels 'for at least three years'.

The corporation's approach was successful over the following weeks. Support of the action decreased slowly at first and then more quickly. By the end of November the corporation claimed that 63 per cent of tenants were paying the increased rents. In mid-January 600 tenants continued to withhold their rent. But in February, with even this support dwindling, the rent strike was called off, 'in favour of other tactics in which the full weight of the association may be employed' (*CDO*, 17 February 1956).

A number of points may be made about the aftermath and consequences of the collective action. Two and a half decades later participants varied in their interpretation of the effects of the protest (Gray 1983). For example, the Labour Party member quoted on page 229 argued

> It was a protest. At the time I thought it was quite successful in the sense that the next time they wanted to put the rent up they talked to us. I can remember that about a year later there was a rent meeting in the community centre. They wrote to us and said the rent had to go up, and they sent someone to explain it. It definitely softened things down. So there was some consultation.

A long-standing labour councillor saw more positive and far-reaching consequences

> half a crown represented something. Whilst it wasn't going to break people, the action was to get the subsidies restored. Indeed, whether it was the Crawley rent strike or not, the Government reintroduced subsidies to new towns soon after the strike. If it achieved nothing else, consultation came out of it. It was quite clear to the Development Corporation that within a few months Crawley was to have its own council as distinct from the parish council. . . . So from 1956 onwards the relationship of the governed by the governing had to change somewhat. . . . Therefore you couldn't turn and disregard and ignore, and consultation became more of a thing of talking between equals.

A senior Crawley New Town official speaking in the early 1970s saw the episode in somewhat different perspective:[13]

> This was a major confrontation . . . [but] . . . the Corporation just played it cool. After this the Tenants' Association faded away. Today, we put up a new increase but there is little reaction.
>
> Most people actually felt the Corporation was a reasonable landlord and did not feel the Corporation was bad. We always sent letters to the tenants

explaining why rents went up. The militant people all begin to mellow over time, as a process. The early days saw the most vigorous reactions of the people, and today there is far less.

The Corporation won its point. We did not lose our nerve over all the fuss, cut down the rent increase or backtrack, and this was important. The pressures could have forced us to compromise but we didn't.

In so far as the campaign was to fight the increase on rent, it failed. Since then there has been no serious organised opposition . . . (to corporation actions) . . . partly because the issues were not truly significant. The rents were fair for the housing, or, perhaps the people couldn't be bothered.

The locality, local state institutions and local social relations changed significantly in the years after the collective action. The rents problem never again became a significant issue. Rents were raised again three years later by 1*s*. 6*d*. per week, and although the CTA was very vocal in protesting at the increases, no collective action resulted. At the time, *The Universities and Left Review Club* in a local study argued 'no one feels he can do anything about it. The old feeling of working-class solidarity seems to have suffered a demise, and working-class people admit their lack of community spirit, their attitude of each for himself' (Hase 1958, 21). This pessimistic radical review concluded that new towns such as Crawley were places 'where class consciousness is theoretically denied, working-class people are consciously trying to elevate themselves, lulled into a dream land of status through possessions.'

Although perhaps accurate as a class analysis, returning economic prosperity had ensured that by the late 1950s many Crawley residents had 'never had it so good'. Their dwellings were of a high standard and wages now generally more than countered rent levels. It is also clear that although there were considerable pressures within government and civil service to push up new town rents, the Crawley action had become a warning restraint limiting what was considered feasible. Cullingworth (1979, 389) quotes a Ministry document which notes that across the board rent increases made it 'peculiarly easy for agitators to whip up the kind of strikes which stopped Crawley industry at the end of 1955'. Although perhaps in a somewhat nebulous way the Crawley action influenced rent levels and the housing consumption experiences of new town tenants both in Crawley and elsewhere. In any event, the corporation was more conscious of the importance of public relations, and political relations in the locality had the new Urban District Council as an at least partially effective avenue through which to work. In addition, the rent campaign had had important if indirect long-term consequences on these very relations acting to crystallize them and make them explicit. Thus Gwynne (1974, 7–8) argues that 'one certain result' of the collective action

> was the formation of a political 'Left' from many assorted elements in the town, whose common enemy was the 'Tory' corporation. As a result of this, from its inception in 1956 the Crawley Urban District Council has been a Labour dominated Council (with the exception of 1969–70 when the Labour Party fell out with the Trade Unions). Everybody who stands for the Council does so as a political party affiliate. In the Council meetings there is constant

reference to the desire for public ownership of the Town's facilities, and especially the houses owned by the New Towns Commission.

The underlying issue of the new town institutions continued to be intensely debated locally and nationally during the following decades. By the early 1960s the building of Crawley New Town was substantially complete. At this stage, despite the original (1946) intentions to transfer assets to the local authority the development corporation was wound up, and its assets and remaining responsibilities taken over by the Commission for the New Towns – a central government body charged with administering a number of completed new towns. Cullingworth and Karn (1968, 26) note that although the Commission was

> announced as a temporary administrative arrangement, the [Conservative] Government reasoning in debates tended to concentrate not on the particular circumstances which made the time unsuitable for a transfer but on the general character of the local authorities which would make them unsuitable to own the assets at any time.

They continue that one of the main disadvantages argued of local authority ownership was that 'their political character would affect policy adversely (particularly on rents)'. Undoubtedly some development corporation officials also argued strongly against the 'political' character of local councils. Effectively then during the following years neither Conservative government nor senior officials in the 'central' local state institutions were willing to allow local social relations to dominate in the administration of new town localities.

In Crawley, however, this strategy was subsequently watered down with the formation of the Crawley Joint Advisory Committee consisting of two members of the Urban District Council's Housing Committee and two members of the Commission for the New Towns' Local Committee. One aim of the Advisory Committee was to achieve 'a greater measure of co-ordination in housing policy and administration including securing and monitoring more or less uniform rents for comparable properties (quoted in Cullingworth and Karn 1968, 81). This state of affairs lasted until the mid-1970s when with changing central government attitudes and continued local pressure the housing assets of the Commission were transferred wholesale to Crawley council. Almost two decades after the collective action public housing in the area was at last owned and administered by a local state institution under local political control. Local social relations and local state institutions were largely in sympathy with each other, and the state of affairs existing in most localities was finally re-established in Crawley.

## 6.8 The state and housing consumption

Despite being over very different issues, the three housing actions described above have a number of features in common. In all three cases local social relations and the nature of local state institutions were of crucial importance in influencing the form and course of the housing action. For example, a central reason why all three actions took the form they did was the inability of local state institutions to adequately respond to and meet local demands. Housing consumers had no option but to address much of their action either outside or against local state institutions. Local social relations were significant in fostering a collective form of action – for example, in two cases people shared common experiences and identities both inside and outside the home. In these sorts of ways specific localities *at particular points in time* (as we saw, Crawley as a locality changed radically within a decade) appear as key formative contexts within which housing consumption issues and actions emerge in particular ways.

Each episode also needs to be understood as something with a complex pre-history and equally complex wider implications both for housing consumers themselves and for the shape of housing consumption. Interestingly, however, in two of the cases state intervention in housing consumption was an immediate cause of an action occurring, while for Brighton it might be argued that the lack of intervention was the root of the issue.

On the surface at least all three collective actions appear to have failed in their immediate objectives: the Brighton squatters left the buildings they occupied without a guarantee of adequate permanent accommodation; Crawley did become the location of a new town; the rent increases were successfully (for the Corporation) implemented. However, such a superficial assessment ignores the longer-term consequences – both local and national – of each of the actions. At this level 'success' and 'failure' are too crude as measures of assessment.

A related point here concerns Saunders's (1981, 276) view of urban struggles as 'typically fragmented, localized, strategically limited, and politically isolated'. Not all of these descriptive characteristics appear relevant to the three collective actions described above. For example, although taking place and based around action in local areas, the squatting campaign was hardly localized in the sense of being restricted to a single locality. Moreover, in Brighton neither was it localized in time. Similarly, neither the Brighton activists nor the Crawley rent strikers were only interested in 'strategically limited' aims. The ultimate objectives of some of the participants included, in one case, the removal of private ownership of property and, in the other case, a restructuring of state intervention in housing.

In addition, even if we accept Saunders's characterization as at least partially accurate, to do so also tends to blind us from more nebulous but none the less important attributes and implications of all three housing consumption actions. In all three instances relations existed between housing consumers and the British state and between the local and the national. These relations are often only glimpsed and hinted at when local studies of housing consumption actions are made – they may be beyond either any easy empirical demonstration or the appreciation of the 'actors' involved. None the less, these relations appear to have flowed and spiralled backwards and forwards – from local to national, from housing consumer to the state – in complex patterns of cause and effect.

These relations are best seen as continuous, although their shape and form might vary over time. For example, the three issues and actions described above are but instances (albeit particularly interesting) of the considerable range of housing issues and actions which have occurred in both Brighton and Crawley throughout the post-war period. Both localities, for instance, have been the scene of a range of collective actions over issues such as maintenance and repair in the public sector, empty property, homelessness, tenants' rights, landlord duties and obligations in the private rented sector, rent levels, housing shortages, environmental change, and so on.

The comparative study of a range of housing actions in various localities and at different issues and times might, of course, be further developed and extended. Apart from Brighton and Crawley, our other two British case study areas, Sheffield and Norfolk, have been the location for a wide spread of issues and actions, the study of which would undoubtedly extend our understanding of what shapes and conditions housing consumption issues and the responses of consumers. For example, during 1967 and 1968 Sheffield was the site of a well supported local authority tenants' movement and rent strike against the attempts by the Labour Party controlled city council to implement a central government directive to increase rents (Hampton 1970, Dickens and Goodwin 1981). The role of trade unions, Labour Party and other political groupings in this action was in stark contrast to what occurred in the Crawley rent strike.

Against the value of further studies of specific localities, it does appear to be the case that no number of local studies will be able to fully penetrate the range of relationships isolated above. In part this is because the national level and the national state are beyond the analytical comprehension of research limited to the local level alone. In this concluding section, therefore, the aim is to look at these relationships. In particular, the focus is on the state and the role it plays in the evolution of the housing question in countries such as Britain and Sweden.

Our starting point is the view that conceptually more important than state institutions, which in themselves are empty and without power, are the social relations of a particular state. These social relations are, in turn, an expression of the balance of social forces in a society at a particular time and in a specific economic, social, political and ideological context. As Jessop (1982, 221) argues, state power and action is 'a complex social relation that reflects the changing balance of social forces in a determinate conjuncture.' It is then real historically specific relations between people that gets things done.

This suggests that what the state does over the housing question hinges on the struggle in and around a particular state. This 'war' may be continuous, but the social forces victorious in a particular battle will push capitalist housing processes in a particular direction with particular consequences. The housing question itself will vary over time and space according to changes in state power and activity, state social relations, and ultimately the wider balance of social forces. Housing consumption is a central component of the housing question and also a very problematic process. Ultimately it dissolves into issues of power, and access and control of scarce resources. In turn, these are issues of social relations between people, social groups and institutions. Such issues often, by their nature, involve tension and conflict. In part this is because of the competitive character of the housing consumption process. Indeed, it is difficult to envisage any society (whether, for instance, capitalist or socialist) where housing consumers do not, at times, conflict and compete with each other and the providers of housing. However, housing consumption in capitalist societies carries additional difficulties.

As perhaps most obviously seen in the unfettered capitalist economy and society of nineteenth-century Britain, the long-term problems endemic in the production, finance and provision of housing create a series of difficulties in the area of housing consumption. At worst, some people remain without a home of any kind. Perhaps more general are the problems people may experience in paying for housing, which, for instance, spring out of the relationship between wages and housing costs. Despite the necessity of housing consumption in capitalist societies, paradoxically, unrestrained capitalist housing processes may create intense housing consumption problems for consumers and also capitalism.

The response of national states such as those of Britain and Sweden to these problems is often made more difficult by the nature of housing consumption. Housing consumers are not passive receivers of the consumption characteristics imposed on them. Housing consumption issues and actions and the social relations in, over and around housing consumption are a continual source of latent if not manifest pressure on the national state. Consumers, through their social relations, may challenge the housing consumption experiences imposed upon them from above particularly if, for whatever set of reasons, these are not to their satisfaction. In the last resort, as a number of housing consumption actions demonstrate, the governability of society is at risk.

Against this background, what sense are we to make of the national state's role in housing consumption? In theory housing consumption might be pushed in any of a diverse array of directions. For instance, through the use of law and ultimately physical coercion tenure 'rights' might be swept away and another set of consumption attributes imposed on housing consumers. We might argue that this indeed has happened at times in the case of the British private rented sector and during some 'slum' clearance. Typically, the British and Swedish states have been more restrained. (Although British legislation providing for 'housing action areas' gives statutory authorities startling powers to curtail property owners' rights.) But this restraint we see as a reflection of, first, the balance of social forces in the two countries; second, an expression of the fundamental importance but paradoxical nature of housing consumption; and, finally as a consequence of the pressure exerted by housing consumers themselves.

Housing consumption is, then, one aspect of economy and society where capital and labour may reach a compromise largely satisfactory to both sides. From capital's viewpoint, such necessary reactions should not prove fundamentally disadvantageous. For example, Jacobs (1981, 46–7) argues for the specific case of British local authority housing: 'In the final analysis, given a revolutionary situation, it cannot be believed that working-class housing tenure will in any way prove critical in determining the outcome of class struggle.' This can be put another way. Those radical commentators who bemoan the generally passive and inconsequential social relations which *appear* to surround housing consumption, fail to explain fully the conditions under which the social relations of housing consumption might be revolutionized and so create the conditions for radical social and economic change; the existence of *any* significant social relations clearly depends on much more than just the housing system.

How then have capital and labour compromised over housing consumption in

Britain and Sweden, and to what effect? In both countries state action at the national level has effectively nullified or muted many (although by no means all) of the origins of housing consumption issues and consequently the need for action by housing consumers themselves. Especially for much of the post-war period, the compromise and state action in both countries have resulted in significant improvements in both material and normative housing conditions for most sections of the population (see, for example, Donnison and Ungerson 1982). In turn, some of the factors lying behind locality-based housing consumption issues and actions have been swept away.

However, there remain important differences between Britain and Sweden in the nature of this national compromise. Chapter two examined the general nature of the capital–labour compromise in Sweden, while chapters three and four discussed the impact this compromise has had on housing provision at the national level. In Sweden, the demands made by labour have tended to be on all fronts – involving economic *and* social and political relations. Moreover, the more homogeneous character of Swedish labour has meant that most people have been included in the compromise, although there are some noteworthy exceptions to this generalization. Some people in minority groups in Sweden are housed in poor and unmodernized or overcrowded accommodation, or may even be homeless. In other cases, although members of groups such as 'low-status immigrants', 'multi-problem families' and the 'socially handicapped' may be in physically satis-factory dwellings, they may have a poor choice in where they live and have little security of tenure. For what are often complex reasons some minority groups are, then, badly treated by the Swedish state and only partly included in the national compromise between labour and capital (Wiktorin 1980, 1982).[14] However, the scale of such housing consumption problems is very small relative to both the size of the Swedish population and to similar problems in Britain.

It is, then, generally the case that when compared to Britain the total 'residen-tial environment' and housing conditions (Popenoe 1977), standards and 'rights' are good, and the social relations experienced by housing consumers in and around their dwellings usually less fettered. A useful illustrative example is to be found in Egerö's (1979) account of the 'model' town of Örebro. In addition, the importance of housing to the Swedish labour movement is well demonstrated by the influential labour controlled building firms and housing co-operatives (which are development as well as consumption organizations, see chapter three); the fact that tenants' unions are an accepted part of the wider labour movement; and, the strength of other housing consumer organizations. Thus, although many individ-ual housing consumers are not actively involved with such organizations (with, for instance, only about one in three tenants being members of tenants' unions) people in most housing tenures are represented in well organized national bodies which have important lobbying or representative power.

At some sacrifice to capital, although equally (as we have seen in previous chapters) also to its benefit, the potential reasons for local struggle have been largely removed at the national level. Indeed we find that locally based housing consumption issues and actions are comparatively infrequent in Sweden. When they do occur, they are often over relatively minor and easily resolvable matters such as allocation policy or estate standards. Because political struggle has been worked out at the national level, potentially political local issues and actions are usually transformed into essentially technical and apolitical concerns. It should be noted, however, that against this generalization in Sweden's largest cities, such as Stockholm and Göteborg, 'alternative' groups have a tradition of lobbying and collective action (ranging from demonstrations to squatting) over a range of local issues, including housing-related ones such as the demolition or change of use of residential blocks in specific localities.

Perhaps the most serious form of local housing problems in Sweden are those of the spatial segregation of different social groups (Rudvall and Swedner 1975, Danermark 1983). Such segregation, of course, is in contradiction to much of the ethos and ideology of the Swedish state. Danermark (1983) provides evidence for three Swedish towns that segregation on the basis of class, income and family differentiation is widespread. Similarly, a more specific study (Flemström and Ronnby 1972) details how local politicians, builders and architects created a notorious 'dump' or problem estate in Malmö. The range of minority and marginalized groups (such as immigrants, the long-term unemployed, 'problem' families, and poor 'social help' cases) occupying the estate were able to do little to improve their housing consumption experiences – either because collective action and protest was non-existent or absorbed and neutralized by local state institution.

Particularly since the mid-1970s an explicit housing policy goal for the Swedish state has been to reduce segregation. For example, the Swedish government instructed the Housing Commission that in planning the population composition of housing areas the starting point was to be 'an effort in the direction of a balanced composition of households, as a means of achieving the social goal of contacts and co-operation between people from different population groups' (quoted in Danermark 1982, 6). For a range of reasons, including perhaps competition for housing of differential quality by divergent social groups, attempts to reduce segregation appear only partially successful.

Despite such problems, the differences in housing consumption between Britain and Sweden are startling (chapters three and four). In contrast to the situation in Sweden, the British labour movement has consistently stressed economic demands over and above other areas. Labour in Britain, unlike Sweden, has intervened directly in housing *per se* relatively little. Moreover, British labour has had a less unitary form than Swedish labour, being subject to a number of divides and divisions. The upshot of the British national compromise has been the development of a generally more market-orientated housing system, emphasizing owner-occupation, offering often the best housing to those sections of labour most able to achieve their economic demands. For such groups, housing consumption is often not a contentious issue, and there is usually little need for consumption actions. As Jacobs (1981, 43) notes, although perhaps in a too sweeping manner, 'owner-occupiers may not indulge in radical protests but, given their highly privileged position in the housing market, have had little cause to do so.' Of course, as Saunders (1980) and Kramer and Young (1978) demonstrate, as and when the need arises in specific localities privileged owner-occupiers are often well able to resist what they view as detrimental change to their housing consumption experiences. In turn, labour least able to make or achieve economic demands nationally has tended to gain little out of this housing system. We might include here the unemployed, black people, marginalized workers, the unskilled, and so on. Such generalizations may also be relevant within tenures. For example, many disadvantaged groups find that owner-occupation does not guarantee adequate housing consumption experiences, and may actually operate as a depressing drain on their already less than satisfactory social relations (Merrett with Gray 1982).

Even in late twentieth-century Britain many such people still experience physically inadequate housing – both in absolute and relative senses – in which they lack security and over which they have little control, while others are home-less or cannot afford the housing costs imposed on them. The continuation of such housing consumption problems in Britain says a great deal about the national compromise achieved, the segmental nature of British labour and the balance of social forces in the British state. Thus the continued existence of major unmet housing need points to the room to manoeuvre available to the British state at the national level, how radical is the intervention to separate housing consumption from capitalist market processes, and consequently the potential for locality-based housing consumption issues and actions.

It is important to stress that national compromise of the sort identified above is not static and unchanging. If a current national compromise is unsatisfactory to either capital or labour we may anticipate pressure to evolve the housing question more to its own favour (and, equally, continual pressure from the other side to maintain and enhance its own present advantage). In the British case, we might interpret the situation during and after the First World War and following the Second World War as examples of labour gaining some advantage in the balance of social forces and concomitant movements in the housing question in its favour. Housing provision and consumption improved for many people. Often, however, this was not without the active housing struggle of people in specific localities (such as Glasgow in 1915). Conversely, the inter-war economic depression and slump of the mid-1970s onwards weakened labour's position which, when com-bined with electoral victories favouring capital, represented a substantial shift in the balance of social forces and a worsening of the housing question. Material and normative housing conditions and housing consumption experiences for many people ceased to improve and actually worsened.

Britain and Sweden allow other interesting comparisons to be made over the state and housing consumption. As might be anticipated, state form and the nature of the national compromise is important in determining how law and tenure – two seemingly important and power tools for controlling housing consumption – are viewed and used. In Sweden during some periods home ownership has been viewed by governments as a socially divisive tenure form contributing to potentially destructive social relations. In contrast, in Britain the dominant image of owner-occupation is that it allows free and unfettered social relations, beneficial to individuals, families, state and society. Home ownership in Sweden has often (although not always) been constrained, partly through the use of law and in the allocation of resources, in the presumed interests of the greater social good. The opposite trend has occurred in Britain. With the full sanction of the law, home ownership has increasingly been encouraged as socially, economically and politically the most advantageous tenure. Conversely, public sector housing has tended to have been treated in the opposing way in either country.

In both cases, however, it is assumed that if housing tenure is got right then most other aspects of housing consumption and related local social relations will fall into place. Such attempts to regulate housing consumption through the medium of law and tenure are problematic. Success will depend not only on the housing consumption experiences produced with different tenure forms (which are not, as often assumed, homogeneous over either time or space) but also on housing consumers themselves, local social relations, local state institutions and other aspects of national economy and society.

This returns the discussion more directly to the issue of the locality and local social relations. Clearly, in so far as a national state and national equilibrium in social relations fail to filter down to dominate in the locality, there remains sometimes considerable scope for divergent local processes and outcomes. Indeed, while governments are forced to confront those non-local dimensions of the housing question determined by the production, finance and distribution of housing under capitalism, at the same time (and as the case studies from Brighton and Crawley illustrate) housing consumption issues and actions emerge under new guises in various localities as a persistent and continued test of the national equilibrium.

In Britain, two alternative policy strategies appear to have been utilized by central government to reduce the significance of locality-based housing consumption – and at a stroke to come to terms with the spatial variation in the social relations of housing consumption. Thus local state institutions may function as an intermediary between the national and local social relations, as a means of fine tuning the local implementation of national policy in order best to meet local needs and demands (and stop the implementation of locally inappropriate policies). Local authority housing is probably the best example here. An opposing strategy is the introduction of forms of housing consumption which are essentially non-local. Owner-occupation, in this way, may function to sever some of the links between housing consumption and local social relations (and hence reduce the need for local state institutions to be involved in housing consumption). Neither strategy is without its difficulties.

Local state institutions acting as an intermediary between the national and local suffer the potential problem that at times they may be effectively captured by the locality itself. Local state institutions may be in a contradictory position, an object of a tug-of-war between national state and locality. Elliott and McCrone recognize this when they argue:

> It is essential, when considering institutions – the frameworks of local government or the health or housing or welfare agencies – to appreciate that the liberties or rights they confer have been won by struggle. They were not bestowed by benevolent rulers but ceded gradually and grudgingly by local and national elites confronted by sections of the citizenry anxious to secure

for themselves some say in decision-making, some improvement in their material circumstances, some basis for fuller citizenship. How those institutions and agencies work, how they respond to citizens and clients is much affected by the particular histories of those agencies. . . . The practices and procedures with which they operate, the commitments which they acknowledge are the outcome of prior struggle. Current efforts to extend or alter them are constrained by those legacies. (Elliott and McCrone 1982, 141)

Local social relations may dominate over and above what is deemed 'appropriate' at the national level. National policy, for instance, may be rejected in the locality and local state institutions used to hinder its implementation. Poplar, Clay Cross, local opposition to council house sales, resistance to cuts in public expenditure and a host of less reported actions might all be interpreted in this way (Duncan and Goodwin 1982b). The converse situation may apply where the national response is to tighten the management of local institutions so that no scope is left for adequate interpretation of local demand. This was an at least contributory factor in the Crawley New Town housing action. At other times neither national level nor locality may gain the upper hand and local state institutions may operate in an essentially independent and autonomous manner, perhaps on the basis of some 'professional' or bureaucratic criteria, again failing to understand or respond to demands from the locality. Whatever the case, local state institutions may at times be inappropriate tools for managing housing consumption issues and actions in the 'national' interest.

An alternative strategy of using an apparently non-local tenure form, to attempt to separate out housing consumption from the locality may also prove ineffectual. Housing consumption is by its very nature a locality-specific process, and while some aspects of housing provision may be made at least partially aspatial (for example, the present British mortgage system for home ownership) other factors may continually reassert the importance of locality. This is well illustrated by the Crawley property owners' action.

In the particular case of owner-occupation in Britain, the inadequacies of tenure may throw up new locality-specific tensions. A case in point, excellently analysed by McCulloch (1983) are the mortgage strikes which developed in some new suburbs in the late 1930s. Another clear illustration, almost fifty years later, in the 1980s, is the increasing spatial variations in the housing market and housing consumption experiences of home owners (Merrett with Gray 1982, chapters fourteen and fifteen). Thus in some places the spatial concentration of housing consumption problems created in areas of mass unemployment, stagnant and low house prices, and an essentially paralysed sub-market may reassert the importance of the locality even for owner-occupation.

Despite the problematic nature of both local state institutions and tenure form as determinants of locality-based social relations of housing consumption, this is not to suggest that either institutions or tenure are without their effect. It is argued, however, that consequences will be geographically and historically variable. Indeed, attempts to resolve or ameliorate housing consumption problems sometimes throw up new sources of tension, new housing consumption issues and new housing consumption actions. Both collective actions in Crawley may be seen in this way. While we may not always be able to demonstrate empirically that housing consumers, through their actions, are able to change the present compromise over the housing question, it has been argued that the social relations of housing consumption both exert considerable pressure on the national state, drawing boundaries around its actions, and are essentially outside any easy sublimation by the state. Housing consumers may not acquiesce to their consumption experiences unless it is to their satisfaction. Whether or not, of course, action by consumers does have an effect hinges not only on the strength of their social relations and the nature of local state institutions, but ultimately on the balance of social forces in a particular state. But it may, as in the case of Glasgow in 1915, be through housing consumption actions that this balance is re-aligned and with it the housing question. The state's role in housing consumption may, then, be paradoxical. Partly in response to pressure from housing consumers, the housing question, via state activity, may evolve. This evolution, however, opens up new sources of tension and conflict in housing consumption, throwing up new forms of action by consumers and redirected pressure on the state. In this sense the housing question, as a consumption problem, is unanswerable.

## CHAPTER SEVEN

# *Variability, structure and explanation*

## 7.1 Empirical conclusions: variability and structure in housing provision

Ranging between Swedish factory workers making houses in chapter three and Brighton ex-soldiers demanding homes with bomb threats in chapter six, the housing question under advanced capitalism emerges from this book as nothing if not multi-faceted. Yet it is important to sum up what we have learnt empirically and to suggest how we think it can be brought together within a relatively clear conceptual framework. Not only is this important for research (including future research) but it has implications too for the politics of housing.

The empirical research recorded in previous chapters shows quite clearly the importance of variability and change in relation to structures. In chapter three, for example, we were at pains to stress the differences in the British and Swedish house building industries. In both countries housing is produced as a commodity, the aim is to make profits and this must ultimately depend on the exploitation of labour. None the less, *how* this is carried out differs markedly, and these differences have considerable effects on the number, quality and cost of housing made available. In turn, these varying effects have significant effects on political, social and economic relations in the two countries, just as the reasons for the different house building strategies originate deep in the political economy of Britain and Sweden. Chapter four maintains this theme, this time looking at the social organization of housing demand. But whereas chapter three concentrates on the recent past and on variation between places, chapter four also considers variation over time. For instance, state intervention in the regulation of supply and demand was extensively developed in Sweden during the 1940s, and continues even during a relatively 'recommodified' housing system in the 1980s; in Britain the unregulated market became dominant as soon as the mid-1950s. But in both chapters we found it essential to extend the chain of analysis out of housing provision itself and into the social relations of labour control and property ownership, both in state institutions and outside. Particularly important for understanding variability over time in the two countries were the relations between capital and labour as major blocs of economic and political power, and the position and role of land ownership.

The same sort of conclusions emerge from the sub-national comparative studies in chapters five and six. There is also considerable variation in how housing is provided at local level, and this is not just a matter of some passive mapping of national policies over an already uneven surface. Local differences are also, in part, the result of varying economic and political strategies which are socially devised, and these have much to do with the nature of production relations and civil society on the local level. We explored this theme in relation to housing tenure. (The important question of sub-national variability in housing production remains.) Thus, in Sheffield and in rural Norfolk during the inter-war period abnormally high rates of council house building was the favoured strategy for dealing with local formulations of the housing problem. In Sheffield a significant proportion of housing was even *built* outside the commodity form. But this common strategy emerged from strongly contrasting political situations in the two areas; in Sheffield a powerful labour movement had achieved long lasting hegemony over local government, while in Norfolk local government was very much the local executive of the bourgeoisie. This is a good example of the way in which different processes can produce similar results (a warning for empiricist research) just as, in chapters three and four, we saw how the same processes at the structural level can produce different results (a warning for structuralist research). Of course, the housing question in Sheffield and Norfolk had the same structural origin – how was housing to be provided as one resolution of the relations between labour and capital, both in producing housing and in consuming it? Again, to understand variability in what actually happens 'on the ground' research had to extend into the social relations of local political economy. We should stress, however, that these must be seen in relation to what happens outside the local level, in national and international political economies.

Chapter six extended the theme of local variability in relation to conflict over the consumption of housing. It also provided an illustration of how localities can change dramatically. Crawley in 1960 was a quite different locality from the place called Crawley in 1940. The chapter not only shows how people's responses to the forms and levels of housing provision are enormously varied but can also be significant to how housing is provided in the future. This varying type of response and level of significance is partly a matter of when and where these responses happen. It was not just incidental that housing protest in Crawley led to a rent strike while in Brighton protest involved squatters armed with dummy bombs. Similarly, the Sheffield rent strike in 1968 had a far different social meaning to its predecessor in Crawley.

The importance of variability and change in the reproduction of social systems is one major conclusion of the book – and hence the necessity to undertake empirical investigation of how this reproduction is actually achieved or not achieved. But a parallel theme is the importance of relatively stable structures which mould and constrain variability and change. How housing is built may differ significantly between Britain and Sweden, but in both countries it is produced as a commodity, as a means of making profits and this depends on the exploitation of labour. This is not a necessarily given structure, clearly housing production has a quite different structure in Eastern Europe or in pre-capitalist society, for instance. None the less the structure of capitalist production and exchange relations has been given for modern Britain and Sweden and this fact has a massive influence on housing provision in the two countries. Similarly, the forms and levels of state intervention in housing provision may vary greatly between these countries or, for example, between Sheffield and Brighton. But we are still dealing with capitalist states in franchise democracies where the issue is that of the relation between the capitalist commodity system and civil society. How can state power be used, and with whose interests in mind, to reproduce labour power, to regulate class relations, to reduce labour costs, or to compensate those without high cost labour power, and so on? While the nature and form of conflict and its results may vary considerably, this is still a matter of the power to use the structure of bourgeois law, based on notions of the contract and private property ownership.

However, these social structures are not imposed by nature or God, the motors of social change are active people with skills and resources. But people are not isolated individuals. Harry Cowley with his dummy bombs, or Wallenberg with his industrial empire, were also acting as members of social groups and classes constituted in space and time; Cowley's actions were important within the context of social relations in Brighton for a short period, the Wallenberg dynasty reflected and helped produce Sweden's political and economic structure for over a hundred years. Similarly, what people have done in the past (the alliances they have forged, the protests they have made, the forms of state intervention they have caused to happen, the housing estates they have had built and the consciousness they have formed in the process) constitutes the starting-point for what the next generation of people do. Space and time are not simply an 'outcome' of something called 'capitalism', they are intimately locked into the very processes of social reproduction. The problem is to find a conceptual framework in which space and time can be incorporated.

Andrew Sayer summarizes this position very well:

> Social structures are both the medium and outcome of social practices. Actions are not only constrained but enabled by structures (for example, speech by language) which only exist where they are reproduced, that is, their reproduction or transformation is not automatic but contingent upon actions. Actors are not automatons or dupes or mere passive bearers of roles, but possess skills, some of them tacit or unconscious, which are a condition of the most mundane of acts. It is therefore possible to recognise that actions take place in conditions and with resources which pre-exist, and which may not be acknowledged by actors but which are nevertheless a necessary condition of their execution, and also that the reproduction or transformation of these conditions is an (often unintended) consequence of the actions. Thus the twin errors of voluntarism (actors act independently of any constraints) and structuralist determinism (the conditions do the acting) are avoided.
>
> (Sayer 1983, 109)

However, this passage is also a summary of the problem remaining. How are we going to deal with the tension between structure and agency/variation in practice? We turn to one way forward in the next section.

## 7.2  Realist epistemology: a way forward?

The critique of structuralism does not mean that structures do not exist and have social effects. Similarly, the critique of voluntarism does not mean that individual agency, still less variation and differentiation, do not exist and have social effects. Both pre-existing social structures and particular historical and spatial situations are formative to how people act, but equally, both are also socially created by people. The difficult question remains of how to link these dimensions in causal analysis.

This section outlines an epistemological basis for making this link adequately, based on an application of the realist philosophy of science to urban and regional studies (following Sayer 1981, 1982, see also Sayer 1984). An epistemological answer to the problem of explanation can of course only be partial, none the less this is an essential component of any answer. For substantive research results and how others may use them partly depend upon the methods and aims of explanation used by the researchers. How should we organize the mass of empirical and conceptual information created by the research? How should we work in ignoring some information as unimportant and elevating other information to crucial importance? How should this hierarchy be arrived at and what aims should this organization of information have? In evaluating the research results, other researchers are therefore forced to also evaluate theoretical concepts, explanatory methods and existential assumptions. Even the ability to begin research depends on researchers already possessing a certain amount of interpreted information. These issues are clearly not just a matter of which research methods to choose (for example, whether to use comparative analysis or not) nor even a question of which social theory is most helpful (e.g. Marxist or neo-classical views of housing provision). They are also a matter of how concepts and measurements are to be organized and brought together, of how research methods and theories themselves are used. It is a question, in other words, of epistemology.

The implication of the debate about explanation in social science is to find some way of relating structure and agency, and also – in avoiding the deficiencies of both structuralism and empiricism – of more adequately linking conceptual and empirical information. This parallels the conclusions of our own work written in reaction to structuralism in urban and regional studies (see Dickens 1979, Duncan 1981, Duncan and Goodwin 1982a). Our call was for 'conceptually informed historical research'.

This is fine as far as it goes, as a statement of what should be achieved and what should be avoided. But it begs the question – how should this 'conceptually informed historical research' actually be done? The danger of leaving this as a purely prescriptive goal is that research can easily regress into detailed empirical work where informing concepts are only loosely connected and integrated. This has indeed been one result of the reaction against structuralist and empiricist work. At best, this can produce some stimulating work as the best known examples of this approach, the 'cultural history' of Hobsbawm and Thompson, show. Even here, however, analytical consistency is lost (see Johnson 1978); rather research is brilliantly intuitive and the less gifted cannot so easily follow such a path. At worst, such work can decline into assertive historical empiricism. How can we decide which processes are necessary for particular outcomes, which are contingent, and which are irrelevant? How can we create appropriate cut off points for investigation, or allocate particular causal claims to particular levels of generality? A set of tools is needed – not just theoretical interpretations but also an epistemological apparatus to help us link structure and agency, concept and measurement. This is where we have found recent applications of realist philosophy useful.

An essential rediscovery made by realism is that, because facts are theory laden, this does not make them theory determined. True enough, the empirical world can only be referred to by using thought-objects, such as scientific theories or common sense, but this does not mean that what is referred to is entirely *ideal*. Knowledge is produced by ideas, yet the objects and processes it refers to exist outside thought. This insight helps to resolve the concept/fact, structure/agency impasses of empiricism and structuralism. These elements need no longer be viewed as exclusive opposites and explanation is not, therefore, forced to build on one at the expense of the other where in fact both poles are necessary for adequate explanation. Concepts are also empirical (and vice versa). Similarly the structure/agency polarity is misleading where both are independent.

How is this insight put into operation and so related to establishing causality? First of all, theoretical and empirical work can be integrated according to the degree of abstraction involved. Second, specific relations of determination can be ascribed to specific levels of abstraction. Third, it is easier to order and relate information into a causal structure which decides what is crucial, what is secondary, and what is relevant to a particular problem at a given level of generality. We will now go on to justify these claims in more detail.

First of all, what do we mean by 'abstract' and 'concrete'? These terms, fundamental to this discussion, are not synonyms for 'conceptual' and 'empirical'. Rather, they refer to the degree of completeness with which scientific discourse apprehends the real world. The concrete object is a complete combination of many diverse forces and processes, but this need not necessarily be observable and hence empirical. Abstraction in contrast refers to a one-sided or partial aspect of a subject. Again, this may well be empirically observable. This can be made clearer using the example of a house. If we conceptualize a house simply in terms of its outside appearance, this will be abstract in being partial and one-sided as well as being empirically observable. Other abstractions, with different conceptual and empirical make-ups, would see the house as an architectural form, a tenure form, the outcome of production relations in construction, a social signifier. To make a completely concrete concept we would have to apprehend all the interacting relationships in which that house was involved.

How are these categorizations to be related causally in such a manner as to avoid the extremes of structuralism and voluntarism, to produce 'conceptually informed historical research'? This can be made clearer in comparison with positivist epistemology, where causation is equated with the regular succession of what are supposed to be atomistic and in themselves unconnected objects. This has the major disadvantage that no clear distinction can be made between correlation and causation. Related to this, positivism is unable to do much in situations where different processes lead to the same result, where the same process leads to different results, or where correlations have no causal significance, or where there is cause without correlation. None the less, in what has been called the 'scandal of philosophy' scientists using positivist guidelines actually do seem capable of distinguishing between some accidental correlations (for example the good statistical fit between flood levels in the Yellow River and the Swiss divorce rate) and some obviously causal processes (for example the mechanics making the hands of a clock move). This is because, when it comes to the crunch, the scientist has jettisoned the assumption that events are atomistic and in themselves unconnected. Rather, (s)he assumes a structure of causal associations which makes some interpretations possible and others impossible. This, as we shall see, is akin to a 'common-sense realism' and sometimes common sense is quite adequate for causal explanation. But there are two severe problems with this. First, it is not always so easy, as in our trivial example, to find obvious causal mechanism already recorded in common sense – especially when the positivist research process regulates formal conceptualization to an afterthought. Second, common sense specification of causal mechanism remains uncritical and largely unexamined; quite often common-sense interpretations will be incorrect. Indeed, what is the purpose of research if they are correct?

In contrast, realism starts from the supposition that objects and events are *not*, necessarily, atomistic and independent. This follows because some changes can be seen to be changes *in* things – their nature itself may change. Hence, explanation can be freed from positivism's paradoxical reliance on the assumption that events are only related accidentally and so also from the inadequate way around this 'scandal' – the equation of regularity with causal power and thus correlation with explanation.

In place of atomism, realism sees causation as the *necessary* ways-of-acting of an object, and these are seen as existing by virtue of the object's nature. It is these necessary generative mechanisms that produce events, not accidental relationships. Laws will not refer, as in positivist schema, to well corroborated and universal empirical regularities (although, again in a slightly scandalous manner, the scientist has usually settled for far less than this). Rather laws will be statements about mechanisms which may, or may not, produce regularities. For causal mechanisms are only activated through the operation of contingent relations which are *not* necessary to the objects or relations which incorporate necessary generative mechanisms. This is an essential element in the realist account of causality.

This can be made clearer with the standard example of the conductivity of copper. Because of a generative mechanism that is part of its nature (its molecular structure, perhaps) copper necessarily conducts electricity. Whether any one piece of copper at any one time will actually do so, to what degree and with what results depends on a whole range of contingent relations. Is the copper connected to a source, is it dirty, is it connected to other materials producing light, to materials producing heat, and so on? A similar example from the social world is the concept of industrial restructuring, referring to those changes in labour processes which in capitalism are generated by the necessity to maintain labour exploitation, in turn generated by the nature of capital–labour relations in capitalist society. Whether this restructuring is achieved by using mechanization, cheaper labour, more or less women in the labour-force, plant relocation, or something else depends on relations contingent to the necessary capital–labour relations which actually generate the restructuring process. For instance, is a new technology, or a pool of under-used female labour power, available? Industrial restructuring may not even be activated at all. Perhaps there is a monopoly producer, a captive market, or direct political control over the costs of labour. In this case the same process can easily produce different outcomes or even no outcome at all.

This relationship between necessary and contingent factors has three very important effects on how explanation proceeds. First of all it is clear that any one mechanism can produce widely different concrete outcomes. Necessary relations may generate change but how this change becomes concretely manifest depends on interaction with contingent factors. Similarly, different mechanisms can produce the same concrete outcome. These distinctions are not available to positivists and their lack has led to considerable causal confusion in their work. Second, *determination* can be distinguished from *determinism*. Events are caused by generative mechanisms (determination), but because these are activated by combination with contingent relations, the actual concrete outcome is not predetermined (determinism). Third, it remains logically possible that the whole world will change, and so change what are necessary generative mechanisms. This is an acute possibility for social science, because society is socially created – what is necessary is often ultimately a matter of human agency and this is changed historically. Again, behaviour is not predetermined but with *one* already created social world – capitalism for example – historically created necessary relations can be treated as relatively given. The identification and distinction between necessary and contingent relations allows causal analysis to be combined with empirical complexity, and so avoids the structuralist/empiricist duality. It is plain that theoretical statements on the level of abstract generative mechanisms cannot be expected to account for concrete circumstances, similarly it is clear that statistical correlations do not necessarily – or even very often – identify generative mechanisms.

This distinction between levels of analysis also helps clear up one common cause of confusion in social science, the 'arguing at cross-purposes' of apparently rival explanations which we can now see to be complementary at different levels of abstraction. It is equally true, for instance, that a building firm went out of business because of falling demand and that it went out of business because the managing director preferred golf to managing. Rather than oppose both these valid explanations, the problem is to relate these accounts in some causal structure. The distinction between more or less abstract and concrete can be very helpful in evaluating research results; very often the research itself is adequate enough but the wrong claims are made for it. A good example is Castells's *The Urban Question* (1977) where research at the abstract level is assumed to give concrete results. Hall's *Inner City in Context* (1981) lies at the other pole. If nothing else, the level of claim appropriate to the research carried out can be established and this by itself would remove one important source of confusion. It would be even better if the links between these levels could be discovered.

Our discussion so far is summarized in figure 7.1, which centres on the ordering of information from the most abstract concepts to particular concrete outcomes. The diagram shows very well how this approach stratifies the real, and how knowledge of abstract mechanisms must be combined with knowledge about contingently related phenomena in order to explain the concrete in all its variations. It should be clear from this book that 'contingent conditions' should in no sense be considered 'secondary' or 'unimportant', since it is these which are activating and determining where, when, how, perhaps even whether necessary relations and tendencies generate concrete outcomes. Causal mechanisms are only activated through the operation of contingent relations which are *not* necessary to the objects or relations which incorporate necessary generative mechanisms.

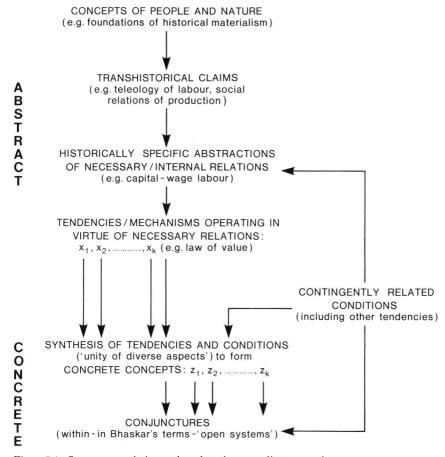

*Figure 7.1*  Structure, variation and explanation: a realist approach

*Source:* Adapted from Sayer 1981.

At first sight this causal structure might seem to imply that every event must be explained via a regress to some ultimate final cause. This is not the case, and indeed the realist account in fact allows considerable leverage in resolving the familiar dilemma between researching everything (ideal but impossible) and researching one situation in isolation (much easier but invalid). It is more possible to establish sensible and logical cut-off points for research − 'sensible and logical' in the way explanation is linked to the real outside explanation.

This leverage arises in two major ways. First of all, the necessary/contingent distinction itself provides one way of identifying different sorts of relevance. Reality is cut up conceptually on a vertical axis, as it were. Second, the real is stratified horizontally by degrees of abstract and concrete. Any one level of abstraction and concreteness will, it is true, be constituted through combinations of generative and contingent processes operating at other, structurally prior, levels. However, this does *not* mean that each level is reducible to a prior level (as structuralism assumes). Each level is irreducible because each − being constituted by a combination of processes − is not predetermined and contains *its own* necessary powers. For example, industrial restructuring in a capitalist and patriarchal society may mean increased 'feminization' of labour. Feminization, however has other consequences not reducible to its constituent processes − particular changes in the labour process or family life for example, which then go on to influence how industrial life actually changes. It is logically and sensibly possible, according to this theoretical interpretation, to study feminization in industry without necessarily involving generative mechanisms of industrial and social restructuring produced by gender and class relations. None the less, only a particular level of claim for the research can then be made; if the researcher wishes to explain why feminization has occurred (as opposed to how) analysis must include consideration of these generative mechanisms.

How are we to judge the adequacy of the way reality is set up in this fashion? As the example shows, this is in itself a matter for conceptual research − the epistemological framework only discerns what we are doing, not how. There is also the further problem that there can be no presumption that real relations are structured just like conceptual relations, so the logicality of a theoretical statement is no guide to its adequacy in describing real structures. However, the possibility remains that conceptual relations, in theories and explanations, can be made to map real ones. Although the thought object and the real object are quite separate the two can be brought into some sort of correspondence in practical terms. We can then begin to distinguish 'bad' theoretical concepts which will divide the indivisible in failing to recognize necessary relations, or base themselves on non-necessary relations.

These prescriptions for undertaking research may look obvious, and so they are in a way. The trouble is that much research has not seen the obvious. How explanation proceeds remains unexamined. A good example of dividing the indivisible is the conception of housing provision as purely a matter of consumption and distribution that has ruled housing research for so long. This is not to say that consumption and distribution are unimportant, far from it, but that housing provision and its variations cannot be properly understood without considering the relations between production and consumption. Research has found this out the hard way. Similarly, the theory of 'collective consumption' provides an example of inadequate abstraction based on a non-necessary relation. Here, collective consumption has been viewed as a given state of housing provision in advanced capitalism, rather than as one historical outcome of owner–consumer relations. This is not to suggest that collective consumption is insignificant as a concrete outcome – it may be very important. But concrete outcomes are the result of combinations of several necessary relations where the actual form of these relations – and hence the outcome – is contingent. Examples of the former might be the relations between building capital and/or those between consumers and money-lenders, although how these combine will be contingent on – for instance – the balance of social power in particular state institutions in a certain place over a given period. How and whether collective consumption results is an empirical matter. The supposition that collective consumption is a necessary stage in housing provision is a weakly based generalization resting on non-necessary relations.

There are several problems with the realist account of scientific explanation and the way in which we have suggested using it. There are several competing interpretations and we have chosen one (Bhaskar's and Harré's realism as refracted through Sayer). More important for our purposes here is the problem of what seem to be *a priori* arguments concerning the necessary make-up of the world. How do we know that the theorized necessary relations are true? How can their validity be tested when they can produce many different real outcomes or indeed where they may never become manifest at all? Does the whole epistemological structure collapse on this point?

This problem can be dealt with in a number of ways. First of all, in some ways this is not a problem at all – or at least not a unique difficulty caused by realism. All explanations ultimately depend on assumed metaphysical or meta-theoretical positions. (For example, statements on the basic nature of people or the basic form of society.) None can guarantee truth and, indeed, these exist only at a very abstract level. So truth – if this means correspondence with reality – cannot be provided. Rather our interest is to gain knowledge about particular societies rather than be satisfied with generalizations about necessary relations. Second, however, this qualification is not a complete answer, for clearly some meta-theoretical positions will be superior to others, just as some abstractions of necessary relations will be more adequate than others.

This returns us to problems of theoretical interpretation where the adequacy of these tools clearly depends on the social theory producing them. The advance provided by realism is that it makes this inevitable interpretation overt and more likely to be examined. The '*a priori*' judgements about the necessary make up of the world are not so much taken on as an act of faith, but more as an act of reason. We happen to have mainly used Marxist social theory in creating these estimations of the necessary, not because of any particular reverence for Marx but because the theoretical development of Marxism seems – usually – to offer the most adequate identification of the social relations we are concerned with. Other identifications are equally possible, as well as various combinations. Marxist abstraction about bureaucracy or gender relations has been notably deficient, for example. The point is, however, that the estimation of the necessary is not just picked out of thin air but results from considerable previous empirical and theoretical research as well as debate between alternatives.

Another linked problem is how to estimate the adequacy of connections between various levels of abstract and concrete. Positivism pretends that a one-to-one relation between abstract and concrete exists, as if descriptions or terms simply 'glue' on to their objects without the practical and possibly difficult process of conceptualizing this interpretation. Consequently, it is assumed that tests (preferably statistical) about pattern correspondence at the level of concrete events produce a 100 per cent truth test. This is not possible, and there are no formal rules able to guarantee a correct choice between explanations. But what can be done is to estimate the relative validity of arguments made for specific conceptual purposes. Realism helps in suggesting both the levels of claim that can be made and the type of information appropriate for assessing claims. It also helps in stratifying thought-objects where a relative test is the ability of causal chains to make sense of concrete events (see also Jessop, 1982). Evaluation of the relationship between necessary and contingent, abstract and concrete is a superior test to the supposed one-to-one relation between fact and hypothesis. The latter promises, but cannot deliver.

In conclusion, then, the realist account of explanation can provide some useful means of checking how we are ordering and evaluating information. Certainly, it is superior to the less examined but equally ordered means provided by structuralism and empiricism. This is not at all to say that any epistemological framework can provide a research blueprint or 'do' the research in some mechanical way. The promise is more one of making it clear what is being debated, what is being claimed, and how information has been assembled. With the realist version of explanation the conceptualization of necessary and contingent relations is critical, for the identification of mechanisms will depend upon careful description of the objects and relations in virtue of which they act. 'Theoretical research' becomes an important stage of research, where empiricism relegates this to an unimportant afterthought and unconscious preliminary. (The facts speak for themselves and theory merely orders them after their appearance.) None the less, it should be clear that the identification and examination of the contingent is also vital to explanation of urban and regional change. For substantive research which seeks to explain concrete events, contingent relations and the way they combine with necessary relations may well be a major focus of enquiry. This stands in contrast to the cavalier attitude structuralism adopts to empirical detail. We have gone some way, through epistemology, to resolving the problem of how to relate structure and agency without determinism or voluntarism, to carry out in practice 'conceptually informed historical research'.

### 7.3 Housing provision, generative mechanisms and social change

The realist approach to explanation provides one way of relating structure and agency while avoiding the inadequate extremes of determinism and voluntarism. This is, however, only one element in the development necessary to keep empirical research in pace with the recommendations made by the philosophy of science. Equally important are theory – the identification of necessary relations and historically specific abstractions – and methodology. As discussed in chapter one, we worked within a Marxist conceptualization of social relations using comparative analysis as a major methodological tool. Neither of these choices was isolated from the epistemological fiat of carrying out 'conceptually informed historical research'. We should also enter the disclaimer that the substantive work recorded in this book was part of the process in reaching these epistemological conclusions, and in this respect the book should be seen as evolutionary rather than definitive.

It is Marxist theory, in social science, which most easily follows this epistemological criterion, at least in so far as the study of social forms and institutions is concerned. By means of well developed abstraction, Marxism postulates generative mechanisms at the historically specific level of the mode of production. These generate causal chains, which in combination with contingent relations as well as other necessary relations not identified by Marxism, can explain the nature and development of empirical events. Social forms can be understood in terms of mechanisms with a real social status but which are not empirically fixed. The difficult question still remains, however, of actually understanding how this empirical condensation takes place. As discussed at length in section 1.4, the methodology of comparative work was a major aid in this respect.

The inevitable dependence on some theoretical statement of what is necessary and what is not will clearly hold its dangers. As we mentioned in chapter one, Marxism has been weak in its understanding of some key social relations outside capitalist production, in particular those of the 'state form' (citizenship and bureaucracy) and gender relations between men and women. Indeed, recent research has shown that the latter are especially important in understanding how housing is provided and consumed (e.g. Rose 1980, Hayden 1981, MacKenzie and Rose 1983). More than that, how the 'production of people' proceeds is a vital element of any mode in production (Murgatroyd, 1983). Thus MacKenzie and Rose (1983) have traced the change from the contiguity of production and reproduction in the pre-capitalist household to their spatial and temporal separation in modern industrial cities. The whole structure of industrial and residential life, including the crucial dependence each has on the other, would be quite different without a particular set of gender relations. In consequence, the relation between women and men has both been changed by, and helped to change, transformations and developments in the mode of production. Housing provision is of course one element in all this. The 'historical compromise' for housing was not just a matter of labour and capital (both in general and in building), land ownership and the petite bourgeoisie. The compromise also depended on, and helped to create, 'the era of the housewife'. And, just like the class relations involved in this housing compromise, these underlying gender relations are not static. The increasing 'feminization' of paid work in Sweden, combined with women's own struggles and views of Swedish society led, among other things, to the mass provision of suburban child-care units shortly after the mass house building of the 'million programme'. The point is, however, that this remains an important area of social relations in understanding housing provision, one which this book neglects. Gender relations may be just as much necessary relations in advanced capitalist society as class relations. But, in just the same way as it would be unwise to see housing provision in isolation from such key social structures, this is not to argue that all housing provision is merely a simple matter of reflected class and/or gender relations. Most usefully, the realist framework allows us to escape this either/or question. How such generative mechanisms actually work, in what way, or even at all, is an empirical question – and the empirical work reported in the book has shown this very well.

Our identification of wider social relations, especially class relations, as crucial for understanding housing provision has a number of political implications. It is changes in these relations which form the quality, amount and cost of housing. Such relations are not, however, mechanically given. They are indeed *relational* and will vary in their nature and effects in different situations. The tension between structure and agency, necessary and contingent recurs in political activity; any political outcome is far from being predetermined or even appropriate. Similarly, epistemologies also have their political implications. Empiricism reproduces the present world in its descriptions, simulations and predictions without understanding how it is created. The question of changing change (as opposed to modelling it) can hardly be addressed. Structuralism also usually ends up in passivity, although sometimes more the passivity of despair rather than acceptance. In this case actions are seen as being predetermined by structures. People must wait for the next structural revolution; for the present they are left with either the pessimism of passive rejection or the release of symbolic outburst. This world view forgets that people must live now and, even if capitalism is inevitably to break down, there will be considerable room for manoeuvre over how this happens and what will replace it. Indeed, these are probably the more important issues. The realist approach implies the possibilities for more meaningful action between these two extremes. Comparative analysis – both in terms of aiding explanation of how structures become varied, and in stimulating images of what may be possible – can do very much the same thing. Actions are not necessarily predetermined nor do they have to simply reproduce structures even if these must be heavily influential. We think that this epistemological conclusion is amply demonstrated by the empirical results of the research recorded in this book.

# *Notes*

## Chapter one

1  This chapter is not the place to back up our epistemological and theoretical working position at length. The issue of realism is developed further in chapter seven. Otherwise, see Keat and Urry (1975) and Sayer (1984) on the critique of empiricism and structuralism; Sayer (1979) for a justification of a modified Marxism in social science *vis-à-vis* phenomenology and positivism; Duncan (1981) for our critique of structuralism in housing research; and, Duncan and Goodwin (1982a, b) on the implications for research on the 'local state'.

2  The terms 'theoretical' and 'empirical' are well understood even if slightly inaccurate for our purposes here. The less well known 'abstract' and 'concrete' (which are *not* synonyms for 'theoretical' and 'empirical') would be nearer our meaning. See section 7.1 for expansion of this point.

3  Advanced capitalism can be defined as the dominance of monopoly multinational capital combined with the internationalization of production based on high levels of control and fragmentation in the labour process, the institutional dominance of interventionist states, political liberalization via representative democracy, and a high level of subordination of non-capitalist modes of production, classes, ways of living and consciousness. The advanced capitalist countries of north-west Europe and North America, and Japan, Australia and New Zealand, are those where this process originates and where it has gone furthest.

   Social democracy can be defined as the institutionalization of 'historical compromise' between capital and labour. This attempts to replace conflict by agreed and balanced social management, defining areas of legitimate interest and control, procedures for comprise and agreed rules of social behaviour. Typically continued private dominance over the economy and over labour at work is balanced by a recognition of union rights, working-class access to state power, and distributive reforms. See Middlemas (1977) and Korpi (1978) for British and Swedish versions.

4  In writing this section we have greatly benefited from Andrew Sayer's comments on an earlier draft. Björn Söderfeldt's conference paper, 'Some methodological remarks on comparative community research' (given at Örebro University College in September 1982) has also been of assistance. We are also grateful to participants at the Urban and Regional Studies seminar, University of Sussex, and the 'Housing question in Australia and Britain' workshop, Australian Studies Centre (both March 1984) for discussion of seminar papers.

5  Thanks to Chris Pickvance for this point.

## Chapter two

1   For example, Murgatroyd (1981, 1982) and Urry (1980, 1981c).
2   Written as part of a newspaper article on the Chartists in the *New York Daily Tribune*, 25 August 1852.
3   The classic work is M. W. Child's (1937) *Sweden: The Middle Way* followed up by, among other influential works, Anthony Crosland's (1956) *The Future of Socialism* (where Sweden was seen as nearest 'the socialist's ideal of the good society' and R. F. Tomasson (1970) *Sweden: Prototype of a Modern Society*. For an opposing viewpoint – where Sweden is now the model to be avoided – see R. Huntford (1971) *The New Totalitarians*. One of the more recent UK government inquiries to use the 'Swedish model' is the Bullock report on industrial democracy (Department of Trade, 1977) *Report on the Committee of Inquiry on Industrial Democracy* Cmnd. 6706).
4   Sources for this section include Duncan (1982a, 1982b), Scase (1976a, and b, 1977), Castles (1978), Korpi (1978).
5   According to the first comprehensive study of monopoly in Sweden, quoted in Hermansson 1979, 16.
6   For an outline of the historical development of the 'tradition' of a strong state see Duncan (1982a). See Sunesson (1974) for the ideology of étatism in the Swedish labour movement.
7   See Dahlkvist (1977) and Korpi (1978) for details. Similar compromise attempts in other countries include the 1936 Matignon Accords in France, and in Britain, the Trade Union–Employer agreements of 1928 and even the ill-fated 'social contract of the 1970s'. None had as much scope, permanency or institutionalization as the Swedish.
8   See Pålbrant (1977) for the interesting case of popular sporting.
9   In 1930 10 per cent of Swedish exports were to Germany, and 27 per cent to Britain. These figures changed to 20/24 per cent in 1939, 47/0.1 per cent in 1943 and 0/16.7 per cent in 1946. See Unga (1970) on the impact of Swedish pre-Keynes Keynesianism.

## Chapter three

1   Ball (1983) qualifies this position.
2   Thanks to Andy Rowe for this point.
3   Newfoundland, Nova Scotia, Prince Edward Island, New Brunswick.
4   For Britain owner-occupiers' housing payments are represented by 'imputed rents', and some subsidies are discounted from these figures after 1973. This will deflate house price rises after this date. The relationship between 'imputed rents' and actual mortgage payments is crude but, in the absence of other suitable information we have taken this as acceptable for describing average trends.

In 1980, 17 per cent of Swedish households received 'housing allowances' (*bostadsbidrag*) and another 29 per cent received 'housing supplements' for pensioners (*bostadstillägg*). These averaged 4317 S kr. (approx £390) and 4416 S kr. (approx £400) respectively. Another 28 per cent of households received mortgage tax relief averaging 5634 S kr. (approx £510). In Britain 7.3 per cent of households received rent rebates averaging £350 per annum in 1982, and 17 per cent rate rebates averaging £90. About 10 per cent of households also received supplementary benefit housing additions, although the subsidy effect is not quantified in our sources. In 1983 all three subsidies were replaced by Housing Benefits, involving cuts in eligibility, amount, and claimant budgetary control (see Erskine 1984). At the same time subsidies in the form of mortgage tax relief to owner-occupiers continue to escalate and are estimated to reach £2750m. by 1984/5.

5 In quantitative terms, non-commodity production has always been more important in Sweden, at around 6 per cent of new completions per annum in the 1970s compared to under 4 per cent in Britain. The British percentage has declined since then while Conservative legislation in 1980 forced British DLOs to act in a quasi-commercial manner.

6 Public housing companies (*Allmannyttigabostadsföretag*) are nominally independent non-profit-making companies or associations, sometimes with charitable status, for the provision of rented housing. In practice, all public housing companies of any significance are controlled by a local authority although in legal terms they remain separate. This is the approximate equivalent of British council housing and amounted to 20 per cent of stock by 1980. Another 4 per cent of stock was direct 'state housing' in the sense of being legally owned by communes and national state departments, etc.

7 Housing co-operatives (*bostadsrättsforeningar*) in Sweden have mostly developed as part of the 'co-operative movement' in close association with the labour movement as a whole. Two co-operatives are overwhelmingly dominant. HSB, the largest, is traditionally connected with the right–centre of the labour movement and the notion of social reform through distribution, although it has significant interests in the building materials sector. The other large housing co-op, RK, is closely connected with the building workers' unions and the union-owned building firm, BPA (the second largest house builder). Co-operative housing accounted for 14 per cent of total stock by 1980.

8 Since 1980 British local authorities have been allowed to make profits out of council house provision. Many do so, and significant numbers use Housing Revenue Account surplus to subsidize the rate (property tax) fund or to pay for local services. See Fielding (1984).

9 Access to co-operatively owned dwellings in Sweden requires a down payment. By 1976–8 this 'transfer price' averaged 19,800 S kr. (approx. £1800). This is treated in market terms and so allows an avenue for capital gains (and losses) by households. Although small in comparison with the owner-occupied sector, these can be quite significant in areas of high demand; for Greater Stockholm equivalent prices were 31,600 S kr. (£2900) and are higher still in fashionable inner-city areas. The transfer prices also act as a market eligibility control so that co-operative housing tenants have a higher income and status profile than in the public housing sector. Interestingly, they have the highest rates of holiday house ownership.

10 There was a ten-year transitional phase for the 'Land Condition' up to 1984. In 1981 the centre–right government rescinded the land condition for redevelopment, although here proposals for state enforced land redistribution are being developed. In 1965–9 63 per cent of new housing was built on land from public land banks, rising to 71 per cent in 1970–4 and around 80 per cent by 1980.

11 A system of housing development certificates for all house building, introduced during the war, was progressively weakened after the late 1950s and finally abandoned in 1963.

12 This is not to deny the significance of other changes in input costs, for instance monetary fluctuations or raw material prices. However, these too are heavily influenced by labour productivity changes, and over the long term will tend to average out between sectors. But short-term effects on particular sectors can be important.

13 NIER figures show a substantial increase, of 10.7 per cent for 1981–3. However, like manufacturing (5.7 per cent) and the economy as a whole (4.3 per cent) this rise is thought to reflect massively decreased work-forces using up established stocks rather than increased labour productivity efficiency as such.

14 1976 was the most recent year when project breakdown data by sector was provided for the smallest firms with under twenty employees. (The centre–right coalition cut

this as part of an 'anti-bureaucracy' drive!) Changes since then are discussed in the text but available data allow for only marginal differences up to 1980.

15 There may be overall short-term stability in the volume of public sector tenders. However, the evidence suggests that individual construction firms still suffer considerable order book instability, while speculative house building is, of course, inherently unstable.

## Chapter five

1 These powers were given through the Acts of 1851, 1866, 1875, 1890 and 1909. For more detail of these and succeeding pieces of legislation see Merrett (1979, 307) and Gauldie (1974, 13). Brief reference will be made, where appropriate, to national legislation in this chapter when discussing both the nature of local variation and the local case studies.

2 Figures 5.1, 5.2, 5.3 and 5.4 provide a county by county illustration of the amount of council houses completed, (a) as a percentage of all new dwellings and (b) as the amount per 1000 population. We use percentage figures since we are concerned with the relative shares between public and private agencies. However there are statistical dangers in working solely with percentages, especially when these refer to low absolute values, so we have also calculated the amount of council dwellings built per 1000 population. Although showing up different types of variation in detail, both sets of maps indicate the importance of sub-national variations in housing provision and give broadly similar pictures. To make comparison easier the counties have been consistently grouped, across all the maps, into the same six classes. Two represent the top and bottom 10 per cent of counties, with those in between being divided into four groups of 20 per cent each. (In some cases it has been necessary to diminish or enlarge classes slightly; for instance, where several counties fall on the same value.)

3 See Bassett and Short (1980) for a wider discussion of different approaches to housing studies.

4 See figure 1.1. Smallburgh Rural District Council no longer exists as an administrative area. It disappeared in the 1974 local government reorganization and its area now comes under the auspices of North Norfolk District Council.

5 These, and all subsequent figures on Sheffield's housing are taken from Sheffield City Council Housing Yearbook 1972 and unpublished data kindly provided by the estates department.

6 Although Jennings gives details of the house building performances of the West Riding County Boroughs, he provides a wrong total for Sheffield's building under the Wheatley and Chamberlain Acts. Our figures are drawn from the records of Sheffield's own Housing Department and these tally with totals held by the Department of the Environment.

7 See for example *Sheffield Star*, 17 August 1960, 18 August 1960, 19 August 1960, 4 October 1962 and 5 April 1963 and *Sheffield Telegraph*, 8 May 1962 and 14 July 1964. See also Sheffield City Council Housing Development Committee (1962).

8 As a cultural and political aside, it is interesting to note that Hyde Park was opened not by the leader of the Labour Party, as was the first phase, but by the Queen Mother. Having first received the sanction of approval from the Labour Movement, Sheffield now sought it from the establishment.

## Chapter six

1 We might include here the dominant ideas of Octavia Hill, including 'Tenants

brought up in slums have engendered slum habits' (quoted in Merrett 1979, 210). Such ideas continued through the inter-war period and into the post-war era. For a relevant review of 'the slum' see Mellor (1977).

2   An account of Harry Cowley and the Brighton squatting movement is in a Brighton *Evening Argus* series of articles between 12 and 20 February 1957. This quotation is from the final article.

3   Hill (1946) provides a detailed and sympathetic account of the London squatting movement. See also Friend (1980).

4   Pollitt H (1946). This pamphlet is a transcript of a speech made by Pollitt in London on 12 September 1946.

5   There was concern in the Cabinet that squatting might spread to the workplace. See Foot (1973).

6   For an examination of subsequent campaigns see Wates and Wolmar (1980) and Bailey (1973).

7   'The Ifield Estate'. Leaflet in Crawley Library. The publisher and precise date of this leaflet are not known.

8   The following description of the inquiry is also substantially drawn from the detailed account in the *Crawley and District Observer*, 8 November 1946.

9   This quote and background information comes from Stanford (1965, 7).

10  From the Foreword by Lewis Silkin (1949) to the New Town Development Corporation's annual reports for 1948–9.

11  This information came from the unpublished 'Summary of development progress, 1st April 1956', issued by the Crawley Development Corporation (1956).

12  For a critical discussion of social planning in the early new towns and empirical material relating to Crawley, see Heraud (1968).

13  This quote comes from interviews carried out in the early 1970s, duplicated by Crawley Council for Social Service (1972), and issued under the title 'People and events that shaped Crawley'.

14  Apart from the references cited in the text, material in this section comes from papers presented to the symposium on 'Housing and State in Sweden and Britain' held at the University of Sussex, 25–6 October 1980. These papers included: M. Franzén and E. Sandstedt, 'State politics and the planning of residential areas: the case of post-war Sweden'; M. Wiktorin, 'Housing policy and disadvantaged groups in Sweden'; L. Hjärne, 'Concerning aims and forms of tenant influence. Some preliminary considerations'; B. Torsson, 'Ten Years of Urban Movement in Sweden. The case of Stockholm'; S. Gromark, 'Ten Years of Urban Movements in Sweden (II): Some notes and notions from the horizon of the city of Gothenburg'.

# Appendix: Project publications and working papers

(SWP = Sussex Working Paper in Urban and Regional Studies, available from The Editor, Urban and Regional Working Papers, Arts Area, University of Sussex, Brighton.)

1  S. S. Duncan (1978a) — Housing reform, the capitalist state and social democracy, *SWP*, 9.

2  S. S. Duncan (1978b) — Housing provision in advanced capitalism: Sweden in the 1970s, *SWP*, 10.

3  J. Backwell and P. Dickens (1978) — Town Planning, mass loyalty and the restructuring of capital: the 1947 Planning Act revisited, *SWP*, 11.

4  P. Dickens (1979) — Marxism and architectural theory: a critique of recent work, *Environment and Planning, B.*

5  P Dickens and P. Gilbert (1979) — The state and the housing question: a local study and some wider issues, *SWP*, 13.

6  S. S. Duncan (1980) — The methodology of levels and the urban question, *London School of Economics, Geography Discussion Paper*, 75.

7  M. Goodwin (1980) — National housing policy, local implementation and the limits to capital, *London School of Economics, Geography Discussion Paper*, 78.

8  P. Dickens (1981a) — The hut and the machine: towards a social theory of architecture, *Architectural Design.*

9  P. Dickens (1981b) — Social science and design theory, *Environment and Planning, B.*

10  P. Dickens (1981c) — Corporate capitalism and the building industry, *Proceedings of the Bartlett Summer School on the Built Environment.*

11  P. Dickens and M. Goodwin (1981) — Corporatism, consciousness and the local state: council housing in Sheffield, *SWP*, 26.

12  S. S. Duncan (1981) — Urban Research, housing policy and the methodology of levels, *Int. Jnl Urban & Regional Research*, 5, 3.

13  S. S. Duncan and M. Goodwin (1981) — The local state and the restructuring of social relations: theory and practice, *SWP*, 24.

14  S. S. Duncan (1982a) — Class relations and historical geography, the emergence of the rural and urban questions in Sweden, *University of Sussex Research Papers in Geography.*

15  S. S. Duncan (1982b)            Land, class relations and the transition from
                                    feudalism to capitalism in Sweden, *London
                                    School of Economics, Geography Discussion
                                    Paper*, NS 6.

16  S. S. Duncan and M. Goodwin    The local state: functionalism, autonomy and
    (1982a)                         class relations in Cockburn and Saunders,
                                    *Political Geography Quarterly*, 1, 1.

17  S. S. Duncan and M. Goodwin    The local state and restructuring social
    (1982b)                         relations, *Int. Jnl Urban & Regional Research*,
                                    6, 2.

18  F. Gray (ed.) (1983)           'Crawley: old town, new town', *Centre for
                                    Continuing Education Occasional Paper*, 18,
                                    University of Sussex.

19  S. S. Duncan (1984)            'State intervention and efficient capitalism:
                                    separating land ownership from development in
                                    Sweden', in Barrett, S. and Healey, P. *Land
                                    policy and problems*, Gower.

# Bibliography

## Books, articles, etc.

Aldridge, M. (1979) *The British New Towns. A Programme Without a Policy*, London, Routledge & Kegan Paul.

Alt, J. (1971) 'Some political and social correlates of County Borough expenditures', *British Journal of Political Science*, 1, 49–62.

Alt, J. (1977) 'Politics and expenditure models', *Policy and Politics*, 5 (3), 83–92.

Ambrose, P. (1976) 'The land market and the housing system', *Urban and Regional Studies Working Paper*, 3, University of Sussex.

Ambrose, P. and Colenutt, R. (1975) *The Property Machine*, Harmondsworth, Penguin.

Anderson, B. (1983) *Imagined Communities: Reflections on the Origin and Spread of Nationalism*, London, Verso.

BPA/RK (1978) *Bygg och bo Kostnad 70-tel*, Stockholm BPA/RIKSBYGGEN.

BS (1983) Bostadsstyrelsen *Bostäder och Boende, 1980*, Stockholm, Liber.

Backwell, J. and Dickens, P. (1978) 'Town planning, mass loyalty and the restructuring of capital', *Urban and Regional Studies Working Paper*, 11, University of Sussex.

Bailey, R. (1973) *The Squatters*, Harmondsworth, Penguin.

Ball, M. (1978) 'British housing policy and the housebuilding industry', *Capital and Class*, 4, 78–99.

Ball, M. (1982) 'Housing provision and the economic crisis', *Capital and Class*, 17, 60–77.

Ball, M. (1983) *Housing Policy and Economic Power*, London, Methuen.

Barlow, J. and Dickens, P. (1984) 'Housing alliances and housing provision in western Europe', *Urban and Regional Working Paper*, 42, University of Sussex.

Barr, C. (1958) *Public Authority Housing*, London, Batsford.

Bartlett School (1980) 'The production of the built environment', *Proceedings of the Bartlett International Summer School*, 1.

Bassett, K. and Short, J. (1980) *Housing and Residential Structure*, London, Routledge & Kegan Paul.

Beirne, P. (1977) *Fair Rent and Legal Fiction*, London, Macmillan.

Benny, M. (1947) 'Storm over Stevenage', in A. G. Weidenfeld (ed.) *The Changing Nation*, London, Contact Publications, 42–50.

Bensusan, S. (1928) *Latter-Day Rural England 1927*, London, Benn.

Beveridge, Lord (1952) *New Towns and the Case for Them*, London, University of London Press on behalf of the Town and Country Planning Association.

Boberg, M., Lorentzon, M., Lundgren, R., Löwendahl, B., Modh, B., Nilsson, K. and Wikner, C. E. (1974) *Bostad och Kapital: en Studie av Svensk Bostadspolitik*, Lund, Prisma.

Boddy, M. J. (1980) *The Building Societies*, London, Macmillan.

Bowley, M. (1945) *Housing and the State 1919–1944*, London, George Allen & Unwin.

Braverman, H. (1974) *Labour and Monopoly Capital*, New York, Monthly Review Press.

Byrne, D. (1980a) 'The standard of council housing in inter-war North Shields – a case study in the politics of reproduction', in J. Melling (ed.) *Housing, Social Policy and the State*, London, Methuen, 168–93.

Byrne, D. (1980b) 'Reproductive politics and class politics in a different place', unpublished paper, given at Institute of British Geographers Annual Conference, Manchester.

Byrne, D. and Damer, S. (1980) 'The state, the balance of class forces and early working-class housing legislation', in Political Economy of Housing Workshop of the Conference of Socialist Economists, *Housing, Construction and the State*, London, CSE, 63–70.

Byrne, D. and Parson, D. (1983) 'The state and the reserve army of labour: the management of class relations in space', in J. Anderson, S. S. Duncan and R. Hudson (eds) *Redundant Spaces in Cities and Regions*, London, Academic Press, 127–54.

Calder, A. (1969) *The People's War*, London, Cape.

Carney, J. and Hudson, R. (1978) 'Capital, politics and ideology: the North East of England, 1870–1946', *Antipode*, 10, 64–78.

Carter, I. (1974) 'The highlands of Scotland as an underdeveloped region', in E. de Kadt and G. Williams (eds) *Sociology and Development*, London, Tavistock.

Castells, M. (1976) 'Theory and ideology in urban sociology', in C. G. Pickvance (ed.) *Urban Sociology: Critical Essays*, London, Tavistock, 60–84.

Castells, M. (1977) *The Urban Question*, London, Arnold.

Castles, F. G. (1978) *The Social Democratic Image of Society: A Study of the Achievements and Origins of Scandinavian Social Democracy in Comparative Perspective*, London, Routledge & Kegan Paul.

Cawson, A. (1982) *Corporatism and Welfare*, London, Heinemann.

Cawson, A. and Saunders, P. (1983) 'Corporatism, competitive politics and class struggle', in R. King (ed.) *Capital and Politics*, London, Routledge & Kegan Paul, 8–27.

Chambert, H. and Skogland, P. (1983) 'A new way of urban building: the 1970s in the post-war perspective', unpublished working paper, Nordplan, Stockholm (trans.).

Child, M. W. (1937) *Sweden: The Middle Way*, New Haven, Yale University Press.

Clarke, S. and Ginsburg, N. (1975) 'The political economy of housing', in Political Economy of Housing Workshop of the Conference of Socialist Economists, *Political Economy and the Housing Question*, London, CSE, 3–33.

Cleaver, H. (1979) *Reading Capital Politically*, Brighton, Harvester.

Coates, D. (1975) *The Labour Party and the Struggle for Socialism*, Cambridge, Cambridge University Press.

Cockburn, C. (1977) *The Local State: The Management of Cities and People*, London, Pluto Press.

Cockburn, C. (1983) *Brothers. Male Dominance and Technological Change*, London, Pluto Press.

Cooke, P. (1983a) 'Regional restructuring: class politics and popular protest in South Wales', *Environment and Planning D: Society and Space*, 1 (3), 265–80.

Cooke, P. (1983b) 'Radical regions? Space, time, and gender relations in Emilia, Provence and South Wales', mimeo, Department of Town Planning, UWIST, Cardiff.

Cooney, E. (1974) 'High flats in local authority housing in England and Wales since 1945', in A. Sutcliffe (ed.) *Multi-storey Living*, London, Croom Helm, 151–80.

Corrigan, P. and Ginsburg, N. (1975) 'Tenant's struggle and class struggle', in Political Economy of Housing Workshop of the Conference of Socialist Economists, *Political*

*Economy and the Housing Question,* London, CSE, 134–46.

Crawley Council for Social Service (1972) 'People and events that shaped Crawley', mimeo.

Crawley Development Corporation (1956) 'Summary of development progress, 1st April 1956', unpublished report.

Crook, T. and Darke, J. (1983) 'Housing', in 'Banishing dark divisive clouds: welfare and the Conservative government', *Critical Social Policy,* 8, 24–5.

Crosland, A. (1956) *The Future of Socialism,* London, Cape.

Cullen, A. (1982) 'Speculative housebuilding in Britain. Some notes on the switch to timber frame production methods', in Bartlett School, 'The production of the built environment', *The Proceedings of the Bartlett Summer School,* 3, 4–12.

Cullingworth, J. B. (1966) *Housing and Local Government,* London, George Allen & Unwin.

Cullingworth, J. B. (1979) *Environmental Planning 1939–1969, Volume III, New Towns Policy,* London, HMSO.

Cullingworth, J. B. and Karn, V. A. (1968) *The Ownership and Management of Housing in the New Towns,* London, HMSO.

Dahlkvist, M. (1977) *Staten, Socialdemoktratin och Socialism: en Inledande Analys,* Lund, Prisma.

Dale, J. (1980) 'Class struggle, social policy and state structure: central–local relations and housing policy, 1919–1939', in J. Melling (ed.) *Housing, Social Policy and the State,* London, Croom Helm, 194–223.

Damer, S. (1980) 'State, class and housing; Glasgow 1885–1919', in J. Melling (ed.) *Housing, Social Policy and the State,* London, Croom Helm, 73–112.

Danermark, B. (1982) 'Methodological problems in the study of residential segregation', paper delivered at the Xth World Congress of Sociology, 16–21 August, Mexico.

Danermark, B. (1983) 'Klass, inkomst och boende: om segregation', *Örebro Studies 1,* Department of Sociology, University College of Örebro.

Department of Trade (1977) *Report on the Committee of Inquiry on Industrial Democracy,* Cmnd. 6706, London, HMSO.

Dickens, P. (1977) 'Squatting and the state', *New Society,* 5 May (40) 219–21.

Dickens, P. (1978) 'Social change, housing and the state: some aspects of class fragmentation and incorporation', in M. Harloe (ed.) 'Urban change and conflict', *Centre for Environmental Studies Conference Series,* 19, 336–96.

Dickens, P. (1979) 'Marxism and architectural theory: a critique of recent work', *Environment and Planning B,* 6, 105–16.

Dickens, P. and Gilbert, P. (1981) 'Inter-war housing policy: a study of Brighton', *Southern History,* 3, 201–31.

Dickens, P. and Goodwin, M. (1981) 'Consciousness, corporatism and the local state: The tensions of council house provision in Sheffield', *Urban and Regional Studies Working Paper,* 26, University of Sussex.

Direct Labour Collective (DLC) (1978) *Building with Direct Labour: Local Authority Building and the Crisis in the Construction Industry,* London, Housing Workshop of the Conference of Socialist Economists.

Direct Labour Collective (DLC) (1980) *Direct Labour Under Attack,* London, Housing Workshop of the Conference of Socialist Economists.

Donnison, D. and Soto, P. (1980) *The Good City,* London, Heinemann.

Donnison, D. and Ungerson, C. (1982) *Housing Policy,* Harmondsworth, Penguin.

Drewett, R. (1973) 'Land values and the suburban land market', in P. Hall, H. Gracey, R. Drewett and R. Thomas, *The Containment of Urban England,* vol. 2, London, Allen & Unwin, 197–245.

Duncan, S. S. (1977) 'Alienation and explanation in human geography', *Discussion Papers in Geography*, 63, London School of Economics.

Duncan, S. S. (1978a) 'Housing reform, the capitalist state and social democracy', *Urban and Regional Studies Working Paper*, 9, University of Sussex.

Duncan, S. S. (1978b) 'Housing provision in advanced capitalism: Sweden in the 1970s', *Urban and Regional Studies Working Paper*, 10, University of Sussex.

Duncan, S. S. (1978c) Review of Popenoe, D. (1976) *The Suburban Environment*, *Environment and Planning A*, 10, 353–4.

Duncan, S. S. (1981) 'Urban research and the methodology of levels: the case of Castells', *International Journal of Urban and Regional Research*, 5 (2), 231–54.

Duncan, S. S. (1982a) 'Class relations and historical geography: the transition to capitalism in Sweden', *Geography Discussion Paper*, NS4, London School of Economics.

Duncan, S. S. (1982b) 'Class relations and historical geography: the creation of rural and urban questions in Sweden', *Research Papers in Geography*, 12, University of Sussex.

Duncan, S. S. (1982c) 'Inner city critique', *Area*, 14 (3), 193–7.

Duncan, S. S. (1985) 'State intervention and efficient capitalism: separating land ownership from land development in Sweden', in S. Barrett and P. Healey (eds) *Land Policy, Problems and Alternatives*, London, Gower.

Duncan, S. S. and Goodwin, M. (1982a) 'The local state: functionalism, autonomy and class relations in Cockburn and Saunders', *Political Geography Quarterly*, 1 (1), 77–96.

Duncan, S. S. and Goodwin, M. (1982b) 'The local state and restructuring social relations: theory and practice', *International Journal of Urban and Regional Research*, 6 (2), 157–86.

Duncan, S. S. and Goodwin, M. (1985) 'The local government problem in Britain: Centralisation and resistance 1979–84', *Geography Discussion Paper*, 12–14, London School of Economics.

Dunford, M. (1983) *Industry and Development in Europe*, No. 1 of 'Exploring Europe' series, Schools Unit, University of Sussex, Brighton.

Dunleavy, P. (1980) *Urban Political Analysis*, London, Macmillan.

Dunleavy, P. (1981) *The Politics of Mass Housing in Britain, 1945–1975*, Oxford, Clarendon Press.

Durr, A. (1980a) 'Brighton's Labour Party: municipal elections 1890–1906', mimeo, Brighton Polytechnic.

Durr, A. (1980b) 'Riots, revolts and co-operation in Sussex 1795–1830', mimeo, Brighton Polytechnic History Workshop.

Durr, A. (1983) 'Co-operation in early nineteenth century Brighton: William Bryan, cabinet maker of West Street', *Sussex History*, 13 (5), 16–22.

ESCC/HBF (1980) *Housing Land Availability. A Joint Study by East Sussex County Planning Department and the Home Builders Federation*, Lewes, East Sussex County Council.

*The Economist* (1941a) 'The land leeches', CXL, 5084, 144.

*The Economist* (1941b) 'Again the leeches', CXLI, 5125, 591.

Edwards, G. (1922) *From Crowscaring to Westminster*, London, National Union of Agricultural Workers.

Egerö, B. (1979) *En Mönsterstad Granskas: Bostadsplanering i Örebro 1945–75*, Stockholm, Byggforskningsrådet.

Ekbrant, C. (1981) 'Bostadssituationen i Sverige 1912–1975', *Statens Institut för Byggnadsforskning*, M81: 1, Stockholm.

Ekbrant, C. (1982) 'Bostadsbyggandet 1900–1945', *Statens Institut för Byggnadsforskning*, M82: 3, Stockholm.

Elander, I. (1978) *Det Nödvändiga och det Onskvärda. En Studie av Social Demokratisk*

*Ideologi och Regionalpolitik 1940–72*, Stockholm, Arkiv Avhandlingsserie.

Elliott, B. and McCrone, D. (1982) *The City. Patterns of Domination and Conflict*, London, Macmillan.

Englander, D. (1982) *Landlord and Tenant in Urban Britain 1838–1918*, Oxford, Clarendon Press.

Erskine, A. (1984) 'Housing benefits: some preliminary comments', *Critical Social Policy*, 9, 99–105.

Esher, L. (1983) *A Broken Wave*, Harmondsworth, Penguin.

Farrant, S., Fossey, K. and Peasgood, A. (1981) 'The growth of Brighton and Hove 1840–1939', *Centre for Continuing Education, Occasional Paper*, 14, University of Sussex.

Fielding, N. (1984) 'Who is subsidising whom?', *Roof*, 9 (2), 11–14.

Flemström, C. and Ronnby, A. (1972) *Fallet Rosengård: en Studie i Svensk Planerings och bostadspolitik*, Stockholm, Prisma.

Foot, M. (1973) *Aneurin Bevan 1943–1960*, London, MacGibbon.

Foster, J. (1974) *Class Struggle and the Industrial Revolution. Early Industrial Capitalism in Three English Towns*, London, Weidenfeld and Nicolson.

Francis, H. and Smith, D. (1980) *The Fed. A History of South Wales Miners in the Twentieth Century*, London, Lawrence & Wishart.

Friedman, A. (1977) *Industry and Labour: Class Struggle at Work and Monopoly Capitalism*, London, Macmillan.

Friend, A. (1980) 'Squatting. The post-war squatter', in N. Wates and C. Woolmar (eds) *Squatting. The Real Story*, London, Bay Leaf Books, 110–19.

Friend, A. and Metcalf, A. (1981) *Slump City. The politics of mass unemployment*, London, Pluto Press.

Gamble, A. (1981) *Britain in Decline*, London, Macmillan.

Gauldie, E. (1974) *Cruel Habitations*, London, George Allen & Unwin.

Geddes, M. (1979) 'Uneven development and the Scottish Highlands', *Urban and Regional Studies Working Paper*, 17, University of Sussex.

Giddens, A. (1981) *A Contemporary Critique of Historical Materialism*, London, Macmillan.

Gilbert, E. M. (1954) *Brighton. Old Ocean's Bauble*, London, Methuen.

Gilchrist, D. (1980) 'The growth of owner-occupation', in Building Societies Association, *The Housing Market in the 1980s*, London, BSA, 9–18.

Gilliatt, S. (1983) *The Management of Reconstruction with Particular Reference to the Housebuilding Programme, 1942–49*, unpublished D.Phil. thesis, University of Sussex.

Gray, F. (1976) 'The management of local authority housing', in Political Economy of Housing Workshop of the Conference of Socialist Economists, *Housing and Class in Britain*, London, CSE, 75–86.

Gray, F. (ed.) (1983) 'Crawley: old town, new town', *Centre for Continuing Education, Occasional Paper*, 18, University of Sussex.

Gray, F. and Lowerson, J. (1979) 'Seaside see-saw', *Geographical Magazine*, March, 433–8.

Green, G. (1981) 'Why defend Sheffield's council houses?', mimeo, Sheffield City Council.

Greve, J. (1971) 'Voluntary housing in Scandinavia', *Centre for Urban and Regional Studies, Occasional Paper*, 21, University of Birmingham.

Groves, R. (1949) *Sharpen the Sickle*, London, Porcupine Press.

Gwynne, P. (1974) 'Organizing community opinion in a growing new town: the experience of Crawley', unpublished paper.

HBF/DOE (1979) *Study of the Availability of Private Housebuilding Land in Greater Manchester, 1978–81*, London, Department of Environment.

Hall, A. (1914) *A Pilgrimage of British Farming, 1910–1912*, London, John Murray.

Hall, P. (ed.) (1981) *The Inner City in Context*, London, Heinemann.

Hampton, W. (1970) *Democracy and Community*, London, Oxford University Press.

Harloe, M. (1981) 'The recommodification of housing', in M. Harloe and E. Lebas (eds) *City, Class and Capital*, London, Arnold, 17–50.

Harloe, M. and Martens, M. (1984) 'Comparative housing research', *Journal of Social Policy*, 13 (3), 255–77.

Harvey, D. (1978) 'The urban process under capitalism: a framework for analysis', *International Journal of Urban and Regional Research*, 2, 101–31.

Hase, J. (1958) 'Impressions of two new towns', *Universities and Left Review Club*, Autumn, 20–3.

Hayden, D. (1981) *The Grand Domestic Revolutions*, Cambridge (Mass.), M.I.T. Press.

Heady, B. (1978) *Housing Policy in the Developed Economy*, London, Croom Helm.

Heraud, B. J. (1968) 'Social class and the new towns', *Urban Studies*, 4 (1), 35–8.

Hermansson, C. H. (1979) *Kapitalister I: Monopol*, Stockholm, Arbetarekultur.

Hill, D. M. (1946) 'Who were the squatters?', *Pilot Papers*, November, 11–27.

Hooper, A. (1984) 'Land availability studies and private housebuilding', in S. Barrett and P. Healey (eds) *Land Policy, Problems and Alternatives*, London, Gower.

Hoppe, C. A. (1976) 'Byggbranschens utveckling', *Institutet för byggdokumentation*, 1976: 3, Stockholm.

House of Commons (1951) Sheffield Extension Bill, *Minutes of Evidence of Select Committee.*

House of Commons (1980) *Environment Committee, First Report, Session 1979–80*, HC 714.

House of Lords (1951) Sheffield Extension Bill, *Minutes of Evidence of Select Committee.*

Howkins, A. (1977) 'Structural conflict and the farmworker, 1900–1920', *Journal of Peasant Studies*, 4 (3), 217–29.

Hughes, V. (1959) *History of the Growth and Location of the Corporation Housing Schemes*, Sheffield, Sheffield Corporation.

Hultén, G. (1973) *Kris i Hyresfrågan*, Uddevalla, Oktober.

Huntford, R. (1971) *The New Totalitarians*, London, Allen Lane.

Hymer, S. (1972) 'The multinational corporation and the law of uneven development', in J. Bhagwati (ed.) *Economics and World Order from the 1970s to the 1990s*, London, Macmillan, 113–40, reprinted in Hymer, S. (1979) *The Multinational Corporation*, Cambridge, Cambridge University Press.

International Labour Organisation (1924) *European Housing Problems Since the War*, Geneva, ILO.

Ive, G. (1980) 'Fixed capital in the British building industry', in Bartlett School, 'The production of the built environment', *The Proceedings of the Bartlett International Summer School*, 1, 107–19.

Jacobs, S. (1981) 'The sale of council houses: does it matter?', *Critical Social Policy*, 1 (2), 35–48.

Jäggi, M., Müller, R. and Schmid, S. (1977) *Red Bologna*, London, Writers & Readers Publishing Co-operative.

Jennings, J. (1971) 'Geographical implications of the municipal housing programme in England and Wales', *Urban Studies*, 8 (2), 121–38.

Jessop, B. (1980) 'The transformation of the state in postwar Britain', in R. Scase (ed.) *The State in Western Europe*, London, Croom Helm, 23–93.

Jessop, B. (1982) *The Capitalist State*, London, Martin Robertson.

Johnson, R. (1978) 'Thompson, Genovese, and socialist-humanist history', *History Workshop*, 6, 79–100.

Johnson, R. (1982) 'Reading for the best Marx: history-writing and historical abstraction', in Centre for Contemporary Cultural Studies, *Making Histories: Studies in History-Writing and Politics*, London, Hutchinson, 153–204.

Karn, V. (1979) 'Pity the poor home owners', *Roof,* January, 10–14.

Keat, R. and Urry, J. (1975) *Social Theory as Science*, London, Routledge & Kegan Paul.

Kemeny, J. (1980) *The Myth of Home Ownership*, London, Routledge & Kegan Paul.

Korpi, W. (1978) *The Working Class in Welfare Capitalism: Work, Unions and Politics in Sweden*, London, Routledge & Kegan Paul.

Kramer, J. and Young, K. (1978) *Strategy and Conflict in Metropolitan Housing*, London, Heinemann.

Lambert, J., Paris, C. and Blackaby, B. (1978) *Housing Policy and the State. Allocation, Access and Control*, London, Macmillan.

Langley, J. (1976) *Always a Layman*, Brighton, QueenSpark Books.

Lee, G. (1964) *The Services of a Building Society*, London, Hodder & Stoughton.

Lefebvre, H. (1976) *The Survival of Capitalism*, London, Allison & Busby.

Lewis, J. and Williams, A. (1984) 'Portugal', in M. Wynn (ed.) *Housing in Europe*, London, Croom Helm, 281–325.

Leys, C. (1975) *Underdevelopment in Kenya: the Political Economy of Neo-colonialism*, London, Heinemann.

Leys, C. (1983) *Politics in Britain*, London, Heinemann.

McCulloch, A. (1983) *Owner Occupation and Class Struggle – the Mortgage Strikes of 1938–40*, unpublished Ph.D. thesis, University of Essex.

Macintyre, S. (1980) *Little Moscows*, London, Croom Helm.

Mackenzie, S. (1980) 'Women and the reproduction of labour power in the industrial city', *Urban and Regional Studies Working Paper*, 23, University of Sussex.

Mackenzie, S. and Rose, D. (1983) 'Industrial change, the domestic economy and home life', in J. Anderson, S. S. Duncan and R. Hudson (eds) *Redundant Spaces in Cities and Regions?*, London, Academic Press, 155–200.

Mandel, E. (1963) 'The dialectic of region and class in Belgium', *New Left Review*, 20, 5–31.

Mandel, E. (1975) *Late Capitalism*, London, New Left Books.

Marcuse, P. (1982) 'Building housing theory: notes on some recent work', *International Journal of Urban and Regional Research*, 6 (1) 115–20.

Marriott, D. (1967) *The Property Boom*, London, Pan.

Marx, K. (1973) *Grundrisse*, Harmondsworth, Penguin.

Massey, D. (1983) 'Industrial restructuring as class restructuring', *Regional Studies*, 17 (2), 73–89.

Massey, D. and Catalano, A. (1978) *Capital and Land. Landownership by Capital in Great Britain*, London, Edward Arnold.

Massey, D. and Meegan, R. (1982) *The Anatomy of Job Loss. The How, Where and When of Employment Decline*, London, Methuen.

Melling, J. (1980) 'Clydeside housing and the evolution of state rent control 1900–1939', in J. Melling (ed.) *Housing, Social Policy and the State*, London, Croom Helm, 139–67.

Melling, J. (1983) *Rent Strikes. People's Struggles for Housing in West Scotland 1890–1916*, Edinburgh, Polygon Books.

Mellor, J. R. (1977) *Urban Sociology in an Urbanised Society*, London, Routledge & Kegan Paul.

Merrett, S. (1979) *State Housing in Britain*, London, Routledge & Kegan Paul.

Merrett, S. with Gray, F. (1982) *Owner-Occupation in Britain*, London, Routledge & Kegan Paul.

Middlemas, K. (1977) *Politics in Industrial Society: the Experience of the British System since*

*1911*, London, André Deutsch.

Miliband, R. (1973) *Parliamentary Socialism*, London, Merlin.

Ministry of Health (1948) *Cost of House-building*, Report of the Committee of Inquiry, 1st Report (Chairman: J. G. Girdwood).

Ministry of Health (1950) *Cost of House-building*, Report of the Committee of Inquiry, 2nd Report (Chairman: J. G. Girdwood).

Ministry of Health (1952) *Cost of House-building*, Report of the Committee of Inquiry, 3rd Report (Chairman: J. G. Girdwood).

Minns, R. (1974) 'Who builds more?', *New Society*, 25 April, 184–6.

Moser, C. A. and Scott, W. (1961) *British Towns*, London, Oliver & Boyd.

Murgatroyd, L. (1981) 'Deindustrialisation in Lancaster', *Lancaster Regionalism Group Working Paper*, 1, University of Lancaster.

Murgatroyd, L. (1982) 'Gender and occupational stratification', *Lancaster Regionalism Group Working Paper*, 6, University of Lancaster.

Murgatroyd, L. (1983) 'The production of people and domestic labour revisited', *Socialist Economic Review*, 1, 85–98.

Murgatroyd, L. and Urry, J. (1983) 'The restructuring of a local economy: the case of Lancaster', in J. Anderson, S. S. Duncan and R. Hudson (eds) *Redundant Spaces in Cities and Regions?*, London, Academic Press, 67–98.

Murie, A., Niner, P. and Watson, C. (1976) *Housing Policy and the Housing System*, London, Allen & Unwin.

Murray, R. (1972) 'Underdevelopment, the international firm and the international division of labour', mimeo, *Institute of Development Studies*, University of Sussex, reprinted in J. Tinbergen (ed., 1976) *Towards a New World Economy*, Rotterdam, Rotterdam University Press.

Musgrave, C. (1970) *Life in Brighton*, London, Faber.

Myrdal, A. and Myrdal, G. (1934) *Kris i Befolkningsfrågan*, Stockholm (extended in Myrdal, A. (1968) *Nation and Family*, Cambridge (Mass.), MIT Press).

Nairn, T. (1978) *The Break Up of Britain*, London, New Left Books.

Neale, R. S. (1981) *Bath, 1680–1850. A Social History*, London, Routledge & Kegan Paul.

New Towns Committee (1946) *Interim Report*, Cmnd. 6759, London, HMSO.

Newby, H. (1979) *The Deferential Worker*, Harmondsworth, Penguin.

Newby, H. (1980) *Green and Pleasant Land*, Harmondsworth, Penguin.

Newby, H., Bell, C., Rose, D. and Saunders, P. (1978) *Property, Paternalism and Power*, London, Heinemann.

North Tyneside CDP (1978) *North Shields: Working Class Politics and Housing, 1900–77*, North Tyneside CDP.

Orlans, H. (1952) *Stevenage: a Sociological Study of a New Town*, London, Routledge & Kegan Paul.

Pålbrant, R. (1977) 'Arbetarrörelsen och idrotten, 1919–39', *Studia Historia Upsaliensa*, 91, Uppsala.

Palm, G. (1977) *The Flight From Work*, Cambridge, Cambridge University Press.

Pawley, M. (1978) *Home Ownership*, London, Architectural Press.

Pinch, S. (1978) 'Patterns of local authority housing allocation in Greater London between 1966 and 1973: an inter-borough analysis', *Transactions of the Institute of British Geographers*, New Series 3, 35–54.

Pollard, S. (1959) *The History of Labour in Sheffield*, Liverpool, Liverpool University Press.

Pollitt, H. (1946) 'The squatters', pamphlet published by the Communist Party of Great Britain.

Popenoe, D. (1977) *The Suburban Environment: Sweden and the United States*, Chicago,

University of Chicago Press.

Pritt, D. (1963) *The Labour Government 1945–51*, London, Lawrence & Wishart.

Queenspark Rates Book Group (1983) *Brighton on the Rocks. Monetarism and the Local State*, Brighton, QueenSpark Books.

Rose, D. (1980) 'Towards a re-evaluation of the political significance of home-ownership in Britain', in Political Economy of Housing Workshop of the Conference of Socialist Economists, *Housing, Construction and the State*, London, CSE, 71–6.

Rowe, A. (1983) 'Mortgage based housing policy: the Prince Edward Island housing market', paper presented to the 12th Annual Conference of the Atlantic Canada Economics Association, Fredericton, New Brunswick, 28 October.

Roxborough, I. (1979) *Theories of Underdevelopment*, London, Macmillan.

Rudvall, G. and Swedner, H. with Nilsson, B. and Warner, B. (1975) 'Boendeproblem: en promemoria utarbetad på uppdrag av boendeutredningen', Housing Department, Stockholm.

Rydin, Y. (1983) 'Housebuilders as an interest group: the issue of residential land availability', *London School of Economics, Graduate School of Geography Discussion Paper*, 6.

SCBR (Swedish Council for Building Research) (1983) *The Swedish Building Sector in 1990: The Need for Research and Development in the Eighties*, G3: 1983, Stockholm.

SIND (1977: 5) *Byggnadsindustri och Byggnadsmaterial Industri*, Stockholm.

SIND (1978: 5) *Byggnadsindustri och Byggnadsmaterial Industri – en Uppföljning*, Stockholm.

SOS (1981) *Levnadsförhållanden, Rapport nr 22 om Ojämlikheten i Sverige*, Stockholm.

SOU (1945: 63) *Slutbetänkande avgivet av Bostadssociala Utredningen. Del I – Allmänna Riktlinjer för den Framtids Bostadspolitiken*, Stockholm.

SOU (1955: 35) *Hyresregleringens Avveckling m.m*, Stockholm.

SOU (1966: 23) *Markfrågan*, Stockholm.

SOU (1968: 7) *Ägande och Inflytande inom det Privata Näringslivet*, Stockholm.

SOU (1972: 40) *Konkurens i Bostadsbyggandet*, Stockholm.

SOU (1977: 43) *Koncentrations Tendenserna inom Byggandsmaterials Industri*, Stockholm.

SOU (1982: 34, 35) *Prisutveckling inom Bostadsbyggandet och dess Orsaker*, Stockholm.

Sainte Croix, G. E. M. de (1982) *The Class Struggle in the Ancient Greek World*, London, Duckworth.

Samuelson, K. (1968) *From Great Power to Welfare State*, London, Allen and Unwin.

Sandström, E. G. (1945) 'Swedish housing and town planning: new ideals in building', *Town and Country Planning*, 13 (50), 69–93.

Saunders, P. (1979) *Urban Politics: A Sociological Interpretation*, London, Hutchinson.

Saunders, P. (1980) 'Towards a non-spatial urban sociology', *Urban and Regional Studies Working Paper*, 21, University of Sussex.

Saunders, P. (1981) *Social Theory and the Urban Question*, London, Hutchinson.

Saunders, P. (1982) 'Beyond housing classes: the sociological significance of private property rights in means of consumption', *Urban and Regional Studies Working Paper*, 33, University of Sussex.

Sayer, A. (1979) 'Epistemology and conceptions of people and nature in geography', *Geoforum*, 10 (1), 19–44.

Sayer, A. (1981) 'Abstraction: a realist interpretation', *Radical Philosophy*, 28, 6–15.

Sayer, A. (1983) Review of Giddens, A. (1981) 'A contemporary critique of historical materialism', *Environment and Planning D: Society and Space*, 1 (1), 109–14.

Sayer, A. (1984) *Explanation in Social Science: A Realist Approach*, London, Hutchinson.

Scase, R. (ed.) (1976a) *Readings in the Swedish Class Structure*, London, Pergamon.

Scase, R. (1976b) 'Images of progress – Sweden', *New Society*, 23 and 30 December, 614–15 and 742–3.

Scase, R. (1977) *Social Democracy in Capitalist Society: Working-class Politics in Britain and Sweden*, London, Croom Helm.

Schaffer, F. (1970) *The New Town Story*, London, MacGibbon & Kee.

Selley, E. (1919) *Village Trade Unions in Two Centres*, London, Allen & Unwin.

Sheffield City Council (1981) *Alternative Economic Policies – A Local Government Response*, Sheffield, Sheffield City Council.

Sheffield Corporation (1955) *Multi-Storey-Housing in Europe*, Sheffield, Sheffield Corporation.

Silkin, L. (1949) 'Foreword by the Minister of Town and Country Planning', to New Towns Act 1946, *Reports of the Corporations for the Period Ending 31st March 1949*.

Skinner, D. and Langdon, J. (1974) *The Story of Clay Cross*, Nottingham, Spokesman Books.

Sklair, L. (1975) 'The struggle against the Housing Finance Act', *Socialist Register 1975*, 250–92.

Smith, D. (1982) *Conflict and Compromise. Class Formation in English Society 1814–1914*, London, Routledge & Kegan Paul.

Söderfeldt, B. (1980) 'Att mäta Klasserna i Sverige', *Häften för kritiska Studier*, 3 (13), 17–41.

Söderfeldt, B. (1982) 'Some methodological remarks on comparative community research', unpublished paper presented at the conference 'Housing and the state in Britain and Sweden', Örebro, September.

Södersten, B. (1968) 'Bostadsförsörjning och bostadspolitik under efterkrigstiden', in Södersten, B. (ed.) *Svensk Ekonomi*, Stockholm.

Springall, M. (1936) *Labouring Life in Norfolk Villages, 1834–1919*, London, Allen & Unwin.

Stanford, E. (1965) 'The public inquiry and the appeal', *Crawley and District Observer*, 3 September.

Stedman-Jones, G. (1971) *Outcast London: A Study in the Relationship between Classes in Victorian Society*, London, Oxford University Press.

Stern, P. (1981) 'Broakes on the brink', *New Statesman*, 4 September, 13–14.

Sugden, J. (1975) 'The place of construction in the economy', in D. Turin (ed.) *Aspects of the Economics of Construction*, London, Godwin, 1–24.

Sugden, J. (1980) 'The nature of construction capacity and entrepreneurial response to effective demand in the UK', in Bartlett School, 'The production of the built environment', *The Proceedings of the Bartlett International Summer School*, 1, 1, 1–6.

Sunesson, S. (1974) 'Den socialdemokatiska statsideologien och fackföreningsrörelsen', in P. Dencik and B. Lundwell (eds) *Arbete, Kapital och Stat*, Stockholm, Roben & Sjögren.

Sutching, N. (1972) 'Marx, Popper and historicism', *Inquiry*, 15, 235–66.

Taylor, J. (1979) *From Modernization to Modes of Production: A Critique of the Sociologies of Development and Underdevelopment*, London, Macmillan.

Therborn, G. (1976) 'The Swedish class structure, 1930–65: a Marxist analysis', in R. Scase (ed.) *Readings in the Swedish Class Structure*, Oxford, Pergamon, 151–68.

Therborn, G. (1981) *Klasstrukturen i Sverige 1930–80, Arbete, Kapital, Stat och Patriarkat*, Lund, Zenit.

Thompson, E. P. (1963) *The Making of the English Working Class*, Harmondsworth, Penguin.

Thorns, D. (1972) *Suburbia*, London, MacGibbon & Kee.

Thrift, N. J. (1983) 'On the determination of social action in space and time', *Environment and Planning D: Society and Space*, 1 (1), 23–58.

Tomasson, R. F. (1970) *Sweden: Prototype of a Modern Society*, New York, Random House.

Trory, E. (1975) *Brighton and the General Strike*, Brighton, Crabtree Press.

Uhr, G. G. (1977) 'Economic development in Denmark, Norway and Sweden', in K. H. Carny (ed.) *Scandinavia at the Polls*, Washington, American Enterprise Institute for Public Policy Research, 214–48.

Unga, N. (1970) 'Socialdemokratin och arbetslöshetsfrågan 1912–34: framväxten av den "nya" arbetlöshetspolitiken', *Archiv för Studier i Arbetarrörelsens Historia*, Uppsala.

Urry, J. (1980) 'Paternalism, management and localities', *Lancaster Regionalism Group Working Paper*, 2, University of Lancaster.

Urry, J. (1981a) *The Anatomy of Capitalist Societies*, London, Macmillan.

Urry, J. (1981b) 'Localities, regions and social class', *International Journal of Urban and Regional Research*, 5, 455–74.

Urry, J. (1981c) 'Deindustrialisation, households and forms of social conflict and struggle', *Lancaster Regionalism Group Working Paper*, 3, University of Lancaster.

Urry, J. (1982) 'Some themes in the analysis of the anatomy of contemporary capitalist societies', *Acta Sociologica*, 25 (4), 405–18.

Urry, J. (1983) 'De-industrialisation, classes and politics', in King, R. (ed.) *Capital and Politics*, London, Routledge & Kegan Paul.

Uthwatt Report (1942) *Expert Committee on Compensation and Betterment, Final Report*, Cmnd. 6386, London, HMSO.

Ward, S. (1975) 'Planning, politics and social change 1939–1945', *South Bank Polytechnic, Department of Town Planning Working Paper*, London.

Wates, N. (1976) *The Battle for Tolmers Square*, London, Routledge & Kegan Paul.

Wates, N. and Wolmar, C. (eds, 1980) *Squatting. The Real Story*, London, Bay Leaf Books.

Wibe, S. (1974) 'Stat, kris och profit', in P. Dencik and B.-A. Lundvall (eds) *Arbete, Kapital och Stat*, Stockholm, Roben & Sjögren.

Wilding, P. (1972) 'Towards exchequer subsidies for housing 1906–1914', *Social and Economic Administration*, 6 (1), 3–18.

Willis, P. E. (1978) *Profane Culture*, London, Routledge & Kegan Paul.

Wiktorin, M. (1980) *Bostad åt Alla?*, Stockholm, Liber Förlag.

Wiktorin, M. (1982) 'Housing policy and disadvantaged groups in Sweden', *International Journal of Urban and Regional Research*, 6 (2), 246–55.

Wragg, M. (1951) 'Starting life in a new town', *Town and Country Planning*, 19, June, 249–52.

Young, K. and Kramer, J. (1978) 'Local exclusionary policies in Britain: the case of suburban defence in a metropolitan system', in K. Cox (ed.) *Urbanization and Conflict in Market Societies*, London, Methuen, 229–52.

Young, M. and Willmott, P. (1962) *Family and Kinship in East London*, Harmondsworth, Penguin.

## Documentary series and periodicals

*Annual Bulletin of Housing and Building Statistics for Europe*, New York.

BBA *Bostads- och Byggnadsstatistisk Årsbok*, Sverige Officiella Statistik, Statistiska Central-byrån, Stockholm.

BO (SM BO) *Statistiska Meddelanden, Bostadsbyggandet*, Statistiska Centralbyrån, Stockholm.

CSO Central Statistical Office, *National Income and Expenditure Accounts*, London, HMSO.

*Crawley and District Observer.*

Crawley Tenants' Association Newsletter (Crawley Development Corporation Records, West Sussex Record Offices, Chichester).

*East Anglian Daily Times.*

Employment Gazette, *Department of Employment Gazette.*

*Evening Argus*, Brighton.

F (SM F) *Statistiska Meddelanden, Företagen*, Statistiska Centralbyrån, Stockholm.

*Financial Times.*

HCS Department of Environment, *Housing Construction Statistics*, London, HMSO.

HLG *Housing and Local Government Papers* (Public Records Office, London).

HR *Housing Returns*, London, HMSO.

*Hansard.*

Ministry of Health *Annual Reports* (1935–1939), London, HMSO.

*News Chronicle.*

NIER (London) *National Institute Economic Review*, National Institute of Economic and Social Research, London.

NIER (Stockholm) *National Institute Economic Review*, Ministry of Finance, Stockholm.

NR (SM NR) *Statistiska Meddelanden, Nationalräkenskaper*, Statistiska Centralbyrån, Stockholm.

PRO CAB Cabinet Records (Public Records Office, London).

SOS Sveriges Officiela Statistik, Statistiska Centralbyrån, Stockholm.

Sheffield Corporation Housing Department, *Annual Reports* (1950–72), Sheffield, Sheffield Corporation.

Sheffield Corporation Housing Committee, *Minutes of Meetings* (1969–72), Sheffield, Sheffield Corporation.

Sheffield Corporation Housing Development Committee, *Minutes of Meetings* (1955–68), Sheffield, Sheffield Corporation.

Sheffield Corporation Housing Management Committee, *Minutes of Meetings* (1955–68), Sheffield, Sheffield Corporation.

*Sheffield Forward.*

*Sheffield Morning Telegraph.*

*Sheffield Star.*

*Sheffield Telegraph.*

Smallburgh Rural District Council, *Medical Officer of Health Annual Reports* (1906–39) (Local History Section, Norwich Library, Norwich).

Smallburgh Rural District Council, *Minutes of Housing Committee* (1915–39) (North Norfolk District Council).

Smallburgh Rural District Council, *Minutes of Council* (1919–39) (North Norfolk District Council).

Smallburgh Rural District Council, *Sanitary Inspector Annual Reports* (1906–39) (Local History Section, Norwich Library, Norwich).

*Town and Country Planning.*

# Author index

# Subject index

abstraction, 246, 248, 249, 250; and comparative research, 29; as level of explanation, 12, 16; and marxism, 37; and theory, 2, 12

Brighton, 3, 14, 207–14 *passim*; as case study, 32, 33, 35, 206, 207, 243; class relations, 208; local politics, 209; local state, 208; squatting, 207–14; urban bourgeoisie, 35–6; vigilantes, 209–12

Britain: construction costs, 74–5, 80, 81–2; construction industry, 94, 96; economic decline, 38; housing production, 69; local variations in housing provision, 147–57; post-war government, 136–7; public housing crisis, 144; reformism, 54, 117–8; speculative housing, 129; squatting, 212–3

capital-labour relations, 14; in building industry, 96, 109; and housing consumption, 235; in locality, 161; in Sweden, 96, 107–9, 115

capitalist state: activities, 15; analysis of, 9; social relations of, 12, 15, 16, 234; state form, 15; variability of, 9

case studies, 4, 31, 32–6; *see also* Brighton, Britain, Crawley, Norfolk, Sheffield and Sweden

central government: definition of, 16

civil society, 12–14, 17, 244; differentiation of, 13–14, 17; social conflict, 17; social relations of, 12; uneven development of, 17

Clydeside rent strike, 204, 205, 241

comparative analysis, 7, 16, 23–31, 234, 254; and checking generalisation, 29–30, 58, 63, 93; and explanation, 24,

25; of housing protest in Brighton and Crawley, 3, 207–32, 243; of housing provision in Britain and Sweden, 2, 57–8, 62–4, 68, 138, 141, 143–4, 235–6, 237, 238, 242; of housing provision in Sheffield and Norfolk, 3, 161–91, 243; re-evaluation of, 24; as research strategy, 28, 31, 234, 253–4; shock value of, 29; *see also* comparative research

comparative research, 2; as explanatory panacea, 27–8, 32; in housing studies, 58–61; and variability of structure, 7; *see also* comparative analysis

contingency, 247, 249; and comparative research, 34; in Sweden, 37, 57, 145; and wider structures, 17

contingent relations: and necessary relations, 10, 248, 250, 252

construction industry, 88–109 *passim*; in Britain, 94, 96; labour relations, 107–9; and speculation, 69; study of, 63; in Sweden, 77, 81, 88–94; variation in, 143

Crawley, 3, 14, 214–32 *passim*; as case study, 32, 33, 35, 206, 207, 243; collective action, 222–32; legal action, 214–22; local politics, 216, 218, 223, 225; New Town Development Corporation, 35, 222–3, 227, 230; property rights, 216–7; public inquiry, 218–9; rents, 224–32 *passim*; social relations, 216; Tenants Associations, 225–7

decommodification, 119–20, 122–3, 130–40; and class relations, 130–2; and crisis, 138–40